AF783025

THE ISLAMIC WORLDVIEW

The quest for a systemic unity of the universe in all of its manifestations is a common topic in Western thought. In *The Islamic Worldview* , Masudul Alam Choudhury shows what Islam can bring to this field of human inquiry. Defining a paradigm of Islamic political economy and world systems, he presents the study of epistemology in the light of general systems derived from the Qur'anic premise. The result is an intellectual endeavour without any dogmatic or religious inhibition that extends the scope of religious and philosophical inquiry.

Masudul Alam Choudhury is Professor of Economics, Director of the Centre of Humanomics and Editor of *Humanomics* at the University College of Cape Breton in Nova Scotia, Canada. His previous book, *Reforming the Muslim World*, was published by Kegan Paul International in 1998.

keganpaul.com

THE ISLAMIC WORLDVIEW
Socio-Scientific Perspectives

MASUDUL ALAM CHOUDHURY

KEGAN PAUL INTERNATIONAL
London and New York

First Published in 2000 by
Kegan Paul International Limited
UK: P.O. Box 256, London WC1B 3SW, England
Tel: 020 7580 5511 Fax: 020 7436 0899
E-mail: books@keganpaul.com
Internet: http://www.keganpaul.com
USA: 61 West 62nd Street, New York, NY 10023
Tel: (212) 459 0600 Fax: (212) 259 3678
Internet: http://www.columbia.edu/cu/cup

Distributed by
John Wiley & Sons
Southern Cross Trading Estate
1 Oldlands Way, Bognor Regis
West Sussex, PO22 9SA, England
Tel: (01243) 779 777 Fax: (01243) 820 250
E-mail: cs-books@wiley.co.uk

Columbia University Press
61 West 62nd Street, New York, NY 10023
Tel: (212) 459 0600 Fax: (212) 259 3678
Internet: http://www.columbia.edu/cu/cup

© Kegan Paul International, 2000

Printed in Great Britain by IBT Global , London

All Rights reserved. No part of this book may be reprinted or reproduced or utilised in any form or be any electric, mechanical or other means, now known or hereafter invented, including photocopying or recording, or in any information storage or retrieval system, without permission in writing from the publishers.

ISBN: 0-7103-0656-3

British Library Cataloguing in Publication Data

A catalogue record for this book is available from the British Library

Library of Congress Cataloging-in-Publication Data

A catalogue record for this book is available from the Library of Congress

This book is a gift to the thoughtful of all times.

Dedication

This book is dedicated to my dearest friend
Professor Muhammad Idris Ali
of Mathematics at the University of Chittagong, Bangladesh,
who passed away so prematurely, leaving a sudden vacuum in the
affection and guidance that I so much needed from him.
May God Almighty rest his blessed soul in His Divine Mercy.

PROLOGUE

24. Seest thou not how
God sets forth a parable?—
A goodly Word[illegible]
Like a goodly tree,
Whose root is firmly fixed,
And its branches (reach)
To the heavens,—

٢٤- الم تر كيف ضرب الله مثلا
كلمة طيبة كشجرة طيبة
اصلها ثابت وفرعها في السماء ۝

25. It brings forth its fruit[illegible]
At all times, by the leave
Of its Lord.
So God sets forth parables
For men, in order that
They may receive admonition.

٢٥- تؤتي اكلها كل حين باذن
ربها ويضرب الله الامثال
للناس لعلهم يتذكرون ۝

26. And the parable
Of an evil Word
Is that of an evil tree:
It is torn up by the root
From the surface of the earth:
It has no stability.[illegible]

٢٦- ومثل كلمة خبيثة كشجرة خبيثة
اجتثت من فوق الارض ما لها من
قرار ۝

27. God will establish in strength
Those who believe, with the Word
That stands firm, in this world
And in the Hereafter; but God
Will leave, to stray, those
Who do wrong: God doeth
What He willeth.[illegible]

٢٧- يثبت الله الذين امنوا بالقول
الثابت في الحيوة الدنيا وفي الاخرة
ويضل الله الظلمين
ويفعل الله ما يشاء ۝

Al-Qur'an, <u>Ibrahim</u> (Chapter 14, verses 24-27).

TABLE OF CONTENTS

FIGURES

TABLES

ACKNOWLEDGEMENT

The preparation of this book has gone through several stages. At each stage a host of people, institutions and sources have greatly contributed towards its successful completion. Most significant among these is the Social Sciences and Humanities Research Council of Canada (SSHRC), which has helped me with a handsome grant for this first part of the major research project entitled, Dynamic Input-Output Analysis of Trade and Development for Members of the Organization of Islamic Conference (OIC). For this grant and the opportunity that it unleashed for me to carry out the two parts of the major research project, I remain greatly indebted and thankful to SSHRC.

My thanks are also to the Islamic University Chittagong (IUC), Bangladesh, where some of the chapters were first presented as invited lectures in 1997. These have since been revised to be incorporated in this book. The lectures could not have been possible without the generous contribution and support of the University College of Cape Breton (UCCB) that allowed me travel grant for the purpose. To both of these caring institutions I remain very grateful.

The manuscript was finally completed during my sabbatical leave at the Department of Finance and Economics, College of Industrial Management, King Fahd University of Petroleum and Minerals (KFUPM), Dhahran, Saudi Arabia. I have benefited from the many support that I received at KFUPM and that made it possible to carry out my major research project and complete this book during my sabbatical leave.

I remain grateful to Kegan Paul International for giving me the opportunity early enough to get this book accepted for publication. As in my first book with KPI so also with this book, I have received expert professional support from KPI.

My thanks are to Professor Gabor Korvin of the Department of Earth Sciences at KFUPM who invited me to present parts of the book as science seminars in his faculty. I also wish to thank my son Mufeedhul Alam Choudhury, a third-year B.Sc Pre-Medical student at McGill University for his expert computer-assisted designing of the many complex figures in this text.

Finally, I would like to remember my wife and children dearly for rendering their caring understanding during my time away from home in the pursuit and dissemination of the theme of unity of knowledge, which comprises the epistemological core of this book.

ILLUSTRATIONS

THE GOODLY TREE

Al-Qur'an, <u>Ibrahim</u>, Chapter 14, verses 24-25.

24. Seest thou not how
God sets forth a parable ?—
A goodly Word
Like a goodly tree,
Whose root is firmly fixed,
And its branches (reach)
To the heavens,—

25. It brings forth its fruit
At all times, by the leave
Of its Lord.
So God sets forth parables
For men, in order that
They may receive admonition.

٢٤- أَلَمْ تَرَ كَيْفَ ضَرَبَ اللَّهُ مَثَلًا
كَلِمَةً طَيِّبَةً كَشَجَرَةٍ طَيِّبَةٍ
أَصْلُهَا ثَابِتٌ وَفَرْعُهَا فِي السَّمَاءِ ○

٢٥- تُؤْتِي أُكُلَهَا كُلَّ حِينٍ بِإِذْنِ
رَبِّهَا وَيَضْرِبُ اللَّهُ الْأَمْثَالَ
لِلنَّاسِ لَعَلَّهُمْ يَتَذَكَّرُونَ ○

THE EVIL TREE

Al-Qur'an, Ibrahim, Chapter 14, verses 26

26. And the parable
Of an evil Word
Is that of an evil tree :
It is torn up by the root
From the surface of the earth :
It has no stability.

٢٦- وَمَثَلُ كَلِمَةٍ خَبِيثَةٍ كَشَجَرَةٍ خَبِيثَةٍ
اجْتُثَّتْ مِن فَوْقِ الْأَرْضِ مَا لَهَا مِن
قَرَارٍ ۝

FOREWORD

Especially in the last two decades, with the resurgence of fundamental Islamic values in various parts of the world, a number of Muslim countries have moved toward transforming their economic and financial systems and social institutions to make them conform more closely with the precepts of Islam. The intense commitment of Islam to human brotherhood/sisterhood and to social and economic justice defines the framework within which this transformation has occurred and continues to unfold.

Generally speaking, the Islamic economic and financial system places great stress on distributive justice and on social and economic equality. This incorporates the principles of redistribution of income and wealth to guarantee a standard of living that is humane, and respect for the basic needs and rights of each individual. This standard must be in harmony with the respect for the dignity of humans inherent in the teachings of Islam. In effect, this requires the organization and realignment of relations between various economic and social institutions and, therefore, demands that the state assume an active role. The resulting powers of government must be consistent with Islamic law, the Shari'ah.

Shari'ah, which developed during the first two centuries of Islam, continued to address the changing needs of Muslim societies through the institution of Ijtihad, or independent reasoning by Muslim scholars on the basis of recognized sources, such as the Qur'an. It was perhaps due to this process that the Islamic worldview manifested itself in all aspects of socio-economic and political life, although not always in clear and coherent manner.

Today, Muslim scholars question the achievement of both the capitalist and socialist economic and social systems and their effects on societies. As part of this process, many are attempting to define an Islamic socio-economic system which would provide a synthesis of Islamic moral and ethical values along with rules and regulations that address the needs of developing and modernizing societies, in social and economic as well as in political matters.

From the Islamic point of view, it is inconceivable to study, understand or apply the Islamic political system in isolation from its social and economic components. Islam as a religion is distinctive in that it views the universe, life and man, with their various and numerous elaborate systems as part of a whole. This emanates from the fundamental principle of Tawhid, the doctrine of the unity of God. It is essential, therefore, to keep this concept in sight in studies related to any aspect of Islam.

At times this holistic view is criticized. Some argue that it contributes to stereotypes, while others suggest that it deprives analysis of some of the tools it needs to perform its task. Professor Masudul Alam Choudhury's work should be able to satisfy both groups.

In this explicit interdisciplinary study, Professor Choudhury assesses economic, social and political developments within a worldview of Islam, which he systematically develops. The thoroughness with which the available quantitative and literary evidence has been studied and the care with which it has been evaluated and analyzed are especially impressive. His conclusions are always judicious and independent; and he is not swayed by the culturally divisive aspects of religion but consistently maintains objectivity and a sense of the universal.

The reader of this book will also clearly perceive the relationship between religion and modernization, a matter of particular importance in Muslim countries. Some very fundamental aspects of modernization, especially the growing acceptance of scientific knowledge, may challenge the existing influence of religious leaders and institutions. Yet Islam, like other religions, has repeatedly shown itself able to embrace and encourage modernization. The Islamic worldview that Professor Choudhury constructs and discusses compels the reader to pay close attention to Islam as a potentially very powerful influence in the areas of modernization and the areas of economic and social development.

For thirteen centuries Islam has provided a divinity-sanctioned political and socio-economic order that has given distinction and meaning to Muslims both as individuals and as a community. Professor Choudhury helps us to understand this and see the possibilities in the future. His work provides not only a solid framework for the Islamic worldview, but also a framework for further inquiry. His book will undoubtedly delight social scientists and scholars of humanities alike and will offer challenges to numerous established assumptions. I consider it a privilege to have been among the first readers of this significant work.

Professor A. Uner Turgay
Director
Institute of Islamic Studies
McGill University
Montreal, Quebec, Canada.

INTRODUCTION

The Islamic worldview is unique and universal across all systems. This permanent nature of Islamic worldview is spelled out in the following verse of the Qur'an (lxxxi, verse 27): 'Verily this is no less than a Message to all the Worlds.' The central premise of this worldview is the epistemology of Divine Unity and the depiction of reality in this framework of unity. This combination of the epistemic view of Unity with the construction of reality in its framework at the highest level of analytical manifestation, is indeed the methodological problematique of all times. It has expressed itself as the undying quest by mankind since time immemorial. The Greeks sought it in the fold of a teleological conception of god, ethics and life. The metaphysical elements of human thought sought it in a numinous god. The modern scientific research programs seek it in the 'theories of everything' or the grand unified theories of matter, energy and forces.

If this quest for systemic unity of the universe in its various manifestations has always been the undying quest of mankind, then what is it that Islam brings so challenging and revolutionary to this field of inquiry? To answer this question we note the distinct nature of the unity conveyed by a numinous cosmic interrelatedness and completeness in all the earlier doctrines that has no exogenously determining agent which upholds a categorical position in creation. In the 'one-many' problem we note that the nature of unity is defined by a plurality of being that is claimed to map into a singular philosophical explanation. Thus, many gods are seen to unify into one god in a cosmic whole (Ruston 1989, Rucker 1983).

The result of such a comprehension of unity in a cosmic wholeness is undefinedness of that Exogenous Being that must singularly define the premise of creation. Many oneness as in the one-many problem, dissolves into a problem of lack of well-definition when seen against the backdrop of whose oneness would it be among the giants here. The Qur'an discards this conception of pluralistic oneness.

In modern physical scientific theory, the universe is given a purely materialistic conceptualization when delineating the original moment of cosmic creation. In this regard Hawking (1988) comments that it is indeed the material characterization of unification of the forces of nature and of explaining the initial state of creation that has boiled down into unresolving conflict between the fields of a large scale theory of the universe and a small scale theory of the universe. The large scale understanding has yielded the General and Special Relativity Theories. The small scale understanding has yielded Quantum Theory. Penrose (1989) points out in his grand systems-oriented perspective of future science the problem of irreconcilability between these two competing conceptions of the universe, which still is claimed to be inherently unified by virtue of its initial conditions. This is an obvious contradiction. It marks a continuation of Darwinism in the natural selection model of competition and individuation. Penrose suggests quantum gravity theory as an alternative, but the essentially materialistic foundation of the sciences in the research program of unification remains imbedded. The deductive nature of logical positivism in such systems is derived from the primacy of mathematical reasoning based on the Kantian type non-synthetic dichotomy between a numinous a priori domain in which resides God, and the two domains – one as a second level of the a priori that is subject to mathematical reasoning, and the other as the sensible or ontic domain of the a posteriori (Kant [1780] trans. Friedrich 1977). Modern science remains unified between the latter two domains while being oblivious of the first one (Carnap 1966). All attempts to unify these deductive and inductive, normative and positive elements of reasoning have failed to date in the occidental and historical syllogism of unitarian theories.

In Islam God is not numinous, as this Exogenous Agent determines the functioning of world-systems through the process of the Divine Laws that are provided for comprehension and application by humankind. The Qur'an says in this regard (II verse 164.): 'Behold! In the creation of the heavens and the earth; in the alteration of the Night and Day; in the sailing of the ships through the Ocean for the profit of mankind................; indeed are Signs for a people that are wise.' The essence of the Qur'anic meta-theory of unity is thereby premised in an epistemological and ontological category that is supra-mathematical and supra-materialistic (Choudhury 1993). But secondly, the reasoning that emanates from this episteme of unity conveys logical constructs for creative explanation. That medium which carries Essence into Cognitive Reality is the domain of the Divine Laws (Sunnat al-Allah) made explainable firstly by the conjoint text of the Prophetic Traditions (Sunnah al-Rasul) and explained in world-systems by the reasoned comprehension of mankind in accordance with the epistemic roots of

Divine Unity. Such is the stage of search (Ijtihad). It is then followed by consensus of the Islamic community that is guided by the learned in Islam (Ijma). The explanatory phases deriving rules (Ahkam) from the epistemic roots are marked by diversities of admissible possibilities as the human action proceeds on while being centred around the pivot of Divine Unity. We thus have the evolutionary stages of knowledge formation from endless processes of combinations between Ijtihad and Ijma. Such a knowledge-induced evolutionary worldview that remains uniquely tied to the origin of unity and its well-definition according to the Divine Laws, characterizes the permanent essence of the Islamic methodology of Divine Oneness, its depiction of unity on world-systems, and its creative possibilities within states of order and meaning.

The distinction between the Islamic meta-theory of unity is precisely the well-definition that this epistemological premise attains in terms of the manifestations of the Divine Laws. The cosmic entirety that is numinously unified in the other doctrines and in the scientific research program on unification, is now given an operational meaning by entering into states of unification of world-systems by means of the Divine Laws. We thereby, obtain the rich and expanding domain of the Islamic Laws in the perspective of world-systems. This perspective is the foundation of Islamic Law, Shari'ah. It is equally social as well as scientific in nature and application. Thus we use the term socio-scientific order in reference to the universal precept of fundamental unity in all systems.

In this work we will develop a relational theory of world-systems as reflected by the rules that will be derived from Qur'an and Sunnah. We will conceptualize it and show how cogently it can be applied to specific examples in terms of its overarching unification derived from the precept of Divine Oneness. A combination of the epistemological characterization of Divine Unity and its externalization in world-systems by the rules of unification in Shari'ah, will be the focus of our interest on Islamic worldview in this book.

SUMMARY OF CHAPTERS IN THIS BOOK

Chapter 1 is a non-mathematical explanation of the epistemology of Divine Unity in a theory of science and systems. A comparative examination is undertaken to bring out the sharp contrast of this Tawhidi system from the mainstream ones. Thereby, a concept of new globalism is developed in terms of the epistemology of unity and unification of knowledge in Islam against that under rationalism in occidental thought and as signified by capitalist globalism in its varied forms.

Chapter 2 introduces the comparative view of scientific methodology in Islamic and occidental perspectives. We point out that as opposed to the steady-state equilibrium and optimal, local and controlled experimental views of mainstream science, Islamic methodology in the sciences looks at the processual worldview with its centrality in knowledge flows that are epistemologically related to the root of Divine Unity. The cognitive world is then shown to be explained by means of a circular causation and continuity model of unified reality. Such a knowledge-induced worldview is shown to be interactive, integrative and evolutionary. A comparative view beyond mainstream scientific theory points out a deep interest in this area today, particularly as ecological concepts of wholeness pervade the theories of the sciences. Here the Qur'anic worldview is shown to contribute fresh light in the midst of its permanence in reality.

Chapter 3 is an in-depth formalization of the universally interactive, integrative and evolutionary (IIE) worldview of socio-scientific systems in reference to Tawhidi epistemology, that is Divine Unity. The Tree Model derived from the Qur'anic chapter, Ibrahim, is invoked to characterize the IIE-model of the Tawhidi worldview and its unification process of knowledge. The chapter is a mathematical formulation of the equivalent two processes, namely, the Shuratic Process or the IIE-worldview. A good number of simulative graphs are included to show the nature of the general systems model emanating from the fundamental epistemology of Divine Unity and taking its meaning in the unification of knowledge within world-systems.

Chapter 4 is a study in the development of the theory of Islamic political economy in comparative perspectives. The emphasis here is on the theory of value in mainstream economics and what it would be in the theory of Islamic political economy in terms of the principle of universal complementarity between moral and material ends characterizing costs, prices and goods in ethicizing market exchange. The Islamic theory of value is contrasted with the Marxist labour theory of value in terms of production, cost and pricing concepts.

Chapter 5 is a further development on the contrasts between the methodology of Islamic political economy as derived from the meta-theory of Tawhidi epistemology and the mainstream nature of Islamic economics. The ethically endogenous methodology of Islamic political economy is contrasted with the exogenous ethical perspectives of Islamic economics viewed within the methodology of mainstream economics. Within the Tawhidi socio-scientific methodology various social contractarian and institutional approaches of mainstream economics are critically examined to bring out the singular nature of Islamic political economy in terms of its unification of knowledge. Several economic issues are thereby examined.

Chapter 6 treats knowledge in economic theory in the sense of interactions using the IIE-model that is established in the earlier chapters. We find a distinctive approach and important implications entering economic theory and the study of political economy by so conceptualizing the role of knowledge. The important issue of money in the context of unification of knowledge premised on Divine Unity leads us to consider money as an aggregate that is endogenously determined on the basis of real economic exchange for goods and services. The case of quantity theory of money is then compared with the endogenous treatment of money in Islam when taken up in the epistemological sense.

Chapter 7 is yet another study of universal complementarity, social well-being and unity of knowledge in globally interactive, integrative and evolutionary systems. Here the Qur'anic ecological and agricultural model is invoked to set the scene of the analytical investigation. The agricultural model being a further abstraction of the tree model treated in Chapter 3 conveys a deeper meaning of 'global' systems in which interlinkages describe sustainability caused by ethicizing market, choices, technologies and institutions. We have treated a number of issues with regards to ecological, inter-generational and demographic sustainability in an economy wide sense with the objective criterion of social well-being.

Chapter 8 treats the subject matter of decision-making as a process study on unification of knowledge evolved from the epistemological root of Divine Unity. Here too a comparative examination of decision-making as a process study, is undertaken. The Islamic process-oriented decision-making model is shown to be characterized as the Shuratic Process. Its inner character is discussed. We show how it delineates the nature of decision-making in Islamic political economy as expounded. Here the nature of endogenously interactive, integrative and evolutionary preferences in the knowledge-based domain are explained. Thereby, the development of the knowledge-induced socioeconomic variables and the social well-being function, are formalized.

Chapter 9 is an application of the principle of universal complementarity in the context of Tawhidi epistemology and its worldview of unification of knowledge. Here we extend the study of social action from a specific reference to Islamic political economy to a general system in consumption, production and distribution. The interactive, integrative, evolutionary model (IIE) is thoroughly invoked and utilized. Several issues of value theory and factor pricing are discussed in the Islamic politico-economic perspectives.

In Chapter 10 we extend the principle of ethical endogeneity derived from the unifying worldview of Tawhidi episteme to the nature of methodological individualism, systemic plurality, and perceptions, all of which are shown to characterize the domain of rationalism. The focus on the topic of 'de-knowledge' is shown as a lateral opposite to the discussion of unification of knowledge in Chapter 3. Hence the Qur'anic Evil Tree is invoked in this chapter just as the Goodly Tree was invoked in Chapter 3. Thereby, all systemic contrasts are generated in the light of a meta-theory of socio-scientific systems according to Tawhidi episteme.

This book is the first part of the author's major research project entitled, 'A Dynamic Input-Output Analysis of Trade and Development in Member Countries of the Organization of Islamic Conference' supported by a grant from the Social Sciences and Humanities Research Council of Canada (SSHRC). This project is in two parts. The first part comprises a normative examination of a knowledge-induced dynamic model underlying the Islamic worldview. The second part is an empirical study of the existing state of affairs with respect to trade and development in the OIC countries. These two parts make up an integrated approach to a policy-theoretic examination of issues of trade and development in OIC membership. This first part provides the philosophy of science underlying the normative perspective of the dynamic model in terms of knowledge flows that intrinsically underlie the interactive, integrative and evolutionary dynamics of the Qur'anic Shuratic Process. The same process is also referred to here as the IIE-model.

This book should be read for a critical appreciation of issues in endogenous ethics, values and systems by students and academics of comparative political economy, political philosophy, philosophy of science, religious studies and systems scientists. It is hoped that the major contribution of this book would be on two fronts. First, it propounds a paradigm of Islamic political economy and world-systems based on epistemological roots. Secondly, it presents the study of epistemology in the light of general systems derived from the Qur'anic premise. Yet at the end, the result is a piece of intellectual endeavour that remains universal in all socio-scientific systems without any dogmatic and religious inhibition.

CHAPTER 1

GENERAL PERSPECTIVES: THE WORLDVIEW OF ISLAM AND THE OCCIDENT

FROM PRESENT TO THE FUTURE

With the coming of the information age mankind has entered an extensively interactive world-system. This world-system works at various levels. At the level of thought, it carries an epistemology of a process-oriented worldview, which Huxley foresaw to be the biological expression in his **Brave New World**. Whitehead referred to such a process view of reality in his **Process and Reality**. At the level of society the interactive worldview carries the seeds of new questions embedded in a post-modernist outlook of the future social arrangement. In this area we are witnessing today the rise of subnational interest groups. At the level of global political economy, borderless trading boundaries are transmitting the nature of managerial and financial capitalism. Here the implications are different from that earlier conceived in terms of the ownership and distributional questions involving labour and capital. At the level of science, new epistemologies for unification of the methodologies of science are being conceptualized. At the level of institutions, the world-system of capitalism is being intensified by a new type of mercantilist hegemony. It is a hybrid between Eurocentricity and regionalism.

Even as we pass this scene of enforcement during the coming millennium, the question crosses our mind: Where lies that human future which is to be embedded in social well-being? Have not the greatest thinkers at every juncture of human history revived the question of the moral contract to underlie the essence of change? Yet was change ever possible by separating the spiritual from the material world? Indeed, some form of morality, ethics or humanism has always grounded the vision of human future at every juncture of social transition. The sciences have not remained separate from such a demand. The important contribution in the history of thought has been the incessant pursuit for unity in the sciences and the categorization of morality inside the methods of science. Roger Penrose says in this regard (Penrose 1989, p. 97): 'Great works of art are indeed 'closer to God' than are lesser ones. It is a feeling not uncommon amongst artists, that in their greatest works they are revealing external truths which have some kind of prior ethereal existence.'

If unification and processual ordering of nature is to be the essence of future socio-scientific inquiry – spanning across society, political economy, institutionalism, science and technology – then new and abiding questions arise on the nature of globalism that is presently on.

QUESTIONS OF GLOBALISM

First there is the inquiry around the following question: Can the globalization of managerial and financial capitalism, trade and regionalism, and the kind of scientific support for these patterns, evolve into an interactive order of ethical linkages within the socio-scientific order? Can globalization of this type realize social well-being as something that is premised on extensive unity of the human race and its moral and material premises? Can science and society reach a unified worldview in the midst of the emerging globalization of this age?

Second, there is the inquiry around the following issue: If the answers to the first set of inquiry are in the negative, then positive answers must be sought afresh in the realm of new epistemologies in the area of unity of knowledge. The methodological individualism and reductionism of all socio-scientific ideas must be changed for a process-oriented world of intrinsic unity. This is of the essence that nothing can be meaningfully explained and realized unless all conditions of the new world-system can be premised on fundamental Unity. We are then aiming at a methodology that emanates from and in turn intensifies the socio-scientific outlook in a biological age in the light of a fundamental and most irreducible Unity of Being.

Of recent we have heard the clamour regarding a knowledge-based economy dawning with the information age, as a megatrend of socioeconomic transformation of the new millennium (Naisbitt & Aburdeen 1990). The knowledge economy is being claimed as the ultimate post-capitalist order and a medium that can equalize the distribution of social and economic benefits to all nations (Drucker 1993). Yet in the midst of these claims resides the concept of human resource development as an input of skills that revolves around economic efficiency and social development according to a neoclassical economic model. Diffusion of human resource development to the poor and the grassroots is being modelled in and around the demand configuration of an economy that is set into motion by the principles, institutions and power of a capitalist world-system. Consequently, there remains a close interrelationship between capitalism as a system of acquisition and ownership on the one hand, and education as a medium to sustain the former on the other hand. Education according to the neoclassical human resource model then becomes a medium that sustains the de-equalizing ownership within capitalism.

However, now the nature of capitalism is extended beyond the simple theme of ownership arising out of conflict between capital assets and labour services. It becomes a legitimation for the ownership of information technology and its knowledge base by the corporate world. The latter form can be referred to as managerial capitalism. Now human resource development in the knowledge economy of managerial capitalism becomes an instrument for sustaining the latter. At the end we find that such a conception of human resource development does not liberate individuals from the throes of inequality and deprivation in as far as capitalism can perpetuate itself in the midst of such unequal partnership, conflict and ownership.

The twin goals, namely of attaining economic efficiency and social equity for human well-being, now appear as conflicting and substituting ones within the model of neoclassical trade-off. In this picture we find that while human resource development must serve the goals of an efficient economy, it must become a powerful instrument in the hands of capitalists. The share of national wealth for capital must consequently remain substantially higher than the share for labour. Hence the trade-off is spelt out in terms of such conflicting trade-offs in the global production menu with a neoclassical conception of human resource. Nothing better can be expected from such a perspective of human resource development in the framework of a knowledge economy beyond accelerated economic growth and its trickle down effect that renders no improvement of the relative scale of well-being among unequal agents transacting in the capitalist global economy.

Yet another perspective of capitalism arising from the powerful property rights of the knowledge economy is financial capitalism. At this juncture, the global community is witnessing a rapid transference of money from national governments and international financial institutions to the multinational banking sector (Bhaduri & Steindl 1985). Financial multinationals are today capable of affecting the global supply of money through issuance of bonds and loanable capital. They are then equally capable of making the global economy highly speculative and risk-prone. We are witnessing the highly speculative nature of the global economy entrenched in such financial issues of promissory notes (Independent Commission on Population and Quality of Life 1996). Even the Tobin tax on international financial transactions does not help out, for an ad volerem tax on the production of economic 'bads' by oligopolies can always be transferred to the consumer by such conglomerates, thus reducing economic welfare (Nordhaus & Tobin 1972).

In the end, global financial capitalism is found to aim at a control of monetary resources while engendering real sector activities in low-wage and resource-abundant economies. As long as the control of financial policies and instruments remain vested with giant multinationals, the reign of speculative fever and the whims of political and economic uncertainty for nation states will always remain within the control of giant corporations at the expense of the grassroots (Korten 1995). The most pervasive causes of such widespread uncertainties are found to be the high rates of interest and exchange rate volatility in developing countries. Policies to control such rates cannot be set independently of the financial and economic policies of industrialized nations. Such policies are in turn determined by the financial policies dictated by large banks and their central banking authorities. An example in this regard is the global merger of large corporations in recent times that have intensified oligopolistic power and have affected the flow of capital and goods across the globe. The recent capital flights from Asian countries is an example testifying the governance of large corporations over the fate of nation states.

Following the debt crisis of the eighties, the IMF too was pulled into a risk-absorption commitment set by the large financial banks. This caused IMF policies on interest rate, exchange rate and balance of payments to be determined by the wishes of the global banking consortium. A glaring example of this is the privatization of Special Drawing Rights and the Euro Currency in the form of preferred bonds that can be held by large financial corporations (IMF 1995).

In the end, the global economy is experiencing nothing new today in the way of ameliorating social well-being, and the new millennium is not expected to be any different from the Eurocentric mercantilist spirit of the industrial revolution. In recent times we have also heard the empty slogans of a new global order, the peace dividend, human rights issues linked with international trade, the reorganization of the United Nations and the commercialization of Rio Earth Summit (Stockholm Initiative 1991, Urquhart & Childers 1996, Parikh 1992, Ongun 1994). Yet for all, the debt crisis is once again found to be linked with the financial uncertainties of nation states, whereas the assets of the poor have suffered the most in this debacle. Examples of the assets of the poor being liquidated in the recent currency crashes in Malaysia and Indonesia testify to this fact.

NEW GLOBALISM

A new perspective of globalization based on jointly realizing social justice, distributive equity and economic growth (efficiency) must therefore be engendered. This is to arise from the common will of the global community, or failing this, by the grassroots in various nations. Social well-being would then be achieved by realizing complementarity between the social and economy ends. The underlying forces that can make this complementarity happen, must be supported jointly by the instruments of science and the organization of polity at all levels of the social structure. Each such level will have to be guided by the same principle of extensive participation and complementarity among the agents involved. Participation and complementarity are attributes that depict interactions and consensus among various agents. Such consensus result in systems of social contracts.

Globalism is then to be redefined to mean a consensual world-system that is causally interrelated with pervasively interactive systems interlinking society, economy, polity and science along with all their sub-systems. An ecological wholeness incorporating such interactive and consensual orders now break down barriers of dichotomy, conflict and disorder. Participation and complementarity replace marginalist substitution, which we saw above to be characterizing the neoclassicism resource allocation. Neoclassical trade-offs are replaced by the globally unified world-systems caused by a unification of knowledge among exchanging systems and their agents. Since interactions and integration define the dynamics of the unification process of global complementarity, and this reflects diverse possibilities, therefore the worldview of new globalism must be a processual one. Being of unifying type across systems, it must be fundamentally epistemological and ontological in essence. Being applicative, it must be governed by concrete instruments, programs, policies, guidance and enforcement.

Such a vision must be epistemologically sensitive within the new global order at every step of its evolution. Its very essence of unity at the roots would contradict the rationalistic basis of both socialism and capitalism. Its morally charged complexity must be opposed to the ethically neutral deterministic order of rationalism.

In this regard we note that Marx started his dialectical thesis on the premise of 'economism' and reduced all social actions to this one-dimensional determinant (Staniland 1985, Marcuse 1964). Likewise, capitalism remains premised on a social contractarian philosophy that is organized around ownership by conflict, an attribute of social Darwinism. Consequently, rationalism must predominate in this order to sustain evolution but in a random plane or to be regimented by hegemony (Kant trans. Friedrich 1987, Hegel trans. Sibree 1956, Heilbroner & Milberg 1995). There is even a claim among some quarters today that a rationalistic understanding of evolution marks the stereotyping of an occidental concept of historicism in all world-systems (Fukuyama 1992).

On the other hand, the epistemology of fundamental unity and the emerging worldview of unification of knowledge from it across hierarchies of agents, variables, relations and systems, outrightly annuls rationalism, its resulting dualism and pluralism (Bergson see Russell 1990). Likewise, 'economism' is replaced by knowledge generation out of fundamental unity in all systems. Thereafter, all materiality gets determined simultaneously by means of the continuous flow of knowledge as input and output of its associated cognitive order. Disequilibrium, conflict and sustained inequality of these systems are resolved by participation in the midst of interactions. Interactions lead to consensus or social integration. Now the attained levels of unification caused by generated knowledge cause fresh evolution of knowledge and their induced material forms. A socio-scientific order emerges epistemologically from the foundations of fundamental unity both at the levels of conceptualization and its application to a reformed world-system in the new global order. Such evolutionary systems have order but complexity in them as they permanently revolve around fundamental unity. Such attributes make them altogether different from the rationalistic world-systems premised on dualism and pluralism. The latter have formed the permanent and historical characteristics of capitalism, socialism and their prototypes (Schumpeter 1950).

Marxism, occidentalism and their prototypes in the socio-scientific order, have for long now abandoned any meaningful reference to the moral precept of unity. Consequently, the resulting social contractarian ideas of these systems have permanently relied on power-driven, conflicting and hegemonic institutions of man fuelled by the human ego. Morality could not be sustained in such systems due to the presence of such unilateral or collectivized power and hegemony. Linearity of processes in such systems resulted from the absence of interactions toward realizing participation as opposed to individualism or hegemony. Likewise in the sciences, as in the case of Newtonian time, a linearity of relations overshadowed the profundity of more complex reality. Yer where complexity is assumed, there randomness becomes endemic. Where order is derived from chaos, there adaptive control is assumed to configure equilibrium by hegemony. All of these states are assumptions of a methodological nicety rather than of realism, such states are required to attain an optimal-equilibrium state in the socio-scientific order that remains devoid of extensively interactive processes. The emerging processes must at the same time unify as well as enrich the evolving ranks of the interactions and consensus through diversities of human possibilities and must be premised on fundamental unity. Now moral social contract becomes the rule of engagement in this new world-system. Its methodology is systemically processual, leading to evolutionary equilibria but never to optimality (Shackle 1972).

In none of these approaches do we find unification of knowledge to be the permanent essence of the socio-scientific systems as opposed to the randomness of rationalism. When such unification sometime appears, as in Kant's theories of reason, fundamental unity is seen to remain dysfunctionally outside of human reality. God comes to be explained by means of theories of rationalism, rather than reason being ontologically premised on revelation that emanates from Divine Unity. The subsequent arguments, analysis, constructions and explanations of systems remain embedded in rationalism in all of the occidental order. Contrarily, the same functions are established powerfully by the epistemology of Divine Unity in the Islamic worldview.

THE ISLAMIC WORLDVIEW

This is where the Islamic worldview takes its roots, for springing into the new millennium with its own socio-scientific explanatory power. Indeed its fundamental premise, namely the precept of Divine Unity has permanently lived its experience in the history of the past and present. It is well-known that all Islamic scholars, no matter whether they were rationalists or religionists (Mutakallimun), looked to Divine Unity for logic, theory and explanations of creation. The difference among them was simply the method of inquiry used in invoking the epistemology of Divine Unity on conceptual and cognitive facts.

Yet Qur'anic consciousness of civilizational change is of a far greater depth than the narrative history of Islam, for through it is established the permanence and uniqueness of the socio-scientific methodology. The phenomenon of the Qur'an, as Malik Ben Nabi calls it (Nabi 1983), is the inhering essence of Divine Unity that is both the epistemological precept as well as the (cognitive) field for understanding globally explanatory comprehension, relationism and applications (Choudhury 1991). It finds its expressions permanently in the intellectual dynamics of the socio-scientific order as in the mundane areas of human life as well. Thus the episteme of Divine Unity resides embryonically in both the essence of matter and mind as a coherent reality without distinction between the secular and the non-secular, the West and the East, Muslims and the other. The Qur'an mentions about this indelible phenomenon as the universal civilizational and essential reality (Chapter lv verse 17-8): 'He is Lord of the two Easts and Lord of the two Wests: Then which of the favours of your Lord will ye deny?' Furthermore (Chapter xli, verse 53): 'Soon will We show them Our Signs in the (furthest) regions (of the earth), and in their own souls, until it becomes manifest to them that this is the truth. Is it not enough that thy Lord doth witness all things?'

The Islamic worldview is thereby, the comprehensive and universalizing, overarching and complementing design of reality that is premised on the epistemology of Divine Unity and is evolved into intellection through the process-orientation model of unification of knowledge in world-systems as derived from the primal source of Divine Unity. In this book we will also refer to Divine Unity by the Qur'anic term, Tawhid. The principal sources of Tawhidi epistemology of life and thought are the Qur'an, the guidance of the Prophet Muhammad (Sunnah) and the authoritative research of the conscious Islamic community on the specifics of interpretation of the above two sources. This conscious search is called Ijtihad. Ijtihad takes place under a detailed method of discourse called the process generated by the institution of Islamic consultation (Shura, hence the Shuratic Process).

The result of Shuratic Process is to come up with consensus on the issues at hand. Such an integrating state is called Ijma. Beyond any state of Ijma, the perpetual evolution of fresh knowledge premised derived from the Tawhidi episteme, leads a preceding interactive (i.e. Ijtihadi) and integrative (Ijmatic) process into creative evolution. The Qur'an refers to this last state of dynamic realization of systemic unification as re-origination (Khalq in-Jadid). Note the following verse of the Qur'an (Chapter X, verse 34): 'It is God Who originates Creation and repeats it: Then how are ye deluded (away from the truth)?'

The Islamic Law or Shari'ah is now seen as being composed of an immutable core and an Ijtihadi outer substance. The core is the epistemology premised on Tawhid. It combines the rules (Ahkam) derived from the Qur'an and the guidance of the Prophet (Sunnah) for an understanding of reality. The outer domain of the epistemic core is spanned by knowledge-induced discourses on specific issues (Ijtihad). They bring about fresh interpretations and enhance earlier ones. The last stage provides the domain of evolutionary epistemology of unification of knowledge premised on the epistemic core of Divine Unity. The totality of the process emanating from the epistemology of unity and carried thereafter to the evolutionary stages, is termed as the Shuratic Process. Shari'ah is thus evolved by means of the Shuratic Process from the core in a creative fashion, while responding to changing demands of the times. This kind of process when taken up in continuity across world-systems, marks the essence of Qur'anic civilizational change. It is at once social as well as scientific.

Hence, both Shari'ah and the Shuratic Process now mean a holistic worldview of interactions, integration and creative evolution that is applied to every aspect of reality. These pervasively embryonic processes apply to the total socio-scientific order, not simply to the political and legal venues, as often misunderstood in Islamic thought (Asad 1987). The realization of such a worldview in all areas of life and thought now constitutes the well-being criterion. About this the Qur'an says (Chapter viii, verse 29): 'O ye who believe! If ye fear God, He will grant you a Criterion (to judge between right and wrong), remove from you (all) evil (that may afflict) you, and forgive you: For God is the Lord of Grace unbounded.'

Within the Islamic worldview as defined above, the new concept of globalism becomes one of politico-economic interactions, integration and creative evolution realized by using the tenets and the rules for the construction of a socio-scientific order that is premised on Tawhidi epistemology. Such a global order is therefore not simply of the nature of geographical continuity, regionalism, or one that is established entirely by international trade within the Muslim world. Instead, it is all these only in concert with the socio-scientific conception and organization that are premised on the unification of knowledge as derived from Tawhidi epistemology. Such a concept of the world-system is termed in the Qur'an as the Ummah (Choudhury 1997). The Qur'anic verses in this regard are (Chapter 2, verses 142-143 interpretations by author):

> ...To God belong both the East and the West: He guideth whom He will to a Way that is straight. Thus have We made of you an Ummah justly balanced, that ye might be witnesses over the nations, and the Apostle (Prophet Muhammad, i.e. Sunnah) a

witness over yourselves; and We appointed the Qibla (direction of worship, broadly speaking the organization of the institution of prayer, worhsip and their concomitant consequences for life), to which thou wast used, only to test those who followed the Apostle from those who would turn on their heels (from the Faith) (takes up a universal meaning from the battle of Badr to the continuation of Sunnah). Indeed it was a change momentous, except to those guided by God. And never would God make your faith of no effect (universality). For God is to all people most surely full of kindness, Most Merciful (Certainty).

The new global order is referred to in the Qur'an as Ummah. It conveys benefits to both Muslims and others. In terms of its socio-scientific essence, it conveys knowledge-induced well-being for both the human world and the great ecological totality. The generic knowledge-induced Shuratic Processes of Ummatic world-system are applicable in the small scale problems as in the progressively interlinked totality of greater orders of systems. In this perspective, the political economy of Islam becomes applicable to the sub-nation, the nation, and the Ummah. In these world-systems, the stages of interactive generated integration with creative evolution are realized through progressive interlinkages. Inherent in such processes is the enabling principle of pervasive complementarity explained and enacted in accordance with unification of knowledge. Islamic political economy now assumes a well-definition in such a globally interactive systemic worldview as a socio-scientific order with interactions, integration and creative evolution across hierarchies of agents, variables, relations and systems.

THE HISTORISTIC DIFFERENCE BETWEEN CAPITALIST GLOBALIZATION, OCCIDENTAL GLOBALISM AND THE WORLDVIEW OF THE UMMAH

With the demise of socialism, with the subsequent rise of a plethora of power-centric groups, with the new drive of science away from materialism into essence, with the reversal of economic power from the West to the East, and with unrelenting questioning against Eurocentric ordering of thought and life both in the East and the West, mankind has today reached the threshold of a post-modern age. The dawning of such an age is marked by paradigmatic questioning against the hegemonic nature of modernity as traditionally defined by neo-liberal rationalism (Ferry & Renault 1992). The conduct of neo-liberal rationalism and its associated form, the political philosophy of democracy, have proven to be power-centric representations of aggregative preferences of voting individuals governed by self-interest and methodological individualism (Sullivan 1982). Both of these lead to the assumption of power out of conflict and of sustaining the same by similar processes. Social Darwinism is intrinsic in such a selfishly organizational gene (Dawkins 1976). Post-modernity opens up a Pandora's box of questions against the philosophy of modernity by its demand for deconstruction of the large and the hegemonic. In Fukuyama's terminology, this marks the rise of the isothymotic spirit of the post-modern age against the megalothymotic one of modernity (Fukuyama 1992).

The question however remains unresolved. For even in Fukuyama's thesis of the end of history, we find a hegemonic convergence towards the modern capitalist transformation. The roots of capitalism that is seen as an unending series of conflicting processes of new becoming from the old orders, is a Hegelian dialectical process carrying the world into its present transformation, namely global capitalism. Along with this transformation has also gone along a convergence in the requisite scientific, technological, economic, social and political orders of the West. It further means that any fresh inquiry in post-modern era would be simply a re-examination of the modernist epistemology within the same methodology. Such a methodology is represented by individualism and pluralism and all that these entail in the realm of thought and applications.

If mankind is to accept the moribund picture of a petrified end to historical novelty under either the modernist or the post-modernist methodologies, both being premised on hegemonic convergence towards global capitalism and its artefacts of power, then there can be no further structural evolution of thought. Contrarily, if this claim of the occidental order is to be questioned seriously by methodology, analytics, explanations and applications that are more profound than the observed ones since the last three-hundred years of Western world-system (Wallerstein 1979), then the world should be ready for a new take-off. This is the claim of Islam as the historistic and civilizational reality that is permanently embedded in the order of things. It regains its momentous expressions at major epochs of history for a reconfirmation. We have noticed this in the recent history of the Ottomans, and we continue to sense it in the reawakening of Islamic movements both at the political level and the grassroots levels (Khomeini 1980).

The idea of historicism in Islam is itself associated with the ever-presencing of the unity of knowledge in cognitive reality and its creative understanding in all systems of life and thought across evolutionary planes of knowledge. Thus modernity in this sense of an ever-becoming historicism means novelty of ever-unfolding reality. The concept of post-modernity is not deconstruction of a hegemonic and centralized modernist way of thinking and organization (Giddens 1983, White 1989) into its individuated components. Rather, in Islamic perspective the meaning of post-modernity is the emergence of the globally interactive worldview premised on Divine Unity (Tawhid) and as this fundamental unity is pervasively formalized and applied in the real world through unification of knowledge as process. An ecological model is thus formalized as being capable of carrying the attributes of interactions (Ijtihad), integration (Ijma) and evolution (Khalq in-Jadid) across hierarchies of agents, variables, relations and systems.

ISLAMIC WORLD-SYSTEM AS THE NEW GLOBAL ORDER

The idea of the Islamic world-system being framed in the midst of knowledge-centred unified systems, and defining in this way the concept of globalism, creative change and historicism, points to its distinct nature over other received doctrines. We know that the origin of occidentalism resides in Greek metaphysics, thereafter sculptured out progressively in the West (Russell 1990) through the medium of its transference and refinement by Islamic rationalists. Thus to study the epistemic roots of occidentalism we need to inquire on the Greek World and trace its presence through important junctures of history that evolved cumulatively into modernity and post-modernity. We need to show as well, how the Muslim rationalists (Kalam) were influenced by Greek thought and then contributed to rationalist thinking in the West. On the other hand, the Qur'anic roots of the Islamic worldview, as explained above, need to be derived from their independent roots in Qur'an and

Sunnah. Here rationalism and its prototypes must be abandoned. They are to be replaced by the precept of Divine Unity, then developed into an explanatory model of systemic unification of knowledge. Thus a distinct concept of epistemological functionality is developed in this non-rationalist framework. In Islamic history the school of epistemologists, called Mutakallimun, adopted such an original approach. It proved to be distinct and often contrary to the Greek World.

In the field of political economy, the same kind of a dialectical method caused Ibn Khaldun's ideas to be premised on social conflict and disequilibrium analysis. The cosmological view of Kalam scholars was based on a materialist-dialectical method. This is reflected in the works of the Ikhwan as-Safa and the Mutazzilites (Nasr 1978). The conceptualization of a theory of political economy in the light of a conflict-centred social disequilibrium model, made Khaldun's methodology simply a forerunner of the latter days' social dialectics, neoclassical marginalism and institutional hegemony.

These conditions were later on explained by classical political economy and Marxism-Hegelian dialectics (Ferry 1992). Marginalism was taken up by neoclassicism and was the cause and effect of a material domain that was subjected to conditions of trade-off, optimality, steady state and full information. Hence in this way some of the niceties but unrealism of utilitarianism were assumed earlier by the Kalam scholars despite their claim of a processual dialectical method. Continued debility in their methodology was caused by their inability in endogenizing unification of knowledge in systems and explaining the cognitive world by means of it (Siddiqi 1979).

The Mutakallimun scholars on the other hand abandoned rationalism. In this, Ghazzali went through the painful task of rationalist experience, but he later on realized the futility of explaining Tawhidi reality by a rationalistic method (Karim undated). Instead of rationalism, Shari'ah became the premise of knowledge generation in Ghazzali's metaphysical methodology. From this arose the distinct concepts of economy, society, institutions and polity. The epistemology of Shari'ah itself was Divine Unity. The study of political economy now became one of studying the dynamics of the world nation of Islam, Ummah. The Shura and Caliphate now became the essential determinants of the political economy of Ummah. Thereby, political economy as a study of social conflict, found in mainstream thought, is replaced by the study of interactions, complementarity and moral processes intrinsic in systems. Ghazzali profoundly invoked Tawhid and its self-same event, Akhira (Hereafter), to embody the knowledge-induced processual attributes into social analysis and social psychology.

Figure 1.1 summarizes the major perspectives of Greek and rationalist thought in Western economy, society, polity and science. It then traces out the areas where occidental developments were influenced in specific ways by Islamic scholasticism. The development of the essentially Tawhidi epistemological basis of Islamic worldview as conceptualized by the non-rationalists and as it projects the new interactive global order – a cosmologically ecological model – is shown to be the distinct worldview of the future (Choudhury 1995).

In figure 1.1, the rightward direction of the arrows (→) shows the progression of schools of thought. The downward direction of the arrows (↑) indicates related developments of the corresponding schools of thought. The upward-downward arrows show interactions of thoughts and systems. Islamic thought is shown to have branched out into two distinct directions – of the Kalam and the Mutakallimun. The abrupt ending shows the end of a particular school of thought.

The Kalam concepts are shown to have experienced a similar nature of rationalistic evolution in the natural and social sciences, institutionalism and polity, as did the occidental schools experience in relation to Greek epistemological roots. Thus, the concept of 'just balance' (Mizan, 'Adl) was taken up in a rationalist sense with assimilation of some Qur'anic essence in it (Mahdi 1964). The universe was seen to be continuous in terms of matter (Al-Farabi trans. Walzer 1985). Farabi's Perfect State, Ibn Sina's dichotomy between Active and Passive Reason, are all similar to the dichotomy between pure and practical reason given later on by Kant (Ali 1989). Such a conception severing God from cognitive reality, spelt dualism and pluralism within the rationalistic methods of the Kalam scholars, and often turned them into pantheistic thinkers (Rahman 1958). The combination of dialectics, perfect state, materiality and pantheism in their concept of the universe, made the Kalam scholars as early utilitarians, who premised their concept of ethics in the humanistic perception of a notion of happiness borrowed from Aristotle (Weldon 1987, Quinton 1989). The Kalam scholars then coated their concept of happiness and freedom by a Qur'anic note of morality and Oneness of God. However, such a divine invocation remained an exogenous prescription, having no endogenous force as we find in the case of a knowledge-centric world-system (Bayrakli 1996).

Al-Arabi too wrote on the science of Tawhid and wanted it to become the endogenous analytical approach in Islamic thought. He argued that Tawhid provides a premise of analysis that is altogether original of its own and needs no distraction by externally imposed doctrines for explaining reality. He wrote (Chittick 1989):

> Two ways lead to the knowledge of God. There is no third way. ...
>
> The first way is the way of unveiling. It is an incontrovertible knowledge, which is actualized through unveiling and which man finds in himself.
>
> The second way is the way of reflection and reasoning (Istidlal) through rational demonstration (Burhan Aqli). This way is lower than the first way, since he who bases his consideration upon proof can be visited by obfuscations which detract from his proof, and only with difficulty can he remove them.

Shah Waliullah developed the method of discovering analytical rules independently in the Qur'an (Jalbani 1985). Imam Shatibi's theory of Maslaha wal-Istihsan and Fakruddin Razi's theory of self-actualization are landmarks on the Shari'ah basis of social well-being. Ibn Taimiyyah's use of the institution of social regulation of markets was a practical example of establishing complementarity between market efficiency and social justice as a corner stone of the study of Islamic political economy (Holland 1982).

The worldview of Divine Unity and its substantive formalism in the socio-scientific study of globally interactive systems, is a rigorously analytical methodology in unification of knowledge. It is seen here to be the crystallization of the interconnected cosmological worldview that the Mutakallimun scholars upheld. But such a cosmological generalization is not an empty holistic concept. The worlds (al-A'lamin) are sub-systems of the cosmological universe; so are the inner domains of such world-systems. The Islamic theory of knowledge thus applies uniquely to all of these at every level of construction and deconstruction.

Figure 1.1: From capitalist globalism to knowledge-centred worldview

GLOBALISM IN OCCIDENTAL WORLD VIEW

Rationalism ⇒ Individualism ⇒ Pluralism ⇒ Modernity ⇒ Postmodernity

⇓

Greek World ⇒ Physiocracy ⇒ Classical ⇒ Neo-Classical ⇒ Micro-Macro

⇓ World-System

Markets Institutions Global Capitalism

⇓

Utilitarianism ⇒ Liberalism ⇒ Neo-Liberalism

⇓

Pluralism Political Philosophy Democracy

⇓

Political Economy
Scientific and Technological Reductionism:
Rationalism, Matter-Mind Dichotomy, Ethical Neutrality

⇓ ⇓

Micro-Macro Conflict in Science Megalothymotic vs. Isothymotic

⇓

Preference Formation, Society, Economy, Polity, Global Order

⇓

Eurocentricity

I. GRECO-ISLAMIC LINEAGE (*KALAM*)

Rationalism with Qur'an Ethical Holism (Cosmology)

⇓

Nationalistic Concepts ⇒ Utilitarianism ⇒ Conjecture ⇒ Dialectics ⇒ Conflict with Divine Laws

⇓

Metaphysics and Science (Al-Kindi, Ibn Sina) Political Economy (Ibn Khaldun) Materiality Pantheism (Al-Farabi, Ibn Rushd)

⇓

Rationalistic Cosmological View of Science and World-System

Figure 1.1 (Continued)

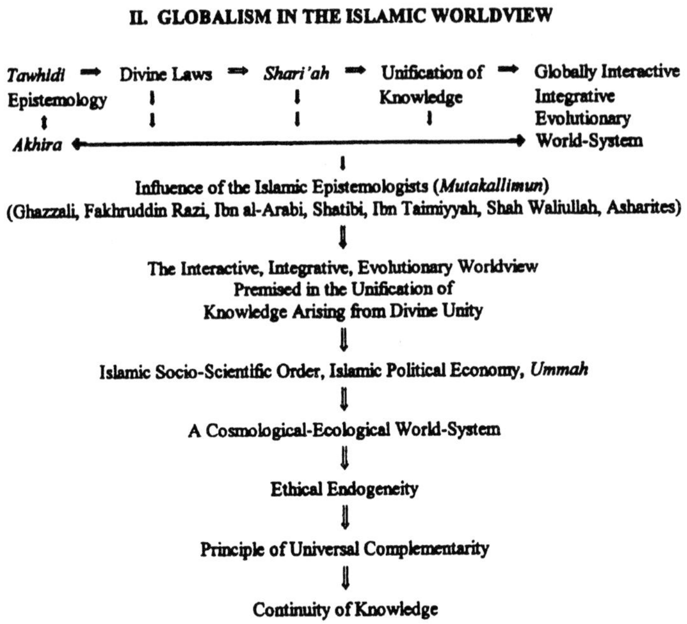

In figure 1.1, the emergence of new globalism is shown to be premised on the age-old Truth of Tawhid in world-systems (Haqq al-Yaqin). This is seen to arise anew as a great epoch in post-modernity. It is shown to come at a juncture when the 'end-of-history' thesis of modernist hegemony is found to seal in the same stereotyping way the transition from modernity whose outlook is based on individualistic (isothymotic) aggregation of social preferences, and the post-modernist, whose outlook is based on the deconstruction of a social aggregate preference relationship (megalothymotic) marking methodological pluralism. Such a stereotype has remained permanent in occidental history ever since its Hellenic inception and through the ages. The perspective is not expected to change with the advent of post-modernity in the West.

In post-modernity, the much popularized slogans of information age and knowledge-economy are seen as mere instruments of global capitalism. Hence they remain as part and parcel of the old idea of capital in modernity, now repeating itself in the form of information capital. Within this same genre of thinking, ecology itself is simply a study of the environment carrying the human and other species with it in some kind of a social contract. The neoclassical methodology of marginal substitution, and the competition caused by individualism of agents in such an order, make the environment-economy general equilibrium model, to be one based on conflict. Complementarity is dispensed within these models when economic efficiency (e.g. economic growth) and distributive equity (e.g. income distribution) start to substitute each other in models of economic growth and resource constraint. An idea of ecology defined in such reductionist models is not the same as that of the overarching cosmological ecology that we have referred to in the context of a systemic worldview.

We have shown in figure 1.1 that because of the inherent absence of interactions in rationalism and methodological pluralism (individualism) within society, science and polity of the occidental worldview, all such systems will move into increasing individuation, as shown. On the other hand, the Islamic world-systems governed by pervasive complementarity, will increasingly become interactive, integrative and evolutionary. This is the new globalism of the Tawhidi worldview as opposed to the old globalism that fades away into uninteresting non-renewal of change at the end of global capitalism and its derivative called post-modernity.

CHAPTER 2

THE QUR'ANIC WORLDVIEW IN THE SCIENCES

Traditional conceptions in science, be these natural or social sciences, are shown to be the result of and leading to controlled experimentation. Thus, the concepts of optimality and steady state that have long now impacted upon the growth of scientific methodology are found to be ideal states, admitting no possibility for interactions. Hence knowledge formation as substantively understood in terms of interactions remains void or conflicting in rationalist world-systems, except due to hegemonic regimentation. Science is thus shown to be partitioned between ideal states caused by a rationalistic perception of the universe and a reality that is made to be devoid of ethical relevance.

The Qur'an shows how the precept of Divine Unity creates a worldview premised in a new epistemology termed as Tawhid, meaning Oneness of God. From this epistemology emanates the nature of unification of knowledge. In the context of this epistemology, the dichotomy caused by science between rationalism and ethical meaning, is rejected. The new methodology creates unification in the strong and extensive sense based on the attributes of knowledge formation that are premised on a model of interactions, integration and creative evolution (IIE).

OBJECTIVE OF THIS CHAPTER

The objective of this chapter is to critically examine the comparative meaning of science as it is understood conventionally and in the light of Qur'anic precepts. We will then briefly develop the alternative scientific worldview presented by the Qur'an in terms of its methodology and application. These will be shown to lead to a universally interactive, integrative and evolutionary (IIE) process that emanates from the foundation of the Unity of God and its application to the study of scientific problems, ethics, markets and globalization (i.e. Ummah = world-system of Islam). The coverage of none of these significant areas is by any means exhaustive here. The very subject matter of methodology, application and comparative study of the theme presented here is in the least of voluminous size. The reader may turn elsewhere for such extensive studies (Choudhury 1994, 1995a; Nasr 1992).

WHAT IS THE SCIENTIFIC VIEW AND METHODOLOGY?

What is the meaning of science as perceived, theorized and practiced since the Age of Enlightenment in the occidental world? In answer to this, we note that the challenge of industrial revolution in Eighteenth Century Europe brought home the need to establish certain ways and means of legitimating the exploitation of human and material resources for the sake of economic growth, for the acquisition of wealth and for the reign of the 'animal spirit' in competing entrepreneurship (Wallerstein, 1989).

Production of goods and services meant to Europe the use of taxing powers by the English, French and Dutch mercantilism for the acquisition of cheap resources from the colonies. This helped to fuel the on-going inventions of the industrial revolution during the Eighteenth Century. It was felt that the aggrandising spirit of capital accumulation, technological change, acquisition of wealth and power, could be reinforced by a free disposition of the human rule over all domains.

Science in the occidental order was born at such a juncture of social psychology. On the one hand, it represented a cause and effect (necessary and sufficient condition) of the prowess of market transformation, power, wealth and technological change that were necessary for science to flourish. On the other hand, the self-serving Eurocentric interrelationships among science, technology, markets and power, reinforced all of these.

From this early need for comprehending the material perspective of the natural world and to make nature, mind and actions subservient to sheer materialistic comprehension, science was born in the crucible of the materially observational world. These in other words were the essence of the Copernican Revolution and Cartesian metaphysics

(Garber 1992). The observational world was made to acquire logical rationalization within the academic discourse of mind with matter. Science became an intellectual regimentation for viewing, controlling, guiding and developing such a linear relationship of causation between materiality and the growth of mind. The observational domain of science is thus a self-reinforcing process between logical reductionism of materiality and the emerging observational categories.

Furthermore, methodological individuation in this mind-matter, moral-material interrelationships in science means that science prevails in the domain where all experiences must exist as quantifiable, measurable and logically explainable categories. The domain of science ends where these very categories cease to be so discerned. Consequently, occidental science is axiomatic in nature, whereby, axioms of science assume two characters: First, they arise from the realm of the materially configured attributes that appeal to perception. This characterizes the domain of rationalism. Rationalism reigns in the temporal extant of perceived faculties.

Second, the axioms are most reduced in number in order to convey both a minimum premise for explaining the greatest range of possibilities, and to preserve the invariance of these axioms (Einstein 1960). Hence, the axioms of science are their most reduced premises of knowledge. All observations, logical synthesis and inferences are subsequently made in light of these axioms in varied problems.

DESCRIPTION OF SCIENCE IN OCCIDENTAL CONTEXT

A definition of science can now be given in its occidental context: Science is the study of relations between a body of theory and its experimental evaluation on the basis of a minimal number of most reduced axioms. It becomes necessary to study the relationships between science and the real world on the basis of a controlled environment that makes the axiomatic relations work.

Let us take an example from chemistry. In the light of the above definition of science, if we are saying that 'water' is made up of two atoms of hydrogen and one atom of oxygen (H_2O), this is just a mathematical way of making the calculations of Mendeleyev's atomic table on valences, hold up for studying the properties of water in its purest state (Heiserman 1992). Such a molecular property of water is thereafter made to be invariant in all states of nature, because the mathematical properties so assigned to water, remain unchanged. Yet if we consider 'water' with the slightest bit of impurity in it, then the above-mentioned atomic character will cease to be observed. The substance called 'water' par excellence, will not be observed. In other words, in order to study water in scientific measurements according to Mandeleyev's table, this substance must be pure and perfect water. All this means that science studies water as a controlled substance that must exist in its purest state in accordance with how the axiom of that scientific category defines 'water.'

In the same way, one would say the laws of motion of a particle according to Newtonian classical mechanics must obey the ideal state of vacuum for the motion. A difference to this classical idea of motion is that of the curvilinear deflection of light around a gravitational field (Skinner 1969). Yet in a state of rarifying gravitational field, such as for an inflationary expanding universe, the Einstein-Schwarzschild law of deflection of light will increasingly fail to hold (Hawking 1988).

Science therefore aims at establishing interrelationships within a system of segmented categories that are subjected to axioms, controls and mathematical statements in ideal forms. The application of science on the basis of these primal attributes of matter, is equally a controlled experimentation. In the midst of all such axiomatic perceptions, the important issue of interactions among categories in the substantive idea of a process, is ignored by science.

One then questions, does science establish an interactively systemic view of the world and nature? Such a systemic view exists in the received theory of science only within a system of related categories existing in their ideal forms. But science remains limited in realizing all possible systemic interactions and integrations. This is due to the fact that systems get reduced to segmented sub-systems by the purpose and application of scientific investigation.

The underlying logical positivitism as the essence of materiality, observation, reductionism and controlled inferences in science were given by Descartes, Bacon, Hume and Russell of many others. Dampier wrote regarding the reductionist deprivation of western sciences and philosophy in the following words (Dampier, 1961, pg. 491):

Even if we take empirical observation as the sole basis of physical knowledge, we thereby select subjectively the kind of knowledge to be admitted as physical; the Universe so discovered cannot be wholly objective. Epistemological science investigates the meaning of knowledge instead of a supposed entity, the external world, and its symbols stand for elements of knowledge. We thus reach a selective subjectivism, in which the laws and constants of nature are wholly subjective.

SCIENCE IN THE FRAMEWORK OF THE UNIFICATION PROJECT

We will now take up a slightly more extensive view of science. Modern science arising from theoretical physics sees the scientific aim to be unification of forces and fields in physics. Scientists claim that this can only be possible if the four forces of nature, namely, gravitation, strong nuclear, weak nuclear and electromagnetic forces, become unified. Unification in turn necessitates that the methodologies of quantum physics (micro-physics) must lead to the principles of relativity physics (macro-physics) and vice versa. Finally, these preconditions also imply that the frames of references, motions and observations of events in space and time, must remain invariant in order to derive unique inferences.

This is also the belief of the recent anthropic principle of theoretical physics on which Breuer writes (Breuer 1990, pg. 8):

> Because there are observers in our universe, the universe must possess properties which permit the existence of these observers.
>
> The structure of the universe and the particulars of its construction are essentially fixed by the condition that at some point it inevitably produces an observer.

Scientific orientation has thus shifted significantly from classical mechanics, relativity, and quantum mechanics, to the present days unification theories in theoretical physics or to entropy theory in thermodynamics (Coveney & Highfield 1990). Modern science is centrally concerned with the quest for axioms, methodology, application and inferences that can establish unification in the sciences. Consequently, the same quest for unification means scientific comprehension in the order of general systems while combining segmented ones (Koizumi 1993). This kind of inter-systemic as well as intra-systemic interactions is increasingly becoming the indelible mark of new science. The axioms, methodology and perceptions in science are consequently changing and are expected to experience further paradigmatic shifts as we come closer to comprehend the unification research agenda.

A NEW DEFINITION OF SCIENCE

We now offer a new definition of science in the light of a relational, interconnected and unifying nature of systemic entirety. This is an idea of Hubner's 'systems-ensemble' expressed as follows:

> By the second historical category, the 'historical system-ensemble,' I mean a structured set of systems, in part contemporary (to the time in question) and in part handed down, which are ordered among themselves in accordance with various relations and within those compass a given society moves at any given time. Scientific systems, that is, theories and hierarchies of theories, as well as the rules governing scientific work, are thus all a part of this collective ensemble that presents us with the world of rules within which we live and act at any given time (Hubner, 1985, pg. 109).

Science in this light is the package comprising epistemology, methodology, axioms, comprehension, application and inferences for those categories of theories that enable inter- and intra-systemic interactions, cohesion and evolution to occur, to be sustained and to be so studied. The methodological and experimental character of science still persists, but now in the mould of interactions, integration and evolution - not in the mould of the ideally perfect and controlled prototypes (Hull 1988).

Yet one must be cautious not to bluntly claim the predominance of Darwinism in such an interactive and evolutionary approach. The exception to Darwinian natural selection principle is made on grounds that such a principle is yet another perspective of the ideal, and consequently, segmented character that life-forms assume through mutations. Once such mutations are completed, other mutations arise to further separate themselves into newer ones. The entire system thus becomes eventually a disjoint collection of mutated sub-systems. They persist by themselves under their own survival power independent of the earlier parent forms. The life of an entire system, i.e. 'systems-ensemble,' is then a continuity of its mutation process leading to optimal and segmented states. In this way, the boundedness of the systems within their own mutated domains once again is of the nature of non-interactions and ideal states. We are then back to the old category of science as a controlled exercise moving from rationalistic construction into observed forms (Dawkins 1976).

UNDERSTANDING OLD SCIENTIFIC TRUISM IN THE PROCESS VIEW OF SCIENCE

In the light of the generalized systemic view of science within the unification process, the examples of water and motion of particles that we brought into the picture earlier, are now re-examined.

Water as a substance is now viewed as the result of interactions among life-sustaining elements. Of these are oxygen, hydrogen, the interactions with other substances that affect water and their own systemic knowledge exchanged with other substances and conditions of the environment. The field of interactions thereby, becomes an important role player in determining ordinarily used substance that we may call 'water.' This negates the concept of ideal type.

Likewise, the trajectory of a particle must be described in the perturbed, and not in the ideal state of the environment. Such a relational trajectory describes the impact of interactions, instead of the ideal condition of motion in vacuum. Perturbations are the result of systemic interactions and vice-versa; whereas they do not affect motion in vacuum.

A CRITIQUE OF THE DEVELOPMENT OF MODERN SCIENCE

Greek Roots of Scientific Epistemology

In conclusion to the above discussions, we note that the methodology of systemic individuation in modern science is epistemologically traced to the times of the Greeks. It has been given a new form only by way of refinements of methods, observation, analysis and inferences. Because of this unchanged epistemology in modern science, we interpret that the view of nature as springing from a primordially mutated state by the principle of survival and taking up form in the realm of materiality, remains entrenched in the process view of occidental science.

Aristotle thought that opposites guide our worldly experiences (Charon, 1975). In this light, deterministic approaches to science have for long now accepted this reasoning, only to be challenged in recent times by the method of fuzzy logic (Kosko 1993). According to this view, binary states of nature, such as, 1 for cold (Truth), 0 for hot (Falsehood), are only end-states of many other possibilities, such as not-so-hot, not-so-cold, not-not-so-cold, not-not-so-hot, etc. For each of these states sub-binary enumerations must be assigned.

In the same light we can critique by noting that Aristotle considered cosmology to be divided into a domain perfection that is of God's and thus separated from the domain of the sub-lunar world that is blemished. The two domains were seen never to interact. Morals and ethical values derived from the upper stratum do not therefore permeate the lower universe. Western science has always maintained this divided outlook. Occidental science thereby, remains bereft of ethics, values and morals. Ethics, values and morals are seen in the occidental order as being outside its fold, unable to address the scientific methods. Science thereby, dichotomizes reality between moral values and purely material ones. These are not co-determined in and by occidental science.

Alternative Approach to Science

In opposition to this perspective of modern science, we are now in pursuit of a comprehension of science that is 'globally' of the essence of relations. This becomes a study of universally interactive processes. It derives its epistemology from the roots of a unifying universe. It establishes itself by cause and effect in this order of unification of knowledge. Unification here means the total of epistemology, methodology and inferences of a universe that inter- and intra-systemically interacts in perpetuity.

An invariant axiomatic premise of knowledge is once again assumed to exist. We find that in spite of the quest for grand unification theories in modern science, its lineage to a pluralistic way of viewing reality between God, man and the universe, to serve material ends and to survive in the midst of all these, has caused methodological inability to attain unification in the sciences (Hawking 1980). This is the case, in spite of the brilliant efforts that have been launched for some time now (Neurath, Carnap & Morris, 1970).

QUR'AN ON SCIENCE

The Qur'an is a book of guidance according to Divine Laws that explain the entire creation in terms of the Unity of God and how this unity reflects itself in creation. Thus, there are two concurrent effects of Divine Unity on creative explanation.

First, it is to establish the most irreducible foundation of Complete Knowledge. On the basis of this primordiality, creation comes about, is sustained and re-originated. God then becomes the Creator and Sustainer of the universe.

The second part of understanding Divine Unity is the manifestation of Unity in creation, through what are known as the Signs of God (Ayath al-Allah). The Qur'an is profuse in establishing belief in Divine Unity through human reflection on the Signs of God. They guide the mind towards an irresistible acceptance of Divine Unity, to the mercy and beneficence of God, to the humility of life in front of the greatness of creation, to the reproductive and endless bounties that God has bestowed in creation for all and which the believer is asked to contemplate upon (Qur'an 2, verse 164). The part on contemplation is inextricably linked to the precept of Divine Unity via the proof of God's sustenance of creation.

The interconnectedness of the two attributes is shown by the Qur'an to span every aspect of creation. It is manifested in reality over endless historical time and is presented as the end-all of existence.

Within this completeness is the divine message that was sent and reinforced since time immemorial by the prophets as Teachers of Unity. These divine messages are claimed by Muslims to be completed in the Qur'an, which was revealed to the Prophet Muhammad.

Within this interconnection of the two divine attributes and the revelation of the text that becomes the recorded groundwork of life's conduct according to the Divine Laws since time immemorial, and is everlasting, exists the guidance that now becomes science. Realization of the scientific spirit of Qur'an commences from the point when reason becomes one of the many divinely created powers for the sole purpose of comprehending and applying the pervasiveness of the Divine Laws to all of life.

The characteristics of interconnectedness, pervasiveness and reason as derived from the primal field of revelation, mean that there is a unique relationship in creation that can be recognized by means of the divinely creative matrix. This matrix of Qur'anic concepts rules and facts once recognized assume an axiomatic character. We will now lay down this relationship.

THE PRECEPT OF DIVINE UNITY AND THE MANIFESTATION OF UNIFICATION OF KNOWLEDGE AS DERIVED FROM THE QUR'AN

The most irreducible principle of Divine Unity, Tawhid, grounds the primal epistemology of the creative order. We will call this premise as the Unity Precept. The Qur'an from the beginning to the end of its message identifies this primal epistemology as Complete Knowledge (Choudhury, 1991).

Next, from this primal origin emanates the Signs of God (Ayath al-Allah). They first take the form of the Divine Laws that are permanent and pervasive in nature across creation. God self-references Himself in the Qur'an as the Lord of the worlds (Qur'an Chapter 1, verse 2). The Divine Laws also take up cognizance in reason and derived rules (Ahkam). They manifest themselves in the form of material things. The realization of all these together recreates the domain of temporal knowledge for a greater understanding of Divine Unity and its functional relationship with creation. Creation then becomes a relational universe.

It is created, sustained and then re-originated in continuity by reference to the Divine Laws (Sunnat al-Allah). Within this order of circular continuity led by the initial impact of divine knowledge on reason and created forms, followed thereafter by their sustenance and re-origination, life forms are seen to become bundles of knowledge-induced entities that never die. Physical death is thereby simply a temporal end not an extinction.

In this context, the indestructibility of the soul can be taken up within this continuity of knowledge occurring in perpetuity. In the same context, the death of physical forms means the emanation of a meaningful diversity that the experience of life and death conveys to our sense of observing the Divine Laws at work. What is to be understood here are the 'deep' ecological interrelationships that exist between man and the cosmos including other life forms, through the medium of Divine Unity. Together they are all accountable to the Divine Laws and are brought back for continuous determination (Qur'an, Chapter 6, verse 38). It is the harmonious nature of these interrelationships that configures the extent of knowledge formation.

Just the same is true conversely of 'de-knowledge.' Flows of knowledge generate diversity of possibilities. Consequently, the knowledge process is transmitted through goodness and piety in such pervasively ecological interrelationships, to the continuity of the soul after death. Thus the knowledge process for scientific investigation marks a continuity from this life to Hereafter through the indestructibility of the soul with death.

In this light of the indestructibility of knowledge formation process through the soul, Qur'anic events such as the world of the soul (Barzakh), Doomsday (Kiyamah), Hereafter (Akhira) and other supernatural existences are capable of deep scientific meanings in Qur'anic framework (Mahmood 1991). While these meanings cannot be expounded in this brief coverage, the following can be briefly noted: The split moment (cosmic in nature=of the nature of Qur'anic time that is identical to the six-days beginning of creation) from Kiyamah to Akhira is the moment of destruction of 'de-knowledge' by the supercardinal measure of accumulated knowledge on the Tawhidi plane. Supercardinality is a concept of hyper-topological extension of Cantor's cardinal measurability (Cantor, 1955). Hyper-topology likewise, is an extension of the idea of supermanifolds appled to non-Euclidean relational nexuses (Dewitt, 1992). The terminal Knowledge at Akhira is once again the Complete Knowledge (=Lauh Mahfuz). Creation in the knowledge plane thus proceeds through a dynamic interactive, integrative and evolutionary process, commencing first from the topology of Complete Knowledge in the Beginning to the topology of Complete Knowledge in the End. These are hyper-topological correspondences of entire non-Euclidean nexus spaces and non-linear functionals to which the scientific emanation of Qur'anic concepts lend themselves. Within this hyper-topology, temporal forms can be explained by approximations using a complex of Euclidean, non-Euclidean, linear and non-linear correspondences among systems (Hirsch, Marsden & Shub 1993, Kakutani 1941).

THE QUR'ANIC UNIFICATION PROCESS

The process of continuity that links the precept of Unity to the Signs of God, the sustenance of life and its recreation as signified by the pervasiveness of knowledge, is referred to here as the unification process. The Qur'anic science of creation is therefore to be understood as the continuity of process that pervasively and endlessly emanates from the origin of divine knowledge. It then generates life forms as embodiments of knowledge flows that are comprehended by the exercise of reason (Aql) and nature (Fitra). This stage is then followed by the circular continuity of the deductive-inductive process tying essence with materiality and thereafter creating more knowledge as essence and so on.

Unification then is the process that integrates life through pervasiveness of the Divine Laws in creation. Creation according to the Qur'an is thus a relational order that interconnects, complements and re-originates across a diversity of forms, each reflecting the richness of knowledge and experience.

If now we call the domain of creation, taken up in its relational character, as the Field of Creation, then the unique scientific process derivable from the Qur'an can be represented as the following chain of continuity:

(Precept of Divine Unity)*→ Creation of Temporal Knowledge → Creation of Cognitive Forms (Reason and

Material Forms)=Signs of God → Re-origination on the Plane of Knowledge-Induced Material Forms.

The asterisk in the above chain denotes the most irreducible, and hence unchangeable premise of all knowledge and forms. If this attribute was not there, creation would become random and full of accidental forms. Endlessly multiple explanations of reality would emerge. This other perception is what we find in all other foundations of scientific epistemology. The randomness of scientific perceptions in occidental order is known to be the legacy of Darwin, Popper, Kant, Hume, Descartes, etc. (Russell 1990).

The above-mentioned Qur'anic cycle is continuous over knowledge flows and represents a process. Its circular continuity through re-origination of knowledge, as is manifested by the indestructibility of soul, denotes the essence of unification that is experienced by creation through the frame of knowledge flows.

By the same idea of process we can write as follows the interrelationship between essence and materiality that incessantly continues to manifest itself in the Qur'anic concept of the relational universe:

(Complete Knowledge)* → Temporal Knowledge Flows → Knowledge Embodied Life Forms → (New Knowledge Flows that Reinforce Divine Unity) → New Levels of Reproduction of Matter Through Diversity → Continuity of the Process.**

In the above chain of relations, ** signifies that of all the knowledge and material forms of life and experience, there is only one that exogenously imparts primal knowledge to all created things. This is the permanent presence of Divine Unity. Thus in the nature of the process shown above, all interrelationships induced by temporal flows of knowledge and between levels of such knowledge flows, become systemic in nature (endogenous = knowledge recreates knowledge). Whereas, Divine Knowledge alone remains overarching and unchangeable, irreducible, and impacting on world-systems (exogenous). In the Qur'anic conception of science, this process worldview is premised on one exogenous root, that is, Divine Unity (signifies primordial Complete Knowledge). Apart from this there exist all other pervasively many endogenous forms, that is, knowledge flows leading to diversities of cognitive forms and their re-origination together.

THE MODEL OF KNOWLEDGE VERSUS 'DE-KNOWLEDGE' IN TAWHIDI WORLDVIEW

One can now go on to construct a similar kind of dynamics on the side of 'de-knowledge'. Since indestructibility of Divine Unity is the irreducible foundation of the universal order, therefore, Divine Laws must control 'de-knowledge' as well. This in other words means that 'de-knowledge' (i.e. Falsehood=Devil=Evil) by itself has no power. 'De-knowledge' is thereby a necessary manifestation of creation in the Qur'an. It is required for the purpose of establishing the indestructibility of Truth and Goodness over Falsehood and Evil. Qur'anic reality as represented in the above processes must therefore, convey the final essence of Reality. This final total reality is made up of Truth and Falsehood as two disjoint conditions of any thing.

Between these two disjoint domains exist fields of temporary observations caused by incomplete knowledge of those forms (Mubah). But as the process of knowledge formation continues, such temporary events are made to well define themselves. Thereby, the trajectories of Truth and Falsehood finally emerge as the only two realities of creation. It is also in this light that Heaven, Hell and Hereafter (Akhira) can now assume scientific meaning for operational purposes. They become topological domains in the ultimate state of complete disjointness between Truth and Falsehood. This state also signifies the fullness of divine knowledge. One idea of such a perfect state was provided by Farabi (Walzer 1985).

THE QUR'ANIC SCIENTIFIC WORLDVIEW

Process of Knowledge Formation and Continuity

The concept of Qur'anic worldview has now been explained albeit summarily. For a greater coverage of the concept of worldview versus perceptions and paradigms, the reader can refer elsewhere (Choudhury 1995b). Summarily again, the concept of worldview is characterized by pervasive interactions intra- and inter-systems, through the process of knowledge simulation. Such interactions arise from the concept of knowledge-induced diversity that presents reality (Signs of God) in various hues and colours, with God as the Bestower of such rich diversities (Qur'an, Chapter 59, verses 21-24). This at once awakens an order of complementarity, instantaneity and simultaneity among the sets of 'goods' and disjointly with the sets of 'bads.'

From such interactions (diversities) arise further creative systems. In turn, the complementarity and transference of knowledge among a diversity of evolving and interconnecting forms generate integration (or convergence, social consensus = Ijma). Through the medium of interactions leading to integration, creation becomes imbued with felicity, whose confirmation in experience at large, causes further enhancement of the knowledge-induced material order. We then have the following Qur'anic chain of attributes that qualify the process-centred worldview:

Just Balance → Just Purpose → Certainty → Felicity → Re-origination.

Now by combining the previous relations with the last one, we derive a complete system of scientific approach in Qur'anic perspectives. This is presented as follows:

→ Tawhid: Complete Knowledge & Emanation of Divine Laws
↑
↓
↑
Just Balance → Just Purpose → Certainty → Felicity → Re-origination
↑
↓ ↓ ↓ ↓ ↓
↑ Temporal Knowledge ← Material ← New Knowledge ← Circular
Flows Order Flows Continuity

In this way, everything emanates from the springs of Divine Laws (Unity of God=Sunnat al-Allah) and returns back to this Divine

Origin (Qur'an, Chapter 42, verse 53). Such a circular continuity, i.e. interactions → integration → evolution (interactive-integrative-evolutionary worldview), occurring incessantly, increases our comprehension of the interrelationships among Knowledge, Creation and Re-origination.

Process of 'de-knowledge' formation

A similar relational model can be constructed for the 'de-knowledge order' to answer the scientific question of individuation and dissociation, rather than of complementarity and balance, i.e. unification of knowledge, which the Qur'anic methodology projects for scientific thought. The two processes, namely, knowledge and 'de-knowledge,' are thus polar to each other, no matter where they are found, that is, in the sciences or in worldly experiences and belief systems. In this way, the criteria of Truth and Falsehood become perfectly disjoint phenomena along the progress of knowledge flows premised on Divine Unity.

RE-EXAMINING SOME BASIC SCIENTIFIC TRUISM AND CONCEPTS IN THE CONTEXT OF THE INTERACTIVE, INTEGRATIVE AND EVOLUTIONARY WORLDVIEW

Some Common Scientific Nomenclature in the Interactive, Integrative and Evolutionary Worldview

We now return to our questions on the molecular equation of water and the case of the motion of a particle in vacuum. An application here of the knowledge-centred globally interactive, integrative and evolutionary methodology of science that we have presented, is to consider water as a substance not in its ideal state, but as a substance experiencing change in the process towards attaining its purity. Interactions among oxygen, hydrogen and the environment are so induced by natural and anthropic responses, that they cannot cause true knowledge to be formed in these cognitive forms. Hence, the realization of the substance called 'water' must be based on this limiting condition of interactions.

The state of H_2O as given to us in chemistry, is an optimum state attained by taking away all impurities and thus ceasing any further interactions to continue. This is an assumed end-state that takes up a mathematical valence in Mandeleyev's Atomic Table. On the other hand, the interactive process does not assume this optimal state pari passu. It aims at describing the stages through which the elements of a substance must interact with other elements during the advance of knowledge flows, before the substance arrives to the stage of being 'water.' In this way furthermore, all other interactions based on the process equation of water, become equally process-based scientific explanations of the advance of knowledge induction on experimental forms.

Next let us take the case of motion of particles. It is now well-known from Relativity Physics and Quantum Mechanics that motion is considered in reference to fields of forces rather than in vacuum. The trajectories of such notions are deduced by curvilinear spaces in the presence of rarified matter. Yet the interactive, integrative and evolutionary worldview of science goes further than this. Motion is now defined by the state-preference configuration of a dynamically moving object under the simulative effect of knowledge flows. Geometric descriptions and topological content now take up the methods of describing the nature of such movement, the direction of motion and the state of the motion acquired at a given point during simulation across knowledge spaces. Yet only in the controlled case of the very localized region, can such spaces be of the Euclidean type – yielding to optimality and steady-state equilibrium.

In either of the above two cases, we view scientific process to be a dynamic circularly continuous movement of change from lesser to higher degrees of certainty. Optimal conditions of much of end-state science are now replaced by the endogenous process view of change, relevance and discursions among anthropic investigators. These see the power of unification in the systems under study and enact laws derived from unification epistemology in the light of the precept of Divine Unity.

The concept of interactive, integrative and evolutionary worldview has universal application in all scientific domains that can be characterized as systems (Choudhury 1996a). In other words, the Qur'anic worldview is a systemic one. Within this systemic entirety, the idea of Shura as a process for example, is extendible from its narrow political meaning given to it by Muslim traditionalists, to the essence of the interactive, integrative and evolutionary process premised on knowledge flows across hierarchies of agents, variables, relations and systems. Most importantly required in such a process are the anthropic observations and explanation of the underlying values, morals and ethics that the Shuratic Process unravels (Qur'an, Chapter 42, verses 50-53).

Some other issues in modern science

Modern frontiers of science are seen to be expanding. Research in medicine is focussing on therapeutics over antibiotics (Cohen & Hogan, 1994). Parapsychology is investigating the meaning of death and supernatural existences in cross-cultural planes. Sensory responses of the brain are being categorized by computers. Ecological and environmental studies are expanding into the area of human ecology that takes up the study of the environment in the context of justice, commons and property rights (Busuttil, Agius, Inglott & Macelli 1990). Theoretical physics and thermodynamics are focussing on unification fields and entropy theory, respectively. Meta-theories of extensive unification are being researched upon in the theories of everything (Barrow, 1991).

The above examples are proofs of the emergence of a new scientific epistemology. This is an area where scientific derivations (Ahkam) from the Qur'an, those that are humanly derived by the effort of knowledge and that still accept the possibility of error and change as part of the diversities endowed in the temporal order by its incompleteness of knowledge, become conceptual, methodological and testable cases of deeply viable content (Davies 1983). We can examine a few more examples here.

MARKETS AS SYSTEMS OF SOCIAL CONTRACTS

Within this order we can also construe markets as systems of social contracts; the energy fields as fields of knowledge-induced interactions; the science-society interactions as a process in endogenous combinatorics that systematize unique laws for both, and so on (Choudhury, 1996b).

Markets as systems of social contracts are seen in the light of the endogenously moral preferences that emanate from knowledge induction and that then determine the consumption, production and distributional menus of the economy. Households, institutions, communities, nations and the global order now vigorously interact to generate this concept of 'ethicising' markets. We then can constructively think of the Ummatic concept of economic cooperation and integration. Markets now become the blessed medium of circulation of goods, capital, human resources and money for the common social well-being.

Such an economy then generates prices that respond to the demand and supply and knowledge-induced preferences for goods, services and technology. All of these co-determine the ethical nature of markets. In such a market order, the principle of co-determination of the menus of consumption, production and distribution of appropriate technological change, money, capital, human and natural resources, ethical balance in all these and among agents that interact for determining the social contracts, is a social function rather than a representation of methodological individualism. The latter is found to characterize the markets of the non-Qur'anic worldview in every other system. Markets are therefore, visible systems in the Qur'anic worldview. They are not governed by the invisible hand principle, and hence, by the nature of competition for sheer self-interest without moral imperative.

CONCLUSION

We find that the same law of an interactive, integrative and evolutionary knowledge-induced worldview configures all systems of the sciences, when these are uniquely derived from the most irreducible premise of knowledge, that of Divine Unity. The worldview itself reflects the process of unification as the meaningful, comprehensible and testable nature of knowledge pervasiveness intra- and inter-systems. The universe of the Qur'an is a knowledge-centred relational order, not an individuating one. This is found to be true for all systems, ranging from the very small to the very large, in the natural, human and social sciences.

The question of Qur'anic science is therefore not a figment of the imagination or an abstract and speculative philosophy. Contrarily, it overarches across an endogenous systems approach and thus opens doors to that ever new epistemology to understand and explain. Indeed, the

Qur'anic worldview has always been there; only the quest for it has taken up different shapes and forms over space and time. Its everlasting newness is endlessly refreshing to the contemplative minds in every new age of science, thought and experience.

CHAPTER 3

THE QUR'ANIC MODEL OF KNOWLEDGE: THE INTERACTIVE, INTEGRATIVE AND EVOLUTIONARY PROCESS

The primal epistemology of the Islamic worldview is premised on Divine Unity, referred to in the Qur'an as Tawhid. The essential precept of Tawhid is the Unity of Complete and Perfect Stock of Knowledge that governs and guides supremely over creation from its beginning to end. Thus from Tawhid as this Stock of Knowledge emanates flows of knowledge, which too carry the essence of unification of knowledge as a process, establishing through it extensive and universal complementarities across interacting agents, variables, relations and systems. Yet such flows of knowledge are never complete and perfect. Thus a perpetual knowledge-based evolution is configured out of the process of interactions, integration and evolution that unification of knowledge brings about.

OBJECTIVE

In this chapter our objective is to develop the interactive, integrative and evolutionary process oriented Qur'anic worldview as a mathematical system. Through it the epistemology of Divine Unity can be shown to be mobilized through unification of knowledge into factual problems of experience. We will show that the systemic world-system of the Qur'anic processual order can only be explained and effectively applied by recourse to abstract mathematical methodology. This is due to the epistemological essence of the Qur'anic worldview, the primacy of the Divine Laws instead of any corporeal abstraction given to God in His Divine Oneness, and due to the extensively systemic outlook that the methodology generates.

THE EPISTEMOLOGY OF DIVINE UNITY AND THE UNIFICATION OF KNOWLEDGE.

We will now denote the Complete Knowledge Stock of Tawhid as a mathematical topology (Choudhury & Malik 1992) by the symbol, Ω. Since Tawhid, Ω, transcends pervasively from the most micro-level to the entire cosmic order, therefore, it must govern and guide the most micro-level knowledge flows as well as their extensive nexuses of complex aggregations.

Let the aggregation of all knowledge flows across a given number of interactions, agents, variables, relations and systems be denoted by θ^*. But θ^* is the result of elementary knowledge flows. Besides, since all knowledge flows arise from Ω, therefore, θ^* is also derived from Ω as the limiting value of a vast complex of elementary knowledge flows. We will show that such elementary knowledge flows as if occurring along branches of a knowledge tree. This is to invoke the Qur'anic verses (Chapter 14, verses 24-27, see appendix). Thus the following elementary branch is possible:

$$\theta^*$$

$$\uparrow$$

$$\Omega$$

Ω is taken as a supercardinal mathematical space of complete knowledge in the topological sense. This topology is said to be supercardinal because although God is boundlessly Great, yet He cannot be simply characterized as infinite, for from Allah (God) come the Divine Laws (Sunnat al-Allah), which generate worldly relations. There must therefore exist well-defined interrelationships of these types. Hence, the topology of Ω is measurable in this sense of its extensively relational nature by a measure that is theoretically meaningful to generate derived functions but cannot by itself be quantified. We therefore call the measure of Ω as supercardinal in terms of the completeness of the Stock of Knowledge in it (Choudhury 1995, Cantor 1955, Russell 1970, Moore

1991, Rucker 1983). It generates flows of knowledge, but by itself remains uncreated.

Although θ^* emanates from Ω throughout the exercise of discourse and reason, it is not the product of rationalism. In order to well define the derivation of θ^* from Ω, we need the precise relevance of Sunnah or guidance of the Prophet Muhammad in such knowledge derivations (Ahkam). Such ways of deriving precise rules are based upon the Qur'anic assertion that the Prophet Muhammad was bestowed a complete form of knowledge during his celestial flight to the realm of Perfect Knowledge, referred to in the Qur'an as Sidrathul Muntaha. The Sidra is the tree of complete knowledge, which the Qur'an describes as being shrouded in mystery but is richly imbued by divine knowledge (Chapter 53, verses 14-16,18). The same kind of the tree is mentioned in the verses on the Goodly Tree in the Qur'anic Chapter, Ibrahim and in the Chapter, Light. One of the greatest feats of Islam, namely the Constitution of Madinah came about after the Prophet Muhammad's mystical experience in the Sidrathul Muntaha (Miraj). The universal message embalmed in this message is that it comprised the Essence of the Madinah Charter. This essence constitutes the ontological knowledge experience of the Prophet Muhammad which he was able to incorporate in his constitution of Madinah. Thus as a principle and essence, the celestial experience across the knowledge tree marks the primordial organizational element of Islamic world-systems.

By a multiplicity of the branches of the tree, there are many flows of knowledge of the type θ^*. We denote a countably finite number of them by the set, $\{\theta^*\}$. Since $\{\theta^*\}$ is a small subset of Ω and there are many disaggregated parts of $\{\theta^*\}$, therefore, with Ω as supercardinal topology, $\{\theta^*\}$ as a neighbourhood within S, itself defines a topology. Although $\{\theta^*\}$ is not a supercardinal topology because of its finite measure (Halmos 1974), yet the complex cumulation of $\{\theta^*\}$ across all possible hierarchies of interactions, agents, variables, relations and systems (whether temporally and spatially known or unknown), yields the supercardinal measure. But the latter being a cumulative result, it can happen only once, otherwise, there would be many such supercardinal states and that would annul the supercardinal concept. The supercardinal measure occurs with Ω in its primordial revealed state and once again in its Complete Form as Knowledge Stock at the End. Such a terminal event is that of Universal Optimality and Equilibrium. It is referred to in the Qur'an as the Great Event of the Event of Supreme Felicity for knowledge (Qur'an, Chapter 9, verse 72): 'But the greatest bliss is the Good Pleasure of God: That is the supreme felicity.' This Great Event (Naba ul-Azim) is referred to as Kiyamah and Akhira (Doomsday and Hereafter, respectively) (Qur'an, Chapter 78).

Hence there is a necessary and sufficient relational mapping of the type:

$$\Omega \rightarrow_{sh} \{\theta^*\} \rightarrow_{\{f\}\in sh} \Omega(=\text{Akhira}),$$

With, lim (s ∈ entire nexuses of interrelations) $\{f\}\,[\{\theta^*\}] = \Omega$,

where 'sh' denotes a particular understanding of Shari'ah with respect to space and time, with $f \in sh[\Omega]$ denoting a set of rules (Ahkam) derived from the knowledge of Shari'ah.

Also, $\{\theta^*\} \in sh[\Omega]$,
i.e. $\{f\}[sh(\Omega)] \in \Omega$,
or $\{f\} \circ sh \in I$,
the identity 'mapping' of Ω into itself through Shari'ah, 'sh.'

The entire set, {f} denotes the cumulative knowledge flows of the temporal domain through all forms of interactions, agents, variables, relations and systems. We thereby note that inverses of 'f' and 'sh' must exist in order to make the extensive and complex interrelationships meaningful. The functional inverses and mappings when taken over the entire chain from the Beginning to the End, also means that the creational inferences remain identical either when emanating from Ω to Akhira or from Akhira to Ω. Indeed the Qur'an makes the belief in Akhira as a principal article of Islamic Faith.

DISPELLING A POINT OF METAPHYSICAL CONTENTION

It might appear to some readers that the above-mentioned characterization of Tawhidi epistemology leads us into a metaphysical futility like that which was experienced during the Eighteenth Century scholastic enlightenment. To dispel this concern, we note that the Qur'an rejects rationalism for belief by rendering its reference to Akhira and the various descriptions of the eternal knowledge domain and Divine Bliss as a part and parcel of the Greatest Signs of Allah upon which Islamic epistemological and cognitive reality are constructed as a circularly reinforced deductive-inductive reasoning. By invoking the measurable mappings and relations between the domain of the Divine Laws and the created cognitive world-system, Qur'an turns such relations into mathematical comprehensions. In this, the Precept (Divine Unity) is inseparably integrated with the Field (flows of knowledge and their cognitive forms in relation to the Signs of Allah). Consequently, all of rationalistic philosophy, particularly the non-functionality of God in Kantian order (Kant 1987, Choudhury 1995), the mechanistic perception of God in Descartes (Descartes 1954), and the loss of essence in Hume's ontic creations (Hume 1988, Sherover 1972), are totally abandoned.

In the end therefore, rationalism is rejected for the epistemology that integrates God with an interactive world-system and creates evolutionary knowledge-induced realities. In this, if Qur'anic realities such as, Tawhid, Kiyamah, Akhira, Sidrathul Muntaha etc. appear as esoteric ideas, it must be remembered that they form mathematically creative realities, for which dimensions do not exist, only unifying relations matter. The greatest ideas of world history have indeed been based on essence rather than materiality in the first instance (Ibn al-Arabi, Imam Ghazzali, al-Tabari, Shah Waliullah – for these see Qadri 1990, Husserl 1964).

THE PRINCIPLE OF UNIVERSAL OR 'GLOBAL' COMPLEMENTARITY

The use of inverse mappings and multiple extensions of branches of the tree model emanating from Tawhidi epistemology, will now be extended to establish the principle of universal complementarity. This principle is a natural corollary to the globally interactive, integrative and evolutionary worldview that is established by the unification of knowledge as derived from the precept of Divine Unity. We proceed as follows:

There exist interrelationships based on the principle of global complementarity among all opportunities found in the hierarchies of interactions, agents, variables, relations and systems. We use figure 3.1 to explain the inherent ideas. Note here the double directions of arrows. Mathematically, these are valid statements. As well as, according to Tawhidi Unity worldview of the knowledge model, there exist continuous recursion in the underlying Shuratic Process that regenerates the knowledge-induced worldview through interrelationships between knowledge flows and their knowledge-induced cognitive forms. Hence, cause and effect (shown by two-way arrows), that is, deductive-inductive reasoning, co-exist.

Now, $F = f_2' \text{ o } f_2$ and $F^{-1} = f_2^{-1} \text{ o } f_2'^{-1}$. Both of these are well-defined, as shown by reverse arrows. We can write, $F \text{ o } F^{-1} = \epsilon$, where ϵ is a neighbourhood of the Unity mapping that signifies the lack of full identification of interrelationships due to prevalence of incomplete knowledge along the evolutionary plane of θ-values. Thus, $(f_2' \text{of}\ _2)^{-1} = f_2^{-1} \text{ o } f_2'^{-1} = \epsilon$. Thereby, f_2^{-1} and $f_2'^{-1}$ exist.

By similar extensions we derive that,
$H, H^{-1}, G, G^{-1}, f, f_1^{-1}, g_1, g_1^{-1}, g_2, g_2^{-1}$ all exist and are well defined, as shown by double directional arrows. Furthermore, all mappings are linked in the necessary and sufficient sense to θ_1 as the common base. Hence by extensions, G and F depend on the same mappings as shown. In this way, an extensive domain of systemic interlinkages is established across the branches shown. Such interlinkages establish the complementarity between G and F shown by the dotted lines (double directed arrows). The same is true of H, and hence of all mappings which are now reduced to complementary maps. We denote such a complementarity by G o F.

Furthermore, in figure 3.2 we show the overarching nature of the above complementary process by extensions of branches of the tree. According to the number of interactions (i, Ijtihad), integration (Ijma) and evolution (Khalq in-Jadid) across agents (j), variables (k), systems (l), the aggregation toward and disaggregation from the common root of θ_j form the branch j of the tree (e.g. agents, j = 1, 2...N). Each of the (j,k,l)-stages has a limit point caused by interactions and integration that generate evolution E to the next stage. The inverse mappings establish the continuous relations between stages of evolution – backwards and forwards. This signifies the formation of systemic interlinkages.

Figure 3.1: Interactively determined complementarities

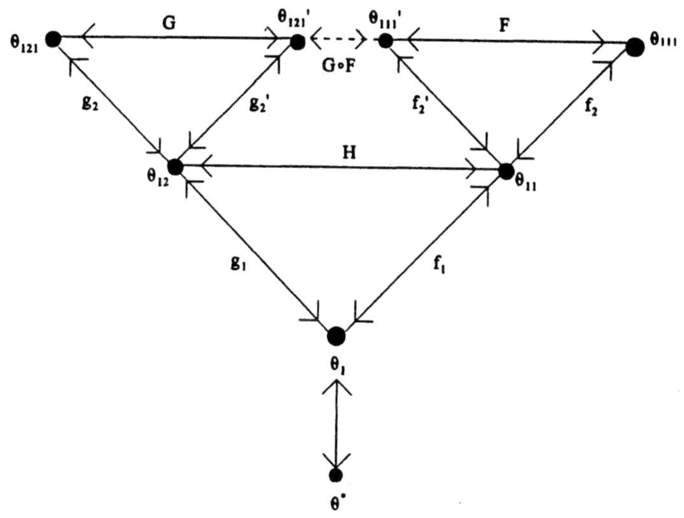

Since each functional mapping is a function of θ-values and G o F includes all IIE phases, therefore, G o F = $\cup_i(\theta_{121}, \theta_{121}'\}\cap\{\theta_{111}, \theta_{111}'\}$ = $\cup_i\{\theta_{12}\cap\theta_{11}\}$ = $\cup_i\{\theta_1\}$, now includes many more of such branches in the compound mappings. Then, G∩F turns out to be as given below in the limiting sense.

The definition of a branch is the function of θ-values at given stages of the interactive, integrative and evolutionary (IIE)-model. But a collection of such branches establishes complementary interrelationships. This is defined by extended versions of G∩F over stages.

The principle of universal complementarity in the knowledge-induced branches leads to the extensions of the above-mentioned formation, all being interlinked due to the common knowledge root of θ_1. Likewise, these are extensively composite mappings of the earlier type, i.e. $\cup_j\{G_{1j'} \text{ o } F_{1j'}\}$. For the more general case of n-number of branches and many generic values like θ_1, we obtain, $\cup_{i'j'}\{G_{i'j'} \text{ o } F_{i'j'}\}$. The multiple θ-values are thus taken across agents, variables, relational systems and stages.

Since stages of systems or hierarchies are linked by consecutive limiting points, therefore,

(1) $\lim(i \to N, l \to l_1) \cup_i\cap\{\theta_{i,j,k,l}\} = \{\theta_{N,j,k,l1}\} = \theta_{N,j,k;l1}$
(l_1; implying given l_1)

(2) $\lim(N \to N_1, k \to k_1) \cup_i\cap\{\theta_{N,j,k,l1}\} = \theta_{N1,j,k1,l1} = \theta_{N1,j;k1,l1}$

(3) $\lim(N_1 \to N_2, j \to j_1) \cup_{N1}\cap_j\{\theta_{N1,j}\} = \theta_{N2,j1}$.

The above sets of {G o F}-interrelations and the corresponding θ-centred mappings are shown in figure 3.3. All of these relations are shown to arise from Tawhidi epistemology.

Figure 3.2: Systemic complementarity across multiple branches of the tree

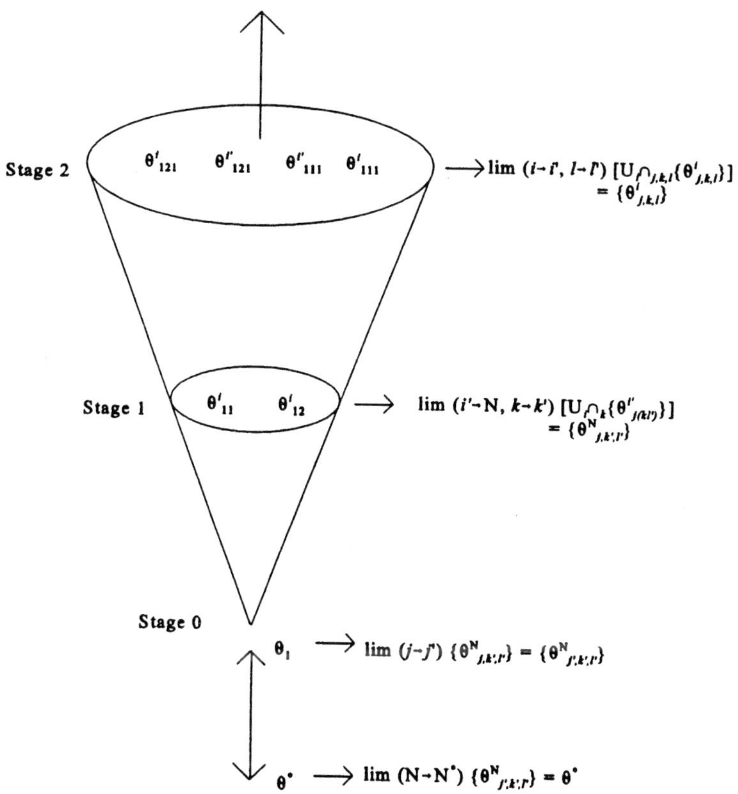

Figure 3.3: Interrelationships across branches of the <u>Tawhidi</u> tree

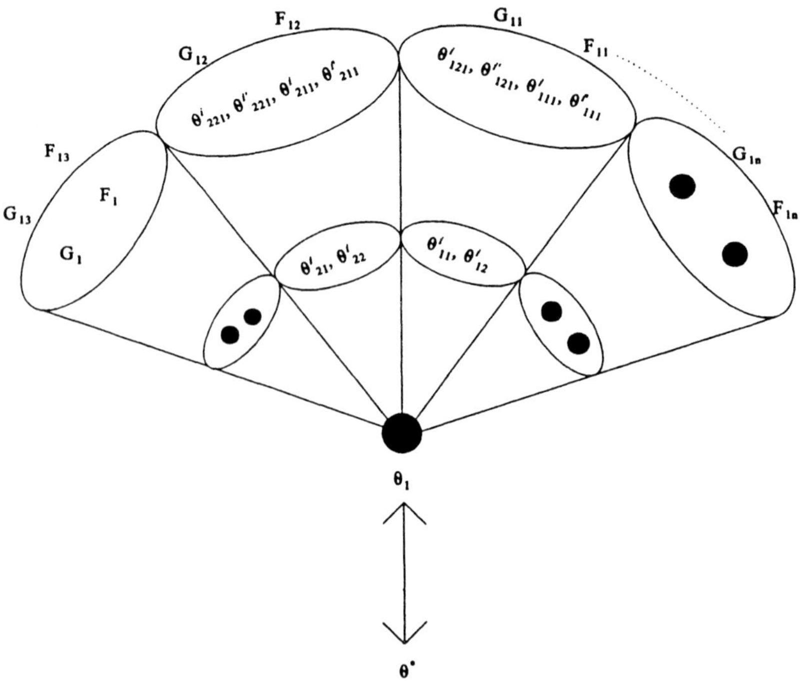

Figure 3.4: Stages of micro-level aggregations and disaggregations

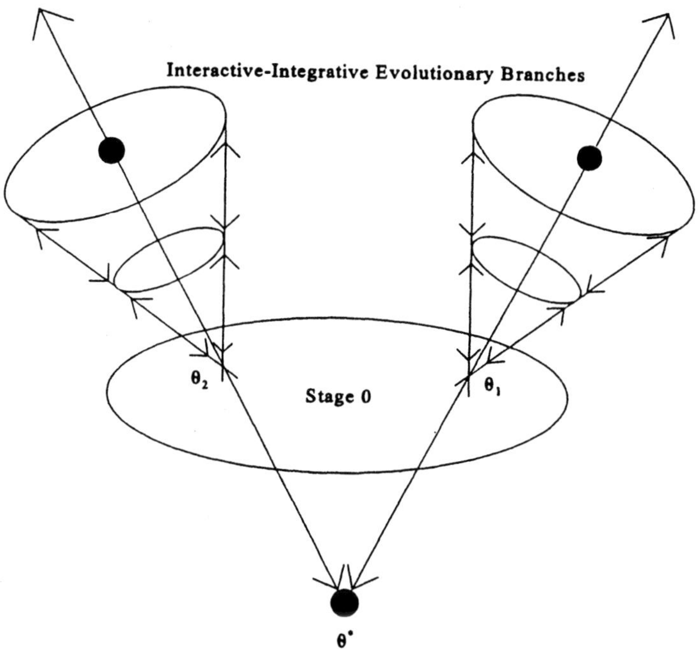

A finer degree of disaggregation leads to a similar analysis. Thus, $\{\theta_1, \theta_2, ...\}$ can be treated in a similar limiting process. Hence, $\lim(N_2 \rightarrow N^*) \cup_{N2} \cap_{j1} \{\theta_{N2,j1}\} = \theta_{N*} = \theta^*(N^*)$, corresponding to N* number of interactions leading to such an integration stage. Here, $N^* = N+N_1+N_2$. Beyond N*, newer evolutions occur. Now θ^* evolves to say $\theta^{*\prime}$. But there is an intermediate step here. Such a step is the relationship of θ to real cognitive facts. In this way, the basis of common θ^* is caused by and is in turn the cause of composite functionals at finer micro-levels. These kinds of stages of aggregations and disaggregations at finer micro-levels are shown in figure 3.4.

We return now to the mappings of θ-values and consider them at a particular hierarchy and stage as mentioned above. Now the intermediate mappings are as follows: $f_1 = f_1'' \circ f_1'$, and the inverses of these mappings exist. Thus, the cognitive variables, X_1 in an intermediate relation (mapping range) is formed as follows: $X_1 = f_1'(\theta_1)$. Thus, $X_1 = X_1(\theta_1)$, $f_1' = X_1$.

Furthermore, $\theta_{11} = f_1''(X_1) = f_1''(f_1'(\theta_1))$.
Thus, $\theta_{11} = (f_1'' \circ f_1')(\theta_1)$. Also, $\theta_{11} = f_1(\theta_1)$.
Hence, $f_1 = f_1'' \circ f_1'$.

The above kinds of composite knowledge-induced mappings between θ-values and their cognitive forms are shown in figure 3.5. These mappings also show the consequent direct cause-effect (necessary and sufficient conditions) interrelationships between evolutionary phases of knowledge. The reverse arrows show the existence of inverses, and hence the extension of the principle of complementarity from the domain of knowledge flows to the domain of knowledge-induced cognitive forms. The entire system of IIE-process is now extended to both of these domains across interactions, agents, variables, relational systems and hierarchies.

Figure 3.5: Knowledge-induced composite mappings

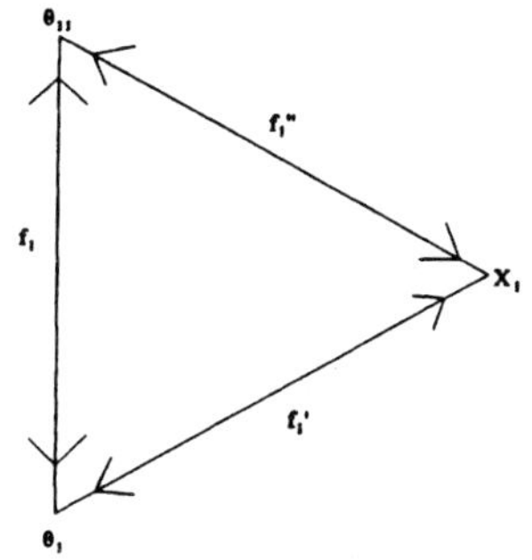

A THEOREM OF SIMULTANEITY BETWEEN KNOWLEDGE FLOWS AND THEIR INDUCED FORMS

The question of simultaneity of (θ,X)-tuples is now addressed. Since there is limitation in knowledge production and perfection in the cognitive world – of humans and the other – therefore, a period of recursive delay is provided by X_1 in the transmission mechanism, f_1. This transmission mechanism is defined by $f_1 = f_1'' \circ f_1'$. In the ideal form of perfection of knowledge and its density, we would have, $f_1 = f_1' = f_1''$. Then, $X_1(\theta) = \theta_{11}$ and $X_1 = f_1$. Now the difference between knowledge flows and knowledge-induced forms disappears.

Finally, since $X(\theta_1)$ and θ_1 occur in the same stage of an IIE-process, which then causes θ_{11} and likewise its cognitive associate, $X_{11}(\theta_{11})$ to occur, therefore, by extension we obtain the following branches of the $(\theta,X(\theta))$-tuples (figure 3.6):

Figure 3.6: Interrelationships among (θ,X(θ))-tuples across branches of the knowledge tree

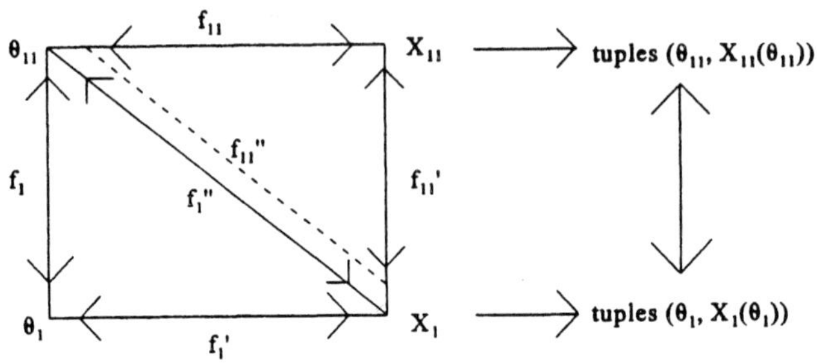

THE TRANSMISSION MECHANISM IN KNOWLEDGE-INDUCED COMPLEMENTARY INTERRELATIONSHIPS

It is clear that the transmission mechanism has now been extended from the domain of pure knowledge flows to the domain of the knowledge-induced cognitive forms. Hence, the transmission process exists between (θ,X(θ))-tuples, as shown by the mappings f_1', f_{11}', f_{11}''. Also then, $(\theta_1,X_1(\theta_1)) \leftrightarrow (\theta_{11},X_{11}(\theta_{11}))$.

The following questions are to be further addressed: Is $f_1'' = f_{11}''$? Thus, is $f_1''^{-1} = f_{11}''^{-1}$? To answer these, let us suppose that these interrelationships did not exist. Then, $(\theta_1,X_1(\theta_1) \leftrightarrow (\theta_{11},X_{11}(\theta_{11}))$. Say that, $h_1(\theta_1,X_1(\theta_1)) \neq h_{11}(\theta_{11},X_{11}(\theta_{11}))$. Taken in parts, $\theta_1 \leftrightarrow \theta_{11}$, $X_1(\theta_1) \leftrightarrow X_{11}(\theta_{11})$. This contradicts the transmission mechanisms in the θ-domain and the X-domain. The principle of universal complementarity is thereby annulled. Hence, $f_1'' = f_{11}''$ and $f_1''^{-1} = f_{11}''^{-1}$. Now all these mappings must be well defined; θ-values and X-values must together be monotonically positive.

It can be noted now how the tuples like, $(\theta_1, X_1(\theta_1))$, $(\theta_{11}, X_{11}(\theta_{11}))$, come about. Since f_1' and f_{11} are the instrumental mappings here for the two tuples, respectively, therefore, depending upon the nature of the topology of the spaces of such variables, such representations must exist, as proven. In the limited version of Euclidean space, the above tuples are simple geometrical points in the positive orthant.

The extended version of the branches in $(\theta, X(\theta))$ - tuples across hierarchies of stages in the IIE-process is shown in figure 3.6. Here the directions of arrows show the endogenous links among the knowledge-induced tuples, $\{\theta, X(\theta)\}$, and the various branches interconnecting with each other via their sets of knowledge-induced nodes denoted by, $\{\theta, X(\theta)\}$. These are causally interrelated with the limiting value, $(\theta^*, X^*(\theta^*))$. The rectangular branches show the hierarchies of interrelationships respecting the tuples.

EXTENDING THE BRANCHES OF THE KNOWLEDGE-INDUCED TUPLES DOWNWARDS TO THE LIMITING NODE

The logic of the $(\theta, X(\theta))$-tuples, or the branch nodes, can be extended downwards by the reverse mapping to define the generic node, $(\theta^*, X^*(\theta^*))$, in just the same way as it was done for the hierarchies of θ-values in terms of θ^*. We note also that by extension of the branches and the transmission mechanism to disaggregated spaces, these will get filled up by points such as, $\{\theta_{ijk}, X_{ijk}(\theta_{ijk})\}$, $\{\theta_{ijkl}, X_{ijkl}(\theta_{ijkl}\}$ etc. We then obtain an extensively spanning domain of $(\theta, X(\theta))$-values across hierarchies of interactions, agents, variables, and systems, all emanating from and converging to the limiting value $(\theta^*, X^*(\theta^*))$, in the sense of the double-directed mappings (i.e. necessary and sufficient conditions).

The interconnected branches arising from $(\theta^*, X^*(\theta^*))$ and going through diversities and complementarities across hierarchies of interactions, agents, variables, relations and systems, can now be shown. In figure 3.7 we show these as the cross-sectional view of a circularly multiple branch nodal interconnections of the kinds shown in figure 3.6.

Figure 3.7: Cross-sectional view of multiple interconnections of branch nodes

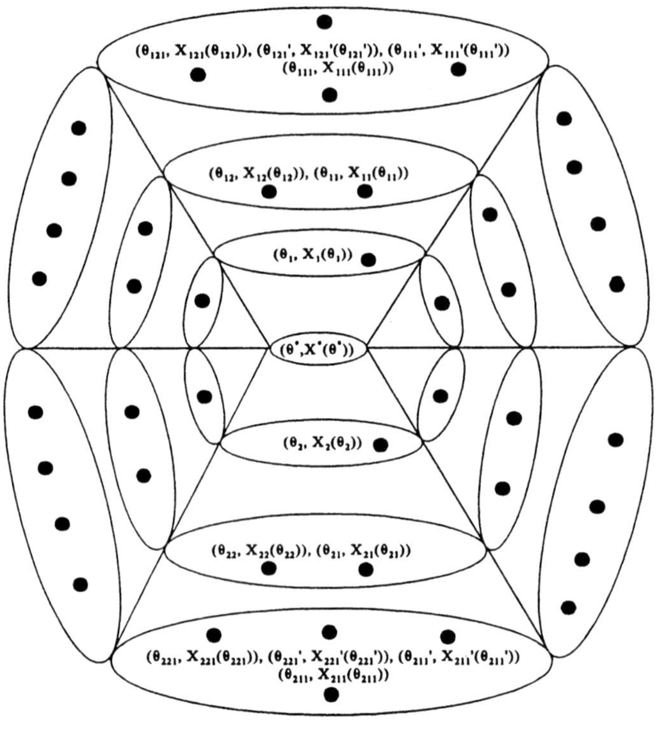

If we are to view the picture in the sense of pervasive complementarities by diversities across hierarchies of interactions, agents, variables, relations and systems, we will get the systemic animation occurring continuously in both the cross-sectional and vertical views of the branches as shown in figure 3.8, diagram 3.8.1 and Diagram 3.8.2, respectively. These diagrams emanate from the spinning motion of the figures analytically constructed in figures 3.6 and 3.7. In figure 3.8, the circular arrows indicate the emerging complementarities and creative evolutions across the hierarchies, causally interrelated to the common node, $(\theta^*, X^*(\theta^*))$, of multiple branch nodes.

Figure 3.8: Evolutionary picture of multiple branch nodes across hierarchies

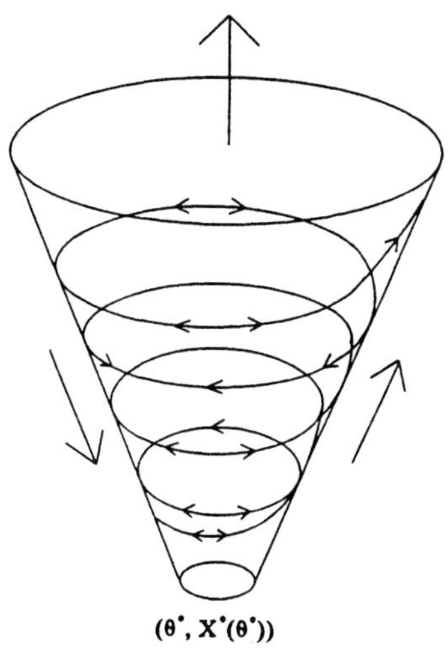

Interactive evolution of branches of the goodly tree seen conically

Diagram 3.8.1

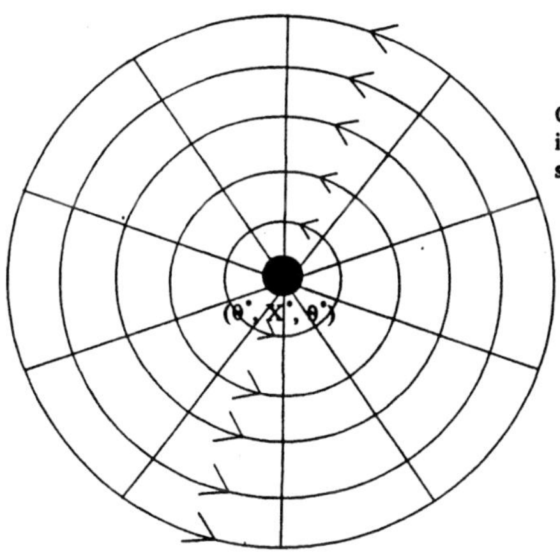

Cross-sectional view of interactions across the cone of spanning branches

Diagram 3.8.2

THE FLOWERS AND FRUITS OF THE TAWHIDI TREE: UNIVERSAL BENEFITS AND FELICITY

Our next topic is to produce the flowers and fruits, that is the benefits and felicity of the branches integrated with the nodes on the trunk of the Tawhidi tree. The fruits are denoted by functions of the $(\theta^*, X^*(\theta^*))$-tuples. In a specific sense this is the Islamic Social Well-Being (Falah and Tazkiyyah), $SW = SW(\theta^*, X^*(\theta^*))$. Once again, we can treat SW as a topological mapping. We can then follow through the same process of disaggregations of $(\theta^*, X^*(\theta^*))$ along with their composite mappings, as done before for the branches and their nodes. Then,

$$SW(\theta^*, X^*(\theta^*)) = SW((\cup_i \cap_{jkl} \theta_{ijkl}), \cup_i \cap_{jkl} \{X_{jkl}(\{\theta_{ijkl}\}\},$$

subject to the fact that each sub-branch and a part of these at very disaggregate levels, also bear their benefits. These other benefits are signified by,

$$\theta_{ijkl} = F_1(\theta_{ijkl}),\ X_{ijkl}(\theta_{ijkl}) = L_1(X_{ijkl}(\theta_{ijkl}))$$
$$\theta_{ijkl} = F_2(\theta_{ijkl}),\ X_{ijkl}(\theta_{ijkl}) = L_2(X_{ijkl}(\theta_{ijkl}))$$
$$\theta_{ij} = F_3(\theta_i),\ X_{jk}(\theta_{jk}) = L_3(X_i(\theta_i))$$
$$X_{ijkl} = H_1(\theta_{ijkl}) = H_1 \circ F_1 \circ F_2 \circ F_3$$
$$X_{ijk} = H_2(\theta_{ijk}) = H_2 \circ F_2 \circ F_3$$
$$X_{ij} = H_3(\theta_{ij}) = H_3 \circ F_2$$
$$X_i = H_4(\theta_i) = H_4.$$

Since SW is a mapping on a topological space that preserves monotonicity between various $(\theta, X(\theta))$-values, therefore,

$$SW(\cup_i \cap_{jkl} \{\theta_{ijkl}\}, \cup_i \cap_{jkl} X_{ijkl}\{\theta_{ijkl}\}) = [\cup_i \cap_{jkl} SW(\theta_{ijkl}, X_{ijkl}(\theta_{ijkl}))] = SW_{ijkl}.$$

SW_{ijkl} denote the flowers and fruits (i.e. felicity and benefits) of various branches across hierarchies of interactions, agents, variables, relations and systems corresponding to the branches integrated at the limiting nodes on the trunk, $(\theta^* X^*(\theta^*))$. As long as knowledge flows in the animate and inanimate worlds remain imperfect and incomplete, SW_{ijkl} will be different from each other. Only in the event of Complete Stock of Knowledge, i.e. in Akhira, can all SW_{ijkl} be optimized. But such an occurrence cannot be the result of only one branch or group of branches based on only one node. We must now continue on to formalize the unification process of knowledge, that is, the principle of universal complementarity, to all other nodes.

Thus $(\theta^*, X^*(\theta^*))$ must evolve, say to $(\theta^{*\prime}, X^{*\prime}(\theta^{*\prime}))$. The entire gamut of formalization showing complementarities, diversities and transmission mappings across hierarchies of interactions, agents, variables, relations and systems, is once again repeated. But now there is an extended series of further linkages. These occur because, $(\theta^*, X^*(\theta^*)) \leftrightarrow (\theta^{*\prime}, X^{*\prime}(\theta^{*\prime}))$. Consequently, the $(\theta, X(\theta))$-values at the disaggregate levels, establish two-directional mappings with the $(\theta', X'(\theta'))$-values, Hence, in Figure 3.9 we show the latices of such mappings that span the entire system of interrelationships in the sense of causality and recursive interrelationships that form composite mappings.

Figure 3.9: Composite mappings of recursive nodes forming the social well-being functionals

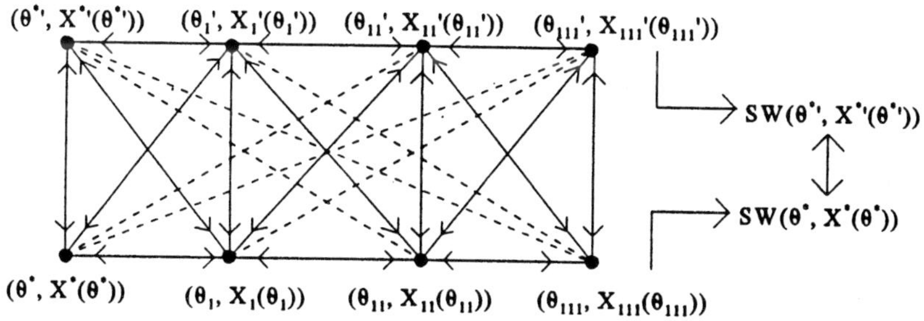

In figure 3.9, the inter-meshing of transmission processes increases with intra- and inter-systemic hierarchies of interactions. The dotted lines show the result of composite mappings with superceding relational implications.

The total SW for both levels is now given by,

$$SW(\theta^*,\theta^{*\prime},X^*(\theta^*),X^{*\prime}(\theta^{*\prime})) =$$
$$\lim(i,j,k,l) \cup_i \cap_{jkl} SW(\theta_{ijkl},\theta_{ijkl}{}',X_{ijkl}(\theta_{ijkl}),X_{ijkl}{}'(\theta_{ijkl}{}')),$$

such that, all the interrelationships shown earlier plus similar ones, apply for $\theta_{ijkl}{}'$, $X_{ijkl}{}'$ and the transmission mechanisms between θ_{ijkl}, $\theta_{ijkl}{}'$, $X_{ijkl}(\theta_{ijkl})$, $X_{ijkl}{}'(\theta_{ijkl}{}')$.

SW is itself a form of transmission mechanism among progressively many hierarchies of interactions, agents, variables, relations and systems. The integrated picture for the two nodes mentioned above and their branches are shown in figure 3.10. Note that due to the increasing measurability of the branches of the tree and its trunk as signified by monotonically increasing $(\theta,X(\theta))$-multiple nodes and their corresponding SW-values, the tree now appears as growing outwards and upwards. The branches are shown to relate with the limiting nodes of interconnections on the trunk in figure 3.10.

Because there exist large numbers of transmission mappings at different stages of disaggregation, therefore, a continuous composition of such mappings will always lead to stage-specific and branch-specific SW as flowers and fruits of such branches and sub-branches. For instance,

$$\lim(i\rightarrow N_1,l\rightarrow l_1) \cup\cap SW(.) =$$
$$SW(\theta_{N1,jkl'},\theta_{Njkl'}{}',X_{Njkl'}(\theta_{Njkl''}),X_{Njkl'}{}'(\theta_{Njkl''})).$$

Similarly, we can proceed by inducing recursive values to the SW(.)-functionals for limiting values of new interactive and integrative stages (Ijma proceeding from the Ijtihadi levels). In this way, after assigning limiting $(\theta,X(\theta))$-values for $N_1\rightarrow N_2$, $k\rightarrow k'$, we write finally,

$$\lim(N_2\rightarrow N,j\rightarrow j') \cup_{N2}\cap_{j'} SW(\theta_{ij},X_{ij}) = \cup_{N2} SW(\theta_{N2},\theta_N{}',X_{N2},X_{N2}{}')$$
$$= SW(\theta^*,\theta^{*\prime},X^*,X^{*\prime}).$$

Figure 3.10: The outward and upward growth of the Tawhidi tree from any limiting node

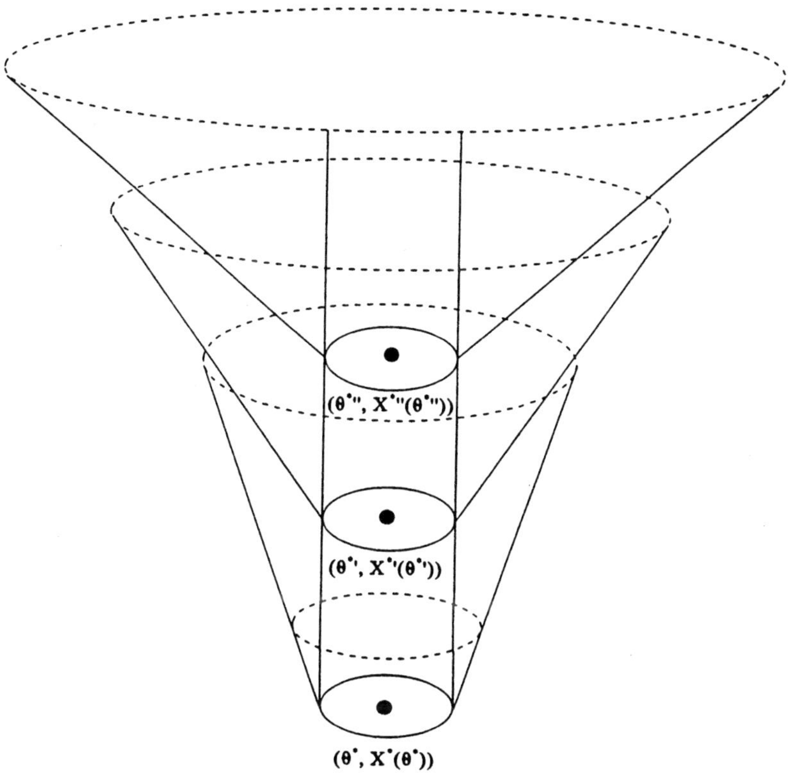

There are as wide a proliferation of SW as there are extensions of the multiple branches and sub-branches. The complementarity among flowers and fruits at any given stage means the creative interlinkages among their knowledge-induced essence. Such flowers and fruits in the Tawhidi tree denote sequences of knowledge flows across hierarchies. The disaggregate levels of $(\theta,X(\theta))$-values, complex as they are, convey the fact that these necessitate human presence and discourse across all systems, and the human capacity to observe, interact, derive rules and organize thought on the knowledge plane of life and thought. Thus the human presence in such IIE-models is more important than the engineering aspect. The engineering application becomes increasingly difficult and uncontrollable due to the extensively complex nature of strings of interrelationships that become all the more complex with the densification of knowledge flows (Wilkinson 1991, Breuer 1991, McCloskey 1985).

The anthropic model is profoundly reflected at finer disaggregate levels; whereas, both the human and engineering systems are taken together effectively at the aggregate level. Hence our engineering version conjointly with the human IIE-process is given by,

$$\theta_1^* \rightarrow_{f1} X_1^* \rightarrow_{f2} \theta_2^* \rightarrow_{f3} X_2^* \rightarrow \ldots$$

the engineering application now becomes increasingly difficult and uncontrollable. Along with this chain, there is a reverse process as well, to imply the necessary and sufficient condition (cause-effect) of the interrelations.

The recursive interrelations signifying the simulation aspect of either the engineering or the anthropic engagement in the knowledge forming world-systems is shown by the following interconnections:

$$\theta_1^* \rightarrow_{f1} X_1^* \rightarrow_{f2} \theta_2^* \rightarrow_{f3} X_2^* \rightarrow \ldots$$

From this chain we obtain the following simulation problem:

Simulate $\{(\theta^*,X^*(\theta))\text{-values}\}$
$SW(\theta_1^*,\theta_2^*,\ldots,X_1^*(\theta_1^*),X_2^*(\theta_2^*),\ldots)$,

subject to all possible interrelationships among the variables including simulated values of SW(.) corresponding to the variables in continuous recursions.

Consider for example,

$$X_2^* = F_1(\theta_1^*, \theta_2^*, X_1^*)$$
$$\theta_2^* = F_2(\theta_1^*, X_1^*, X_2^*) \text{ etc.}$$

as extended by, (i) composite transmission mappings, and (ii) recursions forward and backward.

The arrows in the above expressions indicate creative evolutions starting from elementary states of temporary integration (Ijmas) following interactions in the above-mentioned causal interrelations. The recursive chain shown above indicates that a similar process of IIE repeats itself over stages of evolution. Hence a process, $P_1 = (\theta_1 \rightarrow X_1 \rightarrow \theta_2)$, is followed by a similar process, $P_2 = (\theta_2 \rightarrow X_2 \rightarrow \theta_3)$ etc. Within these processes are interactions and integration that lead $\theta_1 \rightarrow \theta_1^*, X_1 \rightarrow X_1^*(\theta_1^*)$. Then there is evolution of $\theta_1^* \rightarrow \theta_2^*$. The IIE-process is thus shown as a circular causation of unified reality (Tawhid) across all of reality (unification of knowledge) (Choudhury 1994).

We call this circular causation and continuity of the knowledge-induced processes reflecting the meaning of the Qur'anic 'the straight-path' of knowledge-induction as (Sirathal Mustaqim). In the language of the tree model of unified knowledge, we can represent the Sirathal Mustaqim by the trunk, as shown in Figure 3.11. The trunk of the Tawhidi Tree condenses the sum-total of all the essences of the flowers and fruits of multiple branches. Such a trunk of limiting nodal values of knowledge-induced flowers and fruits is interactively integrated upwards from its roots and is creatively evolutionary in reference to the outward and upward spanning branches.

Figure 3.11: The trunk of the Tawhidi tree of knowledge: Sirathal Mustaqim

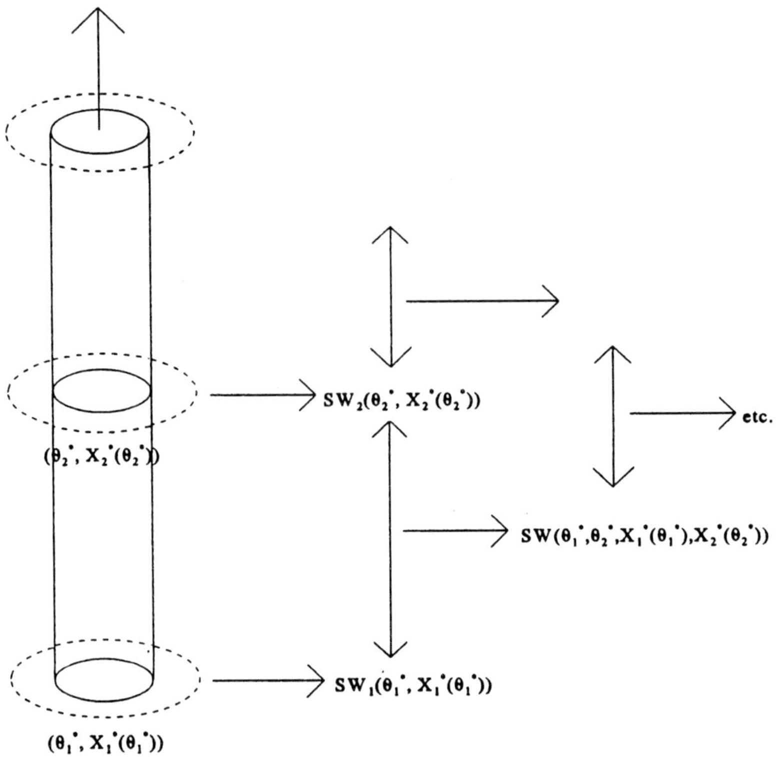

A further simplification can be carried out by putting,

$\theta_N{}^* = \lim\{\theta_1{}^*, \theta_2{}^*, \ldots\}$
$X_N{}^* = \lim\{X_1{}^*, X_2{}^*, \ldots\}$.

Then, Simulate $\{\theta_N{}^*\}$ $SW = SW(\theta_N{}^*, X_N{}^*)$,
subject to, $X_N{}^* = F(\theta_N{}^*)$,
$\theta_{+N}{}^* = G(X^*(\theta_{N-}{}^*))$,

where, (+) subscript denotes the forward recursive values. (-) subscript denotes previous values.

The flowers and fruits of the Tawhidi Tree are shown to configure the region of $(\theta^*, X^*(\theta^*))$-values as shown above.

Since $(\theta^*, X^*(\theta^*))$-values exist simultaneously with knowledge flows, therefore, they are simultaneous creations of S. Through this relation, all disaggregate levels of the tuples are simultaneous creation of S. Furthermore, all branches linked to $(\theta^*, X^*(\theta^*))$, and likewise, the set of values, $\{(\theta^*, X^*(\theta^*))\}$ along with their disaggregations and branches, are simultaneously created by S. This implies that there must exist a lag between the values of $\{(\theta^*, X^*(\theta^*))\}$ across hierarchies of interactions, agents, variables, relations and systems, as signified by the nexus of branches. This is also the implication of the inhering simulation method of the knowledge-based process model. The existence of such lags and simulative knowledge-based processes, implies that knowledge flows remain 'incomplete' and evolutionary. As the knowledge formation intensifies, so also its continuity in the relational order of $\{(\theta^*, X^*(\theta^*))\}$ picks up speed (Choudhury 1997).

The question now is: If Ω simultaneously impacts upon $\{(\theta^*, X^*(\theta^*))\}$-values, then why are such values evolutionary in nature? The answer to this question ties in with the fact that the methodology of deriving rules (Ahkam) of Shari'ah ('sh' as given earlier) – from the Ω-epistemological premise to the cognitive domain, must vary. These in turn would affect the $\{(\theta^*, X^*(\theta^*))\}$-values. Thus in figure 3.12, we show the simultaneous impact of the unique unity among diversities (though not pluralistic) of ways for comprehending Tawhidi epistemology in the socio-scientific order. We imply here that Shari'ah remains dynamic in its evolution pertaining to the changing issues and problems (sh_s-values), although its core remains immutable.

Figure 3.12: Unity within diversity in deriving Shari'ah rules for changing perspectives of issues and problems

$$\theta_1^* \rightarrow_{f1} X_1^* \rightarrow_{f2} \theta_2^* \rightarrow_{f3} X_2^*$$

$$\nwarrow \quad \uparrow \quad \uparrow \quad \nearrow$$

$$\Omega$$

$sh_2 \circ sh_1 = f_1$; $sh_3 \circ sh_2 = f_2$; $sh_4 \circ sh_3 = f_3$ etc. By recursions of these relations we can write,

$$sh_{2n} \circ F_{2n-2} \circ f_{2n-4} \circ f_{2n-6} \circ \ldots \circ sh_1 = f_{2n-1} \circ f_{2n-3} \circ \ldots \circ f_1.$$

We can infer now that only if each $sh_i = sh_{i+1}$ in pairs, i=1,2,...,n, then would each f_i become identical. Thereafter, no evolution would be possible. This is the case of the immutable core of Shari'ah. But other than this singular case, the rules (Ahkam) of Shari'ah remain evolving with the changing issues and problems of space and time, once they are premised in Ω.

ROOTS OF THE GOODLY TREE: A THEORY OF EPISTEMOLOGICAL EXTENSIONS

The Goodly Tree (Qur'an, Chapter 14, verses 24-25, 27) now originates and spans out from the epistemology of Tawhid (Ω). But such a tree also needs roots to make it firm and rich. The monotonic interrelationships among $\{(\theta^*,X^*(\theta^*))\}$-values and the social well-being functionals, $\{SW(\theta^*,X^*(\theta^*))\}$, plus the continuous knowledge-induction in these processes cumulating to Complete Knowledge Stock in Akhira, mean that the mathematical measurability of this cumulative knowledge-induced mass must equal the strength of Ω. This strength is implied by the roots of the Tawhidi Tree. The mass of the roots of the tree thus reflects the supercardinality of Ω, as the cumulative mass of knowledge comprehending the known and unknown creations together compound to the supercardinal measure of Akhira. Now the attributes of Perfect Knowledge, Optimality, Balance of Equilibrium and Supreme Felicity come together to give the final form to the Goodly Tree.

In figure 3.13, we show how the branching outwards and upwards of the Tawhidi Tree must be balanced by the equal mathematical measure of the roots in order for the tree to be firm and rich in bearing its fruits of knowledge. We have shown earlier that the cumulative measurability of all knowledge-induced evolutions in the creative domain, encompassing the known and the unknown, equates to the supercardinality of the Complete Stock of Knowledge, $\mu(\Omega)$, in Akhira. But since, the Tawhidi Stock of Knowledge is completed in Akhira, therefore, the equality of supercardinality at the Beginning and the End is shown in figure 3.13 by the two-way arrows. The supercardinal mathematical measure, $\mu(\Omega)$, as the total strength of the Tawhidi Tree, is thus meant to be the roots of the Tawhidi Tree. This is also true in the epistemological and ontological sense of the Tawhidi Stock of Knowledge. Note that it is the causal relation among all $\{(\theta^*,X^*(\theta^*))\}$ and among all $\{SW(\theta^*,X^*(\theta^*))\}$ that sustain a stable trunk of the Goodly Tree – the Knowledge Tree.

The various roots of the Goodly Tree qualify as the 'attributes' of the Goodly Tree and the interconnected outputs of the attributes. The principal attributes are the Beneficient Names of Allah (Asma al-Husna), which then get intertwined in creating endlessly richer textures out of the Divine attributes. The Qur'an says (Chapter 59, verse 24): 'He is God, the Creator, the Evolver, the Bestower of Forms (or Colours). To Him belong the Most Beautiful Names.'

The removal of indeterminacy being a positive function of knowledge evolution, knowledge flows must therefore be well determined under interactions over stages that lead to consensus formation (Ijma) and thereafter to evolution (Khalq in-Jadid). Hence, indeterminacy called Mubah, has no long-run possibility of evolution of its own. $\{\theta^*\}$ as limiting values of the various sets of θ-values, must therefore be fully determinate. They exclude those θ-values that are revised or rejected during the IIE-process or the Shuratic Process of discourse. For this reason as well, temporary intersections between truth- and falsehood- sets describing the Mubah set, cannot have high dimensionality. Consequently, only neighbourhoods of the corresponding Mubah apply to non-null intersections in the short run.

Figure 3.13: Roots of the goodly tree

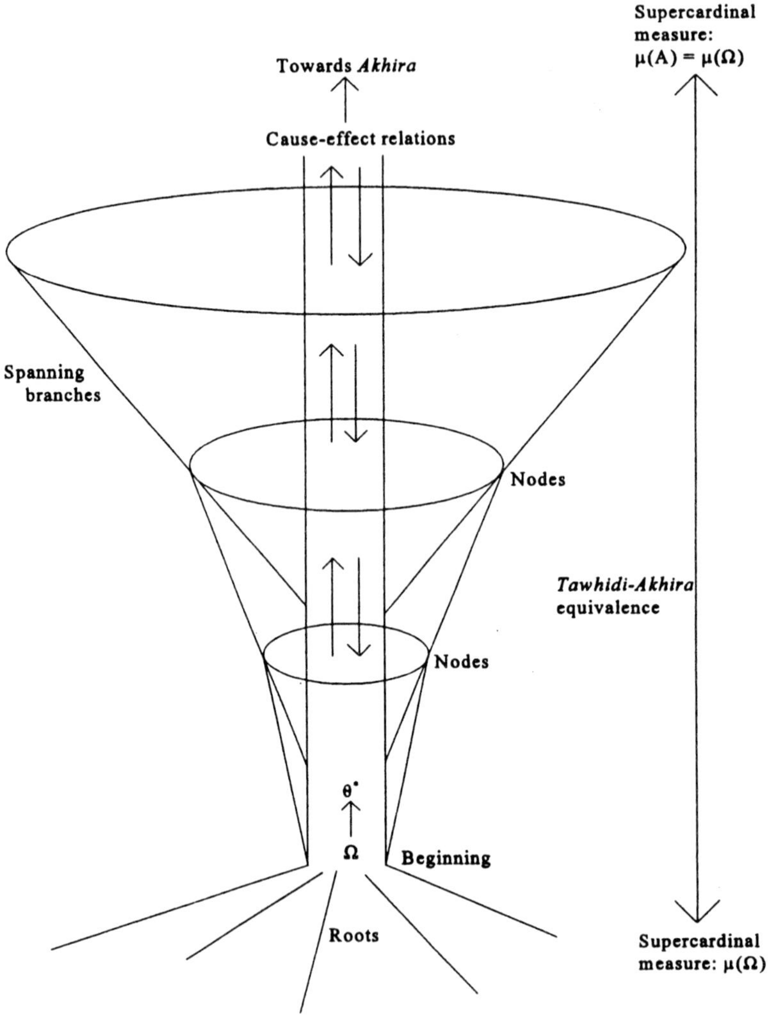

The removal of indeterminacy being a positive function of knowledge evolution, knowledge flows must therefore be well determined under interactions over stages that lead to consensus formation (Ijma) and thereafter to evolution (Khalq in-Jadid). Hence, indeterminacy called Mubah, has no long-run possibility of evolution of its own. $\{\theta^*\}$ as limiting values of the various sets of θ-values, must therefore be fully determinate. They exclude those θ-values that are revised or rejected during the IIE-process or the Shuratic Process of discourse. For this reason as well, temporary intersections between truth- and falsehood- sets describing the Mubah set, cannot have high dimensionality. Consequently, only neighbourhoods of the corresponding Mubah apply to non-null intersections in the short run.

Even apart from Mubah states, a falsehood can be induced by truth to exit from the falsehood- set. A truth can be likewise induced by falsehood. Taken all the cases together as Mubah-like, we can now represent the branches and the Goodly Tree as a general tree model of knowledge and 'de-knowledge' as well. We show these cases of sifting and final knowledge formation in the IIE-model by means of figure 3.14. The Mubah trajectory is shown by M-like ones. Along the directions of evolution of both knowledge and 'de-knowledge,' including all the corresponding tuples and their criterion functions, M-like forms become well-determined. Thereby, they get absorbed either into the knowledge or the 'de-knowledge' sets. Thereafter, the knowledge-induced evolution is once again endogenously recreated in these two disjoint planes of reality. Diagram 3.14.1 shows the above sifting process. Diagram 3.14.2 shows the Mubah movements or the induction of Truth over Falsehood to be moving in cycles

Figure 3.14: Mubah-like movements in the knowledge and 'de-knowledge' characterization of reality: general systems explanation of the tree model

Diagram 1

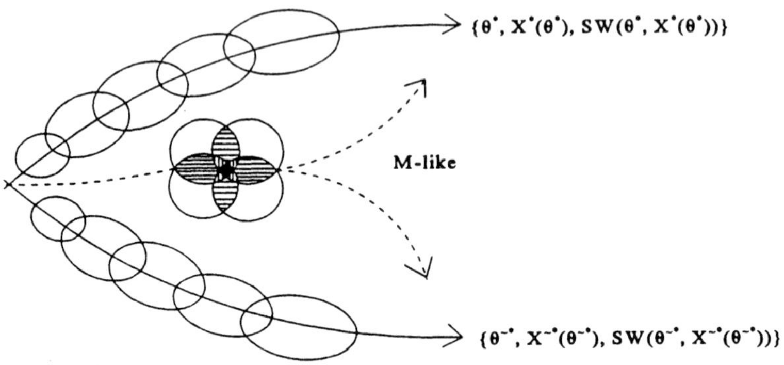

Diagram 2

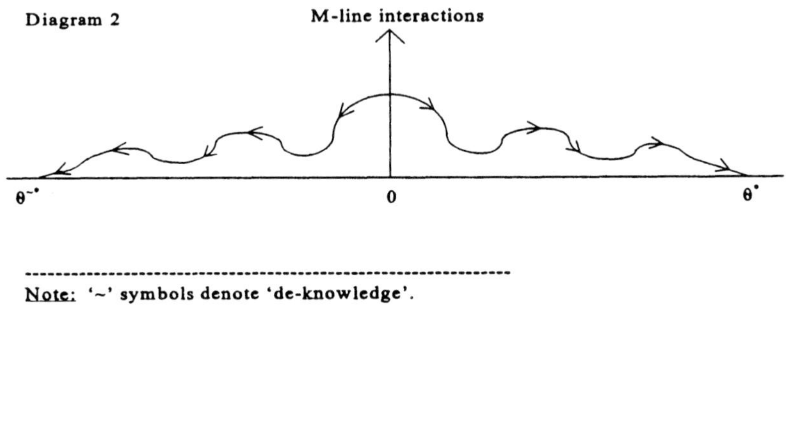

Note: '~' symbols denote 'de-knowledge'.

The basic fact that Ω remains the root of both $\{\theta^*\}$ and $\{\theta^*\sim\}$ on the basis of discerning truth from falsehood, implies that a concept of systemic-identity must arise from either θ^*-values or $\theta^*\sim$-values. These systemic-identities must however be affected by a unity of methodology within their own systems. Thereby, although the methods of evolution of the two disjoint systems represent unity with themselves, the inner structure and the consequences of these systems must remain distinct from each other. It is because of such a structural difference between the two systems and their methodologies, that we call the epistemology of $\{\theta^*\}$ to be premised on Divine Unity (Tawhid) and of $\{\theta^*\sim\}$ to be the disjointness or mathematical complementation of Divine Unity. However, $\{\theta^*\sim\}$ can have no power of its own. Untruth is a created thing of Ω and must therefore, be of the nature of material and cognitive creation of S. The Qur'an mentions about this subordinate authority of Satan ($\{\theta^*\sim\}$) (Qur'an 7, verses 11-18).

We can now represent the above general systems model of Tawhidi authority over both knowledge and 'de-knowledge' in figure 3.15. The principal point to note here is that knowledge and 'de-knowledge' are both created by Divine Laws uniquely in their own spheres to bring out the supremacy of Truth over Falsehood.

The epistemological difference between θ^* and $\theta^*\sim$ is that θ^* submits for its source to Ω. Whereas, $\theta^*\sim$ despite being a created thing of Tawhidi power, denies the primal existence of Ω, and thus claims roots in itself. Furthermore, the epistemological difference between falsehood and indeterminary (Mubah) is that after a due evolution of $\{\theta^*\}$, the indeterminate sets of $\{\theta^*\}$ are transformed into determinate knowledge. This case is shown in figure 3.16. Figure 3.16 shows that Mubah is a short-run phenomenon of intersections between Truth and Falsehood. In the long-run this indeterminacy is not sustained.

Figure 3.15: The general system of Tawhidi supremacy over knowledge and 'de-knowledge' creations

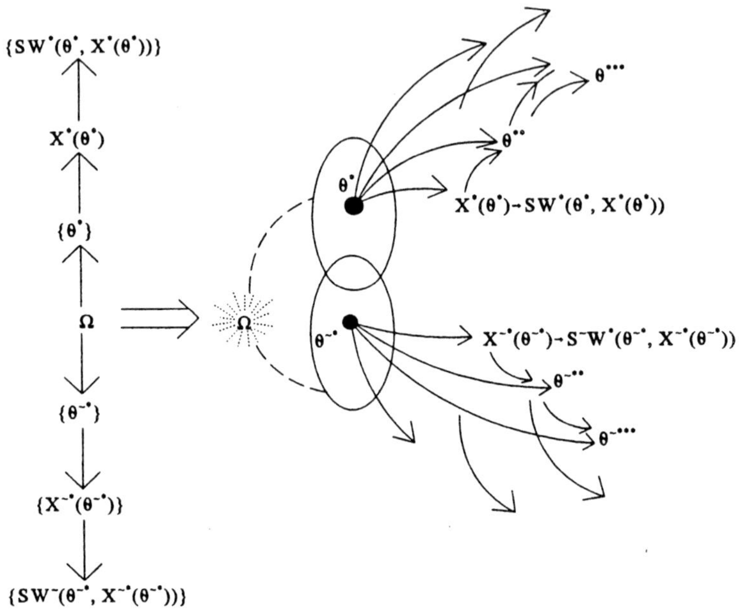

$\{\theta^*\}\ \varepsilon\ \Omega,\ \{\theta^{\sim*}\}\ \varepsilon\ \Omega,\ \{\theta^*\}\cup\{\theta^{\sim*}\}\ \varepsilon\ \Omega,\ \{\theta^*\}\cap\{\theta^{\sim*}\}-\varphi\ \varepsilon\ \Omega$

Note: Symbols with '~' denote 'de-knowledge'

Figure 3.16: The short-run nature of Mubah

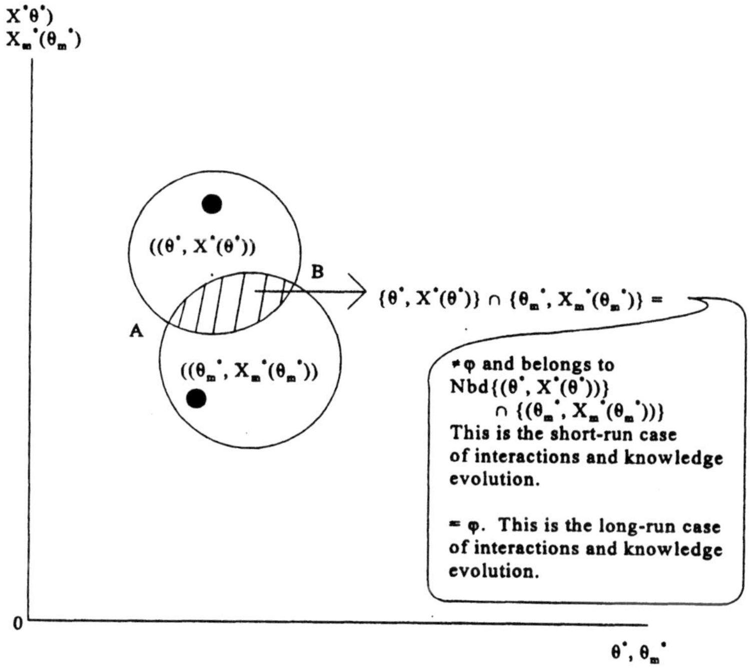

CHAPTER 4

COMPARATIVE POLITICAL ECONOMY: ISLAM AND THE OCCIDENT

The concept of political economy as an academic inquiry has undergone a wide range of interpretations, just as economics has been variously defined between the concept of scarcity and that of resource allocation in both the microeconomic and the macroeconomic sense. Classical and Marxist political economy are seen as the study of the production and distribution of wealth and of the conflict in power among agents involved. Yet different concepts of political economy can be developed. It is our objective here to introduce such an alternative theory of political economy, that which we will call Islamic political economy. We will examine this theory in comparative perspectives.

CLASSICAL POLITICAL ECONOMY

Adam Smith's **The Theory of Moral Sentiments** showed the importance of moral values in the formation of civil society (1976); but his **Wealth of Nations** (1976) was a turn around from such moral moorings toward a study of the dynamics of economic exchange, which were shown to be the rules of competition born of self-interest. The compartmentalizing of the economic function into smaller producing units, called division of labour, made up for the market exchange among competing and efficient agents.

The conflict between the above two works of Adam Smith is found to be based on the marginalization of the moral values among cooperating agents of **Moral Sentiments** after they have been left to the rule of self-interest in the great market place of **The Wealth of Nations**. Hence while human benevolence played a role for small groups of agents, yet in the sense of market exchange, human benevolence was shown by Smith to be unattainable as a conscious value. Benevolence was thus methodologically replaced by self-interest (Coase 1994). The concept of benevolence as a form of altruism, can then be seen as a kind of 'ethical egoism' when placed within the framework of methodological individualism of self-interested agents. That is, if I do good to another that is because I expect a good in return and both of these actions must be quantitatively measurable in the case of market exchange. This is the inference on rational ethical behaviour emanating from the combined reading of Smith's two works. To Smith the measurable return of ethical exchange was the price of the exchange. This aspect of ethical rationality under altruism can only limit the treatment of benevolence to self-seeking behaviour. Then there can be no ethical benefit to be derived other than allocative efficiency of resource allocation. What is reflected finally in the price system with altruistic behaviour is not the essence of the ethical act but the material consequence of the act when entered in exchange. Classical markets thus read only consequentialist results (Sen 1990).

Between these two shades of thinking in Adam Smith, **The Theory of Moral Sentiments** champions the cause of natural liberty in social matters toward realizing the moral laws through the act of cooperation and sympathy as human instinct. Whereas, the same natural liberty is shown to be realized by the rise of individualism and the pursuit of self-interest in the name of the common good in **The Wealth of Nations**. For a good discussion on the dual views of Smith between his two books see Tribe (1999).

The principle of sympathy that characterizes **The Theory of Moral Sentiments** can be felt from Smith's words (1976, pg. 13): 'Nothing pleases us more than to observe in other fellow men a fellow-feeling with all the emotions of our own breast'. Smith goes on in this work (pg. 15): 'Love is an agreeable, resentment a disagreeable passion: and accordingly we are not half as anxious that our friends should adopt our friendships, as that they should enter into our resentments ... The agreeable passions of love and joy can satisfy and support the heart without any auxiliary pleasure. The bitter and painful emotions of grief and resentment more strongly require the healing consolation of sympathy.' The attributes of human nature in consonance with natural liberty can be derived from such passages as the following (pg. 77): 'Nature ... even in the present depraved state of mankind, does not seem to have dealt so unkindly with us, as to have endowed us with any principle which is wholly and in every respect evil, or which, in no degree and in no direction, can be the proper object of praise and appreciation.'

In **The Wealth of Nations**, the natural liberty principle is found to be bereft of benevolence for the multitude of human race. It becomes impossible to attain in large scale systems, such as the market order. Instead, benevolence is replaced by the mechanism of self-interest, which is just the opposite of human attributes such as benevolence and sympathy. Self-interest is now made to depict the result of a grand scale of cooperation among agents who exchange in the market order. Thus, enlightened self-interest is used to describe a form of invisible cooperation that is only implied but not explained as a process in the exchange mechanism. By so dissociating the two aspects of human nature, namely benevolence and sympathy from enlightened self-interest within small and large scale cooperative systems, respectively, but not explaining the process underlying cooperation and exchange, the study of political economy suffered a dichotomy in the hands of Adam Smith. This dichotomy showed up by rendering **The Theory of Moral Sentiments** as a study in human psychology and **The Wealth of Nations** as an independent study of the organization of economic life.

This type of independence and dichotomy of the moral from the mundane is also found to persist in Mill's work with regards to his understanding of political economy. Mill writes (1994, pg. 6-7):

> We have here to consider, not the causes, but the consequences, of the rules according to which wealth may be distributed ... society can subject the distribution of wealth to whatever rules it thinks best: but what practical results will flow from the operation of those rules, must be discovered, like any other physical or mental truths, by observation and reasoning.

To Mill therefore, the study of political economy had nothing in respect to combining the normative with the positivistic aspects of social and economic reasoning. Instead it was simply a pursuit in positivistic and inductive reasoning involving economic consequences.

The limited scope of political economy as perceived in the literature can also be seen by its confined focus on matters of material progress. Henry George writes in this regard (1897, pg. 76):

> Thus the movements with which political economy is concerned are human actions, having for their aims the attainment of material satisfactions. And the laws that it is its province to discover are not the laws manifested in the existence of the materials and forces of nature that man thus utilizes, nor yet the laws which make possible their change in place, form or relation, but the laws of man's own nature, which affect his own actions in the endeavour to satisfy his desires by bringing about such changes.

FROM CLASSICAL TO NEOCLASSICAL POLITICAL ECONOMY

Classical political economy in the mould of its inductive approach to socioeconomic analysis, particularly the analysis of the production, ownership and distribution of wealth and the underlying conflict including market mechanism as a particular case of conflict or consensus, becomes an embodiment of utilitarian methodology. The concept of happiness as in utilitarian philosophy, is equated with material happiness without inquiring on the epistemological, normative or deductive questions of the principles of ownership, the nature of wealth and the laws affecting control and distribution of wealth within a complex of human relations (Quinton 1989). At the least, there was no connection between the epistemological question and the positivistic approach in classical political economy. These questions were independently invoked and remained separate from each other.

In this sense too, neoclassical economics building upon the utilitarian ethics of ownership by efficient allocation of resources and the utilities gained from the consumption bundles of goods and services, becomes a scientific refinement in the same form of a utilitarian political economy, to use a term befitting the original utilitarian outlook on morals and the civil libertarian order (Bentham 1789). Here the role of government is invoked in the allocation of public goods to attain better distributive equity but without removing the inherent conflict among competing ends that remain embedded in neoclassical methodology, that is, the methodological assumption of the trade-off between social justice and economic efficiency and the like (Srinivasan, 1985). Such a neoclassical assumption of self-interested individualism is today also to be found in public choice theory for explaining trade-offs between contending social choices undertaken by governments (Minford & Peel, 1983).

On the issue of price and value, while classical economics considered value to be based on supply price and unit cost of production, neoclassical economics sees value to be determined by demand price arising from the marginal utility of a good/service to the consumer. The existence of marginal utility is a necessary and sufficient condition in optimizing the utility function, subject to assigned consumer preferences. Hence, because consumer preferences determine prices through marginal utility, therefore, price and income also remain exogenously given in neoclassical economic theory. Methodological problems of price determination and hence of economic value arises due to the methodological difference in supply and demand prices, not to speak of the even more troublesome problem caused by the disparate nature of microeconomic and macroeconomic prices (Thurow 1983). If and only if the assumption of competitive equilibrium is assumed, then can supply and demand prices be equated to equilibrium prices. Otherwise, contested markets are the only other option, in which multilateral bargaining is shown to approximate but not to uniquely determine equilibrium prices (Martin 1988). Such an indeterminacy in price determination is to be found in the case of bilateral monopoly and monopsony as in oligopoly, with less than full information among contesting agents (Mansfield 1985, Choudhury 1996a). Now supply and demand prices cannot be equal to each other, and any enforcement of equilibrium price under such a disparate condition of bargaining becomes simply a scientific assumption, not a socioeconomic realism.

A strong consequence of such a scientific nicety is the dual concept of optimality-equilibrium in neoclassical economic theory of perfect and imperfect competition. The presence of polity and social forces along with economic ones in the study of political economy, makes such demand-supply price differences and the attenuating uncertainties all the more a fact of real occurrence. Neoclassical economics has no way of resolving such a situation except to hold on to its scientific nicety of determining expected price by a sheer use of observed probabilities, and to extend utilitarian behaviour to institutions as to atomistic markets, seeking thus compliance of market behaviour with equilibrium and optimality (Shackle 1971). It is because of such deeply methodological problems between price and value that Stigler remarked, the study of the theory of value 'has elicited supreme efforts of the greatest theorists' (Stigler 1960).

MARXIST POLITICAL ECONOMY

Marxist political economy shot out of Ricardo's Labour Theory of Value. It saw in political economy the study of conflict of power underlying the production, ownership and distribution of wealth. Economism was Marx's basis for all human actions. It formed the epistemological premise for all of human praxis in Marx (Stanfield 1985). Every human action was reduced to the level of its economistic explanation. Consequently, even on the question of labour and its alienation by capitalist forces of production and ownership, Marx took the stand that cooperation between capitalists and labour is an untenable thing.

Dead labour was seen to be built into the intrinsic value of things produced. Such dead labour was claimed not to be accounted for in wage determination under capitalism. Marx then argued that because dead labour remained unaccounted for in capitalist production, therefore the marginal productivity of labour was a subjective concept. It formed the capitalist's and not the worker's perception of real value of labour. The difference between such a capitalistic valuation of wage rate and its real value incorporating the use-value of labour imputed in the production of the good, comprised Marx's surplus value.

Alternatively, surplus value can be defined as the excess of gross receipts of the capitalists over variable and fixed costs (Blaug 1968). The two definitions of surplus value given here, become identical when we interpret capitalist prices to be exchange value and take the valuation of output by the capitalists in terms of marginal product as perceived by them. Likewise, variable and fixed costs are measured in terms of exchange-value of wages and rents. Thus the difference between gross incomes and the capitalists' valuation of cost of production at exchange-value prices, is simply equal to the profit component of national income.

Prices for Marx were two-tiered (Cole 1966). Thereby, markets of goods/services must also be two-tiered according to the two kinds of prices. Otherwise, there can be no relevance of markets at all in respect to a two-tiered price theory in the labour theory of value.

First, there was the concept of price associated with use-value, which showed the value of commodities in terms of the total accumulation of past and present labour in their production. Such a value clearly could not fetch a market for itself. For one, the imputed valuation incorporating both dead and active labour, is an impossible task. Second, such a value even if imputed would be extremely high in measuring prices.

Second, the concept of price as exchange-value has to do with the demand of a thing in exchange in the market venue. This is Marx's concept of capitalistic value of commodity in exchange. To Marx exchange-value reflected first, the subjective notion of wages and capital in production cost. Exchange-value was seen to be subjective by virtue of its determination only by and from the capitalist's perception, ownership being skewed in his favour.

We therefore infer that either use-value had nothing to do with the pricing of goods and was thus part of a pure theory of exploitation of labour, or it meant that exchange-value was simply exploitative. This conclusion gives a methodologically non-functional picture of market exchange. Marxist political economy consequently remained a study of the economistic way of reading value in production and not in exchange. This picture provides the supply price concept, not the demand price concept. Yet here too there is a twist: A supply price is not based on the incremental imputation of labour and capital in production. Being a supply price in terms of Marx's concept of value, the production scheme remains severed from the consumption menu, causing thereby, disjointedness between the consumer and producer economic welfare menus (Martinez-Alier 1990). The result is social non-cohesion, non-cooperation among factors of production in the midst of Marx's capitalist-worker-consumer conflict.

There is no mechanism in such a treatment of political economy to either configure markets or to make prices or values as a medium of interactions among sectors and agents. It is for these methodological remises, that Marxist political economy can be seen to evolve into a form of neoclassical replication of efficient national resource allocation. In Marxian economics prices are administered (shadow prices) by the Gosplan, for instance. They give rise to kinked contours of indifference curves along the expansionary trajectory of output. Marginal substitution is prescribed by public authority. Hence prices of factors and goods are accordingly set to denote capital-labour allocations in production (Zimbalist et al 1989). Any change in this configuration of kinked type of resource allocation points is a matter of Gosplan revising its decision on technologically-induced allocations. Consequently, the nature of capital-labour conflicts signified by the prescribed allocations remains inherent in Marxian economics.

The ethical implication of Marxist's social alienation of labour remains to be a case only of an exploitative theory of wages. In this, the use-value of labour is seen as an objectivized and not as a capitalistic commoditized factor. The latter category is equated with Marx's perception of labour in the case of the exchange-value concept in capitalistic valuation of output.

FORMALIZING MARXIST PRODUCTION VALUATION USING USE-VALUE THEORY

A simple formalization on production valuation using use-value concept of price, wage and cost, can be attempted here. According to the use-value labour theory, output Q is produced by labour L alone. Consequently, the use of capital K is imputed in terms of labour. Now the production function F is given by,

$$Q = F(L,K(L)) = K(L)^a.F((L/K(L)),1),\ a \geq 1,$$

implying increasing returns to scale because of the assumed higher productivity of labour over capital in Marxist labour theory of value.

$K(L) = L^b$, $b \leq 1$, because according to the kinked form of the production isoquant contours of socialist allocation of national resources, K(L) and L are gross substitutes. With labour gaining primacy in production, K(L) must therefore be set at a lower level. This assumption is also the consequence of Marx's configuration of the organic composition of capital, defined as the ratio of variable capital to total cost of production. Marx shows this organic composition of capital (= capital/labour ratio) to remain high in value when measured in terms of exchange-value wages, for the capitalist is seen to substitute capital for labour (Blaug pg. 230-31).

Now, $Q = L^{ab}.f(L^{1-b})$, where, $f(L^{1-b}) = F((L/K(L)),1)$ implies that, $P_u.Q = P_u.L^{ab}.f(L^{1-b})$ = cost of production = $w_u.L^c$, for some $c \geq 1$. Here, p_u denotes price in terms of use-value, w_u denotes wages in terms of use-value of labour. Labour is the only primal and active factor of production in labour theory of value. Hence cumulative labour in Marx's use-value theory would be indicated by $c \geq 1$. Thereby, $w_u = A.p_u.L^{1-b+ab-c}$, by approximating $f(.) = A.L^{1-b}$, along the expansionary trajectory of the kinked production isoquant contours. The coefficient A is a constant when it is independent of technological induction as in the case of long-run technological change. Otherwise, in the presence of technological sensitivity, 'A' will act as a technological change parameter (Solow 1970). We note now that as economies of scale continue to be enjoyed in production, we will have, $1-b+ab > c$, but not conversely. Consequently, for $b > (c-1)/(a-1)$, w_u/p_u will be increasing as L increases. It can be noted here that since $b(a-1) > c > 1$, therefore, increasing returns to scale due to labour-using technology is dominated by the coefficient $a > 1$ (not $b < 1$). That is, the production function in Marxist perspective is dominated by labour in the sense that labour now 'substitutes' capital, even though capital is an asset produced by labour induced in it.

Thus, capital formation in the hands of capitalists remains opposed to labour-using technology. These are results of a neoclassical marginal substitution applied to capital and labour in the aggregate production function. Hence, we find that the production menu on which Marx placed so much importance as opposed to consumption menu, is fully explained as a version of neoclassical type production relations. This is true either with kinked (now 'a' and 'b' are set by the state) or smooth production isoquant contours (no particular state intervention).

In the classical long-run case of production, which Marx represented in his approximation of use-value with supply price, $b(a-1) = c$. Now, w_u/p_u will be increasing by the linear monotonic component of labour L. This means that as long as economies of scale are continually enjoyed and finally cancelled, productive labour will continue to contribute simultaneously to wages and prices. But in the event when wages increase proportionately more than prices, as the above result implies to be a possibility, then no rationale exists as to why production will continue to be efficient with increased labour use.

Likewise, when b(a-1) < c in the case of lost economies of scale, increase in labour will decrease the w_u/p_u ratio. Now either both w_u and p_u will decrease simultaneously or w_u will decrease at a rate greater than the decrease (or even increase) in p_u. Labour-using technology must then be replaced, and the labour theory of value will cease to provide answers to efficient production in the midst of a use-value theory. In this case too we find that the coefficient 'a' remains to be the dominating parameter in the labour-capital allocation of resources. Too much labour is being used beyond its productive usage. The marginal productivity remains intact, thus once more proving that Marxist ideas in value theory can be explained by neoclassical economic theory..

The problem in w_u/p_u movements as stated above arises because these are values administered by authority (prescribed by the state). When $w_u > p_u$, it means that labour is extracting a value in excess of its legitimate claim on the basis of use-value prices. When $w_u < p_u$, then too the shadow markets operating on use-value prices do not reflect the true value of labour. There is thus no equilibrating process to cause w_u/p_u = constant. A disequilibrium dynamics in prices and wages therefore persists in Marxist political economy based on the labour theory of value. Marxist labour theory of value forces this equilibrium to occur in a socialist state but cannot functionally explain how it would come about. Equally, the theory fails to functionally explain the disequilibrium situation reflected by various forms of w_u/p_u trends, except by invoking the theory of alienation of labour in capitalism.

DIAGRAMMATIC EXPLANATION OF MARX'S PRICES AND USE-VALUE

Figure 4.1 brings out the above-mentioned relationships. Quadrant 4.1 shows the diminishing but never disappearing economies of scale in a production function with labour as the only variable factor, as implied by Marxist labour theory of value. The shift downwards in the average cost curves is due to labour-intensive technological change. Point 'A' denotes the case of low economy of scale when prices and hence unit cost remains high (c > b(a-1)). Point C denotes the case of optimal economy of scale, where b(a-1) = c. Production and allocative forces around this position of optimal economy of scale suggest the following: When the coefficient '$b < 1$' predominates, then there is increased substitution of capital for labour, and the production technology is capital-intensive. When '$a > 1$' predominates, then there is increased substitution of labour for capital, and the production technology is labour-intensive. Equilibrium from these either sides causes correction for economies of scale to take place – high and low, to allow for marginal substitution between capital and labour. Hence the neoclassical nature of resource allocation is once again embedded in Marxist production menu. The prices of quadrant 4.1.1 denote unit cost values imputed by use-values in production.

Quadrant 4.1.2 shows the p_u/w_u relationships corresponding to A, B and C in quadrant 4.1. Corresponding to A is the case of $p_u > w_u$, shown at the point A′. The case of $p_u < w_u$ is shown by the point B′ corresponding to B. The case of p_u tending to w_u corresponds to points C to C′. The curve A′B′C′ is negatively sloped as shown with the point C′ lying on the straight line OT. As the curve ABC shifts to abc, so does A′B′C′ shift, causing another point C" to lie on a straight line. In the long run, the coefficient 'A' shown earlier in $w_u/p_u = A.L$, will attain stability. Then C′C".. will lie on the same straight line, OT, as shown. This is the case of Marxist long-run equilibrium of capitalist evolution into a socialist and communist state. It is also implied by the long-run nature of equilibrium in classical economics and the long-run technological state in neoclassical economics.

As long as the coefficient 'A' of the equation, $w_u/p_u = A.L$, remains technologically induced, the straight line, OT, will also change slopes, causing C′C".. to be scattered in a region. Such a region D is shown in quadrant 4.1.3, with OT now experiencing shifts as shown by OT_1, OT_2. Corresponding to each of the points of the region D and hence for the whole of D, there are scattered supply prices in the region E. Hence, equilibrium perturbations are caused by such a scatter of supply prices. Consequently, this will cause problem of identification of demand-supply configurations in determining equilibrium price-quantity relationship (Johnston 1984). The price levels shown by the supply curves are now identical with those shown in quadrant 4.1.1. Since the price-quantity relations of quadrant 4.1.4 experience identification problem, therefore, the price-quantity relations in quadrant 1 will also be perturbed in the sense of use-prices imputed by use-value.

Figure 4.1: Equilibrium and disequilibrium in Marxist theory of value

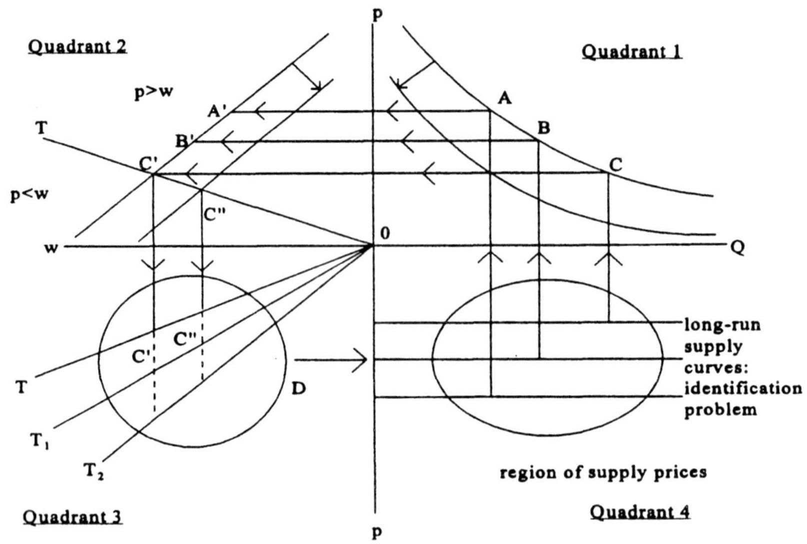

THE ISLAMIC THEORY OF POLITICAL ECONOMY: INTRINSIC VALUE THEORY

In this section we will first introduce the concept of 'intrinsic value,' on which hinges the Islamic theory of value, prices and cost of production. Intrinsic value is a composite of complemented moral-material values found to be inherent in all goods/services by virtue of its primordial createdness and social appropriateness. Such an intrinsic value remains uncreated, and therefore, a primal input qualifying all goods/services. The intrinsic value being primordial in nature, it is neither due to prior labour or capital in production. As an example, consider a rare weed that was suddenly discovered to be of medicinal value. The weed is proven to be valuable because of this intrinsic value in it. However, what brings out the realization of usefulness of the weed is the jointness of use of the land (capital) where the weed grows, and labour (knowledge) that is used to find the weed and discover its usefulness. Hence cooperation between owners and workers becomes part of the extensively cooperative and complementing system conceptualized in intrinsic value theory.

Such an intrinsic value is the God-given primordial value or essence (Fitra) in all things. Its extraction in real world situations is enabled by the exercise of the Divine Laws (e.g. the role of Sunnat al-Allah on establishing a basic needs regimes of development, capital-labour cooperation in joint ventures etc.) that apply to all facets of life. The Divine Laws (Sunnat al-Allah) carry with them knowledge sharing, technological development, institutional cooperation and agent-agent consensus in their mutual interests to approach ventures of social and individual profitability. Enlightened self-interest is now once again invoked, but by the exercise of visible institutional discursions on the basis of knowledge sharing among agents for exploring the common good. The complemented moral-material worth attenuates with the intrinsic value of Godly Bliss in the primal order of all things. This conjoint moral-material realization, the underlying knowledge-sharing, rules and approaches emanating from the Divine Laws (Ahkam) to realize the moral-material worth, are consequences of the primal ordering of socio-scientific actions.

One such institution for realizing the intrinsic moral-material worth of the good is the ethicizing market order. This is the kind of market order that is not hedonically and individualistically exchange oriented. Exchange is fundamental, but now it means exchange of goods/services that have been preconditioned by social discourse, knowledge-sharing, preferences and behaviour formation, choices and instruments of transactions as found appropriate to and emanating from the derivation of rules premised on the Divine Laws and applied to the socio-scientific order.

A SIMPLE FORMALIZATION OF INTRINSIC VALUE THEORY IN ISLAMIC POLITICAL ECONOMY

A simple formalization of intrinsic value theory in ethicizing market exchange is now undertaken for explaining how prices are determined in such intrinsic value theory (Choudhury 1994a). We proceed as follows:

Let θ denote the knowledge premise (Islamic Law = Shari'ah Ahkam = deriving rules from Shari'ah). θ determines the intrinsic value of social well-being, $W(\theta)$, and the value of economic well-being $E(\theta)$. In the economic order, such an identification of value takes the form of unit costs incurred in realizing the complemented moral-material worth by means of a gamut of institutional and market involvements. The total socioeconomic (or socio-scientific) moral-material value is then determined by $V = W(\theta) \times E(\theta)$. An increase in θ through the above-mentioned kinds of interactions premised on the moral law, means that there must be simultaneous increase in $W(\theta)$ and $E(\theta)$. In the social sense, this means that the goals of distributive equity and economic efficiency must co-exist in the midst of knowledge-based resource allocation. Such a knowledge-based process of resource development and sharing that involves large systemic interlinkages among factors and agents is termed as the Principle of Universe Complementarity (Choudhury 1994b).

Since complementarity must be extensive in nature under a unified process idea of the knowledge-centred universe, of which are the specific examples of markets and ecology, political institutions and socio-scientific instruments, therefore, the principle of universal complementarity completely replaces the neoclassical idea of marginalism or the Marxist idea of kinked production isoquants.

Furthermore, $W(\theta) \propto p_w(\theta)$, showing that prices are determined in ethicizing markets. Ethicizing markets are ethically transformed markets under the impact of moral discourse (knowledge formation) affecting consumption preferences, production menus and institutional policies toward enabling consumption, production and distribution to comply with the moral laws underlying these actions. Ethicizing market transformation affects formation of $W(\theta)$. Likewise, $E(\theta) \propto p_E(\theta)$, showing price formation in the midst of ethically oriented economic well-being. Hence, because total well-being is simultaneously related with moral-material complementarity, therefore, $V \propto p_w(\theta) x p_E(\theta)$. Consequently, we have a tripartite mapping interconnecting knowledge (morally invoked discourse), price and value; but note that in the sense of social discourse, which cause creative evolution, old knowledge values lead to new knowledge values and to newly material reconstruction of the socio-scientific order.

The above-mentioned knowledge-based interrelationships in Islamic political economy acting through intrinsic value theory and the methodology of circular causation and continuity model of unified reality is now explained by means of figure 4.2. While it would be too detailed to cover the whole nexus of interrelationships shown in this figure, we therefore limit our details to a subset.

To examine a few of the nexus of circular causation and continuity interrelationships in figure 4.2 we use compound mappings denoted by 'o,' to construct the following relations:

$$f_4 = f_3 \text{ o } f_1;\ f_1 = f_2 \text{ o } f_4 \ldots \ldots \ldots \ldots (1)$$

Thereby, by substituting for f_1 between these expressions we obtain,

$$f3 \text{ o } f2 = I \text{ (identify mapping, as in group algebra)} \ldots \ldots (2)$$

Next, we note that,

$$f_2'' \text{ o } f_1 = f_1;\ f_3'' \text{ o } f_1' = f_1, \ldots \ldots \ldots \ldots (3)$$

whereby, by substituting for f_1' between these, we obtain,

$$f_2'' \text{ o } f_3 = I \ldots \ldots \ldots \ldots (4)$$

and, $f_4 = f_3 \text{ o } f_3'' \text{ o } f_1';\ f_2 \text{ o } f_4 = f_3'' \text{ o } f_1' \ldots \ldots \ldots \ldots (5)$

Figure 4.2: Interactive-integrative-evolutionary interrelationships in the Islamic political economy

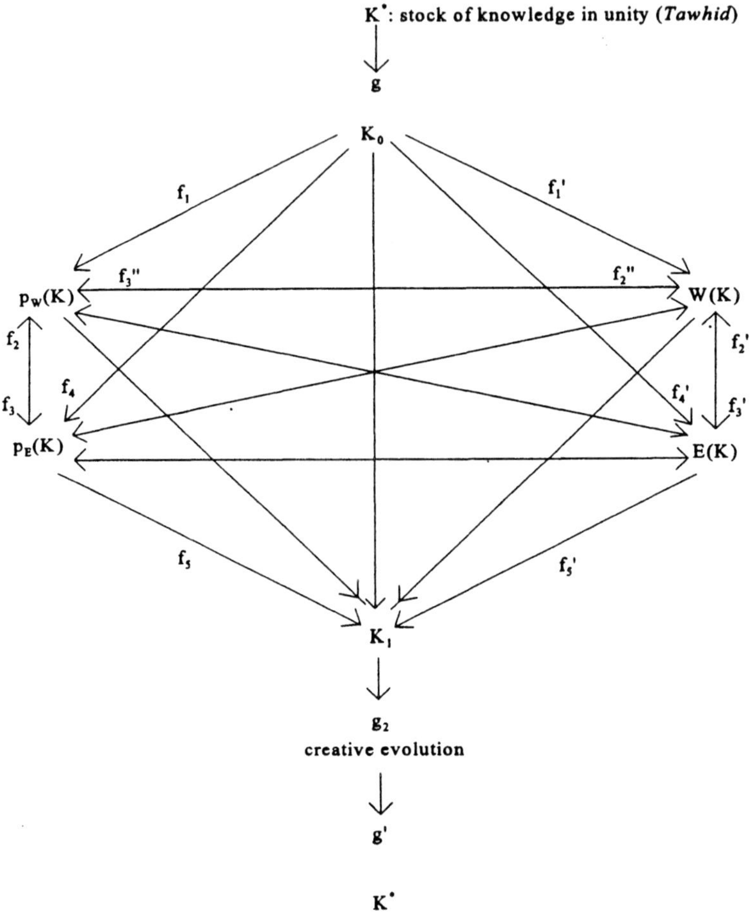

Many other similar circular causation and continuity interrelationships among the various components of the knowledge-induced variables and functions of figure 4.2, can be constructed. Note however, that the passage to θ^* once again, is through the function of flows cumulating to the Stock as the creative evolution proceeds incessantly. The Qur'an calls this supreme function of knowledge in the unification process as realization of Hereafter (Akhira). Now primordial Unity, θ^*, maps into itself in Akhira to 'prove itself.' This is also the result to be derived by using Fixed Point Theorems in unbounded topological sets taking place in the total creative order. The Qur'an affirms the event of Akhira as 'the Sure Reality' (Qur'an, Chapter 59, verse 1).

It can be shown that the mappings starting from θ_0 (an initial knowledge-value impacting upon the political economy) cause a 'globally' pervasive domain of interconnections among the various components. Each relation feeds into the other in circular causation and continuity. Intrinsic value in this interactive, integrative and evolutionary form is thus recreated by a nexus of recursive interrelationships. What is important to note here is that just as prices determine value of the corresponding well-being, so also a given level of social well-being determines the subsequent level of prices as value, and so on.

What does this mean? It means that although a primal value is found to be intrinsic in goods/services, it is discovered and improved upon by greater levels of knowledge that are recreated out of discourse (Shuratic Process = interactive, integrative and evolutionary model of deriving Ahkam from the premise of the Divine Laws = Unity = Principal of Universal Complementarity, i.e. IIE-process) (Choudhury 1993). The same kinds of circular causation and continuity interrelationships in creative planes of evolution of knowledge are found to be recreated among (K,p,w.Q), referred to earlier. This is at once the consequence of the primordial of the Divine Laws playing their central role in the formation of conduct, preferences, behaviour, choices, institutions, technology and markets, as it gets reinforced by the evolving moral-material progress impacting upon the emerging knowledge flows. Such a method, but taken up solely within the domain of positivistic and inductive view of human nature in utilitarian philosophy, is also found mentioned in Mill (pp. 71-82).

From figure 4.2 we can at once deduce that the primal epistemology of this knowledge-based worldview is the extension backward of θ_0 to the spring of Divine Unity, from which springs the fundamental Stock of Knowledge and the Shari'ah. This derivation is determined by the Qur'an and is functionalized by the authentic Sunnah (Prophetic traditions). In this way, θ^* as Stock of Knowledge framed by the Divine Laws (Sunnat al-Allah) is translated into flows of knowledge that determine the temporal praxis by Sunnah. Together with this, primal Unity and its translations in the form of rules of life out of effort (Ahkam and Ijtihad) through evolving flows of θ's, the Divine Unity becomes the unification epistemology of the entire socio-scientific order. Figure 4.2 and its extensions to other issues and problems of political economy and socio-scientific inquiry now form a depiction of unification of knowledge in action. It carries unity within diversity into human praxis, as shown by the multiplicity of mappings through higher plains of knowledge induction in figure 4.2.

Finally, the problem of disequilibrium faced between w_u and p_u in Marxist labour theory of value, as mentioned earlier, is now resolved by taking these values within the discursive praxis (Shuratic Process). W_u can approximate to p_u, these being taken up in the sense of intrinsic value, but only momentarily in the midst of instantaneity of equilibrium along the supply function of output and labour (Haddad 1995). This, however, is a case of no particular realism. Knowledge-induced transformations of socioeconomic variables in the interactive plane, cause dynamic equilibria to arise. Now no optimal-equilibrium points can occur except in the instantaneous sense of the very short run.

CONTRASTING INTRINSIC VALUE WITH OTHER THEORIES OF VALUE

Note next the form of the moral and material conjugation of value in the classical, neoclassical or the Marxist political economy. Let this value be expressed as, $V(M) = W(M) + E(M)$, where M denotes either economism of Marx or self-interested methodological individualism of competing agents in classical and neoclassical economic paradigms. An additive form replaces the multiplicative form of total value in Islamic political economy, because of the substitutional nature of W(M) and

E(M) in the other political economy. The pervasive marginal substitution principle in these paradigms must cause V(M) to increase by marginal substitution between W(M) and E(M). Likewise, relative prices and costs will cause such substitutions to occur. The existence of M implies an optimality in exchange, and hence causes an equilibrium to exist. Consequently, contrary to the knowledge-induced theory of intrinsic value, the classical, neoclassical and Marxist value concepts are all based on such equilibrium-optimality preconditions. Now scientific nicety overshadows social, institutional and socioeconomic realism.

Finally, by defining an ethicizing market exchange as M(K), we not the comparison of values between the Islamic and other cases:

$$V(\theta,M) = V(M(\theta)) - V(M) = [W(\theta) \times E(\theta) - W(M) - E(M)]$$
$$dV = dV(M(\theta)) - dV(M).$$

Under the condition of optimality-equilibrium in received economic theory, including Marxist economism of a socialist state, $dV(M) = 0$. Therefore, $dV(\theta,M) > 0$, solely due to the presence of Islamic moral-material worth, showing the superiority of the knowledge-based intrinsic theory of value over the other ones.

Besides, $dV(M) = 0$ implies that, $dW(M) = - dE(M)$, implying unitary marginal substitution between social justice and economic efficiency. Whereas, in the knowledge-based political economy, $dV(M(\theta)) = (E(\theta)\,(\partial W(\theta)/\partial\theta))d\theta + W(\theta)\,(\partial E(\theta)/\partial\theta\,)d\theta > 0$, because of monotonicity of variables of knowledge induction. Clearly now, each of the knowledge-based terms in this expression must be separately positive.

PRICING IN THE ISLAMIC POLITICAL ECONOMY

A brief explanation is undertaken here of the method of pricing in the Islamic political economy. For greater details the reader may refer elsewhere (Choudhury 1996b). We recall that the allocation space is characterized by perturbations in consumer preferences that in a general systems approach of Islamic political economy makes the production and distributional menus 'fuzzy' on a 'globally' interactive scale. Only in the very instantaneous case can we speak of an equilibrium point. In all other cases, as the interactive, integrative and evolutionary model of decision-making in the Islamic political economy, all equilibrium points become continuously knowledge-induced and hence evolutionary.

In figure 4.3, we denote the decision-making space by neighbourhoods of the type T_1 around 'fuzzy' points such as 'a'. Since 'a' is one of infinitely many similar points both within T_1 and intertemporally, therefore, the entire trajectory, OT_1T_2... is a locus of perturbed points. Consequently, there cannot exist any smooth production possibility curve. Hence prices of the goods, $X_1(\theta)$, $X_2(\theta)$ cannot be determined by any possible 'price line' of the neoclassical genre. Besides, we recall that these goods are complementary to each other extensively. Thus, $dX_1(\theta)/dX_2(\theta) > 0$. The marginal substitution idea is completely replaced by the principle of universal complementarity.

Consider now that the demand function of $X_i(\theta)$ is given by, $X_i(\theta)=D_i(p_i(\theta))$, $i = 1,2$. Since $dX_1(\theta)/dX_2(\theta) > 0$, therefore, $dD_i(\theta)/d\theta > 0$, or, $[dX_i/dp_i(\theta) \,.\, dp_i(\theta)/d\theta] > 0$, $i = 1,2$. That is, each of the interior terms inside [.] must be of the same sign. Therefore, $dp_1(\theta)/dp_2(\theta) > 0$. The meaning is clear: In interlinked markets, the increased demand of any one good causes increased demand for the other good, and conversely. Thus their prices increase or decrease together by mutual demand induction. The prices themselves are simulated by market contracts and not automatic equilibrium of the type found in classical economic theory (Choudhury 1994c, 1996a).

Hence, prices do not read out the value of goods and services in the Islamic political economy. Consequently, the average cost of production too is not a representation of value here. Only the measure of knowledge induction inhering in all socioeconomic variables, stands for value (Fitra). Since Fitra as effect is induced into an ethicizing market exchange, this effect is readable only by such an induction. There is no need for a precise calculation of such a value in the Islamic political economy. Prices and unit costs remain endogenously induced by the Fitra value.

The resource allocation path OT_1T_2 is perturbed by a continuity of regions like T_1 within which K-induced interactions, integration and evolutionary equilibria like E_1, abide.

Figure 4.3: Resource allocation in the knowledge-induced space

Figure 4.3: Resource allocation in the knowledge-induced space

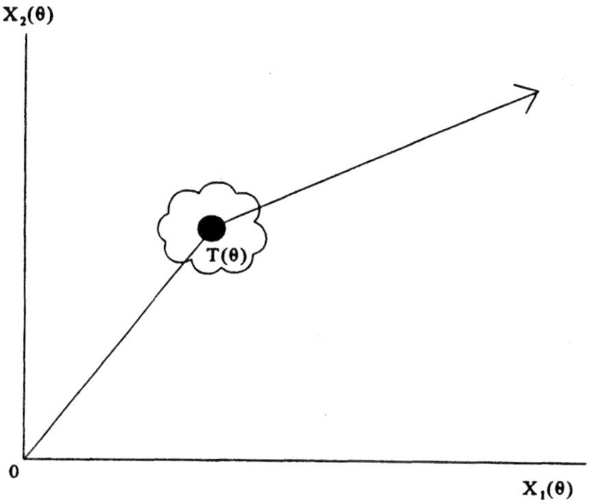

The resource allocation path $0T_1T_2$ is perturbed by a continuity of regions like T_1 within which interactions and integration of decision-making processes lead to temporary evolutionary equilibria like E_1 being θ-induced.

DEFINITION OF ISLAMIC POLITICAL ECONOMY

We can now define the field of Islamic political economy in the light of its analytical features. Islamic political economy is the study of interactive, integrative and evolutionary phenomena arising from the interplay of economic, social, institutional and socio-scientific forces in the totality of human praxis. Its axiomatic premise is grounded on the use of the knowledge-centred methodology. This methodology emanates from the epistemology of the Qur'an, Sunnah and Ijtihad. These three areas combined together help to derive the rules of the IIE-order, thus constituting the process model of political economy, referred to as the Shuratic Process. The pervasively interrelated nature of Islamic political economy is methodologically enabled by the principle of universal complementarity.

CONCLUSION

The principles characterizing Islamic political economy in comparative perspectives enable a vast number of applications that use a combination of deductive, normative, inductive and positivistic approaches. We provide two particular cases of many that have been formalized.

Concept of money in Islamic political economy

The theory of intrinsic value can be shown to apply to a corresponding concept of money. Money is now seen as a social contravention used for realizing the value of goods in exchange. By itself money cannot have value. The value of money is conveyed through the value of exchange transactions. Such a value is a function of the prices of goods/services transacted in ethicizing markets. Money then acquires simply a store of value and is treated as currency carrying a unit of stored value. It is from such a concept of money that the money rate of interest becomes redundant and forbidden in Islamic political economy. When applied to the world of finance and banking, such a currency-money will be interpreted as savings converted into productive investments, which by the preconditions of Shari'ah also happen to be investments in non-speculative outlets.

The institution of banking is now transformed into an investment-cum-management financial intermediary for enabling clients to hold money for convertibility from savings into investment and to control the supply of currency in accordance with the demand for currency required to finance transaction demand. Also banks become participants in joint ventures toward diversifying risk and in directing funds into profitable and productive investments (Choudhury 1991). The end result is a transaction account based on the profitability of investments resulting in the growth of capital. This is contrary to the imputation of interest rates to savings for capital formation and the conversion of savings into promissory notes. Money now becomes real bills for purposes of financing non-speculative investments and are issued as certificates denominating bank loans corresponding to the demand for goods in ethicizing markets.

Socioeconomic development in Islamic political economy

The political economy of development using the intrinsic value theory can be seen as an interplay of endogenous preferences of individuals, households, polity, the market order and development organizations. Hierarchies of interrelationships are now developed of the type shown in figure 4.2. They are now extended to applications with greater details and to wider range of socioeconomic phenomena. Since endogenous preferences provide the groundwork for the interactive, integrative and evolutionary model of interrelationships, therefore, they assume the intrinsic value parameters in this case. Development finance, monetary flows, projects, technological choices and inter-institutional collaborations, are all consequently endogenized by preferences that emerge from the hierarchies of interactions and integration in the dynamic sense of change within the knowledge-induced worldview. Beyond the sheer value implications of prices or labour use, the intrinsic value theory in Islamic political economy turns out to be knowledge flows as substantively defined in the sense of the interactive, integrative and evolutionary model of unified reality.

TECHNICAL APPENDIX:

NEOCLASSICISM AND MARXIST LONG-RUN THEORY OF VALUE IN TERMS OF AVERAGE COST

Since Marxist production menu has been proven to be of the neoclassical genre and the long-run optimal economies of scale are attained by substitution between labour and capital in the production menu, therefore, the following condition must attain:

The total cost of production, C, is given by,

$C = r.\theta(L) + w.L = Q = A.L^{b(a-1)+1}$, as explained in this chapter.

By the neoclassical relations,

$r = p.(\partial Q/\partial\theta) = p.[(\partial Q/\partial L)/(\partial\theta/\partial L)]$
$w = p.(\partial Q/\partial L)$.

Thereby, $w/r = \partial\theta/\partial L = b.L^{b-1}$, is a decreasing function of L, since $b \leq 1$, and since, $\theta=\theta(L)=L^b$ in the chapter. But in the long run, (w/r) must stabilize at the minimum of the average cost. This is also true for reasons of stopping a declining share of labour in output in Marxist production menu. Hence, b = 1 in this long-run case. Now, (w/r) = b = 1.

Hence if we treat average cost in the long run as a measure of value arising from production menu, then there can be no difference between Marxist and neoclassical approaches in understanding this economic value. It is simply that marginal substitution has taken place in favour of labour. This has come about by policy intervention in a socialist state. A market economy will not necessarily generate such a situation. Just like neoclassicism on the side of capitalism, the Marxist long run has nothing new to contribute to the theory of value and it remains devoid of market realism.

ISLAMIC THEORY OF VALUE IN THE LONG RUN IN TERMS OF AVERAGE COST

The Islamic production menu, F(.) is induced by knowledge, i.e. Fitra (interactions and cooperation), θ, among labour and capital. Thus,

$$Q = F(L,K)[\theta], \text{ with, } L = L(K)[\theta], K = K(L)[\theta].$$

Consequently, $w = w(\theta)$, $r = r(\theta)$ as monotonically increasing functions of θ-values.

Average cost of production is now given by,

$$(C/Q)[\theta] = [w(\theta).L(\theta)/Q(\theta) + r(\theta).K(\theta)/Q(\theta).$$

Since, L and K must be jointly productive by induction from each other in the face of complementarity between them, therefore, labour productivity, $P_L=Q(\theta)/L(\theta)$ is proportional to capital productivity, $P_K = Q(\theta)/K(\theta)$. But as complementarity increases, the wage rate, $w(\theta)$ will be inversely related to profit-share, r(K). This implies the progressive transformation of the wage-profit- sharing production menu into a profit-sharing one. Thus, average cost will decline as factor productivity increases within the profit-sharing transformation. But factor productivity must remain higher than the profit-shares, particularly due to the need for retained earnings and internal financing of cooperatives so as to avoid exogenous financial shocks (Vanek 1997, Lutz 1975). In the end, we find that $(C/Q)[\theta]$ must decline.

Only when $\theta \rightarrow \theta^*$ in the long run, then a temporary equilibrium of $(C/Q)[\theta^*]$ can attain. This is subsequently followed by changes in the average cost structure with creative evolutions of θ^*-values. This picture on average cost is distinct from the one presented by neoclassical economic theory and Marxist production menu. In either of these cases the long-run value of average cost must remain optimal due to the steady-state equilibrium (capitalism) or by enforcement in the absence of market realism (Marx). This is a situation that remains structurally valid even with technological change, for its effect is to induce the long-run change. In the Islamic case of value theory of Fitra, ethicizing markets must necessarily be invoked to discover Fitra values in exchangeables. But now there is only temporary equilibria over a phase of interactions leading to integration among workers and owners of capital. But this is followed by creative evolution of the temporary consensual θ*-values, as diversification and complementarity, re-contracting in profit-sharing and cost-sharing, and the need for expansion of operations, drive the θ*-values. Changes in the profit-sharing and cost-sharing re-contracting can generate different kinds of (C/Q)[θ*] structures with varying θ*-values in the IIE-framework.

MARX'S TRANSFORMATION PROBLEM

In table 4.1 (Ekelund, Jr & Herbert 1990) we note Marx's transformation problem – the calculation of prices in terms of the total of cost and rate of profit (= surplus value/(sum of constant and variable cost of capital). Different from the rate of surplus value is the rate of profit (=surplus value/variable capital cost). The total of deviation of prices so calculated from surplus value (= gross revenue - sum of constant and variable costs) is found to be zero although individual techniques and firms may give different price differentials due to variation in the organic composition of capital (capital/labour ratio). Constant capital denotes cost on fixed capital; variable capital denotes wage bills.

The very first error with Marx's transformation problem is the neglect of market forces that can set variations in price differentials. This can very well be due to the choice of technology represented in the variable organic composition of capital. Without this variation, there can be no incentive in market forces to prevail and capital cannot be formed nor wages distributed except by central authority intervening on these matters.

Second, we note that the capital column gives a constant total between constant (c) and variable (v) capital costs. This is the same as to imply that capital costs remain constant. On the basis of this the whole transformation table is constructed. But next inquire as to what it would be if not simply the reallocation of capital but also the X-efficiencies vary, as in the case of continuous re-contracting of profit-shares between labour and capital. Now the average cost of capital would vary. Consequently, the sum of the (price-cost) differentials would not necessarily be zero. Profit rates will vary between techniques and firms producing the same product. This means that the average price level cannot add up to average cost. In our formalization in this chapter we have shown that this equality can happen in the long run with choices of technology that bring about such equilibrium. Thus, equilibrium in the long-run average cost scenario of Marx's production menu is either enforced or assumed by a prescriptive resource allocation mechanism. Otherwise such an equilibrium is impossible to attain.

Table 4.1: Transformation of values into prices

Commodity	Capitals	Capital used up	Cost	Surplus value	Labor value	Average profit	Sales price	Deviation** of price from value
A	80c+20v	50	70	20	90	22	92	+2
B	70c+30v	51	81	30	111	22	103	- 8
C	60c+40v	51	91	40	131	22	113	-18
D	85c+15v	40	55	15	70	22	77	+ 7
E	95c+15v	10	15	5	20	22	37	+17
Total	500*	202	312	110	422	110	422	0

*This total includes a combination of 'stocks' and 'flows' (c+v) and is used to determine the average profit in column 7.

**Although the sales price (column 8) and labor value (column 6) differ for each commodity column 9 shows that the algebraic sums of individual differences is zero.

CHAPTER 5

ISLAMIC POLITICAL ECONOMY, A CRITIQUE OF ISLAMIC ECONOMICS

Our major objective in this chapter is to delineate the development and nature of Islamic economics and critique its overly mainstream leaning in the light of a new field of maturing Islamic socioeconomic reasoning. This is the field of Islamic political economy. We then study selected socioeconomic issues in the light of both Islamic economics and Islamic political economy to show how the methodologies and inferences of these two fields differ substantively.

THE HISTORICAL BACKGROUND OF ISLAMIC ECONOMICS

Just over sixty years ago the study of Islamic economics started in India under the then demand by Islamic movements and scholars in the Indian subcontinent to enhance a distinct socioeconomic manifesto of economic, social and political arrangement. The cry for Islamic economics was thus central among the Islamic movement of the Jamat-e-Islami, which to this day flourishes in Pakistan and Bangladesh. Subsequently, as Muslim scholars took up the advancement of ideas in Islamic economics, it entered intellectual inquiry in Aligarh University, Al-Azhar and recently in various universities of the Muslim countries. The emergence of these countries from colonial dominance after World War II, brought fresh challenge to redefine development in a Muslim framework. Today, an intensification of the same feeling of self-reliance has led to the study of Islamic economics in well-founded international Islamic universities – in Pakistan, Malaysia, Sudan, Bangladesh, Saudi Arabia and other ones.

Yet as the Muslim nations turned to base their revival on Islamic grounds, they faced dire limitations in well-defining the premise of the new worldview. The analytical depth of the literature was lacking or was still in the Arabic language of the scholastics that was not made accessible to the general school of new scholars in the field of Islamic economics. Studies on Islamic economics thus rested on generalities of economic functions and policy issues as they arose. Otherwise, such studies were overwhelmingly socio-religious in nature without workable content. Only recently we find that some of these original works of great epistemological value to social scientists in general are being translated into English and other foreign languages. Yet it also so happened that the translation project that was launched in the Department of Islamic Studies at the National University of Malaysia and in King Abdulaziz University, Saudi Arabia, wrapped up after some time.

In recent years when Muslim scholars wrote on Islamic economics, they had to turn to mainstream economic theories and clothe these up with a palliative of Islamic values. But no new challenge was posed on the epistemological beginnings of a new field of analytical and scientific inquiry. There was no demand from the Muslim scholars to well-define a distinctive field of Islamic economics. The Muslim scholars thus approached the study of Islamic values in neoclassical economic models of behaviour and resource allocation without questioning either the value-orientation of neoclassicism or the possibility of treating Islamic values in such otherwise value-free models of economic behaviour, pricing and resource allocation.

A great intellectual debility thus marked Islamic economics from its very inception. In the beginning this was a paucity of analytical depths for the sake of generality, that did not bear an applicative result on Islamic change in the newly independent Muslim countries. As of now, Islamic economics has become a total slave of mainstream economic theories of neoclassical microeconomics and macroeconomics, Keynesian macroeconomics, and only sparingly of monetarism and rational expectations hypothesis (Khan 1983, Anwar 1987). One can then say that Islamic economics as a field of study is no different from the neoclassical approach to ethical behaviour – if there is any such strange creation as neoclassical ethics other than utilitarianism (Quinton 1989)!

It is equally elusive to treat any trace of ethics in a macroeconomic framework, where there is no ethical decision-maker. Islamic economists have thus escaped the methodological orientations of a new science by borrowing ensemble from mainstream economics. Islamic economics has thus become a study in the piecemeal application of mainstream methods to emergent problems of Muslim thought and societies. Islamic economists have by and large avoided a fundamental invoking of a distinctive epistemology for the discovery of methodology on which would rest its methods and inferences.

In the words of Ludwig von Mises (1976),

> Theory as distinct from history is the search for constant relations between entities or, what means the same, for regularity in the succession of events. In establishing epistemology as a theory of knowledge, the philosopher implicitly assumes or asserts that there is in the intellectual effort of man something that remains unchanged, viz. the logical structure of the human mind.

Whereas, we find that Islamic economics by missing its core orientation on methodology and analytics of this discipline, has missed the epistemological praxis of a new discipline. Even though all Islamic economists unanimously uphold the Unity of God as the premise of Islamic thought in all disciplines (Nasr 1987), yet the normative and positivistic realization of this epistemology generating an endogenous force in the discipline of Islamic economics, has been left unattended. Indeed, classical and neoclassical economic methods of methodological individualism, atomism, value-neutrality, optimization and steady-state equilibrium, despite their time-dependent dynamic nature (Intrilligator 1971), cannot address the endogenous nature of ethics in economic theory.

Yet Islamic economists have not inquired into this methodological problem while using the neoclassical models for explaining Islamic substance. This substance is the central role of Divine Unity generating endogenous force in all systems, of which are the sub-systems of economy, society and polity. More generally, the followers of neoclassical economics and the treatment of economics as an independent field of scientific inquiry (Blaug 1968, Gray 1967), have made it impossible to study economic phenomena in reference to a systems-view of the social, political and scientific universes. Islamic economists inherited this serious debility when they imported the ethics-neutral methods and methodology into their otherwise highly value charged systemic worldview of embedded economic agency, behaviour, institutions, values and legal system (Asad 1980).

A BRIEF EXAMINATION OF MAJOR TRENDS IN ISLAMIC ECONOMICS

The above opening criticism of Islamic economics leads us to briefly categorize specific trends in Islamic economics to date. We will first consider studies within Islamic microeconomics. Within this branch we will take up consumer behaviour, risk-return behaviour, theory of the firm and markets. We will next consider studies within macroeconomics. Within this we will take up monetary models, general equilibrium models and financial models. Our focus will lie on examining whether the endogeneity of values emanating from the epistemology of Divine Unity was possible in these approaches. If not, then to what extent did such approaches fail to address the Islamic worldview? What then is the alternative?

Consumer Theory in Islamic Economics

Studies in consumer theory (Kahf 1978, Khan 1986, Naqvi 1994) have relied on all the aspects of mainstream economic theory of consumer behaviour. Reference to Tawhidi axiomatic premise has been ignored. Tawhid (hence Tawhidi) means the Oneness of God as the Absolute in Knowledge, the Creator and Cherisher of the universe. Islamic values, such as, moderation, responsibility and Shari'ah recommended goods (Halal) while avoiding forbidden ones (Haram), have been simply implied to show that in accordance with such constraints of the consumption set and preferences, a value of blessing and its reward in Hereafter (Akhira) is built into the budget constraints or the Muslim's utility function. The functional dependency of socioeconomic behaviour on such central premises, namely Tawhid and Akhira, are simply implied rather than endogenized as explanatory axioms.

Consequently, the methods of optimization and equilibrium of neoclassical economics have pervaded the analysis and this has left unattended the otherwise rich treatment of decision-making in value-endogenized and contractarian cunsumption sets, resource allocation and the resultant fuzzy-set treatment of such consumption menus (Bowles 1991). The authors in this area of Islamic economics have missed the point, first, by failing to note that a treatment of value-induced problems in neoclassical optimization and equilibrium framework leaves the issue of ethics and morals benign in the system. Second, even though Akhira (Hereafter) and Shari'ah (Islamic Law) are assumed to qualify the basket of Islamic consumption, the methods of optimality and steady-state equilibrium in constrained optimization problems imply ideal Islamic behaviour in individual consumers. The learning-by-doing process towards attaining progressive levels of Islamic consumer preferences is not undertaken.

Recently, in the treatment of Divine Unity (Tawhid) in Islamic individual preference formation, Naqvi treats his axioms of Divine Unity (Tawhid), equilibrium (Al Adl Wal Ihsan), free will (Ikhtiyar) and responsibility (Fardh) as being independent of each other like a basis Euclidean vector (Naqvi 1994). The implication is that these axioms comprise Naqvi's minimal and irreducible set of axioms, by means of which, the author claims that all other ethico-economic realities can be universally explained. Thus the axiom of Unity exists independently of the other ones; the axiom of equilibrium exists independently, and so on (Choudhury 1996a).

Naqvi holds the view unlike many other Islamic economists, that the Unity axiom by itself cannot be sufficient in explaining the total design of the Islamic economic universe. Naqvi then argues that the other axioms need not be deduced from Unity and that these must exist independently in Naqvi's description of the economic universe. This is also the implication of the property of systemic independence of the axioms.

The same implication points out that the author rejects the possibility of any further reducibility of his axiomatic set – that is, to the Tawhidi epistemology (Unity) alone. Rather in his Euclidean configuration of the axioms in relation to the economic space, each of these axioms impact upon economic variables independently and additively to bestow ethical meaning. Ethics then would seem to be an output of this vectorially independent relationship between each of the axioms and the economic variables when taken up singly or in vectors and matrices. Thus, when Naqvi considers ethical forms of consumption, production and distributional menus, the axioms impact upon these activities independently across and within these activities.

The fact of the matter is, that Naqvi wants to treat interdependence among the critical activities by means of ethical values and also suggests an interdependent treatment of utility indexes with production menus (Henderson and Quandt 1971). Yet he holds on to independent basis vectors. Contrarily, in explaining the endogeneity arising from the Unity premise in Islamic social systems, we must hold all axioms to be mutually interdependenct unlike Naqvi's independent basis vector.

Naqvi's basis vectors allow no interactions among themselves, and Unity remains outside the domain of interactions in the economic system. The Euclidean space of vectors leaves ethics neutral, void and silent. The implication is that one can sound ethics exogenously only from outside Naqvi's system; there is no endogenous method to regenerate ethics within Naqvi's system through pervasive interactions among agents, variables, systems and relations. The epistemological meaning and functional centrality of Tawhid in Islamic economics is lost (Choudhury 1991a).

Rationality behaviour in Islamic economics

From the genre of the above type of economic studies we find that rationality axioms of economic theory have entered Islamic economic reasoning par excellence. No thought has been placed either on a concept of bounded rationality in open-ended consumption sets and value-perturbed consumer preferences of the type that emanates from our preceding discussion (Shackle 1971, Simon 1957). There is also no treatment of instrumental rationality, which is a situational way of an agent's response to socioeconomic circumstances as they exist at any moment of decision-making (Lutz 1994, Etzioni 1988).

The full absorption of rationality axiom in the garb of ideal Islamic behaviour of microeconomic agents, makes up for the treatment of cardinal Shari'ah values, Tawhid and Akhira, as axioms that control perfect foresight and given prescriptive preferences without an enforcer or a contractarian basis for enforcement. Since Islamic individual preferences are embedded in social preferences, which are formed by a vast legacy of Islamic social contractarianism (Choudhury 1993a, 1990a), there can be no assumption of transitivity in consumer and social choice sets, which remain open by the force of endogenous interactions within and across such systems and among the axioms, as mentioned earlier (Condorcet et al 1785, Sen 1977, Choudhury 1990b). A combination of the legal and socio-psychological thoughts of the Islamic scholastics, Imam Shatibi, Imam Ghazzali and Imam Fakhruddin Razi (Masud 1984, Karim undated, Noor 1998) points to such social embedding of individual preferences.

Markets in Islamic economics

When the existing methods of Islamic economics as discussed above are carried to the market venue, the market system becomes a consequentialist venue of exchange. That is, the exogeneity of Islamic values may assume that ideal agents exist in society; these then imbue economic transactions in accordance with prescriptive Islamic behaviour. Otherwise, there is no learning-by-doing in the field of ethics and morals to transform market exchange, except by means of regulation, such as by the Islamic social regulatory agency, Al-Hisbah fil Islam (Ibn Taimiyyah 1967), or by state legislation. In the work of Al-Maqrizi we find that this type of social regulation did not work effectively (Allouche 1994). We also find that coercive legislation at many times of Islamic history caused conflicts rather than resolutions of social issues (Iqbal 1986).

Chapra (1992) recently used a concept of the price-filter to theorize that markets should transact in goods that have been approved through a filter system. Consequently, market prices would be governed by Islamically prescribed baskets of goods to the exclusion of all other ones. Such an approach once again is no different from the segmented market approach of labour economics except that it is now transmitted to the markets for goods. It is also no different from the segmentation of the product market between purely public goods and purely private goods. There remains no economic osmosis between such segmented markets. That is, there is no unique transformation of all goods into social goods (e.g. environment). The consequence is of course higher prices overall. But this is not my immediate concern in this critique.

The moral filter to guide preferences in a prescribed segmented markets, assumes compliance of preferences within such differentiated markets, or there must be enforcement on compliance. In all of these, the role of learning to break up market segmentation by moral induction, is replaced by prescriptive behaviour. The latter is simply the case of monopolistic competition of neoclassical economics now being applied to a price-discriminating behaviour of moral agents (Mehmet 1990). Beyond this, preference transformation with learning input remains absent. Markets thus remain either prescribed or consequentialist – responding to the whims of the consumer (Sen 1985, 1987). The absence of the learning process in preference transformation cannot address the case of endogenously ethicizing market contracts (Choudhury 1996b, Buchanan 1975). Thus no new challenge is made in Islamic economics in formulating a most important area of economic theory on an Islamic epistemological basis, namely an endogenous value-induced consumer behaviour, market exchange and choice.

THE THEORY OF THE FIRM

In the Islamic theory of the firm, all the aspects of an optimal firm and resource allocation methods are invoked. Metwally's ideas in this area have gone to the extent of applying Kuhn-Tucker conditions to explain optimization of the firm's resource allocation problem, subject to rational moral agents endowed with well-behaved utility functions (Metwally 1980). Metwally's constrained optimization problem leads to the following result (Metwally 1991, p.68):

> ...the equilibrium condition of a Muslim consumer requires that output consumed and the holding of capital stock should be carried up to some point at which the ratio between marginal utility and price (premium) is the same for all output and capital stock and <u>equals the marginal utility of spending on charity</u>.

The many analytical and Islamic contradictions of the above statement and result can be clearly seen. It is implied that the price for spending in charity is a numeraire, taken by Metwally as unit. Such a fixation of a price for charity remains a given datum throughout any resource allocation. However, this is not a correct postulate according to the Qur'anic view, wherein God-consciousness on charity is shown to increase or decrease according to the continuous formation of Islamic belief in the agent. The Qur'an mentions about such continuous outflow of blessings in terms of multiplying every act of goodness ten-folds. Every act of charity brings about blessings multiple folds like the richness of heads of corn that multiply manifolds (Qur'an Ch. 2, verse 261). The Qur'an also sets a benchmark as to how much one should give in charity. To this the answer provided is, as much as one can (Qur'an Ch. 2, verse 215).

Thus charity is an act that is conditioned by attributes of belief which continuously change, and in doing so, changes the preferences of the agent. The level of belief formation progressively changes the floor of charity giving (Afw). It would then be both impossible to fix a price-numeraire for charity or to hold the rewards of charity constant, except in the instantaneous case of momentary equilibrium. Such a case does not fit a knowledge-induced regime of resource allocation. The method of optimization, equilibrium and rational behaviour borrowed from neoclassical economics, thus cannot fit into the study of Islamic economic behaviour, as otherwise done by the Islamic economists to date.

Firm's behaviour with moral hazard in Islamic economics

Papers contributed in the area of moral hazard and risk-return analysis associate profit-sharing with such conditions. Thereby, it is seen that while fixed interest rate can be perceived by the saver to hedge against risk, the crafty investor will seek the benefit of information asymmetry to gain advantage over the saver. The saver's interest rate thus remains lower than the investor's gains in this asymmetric information problem. If however, the asymmetry was eliminated, then there would not be any need for saving. All would be able to enter the capital market directly to invest. The claim made by the authors (Khan 1985, Taj El-Din 1991, Bashir et al 1992) is that Islamic profit-sharing (Mudarabah) will eliminate the information asymmetry by allowing all to participate equally in risk and return.

The method adopted in the moral-hazard, information asymmetry problem is the analysis of the variable risk-return utility criterion of the investor. Consequently, optimal decision-making of a rational Islamic investor is shown to be fully dependent on the risk-return trade-off.

What is the problem with such an analysis other than the epistemological critique of utility analysis, optimality and equilibrium in morally perturbed social systems, referred to earlier? The additional problem arises from failing to incorporate the continuously varying profit-sharing contracts in which profit-shares are liable to vary among partners. This problem is deepened by treating Mudarabah simply as a partnership between owners of capital and providers of labour, in which case, capital owners may be simply sleeping partners. Instead, the central context of active cooperation between partners that calls for workplace democracy, is not included in the study of Mudarabah in the Islamic economic literature.

Let us see what matters when we do away with the characteristic of sleeping partnership in Mudarabah with variable contracts, and include actively cooperative participation. Now the treatment of the moral hazard problem must reckon with the differential profit-shares to some capital owners and the possibility to transfer capital from one Mudarabah situation to another. Agents now do not know the future expectations of others, and information asymmetry must exist. This will lead either to competition within cooperation or to monopolistic build-up of large conglomerates of Mudarabah. Both of these annul the nature, purpose and usefulness of Mudarabah in the ethical milieu of Islamic socioeconomic transformation.

The problem arises from the very definition of Mudarabah as sleeping partnership and from the methodological impossibility to explain the dynamics of cooperative decision-making in variable contracts. In these latter kinds of contracts, moral hazard cannot be explained by information asymmetry. Rather, increasing and variable contracts with changing profit-shares can increase retained earnings, diversify projects and thus risk. Product- and risk-diversifications are necessary and sufficient conditions for economic interlinkages. Decisions in production menus and technological choices then become interlinked. None of these rich features of 'global' inter-sectoral linkages have entered a comprehensive study of profit-sharing among Islamic economists.

In the Qur'an and the guidance of Prophet Muhammad, we do not find reference to Mudarabah contracts (profit-sharing) or Musharakah (equity-financing) per se. In fact, taking out the central attribute of cooperation and social well-being from the Mudarabah/Musharakah contract would qualify these as pre-Islamic practices that existed in Arabia before Prophet Muhammad (Siddiqi 1991, Ismail 1989). What is stressed instead, is the cooperative venture carried out in the absence of interest-bearing financing and spending in all the good diversities of life as identified and approved by Shari'ah. The principal socioeconomic values emphasized in these Islamic sources are spending in diverse kinds of goods recommended by Shari'ah for attaining justice ('Adl), purpose (Maqasid) and social well-being (Falah) in society at large (Qur'an Ch. 5 verse 115, Ch. 3 verse 191, Ch. 10 verse 31).

FINANCIAL AND MONETARY STUDIES

Islamic economics in financial and monetary studies has not progressed beyond a general delineation of interest-free loans, profit-sharing, equity-financing and secondary instruments devoid of interest (Ariff et al 1990). The more centrally important issue of treating financing in a general systems approach incorporating real economic activities, sectors, financial instruments and their combinations, has evaded the attention of Islamic economists. Consequently, the concept of endogenous money so central in understanding the relationship between real economic activities and the nature of money demand and supply, has not been invoked by Islamic economists.

The focus in monetary studies instead has been on adapting Tobin (1969) and Tobin & Brainard (1968) q-models to explain money demand and supply, price stabilization and economic growth in an Islamic economy. Little attention is paid to explain how such approaches are able to replace the rate of interest in the utility function for money and real assets, and how instead, the profit-sharing ratio (rate) can be set complementary to money and real assets in a social well-being model of the Islamic economy. Consequently, the important question on the nature of inflation in an Islamic economy remains unattended, while price stabilization attained by increased central bank financing of Mudarabah/Musharakah drive rates of return low.

The q-ratio is seen as a function of discount rates and the internal rate of return on projects (Zaidi et al, Khan et al 1987). In all of these approaches to monetary phenomenon in Islam there has occurred a confusion in accepting the otherwise untenability of discounting and internal rates method of capital valuation in Islamic project financing (Zarqa 1983). Besides, money supply to finance investments based in the q-rate as a function of discount rate, reverts itself to the nature of the prime rate of interest set by the central bank.

Fiat money models for the Islamic economy have been shown to depend upon a sequence of marginal cost of producing these fiat money (Jahri 1980). But the rate of return in the Fiat Money equation has not been determined in relation to the real sector economic activity. Consequently, such rates are either administered by monetary authority, as was the case with shadow pricing of transactions in the Soviet Gosplan, for example, or they are narrowly defined marginal costs of production of bullions, in which case real sector linkages cannot occur by the very method of marginalism.

Thus in all, monetary studies of Islamic economics have failed to study the general systems of interrelationships between money, price and economic activity. Consequently, inflation rate and macroeconomic stabilization policy have continued on to be addressed as exogenous monetary effects, instead of being studied in the light of endogenous money where the supply and demand for money are governed by rates of return in the real sector (Choudhury 1999).

Much of monetary theory among Islamic economists have thus been simply borrowed and adapted to changed assumptions in the light of Islamic values, while exogenously eliminating interest rate and replacing it with the rate of return. Yet the question as to how such monetary specifications come about through general systems of interrelationships, has not been studied in the Islamic economic literature. Monetary aggregate as a function of the q-ratio, a discount rate or administered prices in terms of unit cost of producing bullions by the central monetary authority, indirectly cause a disguised form of shadow interest rate to appear in the money supply function (Khan 1991). Interest rate itself as a monetary phenomenon, cannot thereby be phased out either in the exogenous monetary system or in a system that does not comprehensively function as a general system interlinking the monetary sector with the real sector.

Other studies have remained silent on the special nature of money in Islam either in terms of its endogenous nature or in reference to the epistemological relationship of value as reflected in money in Islam (Siddiqi 1983, Chapra 1985). Siddiqi has argued for a restitution of money supply in terms of Mudarabah demand for investment. This is a good argument if the impact of Mudarabah on mobilizing resources can be extended economy-wide or if Mudarabah/Musharakah (profit-sharing & equity-participation) could be qualified as cooperative and active participation among shareholders rather than being simply a management of idle funds pooled in by partners. An example of the former type has now days emerged in the case of Employee Savings and Ownership Plan (ESOP), Universal Savings and Ownership Plan (USOP) (Ellerman 1991).

MACROECONOMIC STUDIES

Macroeconomic studies in Islamic economics have not gone beyond sheer econometric estimation of interest rate relationships in the savings function in Islamic countries (Metwally 1989), or in a version of the Keynesian general economic equilibrium including Islamic variables (Choudhury 1986, 1989a). Recent advances in macroeconomic theory, such as rational expectations (Lucas et al 1978) and micro-foundations of macroeconomic theory (Phelps 1970), have not been matched by advances in macroeconomic theory in Islamic economics. For instance, areas such as the micro-macro interface to incorporate ethical decision-making in a macroeconomic framework, has by and large remained neglected (Hayek 1999, Tschiderer 1996).

The understanding of incomplete information in macroeconomic forecasting and adaptive lags in an institutional framework of decision-making to be found in the legacy of learning process in Shari'ah , has remained by and large neglected within the purview of Islamic economics. This has resulted in the study of Islamic economics, just as much as of mainstream economics, in isolation of endogenous institutional matters. Contrarily, the place of institutionalism and social contractarianism remains a central and a much needed one in the

Shari'ah induction of preferences, resource allocation and the general socioeconomic system (Ahmad 1986, Choudhury 1994a).

In the case of the wealth tax, called Zakah, which is mandated in Islam for amelioration of specific target groups of recipients (Qur'an Ch. 2, verse 177), a macroeconomic system has no method of disaggregation from the level of aggregate policy variables to microeconomic target groups of expenditure. Likewise, macroeconomic aggregation is not a lateral aggregation of microeconomic spending variables. Consequently, treatment of an aggregate value of Zakah in macroeconomic models does not serve the policy purpose of this blessed spending on poverty alleviation, equality, social stability, social harmony and socioeconomic development. Yet this fact has escaped the attention of almost all Islamic economists in their macroeconomic studies (Kahf 1982a, 1982b, Ariff 1982).

In the economic literature we have public choice theory to explain the rational choice foundation of institutions (Buchanan et al 1962). Yet this does not suit the moral social contractarianism of Islam (Choudhury 1993b). Next we have Tinbergen social orders to study institutions and the economy (Tinbergen 1987). Here too methodological recourse to optimal systems make Tinbergen's social orders closed and competing ones.

At the end we see that there is much scope for Islamic social and scientific worldview to contribute significantly to the area of institutional foundations of macroeconomics. It would then combine the micro-macro foundations in an enlightening way. We would move away from prescriptive models of behaviour, optimality and steady-state equilibrium models to normative-positive models of endogenous behaviour and policies explained in extensively simulative models of systemic interactions (Smith 1992, Koizumi 1993, Shakun 1988).

ISLAMIC POLITICAL ECONOMY

The last area of inquiries mentioned above comprises the field of Islamic political economy (Choudhury 1992a, 1997b, 1997c, 1997d, 1997e, Choudhury et al 1992). To a brief study of this academic field we now turn. We will take up all the above-mentioned areas and show how the methodology of Islamic political economy addresses them in ways altogether different from the methods of Islamic economics as they are borrowed and applied to certain value orientations of Islam relating to economic matters. The methodology of Islamic political economy itself will be shown to be of significant worth in the general advancement of scientific, social and institutional thinking. Hence we will use the terminology, socio-scientific order.

Islamic political economy is an epistemological examination of socio-scientific phenomena in the light of the pervasively interactive worldview presented in the Qur'an (Choudhury 1995a). The social rules and conduct of agents (Ahkam) underlying this Qur'anic holistic worldview, is then instrumentalized by the guidance of Prophet Muhammad (Sunnah). The discursions involving Qur'an and Sunnah are then taken up in the midst of pervasive human interactions called the institution of Shura. The Shura as a universally interactive and hence consultative order, generates a process. This process leads from interactions called Ijtihad, to social consensus (or majority agreement) called Ijma. We will also call the joint process of interactions and consensus as interactions-integration. From every state of Ijma evolve new rounds of interactions, followed by new integrations and new evolutions.

Fundamental in such rounds of the Shuratic Process – the interactive, integrative and evolutionary process (IIE-process) – is the unifying outlook of the universe and its sub-systems. Such a pervasive and universally systemic understanding of the Shuratic Process is derived directly from the Qur'an (Ch. 42, verses 49, 51-3). This unifying worldview is derived from the epistemology and ontology of Divine Unity. Its expression in the real world is regenerated by the flow of knowledge signified by interactions leading to unification (integration) and enhancement with new rounds of knowledge (evolution). We thus have the epistemology of Divine Unity and the unification process of knowledge emanating from Divine Unity. The epistemology of Divine Unity remains exogenous but ever present in all sub-systems qualified by extensive interrelationships, i.e. in all processes. Such an epistemology is referred to here as the Stock of Knowledge by virtue of its completeness and absoluteness in the total creative frame of the universe.

Unification of knowledge as flow within all systems and processes causing IIE-phenomenon to appear, is endogenous in nature.

Hence all socioeconomic variables, instruments, institutions, preferences and behaviour induced by the flows of knowledge causing unification of systems, relations and processes to occur, become endogenously interrelated.

Underlying precepts and assumptions of Islamic political economy

Certain fundamental precepts and methodology thus lead the way for Islamic political economy. These are as follows:

First, there is a simple formalization of the Shuratic Process (IIE-process). This constitutes an overview of the methodology of Islamic political economy.

Second, as in the jargon of classical economic school, Marxism, and neoclassical economics, we must first address the problem of 'value,' which Stigler said 'elicited the supreme efforts of the greatest theorists' (Stigler 1960). The concept of 'value' emerges in an altogether different way in Islamic political economy (Chapter 4).

Third, we must explain the principle of universal complementarity and show how this concept of pervasive interlinkages and endogeneity of knowledge-induced variables, systems and relations, emerges from and reinforces the unification of knowledge.

Fourth, we must show how analysis and inference are organized in this pervasively endogenous system of complementarities (IIE-process). We must invoke a knowledge-induced simulative design of systems.

With these precepts acting in concert with each other, Islamic political economy becomes the study of the Shuratic Process or the IIE-process interlinking the economy with institutions, polity, society and science. The agency of decision-making at all levels is taken up in the light of knowledge-induced interlinkages. Islamic political economy is thus a study of systems of socio-scientific interrelationships governed by the principle of universal complementarity as the explanatory form of unification of knowledge (Choudhury 1994b).

A BRIEF LOOK AT THE METHODOLOGY OF ISLAMIC POLITICAL ECONOMY

The methodology of Shuratic Process or the IIE-model, hinges on the following critical factors: First is the epistemology of Tawhid , that is Oneness of God in the sense of the Absolute and Complete Stock of Knowledge. Second is the flow of knowledge emanating from the Stock that brings about the unification of knowledge in all induced cognitive forms. Third, such a unification of knowledge carries the prototype of unity of the Stock and thus complements sub-systems together. Fourth, universal complementarity of this type occurs by the process of interactions leading to integration followed by creative evolution to higher planes of knowledge. Fifth, flows of knowledge remain in the creative form in perpetuity. Hence, optimization and steady-state equilibrium methods are necessarily replaced by simulation methods across domains of knowledge-induced forms. Sixth, the completion and closure of the knowledge-induced Tawhidi universe is realized in the Event of Hereafter (Akhira). This is the Event of cumulation of all kinds of systemic knowledge flows resulting in the supercardinal measure of the Stock (Choudhury 1995b, Cantor trans. Jourdain 1955).

A simple formalization of the IIE-model

The epiphenomenon of circular causation and continuity is explained formally by the relational string (1) (Choudhury 1994c). This also shows the intrinsic closure of the Tawhidi topological universe in relation to its equivalent representation, Akhira (Ω). It is important to take recourse to this formalization due to the complex relations that comprise the Shuratic Process worldview. It would otherwise be too extensive and methodically merely descriptive rather than precise to belabour through a long non-technical rhetoric. One recalls Samuelson's remarks with regards to his own mathematical as opposed to a non-technical approach in his treatise, **Foundations of Economic Analysis** (Samuelson 1970, p. 6):

> In the beginning it was hoped that the discussion could be made non-technical. Very quickly it became apparent that such a procedure, while possible, would involve a manuscript many

> times the present size. Moreover, I have come to feel that Marshall's dictum that 'it seems doubtful whether any one spends his time well in reading lengthy translations of economic doctrines into mathematics, that have not been made by himself' should be exactly reversed. The laborious literary working out over of essentially simple mathematical concepts such as is characteristic of much of modern economic theory is not only unrewarding from the standpoint of advancing the science, but involves as well mental gymnastics of a peculiarly depraved type.

Exactly the same rationale applies to the rich formalization of the Tawhidi worldview. We will restrict our formalization at a simple level. We thus begin with the primitive string relation:

$$\Omega 6_s \{\theta_s\} \rightarrow_I \{\theta_1\} \rightarrow_{f1} \{x_1\} \rightarrow_{g1} \{\theta_2\} \rightarrow_{f2} \{x_2\} \rightarrow \ldots \rightarrow \Omega \quad \ldots\ldots (1)$$

Here, Ω denotes the topology of the Tawhidi Stock of Knowledge.

s denotes the instrument of Shari'ah -mapping of Ω 'onto' the experiential world. This advances rules of Shari'ah as, $s(\Omega) \supset h(\{\theta_s\})$, since only parts of Ω can be mapped 'onto' the experiential world (Qur'an Ch. 72, verse 26).

I denotes the mapping of Shari'ah , $\{\theta_s\}$, 'onto' specific issues and problems of the experiential world by means of discourses called Ijtihad. Hence, $I(\{\theta_s\} / \Omega) = \{\theta_1\}$, in the first set of rounds of interactions denoted by 1. This set comprises many rounds of interactions leading to a consensus. At the point of consensus (or majority), creative evolution occurs and causes new sets of interactions and integration to occur and continue.

The totality, $E = \{\Omega, \theta_s, \theta_1\}$, is the extended Islamic epistemology (E-episteme) at any round of interaction. It is also written down in terms of Ω signifying the Essence of the Qur'an ; $\{\theta_s\}$ signifying Shari'ah as the explanatory part of the Qur'an ; $\{\theta_1\}$ signifying the constructive simulation of the Divine Laws to life through human volitions. Since $\{\theta_1\}$ are primarily induced by Ω through $\{\theta_s\}$, and these latter ones are functional carriers (instruments) of the Divine Law, therefore, there are attributes that mobilize the knowledge flows, $\{\theta_1\}$. These attributes are

A = {Justice, Purpose, Certainty, Well-Being, Creative Advance}. In brief therefore, we can write, $\{\theta_1\} = \{\theta_1(A)\}$.

$\{x_1(\theta_1)\} = f_1(\{\theta_1\})$ is the knowledge-induced experiential form during sets of rounds of interactions, 1, leading to a consensus. Clearly, $\{x_1(\theta_1)\}$ are premised on the E-episteme.

We now have the well-being that is generated by the knowledge-induced tuple, $\{\theta_1, x_1(\theta_1)\}$[A], meaning that A induces the tuple as a whole. From now on this will be implied, and we will suppress the [A] term. The social well-being is given by, SW = $SW(\theta_1,x_1(\theta_1))$. SW(.) is post-evaluated jointly by interactions of the preferences of polity and of the ethicizing preferences of agents in the market order, the socio-scientific order and the like. These agents are induced by the knowledge formation process shown in (1). Thus, such interactive preferences are continuously simulated by knowledge flows as interactions and integration proceed. The agents and agency specifically configuring the variables are denoted by $\{x_1(\theta_1)\}$. Note that for the sake of simplicity, we have suppressed many of the subscripts that should go with the θ_1-variable to signify agents, interactions, systems, relations etc.

At the point of post-evaluation of SW(.) in terms of $\{\theta_1, x_1(\theta_1)\}$, creatively evolutionary sequences of similar orders arise. Thus, interactions leading to integration in a set of rounds of interactions denoted by 1, finally lead to evolution. The IIE-model is now signified by the emergence of $\{\theta_2\}$. The sequences of tuples, $\{\theta_i,x_i(\theta_i)\}$ and their social well-being criteria denoted by $SW_i(\theta_i, x_i(\theta_i))$, continue on in the Shuratic or IIE-framework.

The string (1) so shown, describes how the Divine Laws of Unity are simulated in the framework of IIE to establish extensive complementarity in the experiential world by means of flows of knowledge. Since all inputs and outputs of this system are knowledge-induced, therefore, universal complementarity is established in this order by means of unification of knowledge. The f's and g's denote the derivation of rules and functionality, called Ahkam , from the E-episteme. The sequences, $P_i = (\{\theta_i\} \rightarrow_{fi} \{x_i\} \rightarrow_{gi+1} \{\theta_{i+1}\})$, i=1,2,,.., shown in the string (1), comprise the Shuratic Processes. The IIE-methodology is realized both within these sequences as across them. Hence such strings of recursive interrelationships comprise a circular causation and continuity model of unified reality.

Many generalizations of string (1) including the treatment of the mathematical complementation of knowledge have been studied (Choudhury 1995a). These issues are too detailed to introduce here. The point to note is that there is pervasive and inherent endogeneity manifest in the underlying general system of interrelationships either in the knowledge or the 'de-knowledge' planes (see Chapter 10). These two domains remain mutually disjoint however. The study of such pervasively endogenous processes may appear to be afforded by the methods of rational expectations hypothesis (Minford et al 1983). The problem however would arise from the premise of long-run optimal and steady-state of adaptive models of information flows in REH and the linear simplification of the otherwise non-linear models both in information flows and the Bayesian-type coefficients with their own stochastic properties. The end result of the linear processes, of the expectational equilibrium simplifications and the profuse use of the utility functions, make these to be models of the neoclassical class (Turnovsky 1995). Even in endogenous growth models we find that the introduction of every new asset generates marginal substitution among themselves, which is a neoclassical attribute (Romer 1986).

In the final analysis, there always exists marginal substitutions between groups of goods in such models. Complementarity is never a permanent and 'global' feature of such models just as marginal substitution is not the property of the string (1) – i.e. of the IIE-model. The very assumption of long-run steady-state optimization in REH makes this method unuseable in the study of IIE-general systems on epistemological grounds.

THE NATURE OF FALSIFICATIONISM IN TAWHIDI SPACE

In Popperian methodology that has been stereotyped in the sciences, it is essential for a scientific viability of an idea to be falsifiable (testable with possibility of criticizability, rejection and renewal) (Popper 1982). Elsewhere I have argued that falisificationism does not apply in the domain of the absolute, that is Ω(equivalently Akhira) (Choudhury 1993a). Now self-referencing as opposed to criticizability, takes over as the scientific methodology affirming and confirming the existence of limiting text (Post 1988). But within the region of flows of knowledge emanating from the Stock of Knowledge, an infinite diversity of methods and possibilities is confirmed by the Qur'an. However, the singular character all these diverse relations are the positively correlated interrelationships among them in reference to the law of unity of knowledge (unification of knowledge and systems). Consequently, falsification applies in the temporal domain of the flows of knowledge in respect to the Ijtihadi principle of discoursing and discovering diverse alternatives without permanently confusing a Truth (θ) with a False (θ~) statement and vice-versa. Revisions are acceptable within the framework of Tawhidi unification of knowledge.

PRINCIPLES AND INSTRUMENTS OF ISLAMIC POLITICAL ECONOMY

In Islamic political economy the principles have been shown to be premised on the primal epistemology of Tawhid including Sunnah (guidance of Prophet Muhammad). This crowning principle then links up with the fundamental issues of Property Rights and Entitlement (includes work and productivity). The instruments emanating from the principles, and thereafter, reinforcing the same to finally realize states of social well-being, are taken to be (i) Mudarabah/Musharakah as interactive cooperative and participatory ventures; (ii) avoidance of interest-bearing transactions (Riba); (iii) the institution of wealth tax for realizing justice and goodness in the act of distribution (Zakah); (iv) the avoidance of waste in both consumption, production and resources (Israf). These instruments and principles can be shown to be interactively interrelated. The instruments can be further extended to more of the same types for specific problems of Islamic political economy. Thus a vastly simulative system is generated in terms of the interrelationships, all being premised on the E-episteme. See figure A5.1 in the appendix.

THEORY OF VALUE IN ISLAMIC POLITICAL ECONOMY

In Islamic political economy, neither prices nor unit costs of production stand for any measure of value. The possibility of the utility function and its associated marginal utility of consumption goods, is ruled out on epistemological ground of universal complementarity in the IIE-model. This principle annuls all the ramifications of marginal substitution or limited complementarity in the case of multiple goods in neoclassical economics. Marxist labour theory of value is ruled out, because in it labour appears as the most reduced factor of production. On the other hand, the Absoluteness of Divine Unity is taken as the episteme of Islamic political economy.

All prices, wages, profits and quantities are qualified primarily by knowledge flows that emerge from the Shuratic Process as interactions and integration between polity, economy and society. These generate interactive preferences on the basis of Shari'ah values and are carried through a social contract into the markets and agents by means of rules and instruments. The result is value induction in a general system of interactions among the consumption menu, the production menu, the distributional menu and the related policy instruments, institutions and socioeconomic variables in these. Dynamic basic needs regimes of goods and services are promoted in the light of the principles and instruments of Islamic political economy (Hasan 1986). Above all these, a creatively dynamic purview of interactions and integration in the social action of the Islamic political economy is preserved. Thus knowledge flows induce all the inputs and outputs in these systems as shown in the strings of interrelationships (1).

All goods and services that are Shari'ah determined and promoted in the market order, are seen to be ethicizing goods (social goods) in the light of the principles and instruments of Islamic political economy. Consequently, unit cost of production and the labour/capital ratio (which is Marx's version of organic composition of capital) (Ekelund Jr et al 1990), are fundamentally determined by the use of labour and capital in the intrinsic essence of value as benefit that is embedded in all related goods and services. Such a benefit is termed in the Qur'an as Fitra (a combination of profit and felicity). Unit cost, prices and labour/capital ratio cannot be determined solely by labour or capital alone.

Therefore, since knowledge must remain the root of value, its measure must be determined by valuation using the social well-being function, which itself is simulative in the string form of the IIE-model. Thus Fitra value (F-value) of exchange is the induction of all variables by the knowledge flows. It is properly determined in ethicizing markets under knowledge-induced preference formation emanating from the Shuratic Process (Choudhury 1992b, Sen 1985). This concept of value can also be inferred from the fact that social well-being is the aggregate in a non-linear sense of all the elementary values that can coexist in complementary form in an ethicizing market exchange through the Shuratic Process of Islamic political economy. It would otherwise be incomplete to read value in any other way, since the bundle remains interdependent.

Besides, the string model of the IIE-framework shows that all of its inputs and outputs are functions of knowledge flows. Consequently, the effectiveness of knowledge must be evaluated. This gives rise to creative evolution emanating from interactions and integration that first lead to certain limiting values of knowledge flows. The juncture of evolutionary epistemology here is characterized by the valuation of the social well-being function.

In the case of wage rate, neoclassical economics determines this in terms of the real marginal productivity of labour or the marginal expenditure of labour-use in monopsony (Mansfield 1985). Marxist economics equates wage rate with the unit cost of production, given labour as the primal input. In Islamic political economy, wage rate is determined by the classical form of labour market simulation in the presence of a dynamically interactive and consensual social action. While wage rate is simulated in such a classical sense with ethical perturbations of the labour market, the principle of universal complementarity simultaneously determines the simulated value of rates of return (profit rates, profit-sharing rate, yields etc.). Furthermore, since simulated unit cost of production in complementary frames of references determines prices of goods and services, therefore, the valuation of multi-market prices must likewise proceed in the same breath.

We have thereby, a general system of simulated valuation emerging through the IIE-process according to the principle of universal complementarity. It would therefore be inappropriate in such a general system of interrelationships to target simply labour as a premise of value or anything other than the valuation of knowledge flows. This valuation is simulatively performed by means of the social well-being function in the knowledge-induced variables. Its methodology being premised on the principle of universal complementarity, is none of any of the following: of the utilitarian type, utility based, determined by rationalistic preferences, or a Marxist labour theory of value based on the capital-labour conflict-based alienation idea (Cole 1966).

THE PRINCIPLE OF UNIVERSAL COMPLEMENTARITY

The principle of universal complementarity is the natural cause-effect (i.e. necessary and sufficient condition) of the unification of knowledge in Tawhidi worldview applied to all of socio-scientific order. It is applied here to political economy for explaining resource allocation, pricing, preference behaviour and evolutionary ethico-economic equilibrium (Choudhury 1990c). Within this purview of social action are taken up the gamut of all economic variables.

Unification of knowledge in the Tawhidi worldview is dynamically established by pervasively systemic interactions leading to integration (consensus or majority). This is followed by creative evolution of more of the same. Therefore, the Shuratic Process (i.e. IIE-model) plays the central role in determining the necessary and sufficient condition of the principle of universal complementarity. The principle of universal complementarity totally replaces the mainstream economic (broadly scientific) idea of marginal substitution. Consequently, no neoclassical concept and its prototypes as they are so centrally affected by the idea of marginal substitution, can enter any aspect of Islamic political economy (Choudhury 1996c).

ORGANIZATION OF ANALYSIS AND INFERENCE: THE QUESTION OF CAUSATION

With the principle of universal complementarity and its equivalence, the unification of knowledge in the Tawhidi worldview, altogether new methods of preference formation, resource allocation and pricing occur. We will now examine these briefly.

Preference Formation

The Islamic theory of social action in the Tawhidi worldview commences from a textual reference to the E-episteme. This underlies

Shari'ah. A progressive Islamic movement, Islamic state, institution or educational system, establishes this epistemological order in the polity box (appendix figure A5.2). The organized form of agents in polity uses the texts to progressively establish institutions and mechanisms of evaluation and consensus formation through discourse in the broad socio-scientific environment. The assumptions of polity action in the socio-scientific order are minimal. This nature of minimal axioms has been supported by Ghazzali and Ibn al-Arabi (Karim undated, Chittick 1989). Minimality assumptive conditions also constitute the foundation of science (Nagel 1981, von Mises 1976). These minimal axioms as assumptions are taken here as follows in Islamic political economy:

First, it is assumed that agents in the political economy invoke a natural sense of acceptance of the A-attributes stated earlier, as the carriers of the Tawhidi worldview. These attributes are consciously instilled in society by the Islamic movements, Islamic state, institutions and education system.

Second, due to the first assumption, a coercive action in social action becomes irrelevant. The Islamic order must however, protect the rights and privileges of its members, as this responsibility has been vested upon the institutions, state or movement by general citizenry in accordance with Shari'ah and a Shuratic Process. An Islamic order as in the polity box, comes about by a grassroots participatory Shuratic will.

Third, governments and state intervention in any public affair is minimal beyond security, protection, social guarantees organization, dissemination of knowledge in the socio-scientific order and enforcement of rules (Ahkam), all developed by means of invoking Shari'ah and the Shuratic Process in all affairs. The implication then is, that Shari'ah and the Shuratic Process cannot be limited to the domain of social, economic and political matters alone. These are equally extended to the whole socio-scientific order using complementary strings of discourses in all constituent groups. The Qur'an is quite clear on this universal implication of Shari'ah and the Shuratic Process in terms of their pervasive complementarities and interlinkages for the universal good (Qur'an Ch. 14, verses 24,25,27). The Mutakallimun (Islamic epistemologists) upheld this view (Jalbani 1985, Karim undated, Faruqi 1977, Muslehuddin undated). The Muslim rationalists rejected it (Qadri 1988). Shariati brings out the implication of such an approach on Islamic social thought (Yadegari 1984).

From the polity box emerge preferences of polity to impact upon the economic order comprising consumption, production and distribution menus and all the agents, agencies, variables and relations that these involve. The objective here is to transform the preferences of agents and agencies in accord with the E-episteme. The economy thus responds with its transformed preferences in accordance with their induction by the A-attributes. This generates F-value and delivers social goods and services as a result of the impact. The impact process emanating from polity to the socioeconomic order is called an Action. The evaluation of the social goods, given the transformed preferences, is carried out by the social well-being function in polity. The preferences of polity are thus interacted and combined with the correcting, reinforcing or revising preferences of agents and agencies to form the final interactive preferences. These determine the F-value, the progressive transformation of ethicizing markets, their simulative knowledge-induced ethicizing market exchange, the associated variables and relations and the social well-being.

The evaluation of social well-being and its implication in the level of F-value in the Islamic political economy, called social Response, now sets the post-evaluative state of polity. Policies and programmes of delivery are accordingly changed in polity to simulate the interactive preferences till social consensus (integration) is reached through sequences of Actions and Responses. Accordingly, a dynamic social equilibrium point is attained. The social well-being function is thus evaluated, and further evolutionary knowledge-induced social actions are progressed by the on-going Shuratic Process.

The implication in none of the parts of the Islamic social action is that Shari'ah is changed by a rationalist philosophy or that the Shuratic Process becomes a neo-liberal political philosophy of democracy. Limitations against the neo-liberal order are well established in the literature (Sullivan 1989, Sen 1970, Taylor 1967, Parsons 1964). Changes and revisions proceed on at two levels. First, the rules of implementing Shari'ah, called Ahkam in the affairs of life (Muamalat), must always change, carrying interpretations even though Ahkams are premised on the immutability of the E-episteme. Second, based on the assumptions given above, if the process departs from Shari'ah and the Shuratic Process, no coercive action can prevent this process of devolution. When the latter process occurs, the Shuratic Process as a universal epiphenomenon continues on to persist though – but now in the socio-scientific domain as a scientific worldview. Human synergy is continuously invoked in the political economy as in the scientific realms, to create newer worlds of possibilities (Nasr 1996).

Resource Allocation and Pricing

The neighbourhoods of social action as sub-sets of the grand socio-scientific universe where the interactive, integrative and evolutionary epiphenomenon appear, are characterized by $\{\theta, X(\theta), \succeq; SW(\theta, X(\theta), \succeq)\}$. Here $\{\theta, X(\theta), \succeq\}$ denotes neighbourhoods of IIE-points. S(.) denotes the associated social well-being function. $\{\succeq\}$ denotes such IIE-preferences evolving from the Shuratic social action. Now no points of the consumption, production and distribution sets are steady-state ones. Consequently, no well-behaved neoclassical production and consumption possibility curves, indifference curves and social welfare maps, exist. Hence we abandon the neoclassical nicety of exogenous preferences, optimal convex sets for resource allocation and their utility and social welfare functions. Rather, all social allocations, pricing and social criterion functions are simulative ones in and across neighbourhoods, as defined.

We note that the ethical basis of decision-making, individual and institutional preference formation under a social contract, and the determination of all politico-economic relations in light of the ethical premise, makes the microeconomic foundations of macroeconomics, a feature of aggregation in Islamic political economy. Yet we cannot consider a dichotomy between micro and macro methodologies as a tenable postulate of Islamic political economy. There is an interface between the preference formation basis and the interactive coordination perspective in the Shuratic Process. This makes the methodology of Islamic political economy to emerge from an altogether different epistemological orientation than that of mainstream economics and Islamic economics. This E-episteme delineates a socio-scientific universe of interactions, integration and creative evolution, which when applied to the nature of Islamic political economy means a micro-macro interface (Choudhury 1991b).

Question of Opportunity Cost of Resource Allocation

No neoclassical idea of opportunity cost of resource allocation can exist in Islamic political economy. Instead, we define relative unit cost of allocations among complementary possibilities rather than among substitutes, by means of the relative social well-being indices. Such an index may be taken up in simple or complex forms depending upon the nature of institutions and problems (Choudhury 1993b, 1992a).

The social well-being functional is thus a possible mode of evaluation of F-value in terms of $\{\theta, X(\theta), \succeq\}$. Thus if we consider the resource allocation problem (see appendix figure A5.3) in $\{\theta_i, X_i(\theta_i)\}$, i = 1,2, the concept of a so-called 'opportunity cost' denoted by r, for choosing the complementary 1=1 with i=2 in two possibilities, is the difference between the ratios of the goods and their effective prices (determined in ethicizing market clearance).

Such a ratio, r, is computed as follows:

$$r = dD_1(\theta_1 \cap \theta_2, X_1(\theta_1 \cap \theta_2), X_2(\theta_1 \cap \theta_2)/dD_2(\theta_1 \cap \theta_2, X_1(\theta_1 \cap \theta_2), X_2(\theta_1 \cap \theta_2) > 0.$$

$D_i(.)$ denotes the effective demand of the two goods i=1,2. $\cap$ denotes the complementary nature of these goods in the Shuratic Process underlying allocation and market exchange characterized by interactive preferences.

In terms of relative prices we can write, $D_1/D_2 = f(p_1/p_2)[\theta]$, with $\theta=(\theta_1 \cap \theta_2)$. This is monotonically related to $p_1(\theta)/p_2(\theta)$, as θ-values increase in the IIE-model, either as demonstrated by the string model (1) or by the social action model. It can be shown by simple differentiation that,$d(p_1(\theta)/p_2(\theta))/d\theta > 0$, implying that, $(dp_1(\theta)/d\theta)/(dp_2(\theta)/d\theta) > 0$. Thus the nature of social goods, such as dynamic basic needs baskets consumed and produced in the Islamic political economy would suggest, that $p_1(\theta)$ and $p_2(\theta)$ increase or decrease together but not necessarily by the same percentage. Since $p_i(\theta)$ is positively related to unit cost of production, therefore, relative unit costs will also be complementing each other.

In a dynamic basic needs regimes of Islamic political economy, prices of such complementary goods will stabilize downwards within such regimes with elastic demand curves. Now the growth of knowledge in the Islamic social action means its ordering in the light of the basic needs regimes of development. There is indeed a saying of Prophet

Muhammad pointing out that market prices are not to be unduly interfered with. This principle was reflected in the politico-economic ideas of Ghazzali and Ibn Taimiyyah (Islahi 1995). The difference between the two is that Ibn Taimiyyah invoked Shari'ah to establish a social regulation of unjust market transactions (Al-Hisbah Fil-Islam) (Holland 1982).

The 'opportunity cost' in Islamic political economy of choosing social good 1 with good 2, is given by,

$$|r_1 - r_2| = |(d(p_1(\theta)/p_2(\theta))/d\theta - d(p_2(\theta)/p_1(\theta))/d\theta|.$$

When this difference is positive, good 1 is chosen 'relatively more' than the complementing good 2, and vice versa. In either case, the existence of the principle of universal complementarity in the knowledge-induced unification worldview, will determine prices in ethicizing markets where other than simulation, no steady-state equilibrium exists – except for the instantaneous case of ethico-economic equilibrium (Haddad 1995). Then too, resource allocation points do not lie on well-behaved frontiers of the neoclassical genre and its prototypes. It can be shown that the evolution of ethicizing instantaneous market equilibrium points is tantamount to moving cobweb equilibria under the impact of θ-values (Choudhury 1994d).

Simulation of Knowledge-Induced Social Well-Being Functional

The simulative nature of all the politico-economic variables in the knowledge-induced social actions of the Islamic political economy suggests that the objective criterion in this system can be stated as follows (Choudhury 1995c):

> Simulate $\{\theta\}$ $SW(\theta, X(\theta); \succeq$
> subject to, $\{\theta\}$, $\{X(\theta)\}$, and $\{\succeq\}$ being interactively, integratively and dynamically determined both in terms of each other and within themselves as $\{\theta\}$-values evolve.

The simulation path towards attainment of a given instantaneous equilibrium to be evolved to further similar ones can now be constructed. The Shuratic Process works here for the Islamic political economy by invoking Ijtihad (interactions), Ijma (consensus or majority = integration) and Khalq in-Jadid (creative re-origination) through Bayyanah (unravelling of knowledge). All these points are well-supported by the Qur'an (Ch. 4, verses 59, 65, 69; Ch. 10, verse 4; Ch. 98, verses 1-5). We show the knowledge-induced simulation path of valuation in the Islamic political economy in figure 5.1:

Figure 5.1: Simulation of knowledge-induced general systems

X_i, θ_i, i=1,2,... denotes the sequence of iterated knowledge-induced values and their SW(.) functions. The convergence to (θ*,X*,SW*) is thus shown during a particular stage of IIE.

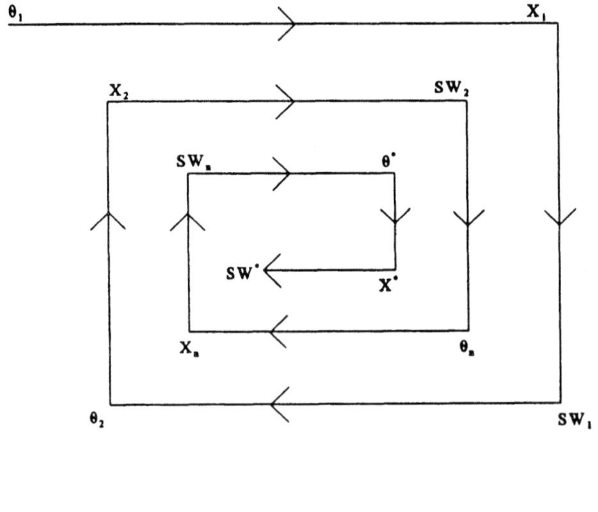

TREATMENT OF OTHER SOCIOECONOMIC VARIABLES IN THE ISLAMIC POLITICAL ECONOMY

The general theory of E-episteme applied to the socio-scientific order that is particularized in this chapter by the example of Islamic political economy, can be extended to all fields within this system. Comparative development, institutionalism and economic integration, community socioeconomic development, are just some of the many themes that have been examined (Choudhury 1993c, 1989b, 1997f). In what follows we will treat money and risk-diversification in the framework of the IIE-methodology replacing the neoclassical orientation of Islamic economics.

Money and Finance

The pervasively interactive, integrative and evolutionary nature of Islamic political economy and the endogeneity of ethics in the inherent social action premised on Shuratic Process, implies that money must be one such endogenous variable in the system (Choudhury 1991c). Money as an endogenous aggregate is simply a contravention of valuation and monetization of real socioeconomic activities. Thus a quantity of money can be established by the central monetary authority in response to a demand for funds at the commercial banks for financing real socioeconomic activities. The presence of speculation is annulled in money demand and supply by removing from the investment portfolio all those kinds of activities for which adequate degree of short to medium run feasibility does not exist and where strict evaluation of the project is maintained in the light of the social well-being function. Thus the use of promissory notes or speculation in the Islamic political economy is minimized. The nature of endogenous money makes money a direct function of rates of return or the profit-sharing ratio across bundles of real projects. These rates are determined by conditions prevailing on prices and unit cost of production, as discussed earlier. Consequently, prices and rates, and thereby, the demand and supply of money for purposes of monetization of real sector activities, negate a real prospect of inflation linked with speculation, expectation, excess demand and credit expansion money multiplier. Profit-push inflation may exist, but is easily controllable by mobilizing resources toward socially productive ends. With an inherent price stability arising from the nature of endogeneity in the Islamic political economy, monetary policy for stabilization loses its relevance although endogenous money remains an important contravention. The need for money is simply for valuation and transaction of real sector activities.

Price stabilization is a developmental policy in the Islamic political economy. It is not a monetary one as construed by the theory of exogenous money or a plastic-card theory of endogenous money (Desai 1989). Some Islamic developmental policies mobilized by endogenous money are as follows: A dynamic basic needs regime of goods and services is to be promoted. The Islamic polity is to promote development and dissemination of knowledge pertaining to the complementary worldview in consumption, production and distribution within the Islamic social action plan. The banking system is to be guided by a Shuratic Process in generating money for endogenizing the real socioeconomic activities for meeting the social well-being in the Islamic political economy.

One can now obviously see that the treatment of money, monetary policy, the banking system and the valuation of assets by means of exogenous money, departs in a substantive way from the received treatment of money in Islamic economics. Besides, the Islamic theory of endogenous money as 100 per cent reserve requirement or fiat money based on the gold standard, is not of the type construed in Quantity Theory. In the latter case, interest rates are allowed to prevail in securitized markets and there exists the permanent fear of inflation in the money-price relationship of the fundamental equation of exchange (Friedman 1989). The same do not characterize the endogenous monetary relationships in their relationships with the real sector.

Risk-Diversification in Islamic Political Economy

Risk-diversification is studied in the Islamic political economy by linking economic diversification in complementary multimarkets of products and services to securitized capital markets. The cooperative institutions and instruments of Islamic political economy earlier mentioned, and now the rate-of-return (profit rate, profit-sharing rate) induction of securities by means of the quantity of endogenous money, interactively integrate according to the Shuratic Process. Such real sector interlinkages help in diversifying risk in the capital market. Speculation is avoided. We now see that the principle of universal complementarity is furthered by means of economic and risk-diversification. This kind of cause and effect between the principle of universal complementarity and diversification is inherent in the nature of resource allocation and mobilization in the Islamic political economy.

How is risk-diversification measured and how does this measure enter the social well-being functional? Since the neighbourhood values of $\{\theta, X(\theta), \succeq\}$ denote multiple possibilities, therefore, the variance of the points in such a neighbourhood is now related to the squares of distances around a particular consensual value, $(\theta^*, X^*(\theta^*))$. This is not necessarily the mean-value. Likewise, resource allocation in a non-utility criterion function rules out the marginal approach to risk-return analysis. In the decision-making problem, the use of the risk-factor as a neoclassical measure is replaced by the consciousness to increase knowledge in the IIE-system. However, there is necessarily a negative relationship between risk and return. Indeed, the Qur'anic worldview leads society into increasing certainty with the advance of knowledge premised on the Tawhidi core (Qur'an Ch. 10, verse 32).

Risk is therefore a relative concept of the measure of the sum of squares of distances of a socioeconomic variable around an instantaneous limiting value of the variable at a given stage in the Shuratic Process. The recursive values come near to diversification with increasing complementarities, as knowledge advances in an evolutionary fashion and consequently the possibilities unify more intensively. Risk is also a negative function of the speed with which knowledge-induced convergence occurs at the given stage of the Shuratic Process.

We now write down,

risk, R(.), of a tuple, $Y(\theta) = (\theta, X(\theta))$,

say a Mudarabah/Musharakah profit-sharing rate, as,

$$R(Y(\theta)) = \lim(\theta \to \theta^*)[Var(Y(\theta) - Y^*(\theta^*))],$$
$$\text{where, } Y^*(\theta^*) = \lim(\theta \to \theta^*)[Y(\theta)].$$

Corresponding to $Y^*(\theta^*)$ as the socioeconomic induction of F-value, $\{\theta^*\}$, we have the evaluative social well-being function, $SW(\theta^*, Y^*(\theta^*))$.

This implies that the F-value is maximized at the temporary and evolutionary equilibrium point $Y^*(\theta^*)$ when risk is minimized at this point with the attainment of $\{\theta^*\}$.

The evolutionary equilibria and optima of these instantaneous types are different in the epistemological sense from those in the literature (Grandmont 1989, Osborne et al 1994). In the case of Islamic political economy, knowledge-induced evolutionary equilibria are the cause and effect of unification of knowledge. Hence such evolutionary equilibria invoke extensive complementarity (participation). As opposed to this perspective, those in the mentioned economic literature are the result of competition, utility analysis, and hence at best of bounded rationality (Simon 1957). This difference in concept is a significant one, as it causes a major departure in the methodology of analysis and its institutional and policy implications.

It can be readily shown that, $\lim(\theta \to \theta^*)[dR(.)/d\theta] = 0$, in the instantaneous sense for any stage of dynamic convergence in the IIE or the Shuratic Process. This results from the fact that evolution of knowledge opens up possibilities for novelty, and hence to diversities and complementarities along evolving basic needs regimes of development.

One can use the simulation picture of figure 5.1 to explain the meaning of variance about the limiting point in figure 5.2.

The type of iteration and convergence during phases of IIE of figure 5.1 is now transported to figure 5.2 to show in the three-dimensional diagram, various such sequences of the IIE in evolutionary planes. The evolutionary trajectory is shown by OW. The projection of OW in $\{\theta, X(\theta)\}$ is shown by OT. The process of evolution is through fuzzy neighbourhoods like S_i, i=1,2,.. The dispersion of values is shown around points like a, b, etc.

The risk-return utility analysis on the other hand, makes the optimal risk condition a permanent condition of rational choice. Note that optimality of resource allocations along the well-behaved risk-return set is a long-run phenomena, similar to the long-run nature of the production possibility surface and the consumption possibility surface. Such optimal and steady-state equilibria remain intact from one surface to another along the trajectory of technological change in the long run. Technological choice of such type that is either exogenous or endogenous in the optimal decision-making plane (Becker 1989,

Turnovsky 1995), does not structurally change this optimal-equilibrium property of well-behaved neoclassical surfaces.

Figure 5.2: Construction of the risk-measure

The type of iteration and convergence during phases of IIE of figure 5.1 is now transported to figure 5.2 to show in the three-dimensional diagram various such sequences of the IIE in evolutionary planes. The evolutionary trajectory is shown by OW. The projection of OW in $\{\theta, X(\theta)\}$ is shown by OT. The process of evolution is through fuzzy neighbourhoods like S_i, i=1,2,... The dispersion of values is shown around points like a, b , etc.

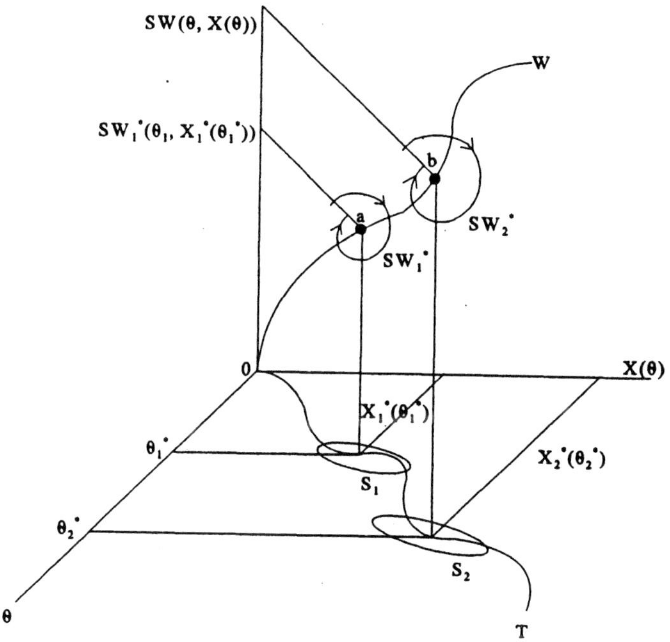

$SW_2^* = SW_2^*(\theta_2^*, X_2^*(\theta_2^*))$
$SW_1^* = SW_1^*(\theta_1^*, X_1^*(\theta_1^*))$

AN EMPIRICAL CRITIQUE OF ISLAMIC ECONOMICS

There are now forty-eight Muslim countries as members of the Organization of Islamic Conference (OIC). Most of them are not democratically governed and the vastly diverse economic status, ranging from the poorest countries (Afghanistan, Somalia, Sudan, Bangladesh) to the capital surplus countries (Saudi Arabia, Kuwait, Emirates), makes the poorer ones subservient to the financing decision of the rich members in the Islamic Development Bank. It is obvious to note that foreign trade financing of IDB could not benefit Iraq after the Gulf War due to the United Nations Embargo that was enforced strongly by the Arab countries. Consequently, a self-reliant cooperative decision-making is replaced by ethical egoism as in a public choice model of international governance (Ansari 1986, Choudhury 1997d). The absence of both collective decision-making and bold participation among OIC members has overshadowed the prospect of realizing a Shuratic Process. No particular model of the Islamic political economy could thereby emerge for the realization of collective wisdom, such as Islamic economic integration, significant inter-country trade in the Islamic bloc, effective coordination of macroeconomic policies and selection of cooperative multi-national projects.

Table 5.1 on project financing of the Islamic Development Bank shows that profit-sharing and equity financing, which should form the back-bone of Mudarabah/Musharakah mode of financing, have remained low historically. We also note that the Islamic Banks Portfolio has remained volatile, comprising only 5.5 per cent of the total IDB project approvals between 1976 and 1995. These statistical figures point to weak coordination among the national economies of the inter-countries with market-driven Islamic economic instruments.

The bulk of the IDB financing has gone into foreign trade financing. But this has not contributed to inter-country trade among Islamic countries. According to the IDB Annual Report (1994-95), only about 10 per cent of OIC countries' world trade flows among themselves as opposed to 58 per cent with the industrialized countries and 37.6 per cent with the developing countries. The Islamic countries undertake only 7 per cent of world trade.

We also note that the bulk of the trade financing has been in import financing, whereas long-term trade financing remained at a low of 2.87 per cent of total trade financing between 1976 and 1995. These further point to the weak linkage between the trade-financing instruments and long-term development in Islamic countries.

Now how can Islamic political economy deliver that which Islamic economics could not in terms of Islamic transformation? While Islamic economics is an overly neoclassical and macroeconomic study of Islamic markets, resource allocation and institutionalism, Islamic political economy calls forth for 'global' interrelationships pronounced by the interactive, integrative and evolutionary worldview of Islamic methodology in science, society, economy and polity within an endogenous knowledge-model of the Ummah. Here for example, Islamic common market, capital market, production and transformation of individual preferences through polity-market interactions and convergence, etc. become the overview of Islamic transformation. In the positive global scale this is a prescription for the grassroots sub-national Islamic movements to collaborate efforts to realize the transformation.

SUMMARY

In summary therefore, no perspectives of Islamic economics, either as an intellectual background for change in the Islamic world or as provider of effective financial instruments, have emerged. All this has happened particularly due to a lack of participatory change and effective economic and political interlinkages on all fronts. This is the worldview that Islamic political economy upholds upon its E-episteme.

Table 5.1: Islamic financing data, Islamic Development Bank, 1976-1995 (ID Million, 1 ID = 1 SDR)

Financing Sources	Total	1991	1992	1993	1994	1995
Loan	974.88	44.49	63.75	74.72	87.06	57.51
Equity	212.85	3.75	3.46	20.72	4.97	11.10
Leasing	689.27	41.35	23.09	10.70	90.89	173.92
Instalment Sale	593.04	47.69	32.10	87.40	41.77	44.98
Combined Lines of Finance	198.37	15.18	2.30	8.60	13.50	6.00

Project Financing	2,686.55	152.46	124.70	202.14	246.00	293.50
Technical Assistance	69.95	0.97	4.94	6.40	6.35	2.03
Ordinary Operations	2,756.51	153.43	129.64	208.54	252.35	295.53
Import Trade Financing Operations	7,161.08	353.04	352.01	250.73	311.39	379.01
Longer Term Trade Financing Scheme	230.25	19.59	46.75	29.69	35.27	40.51
Islamic Banks' Portfolio	619.17	78.04	131.71	41.50	127.68	192.51
Trade Financing Operations	8,015.62	450.67	530.43	321.92	474.44	612.03
Special Assistance Operations	365.58	25.34	37.42	12.11	15.68	3.95
Total Approvals	11,137.70	629.44	697.53	542.58	742.47	911.49

Source: Islamic Development Bank, **Annual Report 1994-95** (Jeddah, Saudi Arabia)

CONCLUSION

In this chapter we have undertaken a critical study of the nature of Islamic economics as it has evolved within mainstream economics and has thus been found to have been unable to contribute anything challenging that can be claimed to be of a substantive Islamic genre in new economic reasoning. We have alternatively evoked an overview of the nature of the academic field called Islamic political economy as a vastly interactive study of socio-scientific epiphenomenon premised on the immutable epistemology of Divine Unity. We have thus formulated a consistent and workable framework of analysis on the plane of unification of knowledge premised on Divine Unity at the core.

The study of Islamic political economy was then used to critique Islamic economics. Alternative explanations of several of the issues tackled by Islamic economics were given in the light of Islamic political economy. We have not claimed a detailed explanation of this field. We also realize that in earlier economic and scientific literature there has existed the treatment of knowledge and the inherent incompleteness of the human universe (Boulding 1967, Hayek 1937, Kirzner 1997). But our standpoint on the pervasively knowledge-centred field of Islamic politico-economic study was premised on the epistemology of unification of knowledge, which other approaches have failed to establish due to their wandering in areas of social Darwinism (Neurath et al 1970).

Empirical evidence was provided to show that Muslim countries using the instruments of Islamic economics have not benefited from them. The need for thinking academically and positively in the light of Islamic political economy is thus mandatory for the Islamic countries. This undertaking should involve intellectuals, students, policy-makers and the public at large arising from the sub-national grassroots levels.

APPENDIX

Figure 5.A1: Principles and instruments of Islamic political economy

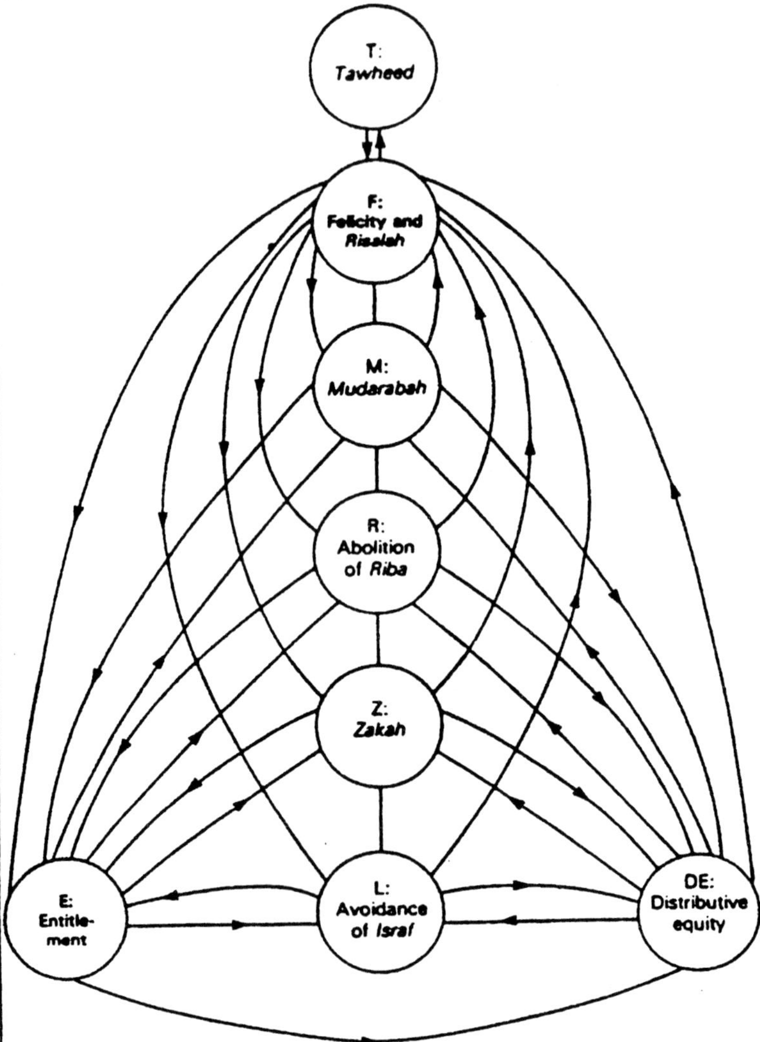

In this figure it can be seen that a great many possible combinations can be formed among the Islamic principles and instruments. The key aspect is the return of all such circular flows (shown by arrows) to the crowning principle of *Tawheed*, and this is only possible by way of Islamic conscience formation and subsequent benefits through the realisation of the understanding of felicity.

Figure 5.A2: Interactive, integrative and evolutionary nature of social action in Islamic political economy

$\{\succeq_P\}$, $\{\succeq_M\}$ are preferences of polity and market, respectively.
$\{\succeq\} = \{\succeq_P\} 1 \{\succeq_M\}$ is the interactive preference.

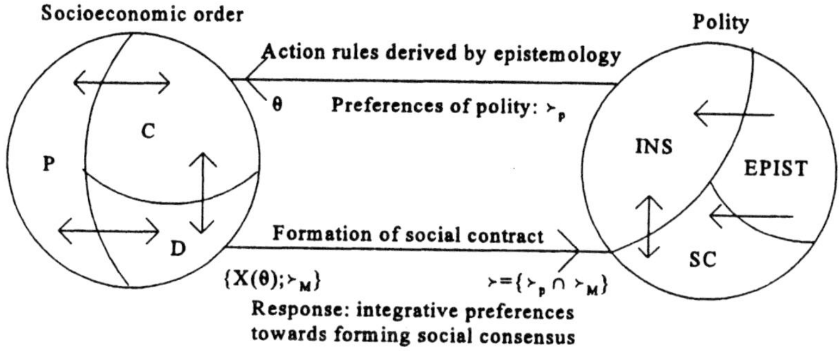

$\succ_p$ and $\succ_M$ are preferences of polity and market, respectively.
$\succ=\{\succ_p\} \cap \{\succ_M\}$ is the interactive preference.
$\{X(\theta);\ \succ_M\}$ is the set of market variables determined by $\{\succ_M\}$ alone.
$\{X(\theta);\ \succ\}$ is the set of market variables determined by preferences formed by interactions and consensus (or integration), $\{\succ\}$.

Figure 5.A3: Resource allocation in the Islamic political economy

In this 3-dimensional diagram the impact of θ-values on $X_i(\theta)$ is shown. Note the evolution of the fuzzy space of actions, S, in the IIE-framework. This evolutionary fuzzy bundle is made up of interactive trajectories like T_i, T_i', i=1,2,... The evolution of the knowledge-induced fuzzy spaces is shown by S_1 to S_2 along the trajectory OT.

In this three-dimensional diagram the impact of θ-values on $X_i(\theta)$ is shown. Note the evolution of the fuzzy space of actions, S, in the IIE-framework. This evolutionary fuzzy bundle is made up of interactive trajectories like T_i, T_i', i=1,2,... The evolution of the knowledge-induced fuzzy spaces is shown by S_1 to S_2 along the trajectory OT.

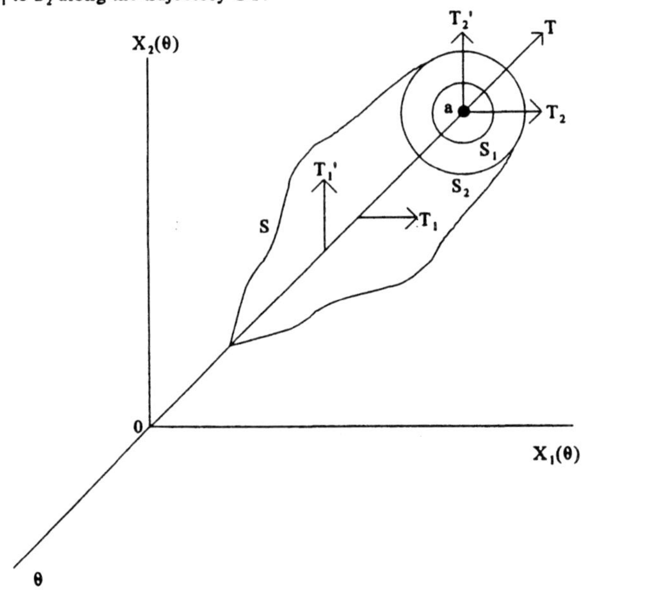

CHAPTER 6

KNOWLEDGE AND INTERACTIONS IN POLITICAL ECONOMY AND ECONOMIC THEORY

Our objective in this chapter is to show that a substantive theory of political economy can be developed by introducing strong interactions and knowledge flows in a complex of interrelationships concerning economy, society, science and ecology. This approach to a systemic understanding of interactions and knowledge in the political economy becomes a powerful methodology. We will show that this approach is to be found singularly in the methodology of Islamic political economy and has not been adequately addressed either in economic theory or in the literature on political economy. We will investigate the literature on the place of knowledge in economic theory against the extensively and strongly interactive worldview of political economy that we will propound in this chapter.

I

CONCEPT OF KNOWLEDGE IN HUMAN CAPITAL THEORY

In the neoclassical approach to human capital theory, education is treated as an efficiency-generating capital good that could exist either in the form of investment or consumer good. The bulk of Economics of Education hinged on the valuation of decisions undertaken by rational agents on the basis of their perception of the kind of good embodying education. The result was a re-creation in Economics of Education of the entire body of neoclassical methodology that at the end left the educational good deprived of its intrinsic social valuation.

Even when psychic returns to human capital were measured this took the form of non-pecuniary or spillover benefits for which the proxies were measured 'residuals' in the production function with quality-corrected labour input (Denison 1962, Grilichez 1970). In spite of such a claim regarding educational returns, some have already disputed the neoclassical methodology of opportunity cost on which the valuation of educational returns is based (Rhoads 1985).

The intrinsic utilitarian comprehension of human capital puts it against the analysis of utility and social welfare optimization with or without the first-best conditions of Pareto optimality. In such a situation of constrained optimality the methodological state of attained full or bounded rationality and the ensuing information flows, leaves the decision-maker completely devoid of a scope for changing the dimensions of choices, preferences and dynamic re-organization of resources and institutions. States of nature are given and assumed to be unchanging during the period of decision-making and its effects. Even though the argument is sometimes meted out that there are no unique equilibria and optima along the social welfare surface (Arrow 1963), and that different choices and technologies can lead to different configuration of optimum, and hence of re-organization of resources, institutional changes etc (Rawls 1971), the methodology still remains constrained by the optimum-equilibrium conditions.

This in turn implies that no further possibility of changes of preferences can be incorporated at and around the equilibrium-optimum points. Hence, in all states of resource allocation, whether these are governed by full information, imperfect information, bounded rationality, certainty or uncertainty, the methodology of treating technologies and preferences exogenously is intrinsic to the entire body of rational economic analysis embodying neoclassical economic theory and its prototypes (Shackle 1971). Endogeneity of preferences and technology loses its relevance in all such optimal-equilibrium analysis of resource allocation and utilitarian approaches to human capital theory.

The end-result of the above kind of optimal resource allocation problem with exogenous preferences and technologies is that learning-by-doing 'at large' along the social welfare function or the expected utility function, is ruled out. Learning, if interpreted as a movement along the outwardly moving production possibility curve or the indifference curves, is merely a phenomenon of repetition of the same adaptive behaviour of rational agents along different regimes and re-organization of resources. The stable nature of the Engel curve and growth path is the result of such assumptions.

Two problems appear from such a methodological treatment of optimal resource allocation with exogenous preferences and technologies. First, because neoclassical economics holds that movement from one regime to another (shifts in the curves) is a long-run phenomenon because changes in the social world are assumed to appear in marginal increments and within a market 'period' (Stigler 1966, Dasgupta 1985), therefore, the nature of exogenous preference surfaces are long-run realities of resource allocation as well.

Second, the absence of learning at or around the optimum-equilibrium resource allocation points in an extended sense (at large) and not simply in the instantaneous sense of point-wise optimality (utility, social welfare or cost-benefit analysis), premises resource allocation on the pervasive neoclassical principle of marginal substitution. Opportunity costs are inherent in choices among alternatives. Marginal substitution now conveys the fact that changes in preferences or technologies cannot be generated by the experience of optimizing and ultimately non-learning agents in the long-run case of resource allocation. Thus, the non-learning preferences, technological exogeneity and constrained resource allocation problem, all become the governing structural characteristics of a neoclassical treatment of human capital (Romer 1986). This is an abiding feature of neoclassical economics both in the short-run and long-run.

KNOWLEDGE AND INTERACTIONS

Knowledge in this chapter will mean inputs that excite systemic interactions among agents and relations of both the human world and the non-human world. In the latter case, the broader scope of socio-scientific investigation cannot ignore the inherently interacting experience of the non-human world (Smith 1992). An example of such a domain is physical and human ecology. These learn by the interactive processes both within their own domains and between themselves (Hawley 1986).

Besides understanding knowledge as the cause and effect of interactions leading to resource formation and its allocation, we must also understand the motive for acquiring this kind of experience in the human world. We must formalize the structure of knowledge formation as interactions proceed across different states of nature. Without these basic facts, there cannot exist a purposive social valuation of resource allocation on the basis of knowledge, as we found to be the case with Economics of Education. Hence we must further characterize the knowledge-formation process in extensively interactive systems of purposive type.

Knowledge Formation: Rationalist Regime

Knowledge formation can take two forms in the strongly and extensively interactive domains. The first kind of knowledge formation is governed by rationalism. Here non-convergence of rationalist behaviour (different from rationality) (Shakun 1988) in a discursive medium gives rise to complex processes that have no order in them. As a result, an entropic relationalism is developed among the agents and the socioeconomic world including the institutions that enforce policies. Dissent is now seen to be the cause of non-interactions among the agent-specific preferences, even though the basis of emergence of such preferences can be limited interactions. Such is the nature of social Darwinism (Dawkins 1976). But in the limit, rationalist and differentiating preferences result in a bundle of processes that cause increasing degrees of non-convergence. We then have the idea of complexity in the socioeconomic system out of randomness and entropy. That is, emergence of processes in such a system is caused by limited interactions leading to greater degrees of entropy, independence and finally individualism. At the end, the system gets characterized by atomistic preferences. Such is a description of individualism, which when further extended from the level of individuals to all other entities of the political economy, spells out the substantive meaning of methodological individualism (Georgescu-Roegen 1971). In such limiting states of knowledge, interactions cease to exist. Besides, the eventual evolution of individuating trajectories comes to be described by a linearized or adaptive envelope of optimum-equilibrium states, despite the fact that these may be of the evolutionary type (Osborne & Rubenstein 1994, Nelson & Winter 1982).

Knowledge Formation: Integrated Regimes

The second kind of knowledge formation is based on interactions that derive convergence from systemic complexity conveyed by interacting processes. But because the system progressively accumulates flows of knowledge in it, the resulting dynamics cause convergence point to evolve in continuum. The denser is the set of knowledge formation measured by the intensity of interactions, the faster will be the simultaneous evolution of new processes of earlier types.

The characterization of knowledge-formation in the system of complexity with order in it is described by the following string:

$$\lim\,(i=1\rightarrow N_1)\{\theta_i\}=\theta_{N1};\ \lim(j=N_1\rightarrow N_2)\{\theta_j\}=\theta_{N2};\ \ldots;$$
$$\lim(k=N_{n-1}\rightarrow N_n)\{\theta_k\}=\theta_n\ldots\text{etc.} \qquad (1)$$

Here, $i=1,2,\ldots, N_1$, denotes the first round of interactions leading to a convergence in the sequence vector, $\{\theta_i\}$. $j=N_1\rightarrow N_2$, denotes a subsequent round of interactions evolved from the previous round, and so on for $k=N_{n-1}\rightarrow N_n$, etc. Thus, each set of interactions leads to a convergence that is subsequently followed by evolution and more of the same kind of process. One can note here that the knowledge flows, $\{\theta_i\}$, can be extended by including very many other indexes corresponding to agents, systems, variables, relations etc.

The above kinds of evolutionary knowledge sequences can be depicted as follows:

$\{\theta_i\}$ $\{\theta_j\}$ $\{\theta_k\}$ .. etc

   $\{\theta_{N1}\}$ $\{\theta_{N2}\}$ $\{\theta_{N3}\}$ .. etc

. . . .

   $\{\theta_{n-2}\}$ $\{\theta_{n-1}\}$ $\{\theta_n\}$ .. etc

. . . . $SC\{\theta\}$

Similarly we have sequences of $\{\theta'\}$.

Here $SC\{\theta\}$ is a supercardinal transformation (see Chapter 3) of all cumulative values of $\{\theta\}$, with the progress of knowledge across all its verities and systems in the extended evolutionary form. Similarly the supercardinality concept, SC{θ′} of {θ′}can be defined. See later in this chapter for more on these supercardinal mathematical measures.

If we continue on in the interactions, integration and evolutionary epiphenomenon as described by (1), the sets of knowledge flows become limiting coalescing values of a collective of shared knowledge space. In the final instance, what we derive is an ever extended tree of interconnected knowledge flows arising from increasingly integrated systems of agents, variables, relations, systems etc. Thus, while complexity increases as the IIE-processes emerge, there is continued manifestation of evolutionary convergences in the systemic trajectories (Choudhury 1993). Such a phenomenon attained in the knowledge plane is quite contrary to the idea of interaction, complexity and convergence given in mainstream economic theory or political economy. Let us examine this issue briefly.

Note what Boland (1991) remarks on the testability and verifiability of an economic theory. According to him a higher and more explanatory universal axiom establishes a stronger empirical field and adapts to a greater degree of falsifiability. The emergence of economic theory is thus of a Popperian nature (Popper 1982). Now if the logic of such a falsifiability is carried far enough the following problem arises: The changeability of axioms with falsifiability that increases the complexity of the system, also atomizes the system into competing groups of theories and predictions. Finally, convergence to a mutually acceptable axiomatic premise ceases to exist.

An example of such a rejection of falsifiable theory is reflected by the conflict between Keynesianism and monetarism on the issue of price-output stabilization. The question settled one way or the other sensitizes the consequential policy issues that hinge on the emergent prescriptions. Such contending sways between the two theories in a disequilibrating fashion, have proved to be extremely costly in terms of policies dealing with stabilization during inflationary regimes (international Keynesianism, see Frenkel et al 1989) or in terms of interest rates and exchange rate volatility in monetarist regimes (Bordo 1989).

AN EXAMPLE OF SYSTEMIC PROBLEMS RAISED BY NON-CONVERGENCE IN RATIONLIST ECONOMIC REGIMES

To examine our implications on the inconsistency between testability, falsifiability and universals in economic methodology, we will study the inferences obtained from the quantity theory of money.

The quantity theory of money yields the identity (equation) of exchange, MV=PT, where, M denotes the quantity of money in the economy; V denotes the velocity of money circulation; P denotes price level; T denotes the number of transactions of money in goods and services. The unresolved question in the above identity is this: Which variables primordially affect money and price movements in a causal sense? Does price increase cause money supply to increase or vice-versa? The circular argument continues on without a resolution (Laidler 1990). In the meantime, price and money increases continue on to adversely affect the production of real goods and services. This can happen either due to a contraction of the quantity of money (monetarism) or due to an increase in the same (Keynesianism). There is no third factor here to act as the numeraire that can set an acceptable level of prices and quantity of money.

The real goods and services as a third factor do not enter the exchange equation in the valuation of money and price relation. This process of non-convergence in the equation becomes all the more acute with further disaggregation of the exchange equation with different categories of money in it and with interest rate sensitivity on money (Friedman 1989).

It is to be noted also that although disaggregation of the quantity equation to different monetary markets can increase the complexity of the relations, yet the degree of entropy increases at the same time. Now a way to restore stability in the segmented monetary markets would be to neutralize the effects of different kinds of money inter-markets. The result then is increasing independence of the monetary markets and linearization of the total exchange equation.

The above argument can be formalized as follows: Let there be n-number of monetary markets for say M_1, M_2 , ... etc kinds of money. Now,

$$M_s = (P/V_s).T(i_1^s, i_2^s, ..., i_n^s, Y_s, u_s) \quad \ldots\ldots\ldots\ldots\ldots\ldots \quad (2)$$

denotes the exchange equation for the sth kind of money in its own market. $i_1^s, i_2^s, ..., i_n^s$ denote the interest rates or rates of return associated with sth money market. Y_s denotes the GDP associated with the use of money in the sth money market. V_s is the velocity of circulation of M_s, s = 1,2,3,...n. u_s denotes all other explanatory variables associated with sth money market relation.

The total quantity of money, M,

$$M = \Sigma_{I=1}^{n} M_s, \quad \ldots\ldots\ldots\ldots\ldots\ldots\ldots\ldots \quad (3)$$

can now be written down in two forms:

1. $\mathbf{\Sigma_{I=1}^{n} M_s',}$

M_s' denotes independent monetary markets (s) obtained after segregating the M_s exchange equations. As a result there now exists no possibility to choose a higher level of 'universals' as mentioned by Boland, that can predominantly explain the whole monetary-real goods system.

2. $\mathbf{M_s(i_1^1, i_2^1, ..., i_n^1, ..., i_1^n, i_2^n, ..., i_n^n, V_1, ..., V_n, Y_1, ..., Y_n, P, u_1, ..., u_n).}$

Here independence of the monetary markets is not assumed, but interactions are entropic, particularly because of the presence of interest rates. Interest rates thus fail to be 'universals' as monetary instruments, which the monetarists would otherwise like to uphold.

A higher level of 'universals' for monetary stability is therefore left to real outputs, but such a choice would be neutralized by the effects of the term-structure of $\{i_1^1, i_2^1, .., i_n^1, .., i_1^n, i_2^n, .., i_n^n\}$, as the monetary instruments.

The inference to be drawn from (3) therefore, is that Boland's claim that falsifiability increases in complex systems is acceptable; but a higher level of universal remains non-existent in the quantity theory of money. Hence, there is no well-defined relationship between 'universals' and falsifiability in the case of the exchange equation.

We also find that falsifiability leading to independence of the monetary markets, each being governed by its own competing quantity equation, does not generate a rich quantity theory of money. Our claim here then is that for reasons of stability of relations in a monetary equilibrium equation with respect to the real sector, outputs and their prices must be made the critical numeraire variables for determining the quantity of money. Subsequently, rates of interest as monetary policy must be rejected in view of their entropic consequences on the real economy. By doing so, the quantity equation can be relieved of its indeterminateness, and money can become a stable contravention of valuation of real transactions. Money is not the result of promissory or speculative notes.

There will still be a need for a reference numeraire to cause a systemic tatonement process to occur. But unlike the case of a Walrasian economic system, wherein the numeraire is currency money (Morishima 1964), in the IIE-system that we have introduced in expression (1), this must be a knowledge-induced choice of goods that enable maximum complementarity in the general socioeconomic system. A candidate for such a real sector numeraire can be a basket of basic needs whose price index remains fairly invariable because of the elastic nature of the demand curve for the bundle (Choudhury 1997a, Haines 1987).

THE STRUCTURE OF PROCESS IN THE INTERACTIVE WORLDVIEW

Now returning to expression (1) of the IIE-model, we find that there are a number of important implications arising from our above inferences relating to the exchange equation taken as an example. The pervasiveness of interactions means that the sharing of information along the path of resource allocation and socioeconomic relations, generate 'global' diversities. 'Integration arising from interactions' means that diversities lead to 'global' complementarities among themselves. 'Evolution' means that the same process is extended across various states of nature, agents, relations, variables, institutions and systems, making the combination of such processes to describe endogenous transformation of knowledge and knowledge-induced socioeconomic entities.

The knowledge-centred IIE-methodology becomes altogether contrary to the neoclassical paradigm. While neoclassical economics is centrally governed by scarcity and marginal substitution as a principle of pricing, resource allocation and capital formation, contrarily the IIE-methodology is centred around the principle of universal (i.e. 'global') diversity and complementarity in evolutionary domains of knowledge-centred systems. Knowledge flows in such systems thus become an endogenous reality.

We have now also negated the relevance of the neoclassical human capital basis of education and knowledge in the IIE-model. We have argued that on the basis of the IIE-model, the cause and effect of marginal substitution, exogenous technology and preferences, cannot provide a substantive meaning of knowledge, interactions, learning and evolution in a politico-economic order. At the same time, since optimality and equilibrium are the twin consequences of the neoclassical model and of the individuated model of methodological individualism, therefore, these two models reflect themselves in the 'core' of economic theory (Debreu 1959).

Knowledge and Interactions in the Austrian School of Economics

The idea of 'creative destruction' in Schumpeter's theory of economic development (1962), the evolutionary knowledge concept of Hayek (1945), the epistemological thinking reflecting rationalist praxis in von Mises' meta-theory of economics (1976), and in present times the dynamic entrepreneurial model studied by Kirzner in the Austrian context (1997), are well-known. We want to investigate now as to how these models differ or compare with the knowledge-centred methodology of IIE-worldview.

The indefinitely evolutionary nature of Schumpeter's model of social becoming and historical revisionism is like the Marxian-Hegelian dialectical model of infinite regress (Luc Ferry 1992). Hayek's model although evolutionary in nature, becomes finally of an equilibrating type. But in the process of equilibration, no analytical explanation is given as to how new processes can arise from the earlier forms of equilibria. Von Mises' idea of economic praxis reduces his model to an institutionally and historistically benign form. It thus becomes devoid of the nexus of interactions that go on between economy and the socio-scientific order (Koizumi 1993). A relapse into the knowledge-neutrality of neoclassical methodology thus becomes endemic in both the Hayekian and Misean models of economic praxis.

Other forms of models for endogenous decision-making and institutions within the neoclassical economic theory have been propounded. For instance, endogenous institutional models sharing the utilitarian perspectives of social contractarianism have been presented by Harsanyi (1955). Political cycles are explained by public choice theory (Nordhaus 1975). Imperfect resource allocation is shown to be corrected by government intervention for improving social welfare in what Srinivasan calls neoclassical political economy (Srinivasan 1985). Sen treats entitlement questions in his neoclassical starvation set (Sen 1986). Becker treats a theory of family decision-making in the light of optimal allocation of household time in various kinds of substitutable activities (Becker 1989). A neoclassical theory of the state is defended by North (1981).

In all of these approaches the continuance of neoclassical reasoning causes institutions to become lateral aggregates of individual preferences. The resulting civil libertarian perspective of total utility function that now emerges is reflective of methodological individualism, as is the case with neoclassical rational choice. Thus, once again the issue of endogeneity of learning within institutional behaviour is annulled when the assumption of optimality and equilibrium is invoked. The principle of marginal substitution and exogeneity of preferences and technologies once again appear as cause and effect of full or bounded information attained by the economic system. Consequently, knowledge and interactions cease to exist.

Boulding too wrote on evolutionary socioeconomic systems that learn like amoebas in a Darwinian state (Boulding 1967). Consequently, amoebas in the process of establishing their life-forms are shown to enter competition that causes the survival of a few on the death of others. Competition thus becomes the feature of resource allocation in Bouldings model as in Hayek's. Whereas, competition leads to pricing of goods in the midst of scarcity of resources, which in turn is the cause and effect of a constrained optimal resource allocation state. Economic competition now appears as yet another natural consequence of scarcity, constrained optimization, equilibrium, and hence, loss of interactions and systemic knowledge-formation as otherwise would be true of endogenous phenomena in the knowledge-induced politico-economic order.

On the contrary though, it is interesting to note the self-organizing model of behaviour applied to complex models with order in them. Krugman has examined such self-organizing models for international trade (Krugman 1996). Yet I am afraid to note in Krugman's treatment of punctuated equilibrium as stable equilibrium, that this may defy or postpone evolutionary characteristics, and hence impede the knowledge-formation interactive processes of trade and development in a globalizing environment.

In a recent article, Miller (1997) traces the role that economic and political science have played in influencing theoretical developments in either. The author points out that non-economic factors that arise from institutional and voting behaviour bring with them common knowledge that affect the aggregation mechanism in economic and political theories. In such a case, the policy space with multiple dimensions is seen to present inhering instability. Convergence as a form of preference aggregation is then affected either by large sets of voters agreeing together or by institutions affecting convergence by a complex set of rules on binding agreements. The author also refers to the use of repetitive non-cooperative game-theoretic approach in the study of hierarchies of evolutionary equilibria that can appear in the multi-dimensional political space. Hence we find that only as recent as now, the 'core' of economic theory premised on optimum-equilibrium has shifted to incorporate the medium of 'common knowledge' in studying social preference aggregations. Such an emerging area of politico-economic theory is changing the concept of the rational in economic theory. Miller writes for the new political economy (Miller p. 1199): '.... the most powerful determinants of outcome are not the atomistic maximizing choices of individuals, but the groups and institutions that guide and constrain self-interested individual choice.' This view reinforces our claim that the evolutionary knowledge space of the IIE-worldview is determined by discourse and extensive complementarity among agents rather than by rational economic behaviour.

A SUMMARY OF ARGUMENTS

In general, for mainstream economic theory we note that interactions and knowledge have not entered it in an epistemological sense, as they are otherwise to be found in revolutionizing the hard core sciences (Prigogine 1980, Barrow 1991, Hull 1988, Kosko 1993).

In econometric models, interactions turn out to be adaptive and Markovian in nature. They are not a result of discursions. Dummy variables for discursive or non-discursive situations turn out to be mechanistic parameters. Ordinal values of utilities are based on the indispensable presence of substitutes in the utility function, explicit or implied. For example, even in the utility function of money, the variable for real goods is implied as a substitute. Learning-by-doing processes are based on neoclassical models that have been shown here to neutralize interactions at the optimum-equilibrium points (Arrow 1962). In complex models of social behaviour in economics, a limited Darwinian interactive domain evolves into methodological individualism and stereotypes the same process in institutional behaviour as well. The other way of forcing an equilibrium-optimality in such complex and non-convergent evolutionary systems is by hegemony of the dominant player. This is manifested by Eurocentricity (Amin 1976). In Rawls the hegemonic condition is expressed by the need for a terminal perceptor in Rawlsian infinite-games (Wolf 1977, Hammond 1987).

Knowledge and interactions as epistemological entities have thus failed to enter economic theory. This spells the poverty of economic theory in addressing the complex social and economic problems brought about in today's post-modern era (Korten 1996, Drucker 1990, Thurow 1996).

II

UNITY AND UNIFICATION OF KNOWLEDGE IN THE EPISTEMOLOGICAL SENSE

The epistemological questions surrounding knowledge and interactions in the IIE-model bring us to investigate the following questions: What is the precise epistemological premise that causes interactions (diversity) to converge to integration (complementarity) and then creatively evolve to more of the same kind of process (evolution)? What then is the epistemology of the IIE-worldview of complexity with order in it, that makes it different from the random complexity of the rationalist school? Answers to these questions are essential in understanding not simply the inner dynamics of the IIE-worldview but also to explain the differences in the methodology of the IIE-model from the neoclassical model and its rationalist prototypes. To address the above questions and proffer an explanation we proceed with the following theorem:

Theorem

Unification of knowledge as a scientific process is possible if and only if a system axiomatizes epistemological unity in it as the premise of knowledge. In all other systems, randomness or uncontrollable complexity must necessarily arise.

Valuation is possible if and only if measurable knowledge exists. Hence valuation is possible only in knowledge-centred systems with unity and unification. It cannot be a measurable concept in any other systems of complexity.

Proof of the Theorem

Let Ω denote the topological space of Complete Knowledge (Maddox 1970). Because of its non-measurable, unbounded but primarily creative nature that makes it relate functionally with its subsets, Ω is referred to as supercardinal topology (SC) here (Choudhury 1995a, Dewitt 1992).

Being a topology of this type, $\exists$ $\{\theta\}$, $\{\theta'\}$, two non-trivial subspaces of Ω, such that, $\{\theta\}\cap\{\theta'\}=\varphi$, with $\varphi\subset \Omega$ as a null subspace; $\{\theta\}\cup\{\theta'\}\neq\varphi$ properly belonging to Ω.as a subspace. φ denotes the null set.

Because of the openness of supercardinal topology of Ω, any functional transformation of $\{\theta\}$, $\{\theta'\}$ and of the functional relations of their mathematical unions and intersections or of the mathematical unions and intersections of functions of $\{\theta\}$, $\{\theta'\}$, are subspaces of Ω. In this way, $\{\theta\}$ and $\{\theta'\}$ become extended in Ω.

The implication of extension is notable. We derive two disjoint strings from the source of Ω singularly premised on $\{\theta\}$, $\{\theta'\}$, respectively. These are represented as,

$$\Omega \rightarrow \{\theta\} \rightarrow \mathbf{f}(\{\theta\}) \rightarrow \text{etc.} \quad \ldots\ldots\ldots\ldots \quad (4)$$

Hence $\{\theta\}$ begets itself by continuous functionals of the type **f**(.).

$$\Omega \rightarrow \{\theta'\} \rightarrow \mathbf{f}'(\{\theta'\}) \rightarrow \text{etc} \quad \ldots\ldots (5)$$

Hence $\{\theta'\}$ begets itself by continuous functionals of the type **f** ′(.).

Now if the $\{\theta\}$- and $\{\theta'\}$- based transformations are carried on indefinitely, these will finally become isomorphic (one-to-one) with Ω in the supercardinal sense. Thereby in this state, Ω will attain itself, while the supercardinal transformations of $\{\theta\}$, $\{\theta'\}$, say $SC(\{\theta\})$ and $SC'(\{\theta'\})$, respectively, will completely exhaust the dimension of Ω. In such a final state, $SC(\{\theta\}) \cup SC'(\{\theta'\}) = \Omega$.

We now infer the following results: (1) that the creative power of Ω extends over the disjoint subspaces, $\{\theta\}$, $\{\theta'\}$. (2) In the finite cases of functional relations as shown by the disjoint strings, all functional relations of $\{\theta\}$, $\{\theta'\}$ are proper and open subspaces of Ω, and hence capable of expansion in Ω while preserving their disjoint character. (3) In the supercardinal sense, Ω assumes its complete proprietorship of $SC(\{\theta\})$ and $SC'(\{\theta'\})$. Note that SC and SC′ are necessary to establish the universality of Ω. (4) Hence Ω is the universal topology.

Existence of Perturbations in $\{\theta\}$, $\{\theta'\}$ spaces:

Because functional transformations of $\{\theta\}$, $\{\theta'\}$ remain properly open neighbourhoods in Ω in any finite progression of the strings, therefore, it is possible to include temporary perturbations between these values in the penumbra of these subspaces. But with the progression of the strings, the perturbations must nullify themselves. Otherwise the result, $SC(\{\theta\}) \cup SC'(\{\theta'\}) = \Omega$, would not hold. It must therefore be true that perturbations described by, $M(\{\theta\} \cup \{\theta'\}) \neq \varphi \in \Omega$, will have a limiting value of its measure to be zero, as $\{\theta\}$ and $\{\theta'\}$ progress on in the strings. M is therefore measurable 'almost everywhere' in Ω with a measure of zero (Halmos 1959).

We have thus described some of the properties of Ω-topology and its subspaces. Next we will provide a more detailed description of the transformation functionals, **f(.)** and **f′(.)**.

Characterization of Transformation/Transmission Functionals

We will say that there is a measured delay between any given levels of $\{\theta\}$ and $\{\theta'\}$ and in their transformations into different levels. Hence there must be an intermediate stages of existence of $\{\theta\}$ and $\{\theta'\}$, subsequently giving rise to different levels of their own. These intermediate values result from previous values of $\{\theta\}$ and $\{\theta'\}$, respectively. In turn, they act as transmission functionals to subsequent levels of $\{\theta\}$ and $\{\theta'\}$, respectively.

We will denote these intermediate transmission functionals as follows:

$$\mathbf{f}(\{\theta\}) = \mathbf{X}(\theta),\ f'(\{\theta'\}) = \mathbf{X}'(\theta') \text{ etc.}$$

Likewise in continuity, forward (+) (hence backward, (-)) values of $\{\theta\}$ and $\{\theta'\}$ are determined by,

$$\{\theta_+\} = \mathbf{f}_+(\{\theta\}) = \mathbf{X}_+(\theta) \text{ and } \{\theta'_+\} = \mathbf{f}'_+(\{\theta'\}) = \mathbf{X}'_+(\theta').$$

Thus in this way, if we denote the progression of the θ-values by subscripts 1,2,3,... (likewise for θ′-values), we obtain a more detailed description of the strings (1), hence (2) as follows:

$$\Omega \to \{\theta_1\} \to f_1(\{\theta_1\}) = X_1(\theta_1) \to_{h1} \{\theta_2\} \to f_2(\{\theta_2\}) = X_2(\theta_2) \to \text{etc.} \to \Omega \quad (6)$$

An elementary chain in this string can be denoted by the compound mapping 'o' as follows:

$$\begin{array}{ccc} & \{\theta_1\} & \\ \swarrow & & \searrow \\ f_1 & & F_1 \\ X_1(\theta_1) & \to_{h1} & \{\theta_2\} \end{array} \quad \ldots\ldots\ldots\ldots (7)$$

where, $F_1 = h_1 \circ f_1$, etc.

The above characterizations (6) and (7) of the more detailed string (4) suggest that there are cause-effect interrelationships among the $\{\theta\}$-values and the corresponding $\mathbf{X}(\theta)$ (likewise for θ′-values and

$X'(\theta')$-values). While formalizing the two disjoint strings, due cognizance is given to the fact that there can exist M-values as temporary perturbations; but these are annulled as the two strings evolve. Such M-values would be included in the string (6) over a finite run of the string. After that period of evolution the string as shown in (6) will recur.

The above result implies the following:

$$M(\{\theta\}\cup\{\theta'\}) = \begin{cases} h(\theta), \text{ with } \lim (\theta \to \theta^*, \text{ a limiting value}); \\ \text{or} \\ h'(\theta') \text{ with } \lim (\theta \to \theta^*, \text{ a limiting value}) \end{cases} \quad \ldots (8)$$

Now, $\lim(\theta \to \theta^*)[F = M \circ f](\{\theta\}\cup\{\theta'\})$

$= \lim(\theta \to \theta^*)[F = (h \cup h') \circ f](\{\theta\}\cup\{\theta'\})$

$= \lim(\theta \to \theta^*)[(h \circ f)\cup (h' \circ f)](\{\theta\}\cup\{\theta'\}) = (h \circ f)(\theta)$,

since in the limit shown,

$(h \circ f)(\theta')=0$, and $(h' \circ f)](\{\theta\}\cup\{\theta'\})=0$,

because h′ and f are disjoint.

Introducing the Knowledge-Induced Socioeconomic Variables

Between (6) and (7) and using expression (4) we can further write:

$$\begin{array}{lllll} \Omega \to & \{\theta\} & \to_F & \theta_+ & \to \text{etc.} \\ & & \searrow_f & \nearrow_h & \to \text{etc.} \quad \ldots (9) \\ & & \mathbf{f}(\{\theta\}) = \mathbf{X}(\theta) & & \end{array}$$

Hence in continuity of the evolving processes we have evolving sequences of compound mappings between θ-values and **X**(θ)-values of the form, **F = h o f**, for all possible values of these transmission functionals.

The idea of unification (complementarity) as a process that we note in the above system, stems from the well-definition of the strings in the disjoint planes of $\{\theta\}$ and $\{\theta'\}$ and their corresponding $X(\theta)$ and $X'(\theta')$ values, respectively. This is possible if and only if the nature of Ω is such that it perfectly separates $\{\theta, X(\theta)\}$ from $\{\theta', X'(\theta')\}$ and the two streams evolve in their own disjointly unified fashions.

CONTRARY VIEW OF RATIONALIST ANALYSIS

Now replace Ω by rationalist analytics, R, where ontological pluralism and multiplicity must exist. Consequently, multiple strings will emerge. These will each claim its own hegemony by competition and functional independence from the other strings. Now if there is a set of strings of the nature of (1), (4) or (6), within them, there will exist marginalism and replacement between them. Thereby, a different epistemology will exist for each of the many strings within the class of (1), (4) or (6). The same will be true of the trajectories within strings of the type (5). Thus there remains no possible comparison and specification between the strings belonging to the class of $\{\theta\}$ or $\{\theta'\}$ exclusively.

The inference we derive is that such pluralistic and multiple strings contend with each other while the whole system governed by R evolves in this integrated way. This implies the standardization of marginalism within the whole rationalistic structure. The idea that unity exists in this entire R-order means that R as a system maintains its evolution while keeping in tact its own nature and structure. In this structure there exists no unity intra-R-subsystems. Now if any one of the multiple trajectories in R is isolated from the rest, there will be further disaggregation to more elementary strings and the intra-systemic marginalism will increasingly pervade. Such a generalization leads to a final state of atomism, wherein finally, only the individual entity exists as a self-maximized identity.

Formalism in the Rationalist R-Space

We can symbolize the above characteristics of R as follows:

$$\text{Let } \mathbf{R} = \{R_1 , R_2 , R_3 , ...\},$$

with R_i being any of the multiple strings of **R**, i=1,2,.... In the limit of atomism inter- and intra- systems, R_i's reduce to point-sets. Now no intersections can exist between them. Such is a state of perfect methodological individualism among the reduced rationalist systems. Unity now exists only around the monadic points; the intra-systemic idea has disappeared. There exists no unity inter-systems (Choudhury 1998).

Contrast among Trust, Falsehood and Rationalism

A substantive difference has now occurred between the Ω- and **R**-orders. Ω causes the universe to separate into two disjoint categories – of {θ} and {θ′}. Within these there are unities of their own. These are governed by laws of morality and ethical neutrality or by being opposed to ethics, respectively and exclusively. In the R-system {θ} and {θ′} are broken up into many of the kinds and there is no unity inter-systems. As the process toward atomism proceeds, there fails to be unity even intra-systemically. The relationship between R and {θ′}-space and its distinction from {θ}-space is shown in the appendix.

In Ω, {θ} and {θ′} are well-defined – i.e. truth and falsehood, respectively. This is due to their moral and ethically benign or opposing character, respectively and exclusively. There is no such well-definition in **R** due to the multiplicity of R_i , all governed by their distinct rationalism.

The multiple and differentiated nature of **R** as opposed to the overarching power of unity in Ω, makes the latter as the sole cause and effect of epistemological unity even within the disjoint systems of {θ} and {θ′}. In this sense, Ω preserves the unity of both of these disjoint systems as well as of unity in the nature of this disjointness in the entire system. This character of epistemological unity affecting the nature of interactions and integration in continuous circular causation within {θ, X(θ)} and {θ′, X′(θ′)} values, gives the meaning of unification as a process derived from the epistemology of unity. The method of unification remains the same in the <u>entire</u> functional nature of these subspaces, although within given trajectories of these systems behaviour is different.

In this regard we proceed by considering that the entire of {θ′, **X**′(θ′)} turns to be the **R**-system. Now the same kind of atomism premised on methodological individualism appears, and the entire system is governed by the underlying methodology. The Ω-supercardinal space looks upon the two systems – {θ, **X**(θ)} and **R**={θ′, **X**′(θ′)} as disjoint due to the nature of independence and methodological individualism characterizing **R** and unity comprising {θ, **X**(θ)}. This results in disjoint trajectories within **R** = {θ′, **X**′(θ′)} intra-systemically. Now the difference between the rationalist system R and the inter-intra-systemically unified worldview, Ω, is the truncation of **R** by the existence of the $\{\theta, \mathbf{X}(\theta)\}$-space in Ω; but this does not exist in **R** due to **R's** complete atomism and randomization caused by rationalism.

THE PRINCIPLE OF UNIVERSAL COMPLEMENTARITY ONCE AGAIN

The epistemology of unity leads to systemic unification within either $\{\theta, \mathbf{X}(\theta)\}$ or $\{\theta', \mathbf{X}'(\theta')\}$ – both emanating from the premise of Ω via the medium of extensive interactions among agents, relations and variables of the systems. Unification arising from such 'global' interactions establishes integration. Following this, both interactions and integration become evolutionary on the planes of advancing $\{\theta, \mathbf{X}(\theta)\}$- and $\{\theta', \mathbf{X}'(\theta')\}$-spaces. Hence, unification, integration and complementarity among the systemic elements are equivalent terms. Since $\mathbf{M}(\{\theta\}\cup\{\theta'\})$ as defined earlier in expression (8) is a temporary phenomenon in the entire interactive and integrative evolutions in Ω-topology, therefore, complementarity must remain universal within $\{\theta, \mathbf{X}(\theta)\}$- and $\{\theta',\mathbf{X}'(\theta')\}$- spaces in terms of their own separate meanings.

In the **R**-space there is complete marginalism caused by conflict, competition, methodological individualism and independence among its elements. There is consequently a pursuit for optimality of objectives and steady-state equilibrium states in resource allocation. These are considered to be long-run predictable features of the differentiated R-systems (Etzioni 1988). Hence, all such systems are methodologically moved towards a static condition of knowledge in the states of permanent optimality and equilibrium (Shackle 1972). Evolutionary conditions in such cases lead to non-relational worlds. Marginalism thus negates 'global' complementarity, although a semblance of complementarity may be implied in the most instantaneous and partial sense of relations.

Darwinian evolutionary systems that have influenced Popper's thought and to an extent Kuhn's (Pheby 1988), are examples of such limited interactive models that finally lead to competition, independence and methodological individualism. Such kinds of rationalistic perceptions have entered both science and society in the rationalistic order. Thereby, the entirety of rationalist order has become devoid of the essence of complementarity. Hence, interactions, integration and evolution of these systems along a unified path among their elements, remain equally non-existent in the **R**-system in the face of methodological individualism – hence preserving their permanent character of optimality and equilibrium in non-interactive systems.

Such optimum-equilibrium states in **R**-systems are attained in two ways. First, methodological individualism either among atomistic agents or groups axiomatizes completeness of knowledge and information in these systems. Second, if institutional power is assumed to exist, then the linearly aggregate objectives of the agents are dominated by hegemony. In the end we find that none of such perspectives can give rise to social participation where interactions and knowledge flows are endemic.

RETURNING TO THE MONETARY MODEL WITH KNOWLEDGE AND INTERACTIONS

At present, the only area of political economy that addresses the topic of valuation of money in terms of the real economy in the absence of interest rates is Islamic political economy (Choudhury 1992). However, in a corresponding exchange equation the elimination of interest rates is not mechanically attained. It is a methodological issue. Banks now deal in non-promissory notes to finance the real sectoral activities. Thus speculative ventures are rejected in favour of those that can be realized within a given feasibility plan. The financial institutions with the guidance from government, study these feasibility plans in the light of their non-speculative elements and with the aim of replacing interest rates with participatory and trade-financing instruments. A process of discourse is generated between and among the agents of needs and supply, and it is the realization of such discursive activities in the real economy that brings about the presence of money as a contravention for valuation of the prices and net worth of the real transactions and projects. Prices as so determined by the process of discourse thus become the primal indicator of monetary value. The growth rate of the quantity of money now agrees with the growth rate of the price level that in turn is determined on the basis of the growth rate of knowledge in the system. The growth rate of knowledge itself is the net worth of the changes among all variables and relations in the systems under study within the process at a point of evolution. Such changes are evaluated by means of a social well-being function,

$$W(\theta) = W(\theta, \mathbf{X}(\theta), M(\theta)) \quad \ldots\ldots\ldots\ldots \quad (10)$$

We write the IIE-problem involving money and the real economy as follows:

$$\text{Simulate } \{\theta\}[\, W(\theta, \mathbf{X}(\theta), M(\theta))], \quad \ldots\ldots\ldots\ldots \quad (11)$$

subject to recursive interrelationships (interactions) among the vector of variables $\mathbf{X}(\theta)$, the quantity of money $M(\theta)$, and all commonly determined interactive interrelationships on the basis of the complementary knowledge vector, θ, as was mentioned in expression (1) or (4).

There is an important implication here respecting the strictly endogenous nature of money in the system (Desai 1989). This feature of money is explained by the endogeneity of knowledge values and the socioeconomic variables. To regulate the circularity of this open-ended simulation model we well define the epistemology of unity in terms of legal Islamic texts (Shari'ah). This is then combined with the human discourse (Ijtihad) that goes around the issues respecting financial and developmental issues – in the present case that of money, the real economy and social well-being.

The exchange equation of money is now derived as a knowledge-induced cause and effect of the simulation problem given in (11). The money equation looks like the following:

$$M(\theta) = f(\theta, \mathbf{X}(\theta), W(\theta)) \quad \ldots\ldots\ldots\ldots \quad (12)$$

The convergence of the open-ended simulation problem is attained by discourse around the elimination of interest rates in accordance with the Islamic law (Shari'ah) premised on Divine Unity. Islamic Law concerning abolition of interest rates of all kinds as shown by the vector in expression (2) is well-developed in the literature (Khan 1984).

III

SIMULATION OF KNOWLEDGE VALUES

How are knowledge values observed and then simulated in the IIE-model to give rise to socioeconomic variables and their values? We begin by arguing that knowledge-like order is intrinsic in the nature of things (Penrose 1989). It is left for human beings to discover it through the process of anthropic interactions – taken up in a broad sense encompassing the human and natural domains. In political economy, the medium of discovering such embedded knowledge is the interaction that takes places both anthropically and in conjunction with market exchange. Thus if there is an inherent utility in a good or service, and for that matter, in primary and secondary commodities and factor inputs, this value is then understood in terms of the extent to which it can develop extensive interlinkages (unification, complementarity and integration). This follows from the principle of universal complementarity. Such goods, factors, technologies, institutions etc. that generate wide interactions and cause systemic unification to occur and social well-being to be attained, are the ones that get promoted in Islamic market exchange. The consumers, producers and institutions including Government are made to interact and consensually unify on the basis of the benefits that such goods confer. Thus a choice of goods in terms of their interlinking character along with the presence of agents to discover such complementarities, constitute the discovery of the intrinsic knowledge in the goods, services, inputs and economic instruments. Here the epistemology of Divine Unity and hence the process of unification, become the cause and effect of the complementarity process generated by specific choices.

The Engineering Approach to the Simulation of Knowledge Values

Once the choice of goods is made on the basis of the principle of universal complementarity, and thus of unification and the epistemology of Divine Unity, a given ordinal value can be assigned to the perceived level of the complementarity attained. This assignment of ordinal values is done by interacting human agents in concert with the observations received from the ensuing interacting, integrating and evolutionary features of the knowledge-induced choices made. Such ordinal $\{\theta\}$-values emerging by cause and effect in response to the chains of interactive tuples like $\{\theta, \mathbf{X}(\theta)\}$, can thus be simulated through discourse among the agents in concert with cause-effect between these variables, as shown in the strings (1), (4) and (6). The presence of θ-values in the socioeconomic variables included in the vector $\mathbf{X}(\theta)$, makes the tuples $\{\theta, \mathbf{X}(\theta)\}$ evolve simultaneously. Hence, only knowledge-induced simulation is possible in such evolutionary cases; no optimality exists, except in the uninteresting case of the most instantaneous case of unchanging knowledge or hegemonic dominance.

It is seen that two kinds of complementarity emerge from the strings referred to before. First there is the simulation of knowledge through the medium of the interconnecting $\mathbf{X}(\theta)$-values and by circular causation and continuity in this interrelationship. Thus, while there must exist complementarity in the θ-values due to unification and the epistemology of Divine Unity, so also simultaneously there must exist the same property in the $\mathbf{X}(\theta)$-values to generate new levels of knowledge flows. This establishes the overall complementarity in the knowledge-induced socioeconomic variables. The above description provides an engineering perspective on the simulation of ordinal θ-values (Casti 1990). This then simulates the social well-being function in terms of the tuples $\{\theta, \mathbf{X}(\theta)\}$ within the string denoting the circular causation and continuity of unified reality.

The Organizational Approach to Simulation of Knowledge Values

The second approach to simulation is based on the more important and interesting organizational behaviour towards discovering socioeconomic value in the political economy of community. Here we invoke visibly participatory, sharing and coordinating agents that remain actively in decision-making. In this light, even more importantly than the engineering perspective is the anthropic presence in the communitarian approach to organizational behaviour that gets governed by the principle of universal complementarity in the interactive, integrative and creatively evolutionary process. In this sense of predominance of the anthopic presence over the sheer mechanical simulation of knowledge-based engineering systems with ordinal θ-values, markets become visible systems of social contracts rather than of abstract exchanges. Hence programs, policies, dynamic preference changes and decision-making under complexity with the order of unity in them, play central role in determining θ-values.

THE SPECIFICATION OF DIVINE LAWS (SUNNAT AL-ALLAH AND SUNNAT AL-RASUL) IN THE SIMULATION PROBLEM OF ISLAMIC POLITICAL ECONOMY

In all cases of knowledge simulation in the Islamic political economy, the transmission functionals stand for the Divine Laws (Sunnat al-Allah) and their comprehension through the medium of the guidance of the Prophet Muhammad (Sunnat al-Rasul), the reinforcing human discourse (Ijtihad), consensus (Ijma) and creative evolution (Khalq in-Jadid) in the midst of the total IIE-Process (the Tawhidi Process). The epistemology of Islamic political economy is thus premised on the extensive study of this very worldview of the Tawhidi Process itself. It is the process as derived from the Qur'an that annuls the dichotomy between the epistemic (Kantian) and ontic (Humean) perceptions in the occidental philosophy of science and instead develops reality around the unified whole of circular causation (Choudhury 1994, Pheby 1988). Such a process while it emanates from the epistemology of Divine Unity, it also establishes the extensively IIE-epiphenomenon of unified reality. It spells out the principle of universal complementarity among possibilitiues; forms the normative and positivistic body of thought; interlinks the deductive and inductive methodologies; and entrenches simulation method of analysis in the knowledge-induced framework of Islamic politico-economic studies. Within this IIE-worldview all specific problems of the $\{\theta, \mathbf{X}(\theta)\}$-space and $\{\theta', \mathbf{X}'(\theta')\}$-space are taken up.

CONCLUSION

After the works of the Austrian school of economics, the evolutionary economics of Kenneth Boulding, the economic epistemology of Ludwig von Mises and Shackle, and the social causation model of Gunnar

Myrdal, we have not known of revisitation to epistemological questions in contemporary economic theory. This has left a debilitating gap in any new praxis of economic paradigm that could explain the interdependent phenomenon of an increasingly interdependent world. Economics prima facie was always incapable of explaining the ethical core of the human world. An indication of this ethical neutrality in economics arose from the divorce between economics and political economy. Even when the latter was taken up by political economists, it turned out simply to be a study of positivistic phenomena while ignoring the normative ones that essentially address the 'ought' statements of public policy and of the ecological human domain (George 1897, Mill 1994 reprinted).

In this chapter we posed the ethical core of human endeavour to be premised on the knowledge and interactions that ensue from the epistemology of Divine Unity and then spreads itself out in an increasingly complementing world of interlinkages and creative evolution. This is the process of unification of knowledge. Contrarily, the rationalist configuration of economic façade is shown to be incapable of achieving the same results and social explanations. Thus, even though humankind is today entering a world that is increasingly ecological (interconnected) in substance by design, observation, institutions and policy, yet the inherited paucity of appropriate methods in economic theory continues. This does not enable us to address the human ecological worldview by means of economic theory.

Despite our invoking of the IIE-worldview as a new approach to politico-economic reasoning in this chapter, we have not been exhaustive on the subject matter on many issues that are taken up at length in many other places (Choudhury 1995b, 1997b). Some of the important concepts to note are endogeneity of interacting preferences in a general ethico-economic system and to study within the organizational behaviour of firms, corporations and other organistic economic forms that apply suitable financial instruments in society and economy; the role of government in knowledge creation in the IIE-model; and the nature of prices, resource allocation and capital formation under the principle of universal complementarity (Choudhury 1996, Daly 1992). There are many other ones as well.

In the post-modern age with new epistemological questions opening up in science, it is time that economic theorists abandoned their narrow vision of neoclassicism and think anew. Indeed, a robust theory is a strong harbinger to moral and effective institutions, programs and policies. Thus a re-orientation on the basis of new epistemological outlook in economic reasoning remains a pressing human need.

APPENDIX: TRUTH, FALSEHOOD AND RATIONALISM IN RELATION TO THE IIE-WORLDVIEW

The R-space in its entirety comprises of sequences of $\{\theta'\}$-values along mutually independent branches as shown in figure A6.1.

Here the transmission functionals {ABC...}, {ABC′...}, $\{A_1,B_1,C_1 ,...\}$, $\{A_1,B.',C_1' ,...\}$ generate the vector in the $\{\theta'\}$-space. Hence, R is spanned by the vector $\{\theta'\}$, with its usual properties of disjointness and independently lateral aggregation along the different branches. Thus, while the above-mentioned transmission functionals have their interactive, integrative and evolutionary properties <u>along</u> the paths {ABC...}, {AB′ C′...}, $\{A_1,B_1,C_1 ,...\}$, $\{A_1,B_1',C_1' ,...\}$, etc. as shown, nonetheless, there exist differentiation, marginalism and methodological individualism between such branches in the entire R-space. This is the idea of unity in the $\{\theta'\}$-subspace and in the <u>entire</u> system of R-space, yet under the control of, i.e. arising from, Ω.

CHAPTER 7

COMPLEMENTARITY IN THE QUR'ANIC ECOLOGICAL MODEL

The attributes of complementarity reflected in the Goodly Tree (Chapter 3 & 10) are further exemplified by the felicitous picture on agriculture presented in the Qur'an. Note the Qur'anic verse in this regard (Chapter 6, verse 99, also see verse 141):

> It is He Who sends down rain from the skies: With it We produce vegetation of all kinds: From some We produce green (crops), out of which we produce grain, heaped up (at harvest); out of the date-palm and its sheaths (or spathes) (come) clusters of dates hanging low and near: and (then there are) gardens of grapes, and olives, and pomegranates, each similar (in kind) yet different (in variety): When they begin to bear fruit, feast your eyes with the fruit and the ripeness thereof. Behold! in these there are Signs for people who believe.

Furthermore in Chapter 6, verse 95 of the Qur'an appears: 'It is God Who causeth the seed-grain and the date-stone to split and sprout. He causeth the living to issue from the dead, and He is the One to cause the dead to issue from the living. That is God: Then how are ye deluded away from the truth?'

A profound meaning of interconnections in the chain of occurrences starting from the germination of the seed by means of a productive process to its acculturation at the levels of vegetation and fruit bearing, are shown as Ayaths (Signs of God). These explain the process of realizing felicitous outcomes from a chain of useful interrelationships. To this is added the environment of human observations, understanding and reflection on the immaculate design of creation. There is the bestowing of felicity outwardly from the realization of the fruits of such an agricultural system.

With regards to dates, we have the Prophet's saying (al-Jawziyyah, trans. al-Akili 1993): 'Dates are a fruit whose seeds came from paradise. They are an antidote for poisoning, a rich source for increasing semen, and drinking the water of soaked Madinah dates breaks the spell of witchcraft (reported by Ibn Maja). Al-Jawziyyah quotes many benefits of all kinds of pomegranates. The Prophet is quoted as saying (Al-Jawziyyah trans. Al-Akili 1993), 'There is not a pomegranate of yours that is not cross-fertilized by a seed of a pomegranate from paradise.' Al-Jawziyyah continues to mention that grapes being mentioned six times in the Qur'an, is to be considered as one the principal favours that God has bestowed upon creation. Grape is thus considered as a fruit both of this world and of paradise. The Prophet Muhammad loved to eat grapes. Regarding olive there are many benefits. Imam Tirmidhi quotes the Prophet as having said (Imam Tirmidhi quoted in al-Jawjiyyah): 'Use (olive) oil as food and as ointment, for it comes from a blessed tree.' What is important to note from these Ahadith is the centrality of belief in Fitra value (Chapter 5) in the Prophet's medicinal prescriptions. The message goes deeper toward making medical science, as every other area of scientific, social and economic investigations, to be deeply ingrained in Tawhidi epistemology via reference to Fitra value found to be intrinsic in these sciences and in their felicitous outputs.

Consequently, since Tawhid becomes the common premise of all disciplines of life, the systems of human volitions like the devotional integrity of the Prophet's medicine, become interactively integrated on the premise of the unified reality. This is the unique premise of Tawhid. It is functionalized by the methodology of unification of knowledge emanating from the Divine epistemological Stock of Knowledge (Choudhury 1995).

One notes from verse 99 mentioned above, the importance of diversity in the agricultural domain and its implication on felicity and richness. The implication of agricultural diversity is thus naturally interlinked with the principle of complementarity. The latter could not have been possible if diversity did not exist. Yet diversity here does not mean pluralism, differentiation and substitution. Pluralism as a rationalistic idea springs from multiplicity in human perceptions. These are premised on differentiated and contending views among hegemonic groups, or they can arise from the one-many problem of Eastern philosophy, where God is pluralized to take control of independent domains of action (Rucker 1983). Some Sufi writers have also misconstrued diversity with pluralism by relating Islamic architectural and cosmological patterns with disparate religious roots that do not stand upon Unity as explicated by Tawhid (Schuon 1989, Nasr 1978).

Several closely interconnected reflections of knowledge and learning ensue from the first verse. These are first, the augmentation of life by the felicity of goodness as fruits. Second, in the studying of the creative process of cause and effect from the stage of germination to the stage of fruit bearing, there is a deepening examination of the complementary activities. Third is the domain of rich diversity of goodness and felicity that enables the principle of universal complementarity to come about. Fourthly, from among these reflections emanate the positivistic representations of truths that are deductively derived. In this way, the deductive and inductive reasoning are integrated together cyclically. On this integrated deductive-inductive plane, the first reflection is seen to bring about common benefits to all. Such benefits that cause coexistence between vegetation, fruits and their usefulness in a vastly interconnected ecological sense, can be construed as sustainability that keeps the human order in harmony with the ecological order.

This in turn creates an extensive human ecology of life (Hawley 1986). A positivistic inference is thus manifested from the inductive premise. The second reflection brings about moral and ethical meaning to scientific investigation by noting the universal complementarity process in the agricultural domain, which explains a meaningful function of such a moral socio-scientific process. Its origin is primarily on the deductive process of reasoning. Then through diversity but avoiding pluralism, all deductive and inductive reflections are integrated together in a circular fashion to form true moral-material worth when knowledge flows and their induced forms are premised on Divine Unity.

Thus, with the pervasiveness of understanding and realization of such extensive complementarities with diversities – that is of unity in diversity – come about truths that are referred to as 'Signs (Ayaths) for people who believe.' The experience of belief is equated to the consciousness of Tawhid (Oneness of Allah) in the order of reality. A theory of observation is thus laid down in Qur'anic perspective. This is to define a cognitive reality on the plane of one of two possibilities –

truth formed by integration of deductive and inductive reasoning on the plane of complementarities; and falsehood formed by a denial of this unified truth.

Verse 95 mentioned above, now links up with the complementary chains of actions and reactions conveyed by verse 99, and carries the meaning to the circular causation and continuity model of unified reality. Here too, a clear polarity is shown to exist between truth and falsehood: 'That is God: then how are ye deluded away from the truth?'

The Absolute and Complete Premise of Knowledge is shown to be embedded in the Oneness of Allah. Thereby, cognitive reality is derived from the impact and pervasiveness of Divine Laws on the simultaneous creation of positivistic things ('It is God Who causeth the seed-grain...'). Here the deductive process of reasoning ('It is God') leads spontaneously to the creation of cognitive reality ('seed-grain,' 'date-stone,' 'split and sprout'). Through continuity, the pervasiveness of Tawhidi epistemology is shown to be ingrained in the circular process: First is the creation of life out of nothing but by sheer Divine Will (Knowledge) – 'He causeth the living to issue from the dead.' Thus new knowledge flows emanate from old ones. Second is the continued obsolescence of existing knowledge flows – 'And He is the One to cause the dead to issue from the living.' Now when these two processes are joined together, the resultant reality is shown to function on the plane of a continuity of the circular process from knowledge to discovery to re-origination. The Qur'anic verse confirming this circular continuity is (Chapter 10, verse 4), 'It is He who beginneth the process of creation, and repeateth it, that He may reward with justice those who believe and work righteousness.'

The above-mentioned verses are thus clear confirmation of the knowledge-centred essence of reality both at the level of deductive and inductive reasoning. Since the Divine Laws pervade both of these domains uniquely, therefore, they must be unified and be of the same nature. This is of the nature found in conveying reality by means of the spontaneous action between knowledge flows and materiality. It is also for this very reason that we say there is no duality and pluralism in Islam. Matter and mind are cogently united. The moral and material are unified and ultimate reduction is to the root of the most irreducible truth. This is the root of the Oneness of God, Tawhid.

Hence unlike Relativity Physics, for example, that relegates physical reality to the primacy of the speed of light and makes this as the limiting determinant of all inductive things, the Tawhidi worldview emanates from the premise of unification of knowledge and carries on the evolving processes manifesting unified reality. Physical premise is thus abandoned for Completeness of Knowledge Stock in Tawhidi epistemology. In this, unification of knowledge becomes permanently foundational.

Tawhidi epistemology and the resulting methodology of unification of knowledge flows, alternatively referred to here as the circular causation and continuity model of unified reality, is polar to rationalism and to the nature of reasoning derived from it (Russell 1954). The profound difference between these two opposite outlook of life and thought lies in the primal and immanent premise of unity in the Tawhidi worldview. This is then carried through in the order of reality by precise laws, Prophetic guidance, instruments, institutions, preferences and evaluative procedures. The holistic model of the Goodly Tree proved such an encompassing worldview. In the above Prophetic medicinal reference, the same message is being confirmed by the corresponding Sunnah of the Prophet. On the other hand, the premise and continuity of rationalism and its derived perspectives of life are permanently embedded in pluralistic perceptions. The result is conflict, independence, methodological individualism and pluralism among individuating systems. The resulting laws, instruments, institutions and organization of life follow similar kinds of aggregative preferences determining the socio-scientific whole.

In figure 7.1 we show that an identical specification of the comprehensive knowledge model of creation arises from the treatment of the Qur'anic agricultural model, as from the treatment of the model of the Goodly Tree. Besides, we note that there is a natural consequence in organizing the knowledge dimensions of increasing unveiling (Bayyanah) according to a theory of the Seven Heavens and its multiples of seven that the Qur'an mentions about. We also note that such Ayaths (Signs) are found across the Seven Heavens and their multiples (creation embedded in knowledge) as on earth and below the earth. In this way we infer the application of the IIE-process of knowledge formation across the roots of the Goodly Tree as across the branches.

The above inferences for the Qur'anic agricultural model like the ones for the knowledge model of the Goodly Tree can be affirmed from the following verses (Chapter 34, verse 2): 'He knows all that goes into the earth, and all that comes out thereof; all that comes down from the sky and all that ascends thereto, and He is the Most Merciful, the Oft-Forgiving.'

In figure 7.1, we have thus extended the knowledge-induction through the IIE-processes above the earth and into the heavens as below the earth. The common premise of all of these is Tawhidi epistemology. The affirmation of the Supreme Felicity of Tawhid is once again shown in the logical completion of all cumulative knowledge in Hereafter (Akhira). As well as at the roots of the Goodly Tree we have shown the supercardinal measure of Tawhid. This is to imply in the broadest sense of the Tree and its systemic overarching felicity, the fact that creation took its roots from the Divine Authority of Tawhid. Even before the creation of humankind, the cosmological order of creation was placed and this took its roots in the Will of God as the Divine Unity. Through this Will God established His infallible Oneness in all of creation, starting from the primordial state of creation to its present and future. Our IIE-model in respect to the Goodly Tree is once again established as follows:

$$\Omega \rightarrow f_s \{\theta_{jkl}\} \in \Omega \rightarrow f_1 \{X_{jkl}(\theta_{jkl})\} \rightarrow f_4 \text{ Continuity of the IIE-Process} \rightarrow \Omega$$

$$\downarrow f_2$$

$$\{\cup_i \cap_{jkl} \theta_{ijkl}, \cup_i \cap_{jkl} X_{ijkl}(\cup_i \cap_{jkl} \theta_{ijkl}\}$$

$$\downarrow f_3$$

$$SW = SW(\{\cup_i \cap_{jkl} \theta_{ijkl}, \cup_i \cap_{jkl} X_{ijkl}(\cup_i \cap_{ijkl} \theta_{ijkl}\}$$

Figure 7.1: Complementary processes in the Qur'anic agricultural model

Dimension of Complete Knowledge Formation

7. Vegetation, fruits and felicity of Heaven (Jannah):
Supercardinal measure of knowledge-augmented forms in Hereafter
Completion of the IIE-Process
$=\mu(\Omega)$
↑

Dimension 6 of knowledge formation

6. Continuity of the IIE-function:
Goodly Tree in its rich branches and yields
reaching out to the heavens

$\uparrow f_4$

Dimension 5 of knowledge formation

5. Realization of social well-being as a function of
$SW=SW(\{\cup_i\cap_{jkl}\theta_{ijkl}, \cup_i\cap_{jkl}X_{ijkl}(\cup_i\cap_{jkl}\theta_{ijkl}\})$
Yields of the Goodly Tree

$\uparrow f_3$

Dimension 4 of knowledge formation

4. Interacted knowledge flows as complementary benefits,
$\{\cup_i\cap_{jkl}\theta_{ijkl}, \cup_i\cap_{jkl}X_{ijkl}(\cup_i\cap_{jkl}\theta_{ijkl}\}$:
IIE-consequences in knowledge-augmented fruits of the Goodly Tree

$\uparrow f_2$

Dimension 3 of knowledge formation

3. Dates Pomegranates Grapes Trelishes Olives etc.

(as diversities of Ayaths, $\{X_{jkl}(\theta_{jkl})\}$:
Fruits of the Goodly Tree)

↑ ↑ ↑ ↑ ↑

$\uparrow f_l$

Dimension 2 of knowledge formation

1. Seeds of various vegetations and fruits: $\{\theta_{jkl}\} \in \Omega$
(as derived knowledge flows in various systems:
nodes of the Goodly Tree)

$\uparrow f_s$

Dimension 1 of knowledge formation

0. Tawhidi Epistemology: Ω
(The Prophet's reference to seeds of Paradise in the fruits)
$\downarrow \mu$
Roots of the Goodly Tree premised in Ω:
$\mu(\Omega)$

Seven Dimensions of Knowledge Below the Earth as Above the Earth

CONSUMPTION MENU LINKED WITH QUR'ANIC AGRICULTURAL MODEL

In the Goodly Tree model we found that the kind of knowledge-induced interactions that unify the felicitous conditions of life, can occur because intrinsic in them are the basic needs regime of development. In the knowledge-induced worldview, such a basic need is seen to be primarily unification of knowledge premised on Tawhid. Thus, the concept of the basic needs changes significantly from the one in physical needs of human being to one on the primacy of Divine knowledge that enables a social and civilizing transformation of preferences toward acceptance of the physical needs as determined by the primacy of knowledge in the first place. Thus a number of necessary and sufficient conditions must characterize the basic needs regime of development in Islamic perspectives.

First is the pre-condition of the Islamic social economy to have inculcated God-consciousness in individuals and groups towards forming preferences that are premised on simplicity, integrity, goodness and justice. The inculcation of such values require guidance by means of Shari'ah to change human preferences. Hence the mapping f_s assumes an effective role in the Tawhidi knowledge-induced transformation. In the Shatibi-type consumption menu, primacy is given to necessaries, then to comforts, followed by refinements (Masud 1984, Ahmad 1991). In Ghazzali, the essence of freedom of individuals to liberate themselves from the grips of selfishness and to relate our lived experience to Akhira, the highly ethical attributes of demand and satisfaction with moderation, are invoked in the individual consumption function.

In Ibn Taimiyyah's works, the social guidance of markets for correcting distributive inequity and imbalances in the economy resulting due to departure from the Shari'ah norms, is recommended, whereas undue regulation is to be avoided (Choudhury 1997a, Ibn Taimiyyah undated). In Imam Fakhruddin Razi's works, the hierarchy of self-actualization that emanates from human fulfilment is found to be premised on obedience to God (Ubudiyyah). From this plane of knowledge the physical qualities of basic needs fulfilment are determined (Noor 1998).

Obviously, primacy of knowledge-induction of physical basic needs creates an automatic dynamic essence in consumer preferences, attributes of the goods and services now called social good (Lancaster 1966), and in the concept of human fulfilment or self-actualization. All of these emanate uniquely from the Tawhidi premise. Hence such attributes are all interlinked by complementarity. It denotes unification of knowledge in systems once knowledge flows are derived from the fundamental epistemology of Unity. The method of derivation itself is not an individualistic process. Instead, this is derived by the rules of Shari'ah (Ahkam) affecting human behavioural transformation. It also passes through the medium of discourse (Ijtihad) leading to consensus (Ijma). On the basis of such rules and consensus are established policy guidance, instruments, institutions and social evaluative functions. The IIE-process now becomes fully active at the level of consumer preference formation. The knowledge-induced basic needs regime of transformation affecting human fulfilment and preference changes in accordance with Shari'ah rules that cause the Tawhidi worldview to be mobilized in the social economy, is termed here as dynamic basic needs menu (Choudhury 1992).

DYNAMIC BASIC NEEDS REGIMES OF DEVELOPMENT ACCORDING TO THE QUR'ANIC AGRICULTURAL MODEL

In light of the Qur'anic agricultural model, the dynamic basic needs menu is defined by,

$$B(\cup_i \cap_{jkl} \theta_{ijkl}, \cup_i \cap_{jkl} X_{ijkl}(\theta_{ijkl}); \{\succeq_{ijkl}{}^c\}).$$

Here i,j,k,l are as defined before (Chapter 3); 'c' denotes the number of consumers. $\{\succeq_{ijkl}{}^c\}$ are preferences of the cth consumer when induced by knowledge formation in relation to the changing knowledge-induced sets of goods. Clearly, B is a positive functional of the parent social well-being function,

$$SW(\cup_i \cap_{jkl} \theta_{ijkl}, \cup_i \cap_{jkl} X_{ijkl}(\theta_{ijkl}); \{\succeq_{ijkl}{}^c\}).$$

Now two representations of B with SW can be determined. First, in the case of Ghazzali and Razi, the entire B is embedded in SW-functionals. Since both of these are evolutionary with respect to knowledge flows, therefore, they can be denoted by evolving concentric forms as shown in figure 7.2.

It is interesting to note what the structure of each of the evolving concentric maps would be. Each evolution is caused by interactions leading to integration in the IIE-model. These phases are then followed by evolution of knowledge and states at the end of each process (Shuratic Process). Thus, figure 7.2 shows that a knowledge flow, say $\{\theta\}$, leads to the dynamic basic needs basket, $\{X(\theta)\}$. This is the f_1-map shown in figure 7.1. Subsequently, $\{X(\theta)\}$ leads to new $\{\theta'\}$-values and the processes of evolution continue through fresh IIE-rounds. Besides this one-directional movement, it is to be noted that inverse relations exist between $\{\theta\}$ and $\{\theta'\}$. This is true both for the case of a particular functional relation between these, and also in the sense of the circular causation and continuity model, where similar processes appear, disappear and reappear. But by the very IIE-model, the functional $\{\theta'\}\rightarrow\{\theta\}$ must mean that f^{-1} exists. But, $f=g_1 o g_2$. Hence, g_1^{-1} and g_2^{-1} must exist. Thus two-directional interrelationships must exist in the triangle as shown.

This result points out that there are recursive interrelationships both preceding as well as following the interrelationships shown in the triangle. At the end of any of these processes an evolution must therefore precede and follow. Thus the evolutionary concentric forms represent the effect of evolutionary triangles in the sense of such forward and backward cause and effect interrelationships. The spanning concentric forms are shown by the dotted line.

SW(.) must also be evolving in the IIE-model. Otherwise, an optimality of SW(.) would eventually mean the optimality of the B(.), and the two will coincide. This would end the knowledge formation process for inter-systemic complementarity. Therefore, the ecological character of such evolving systems must mean that both B(.) and SW(.) must evolve simultaneously. The outward arrows from SW(.) circle in figure 7.2 denote this growth. This is the implication of the learning process and complementarity that always bind the circular deductive and inductive processes together in the IIE-model. Such a recursive nature of the processual chains also suggests that optimal methods are to be replaced in such methodologies by simulative ones (due to perturbations).

We also note importantly, that since diversities are an essential part of the Qur'anic agricultural model, therefore, the triangles will perpetually be in a rotational phase describing the path of the concentric knowledge-induced forms. Thereby, diverse sequences of θ-values and their induced forms, all premised on Tawhid, will perpetually emerge.

The other possibility for the B-SW interrelationship is to allow for imperfect complementarity followed by progressive change as the knowledge induction picks up effectiveness. Now figure 7.3 shows that the SW(.) and B(.) sets will progressively evolve in the direction of the arrows to increase the intersection. This implies greater complementarity between the two sets with increasing knowledge induction. This latter feature is shown in the diagram with [SW(θ,X(θ))1B(θ,)]. In this way, from limited complementarity we obtain increasing complementarity, and then expanding complementarity as the knowledge formation picks up speed. Finally, in such stages, we revert to the conditions of figure 7.2.

Figure 7.2: Monotonic interrelationships between basic needs and the social well-being function

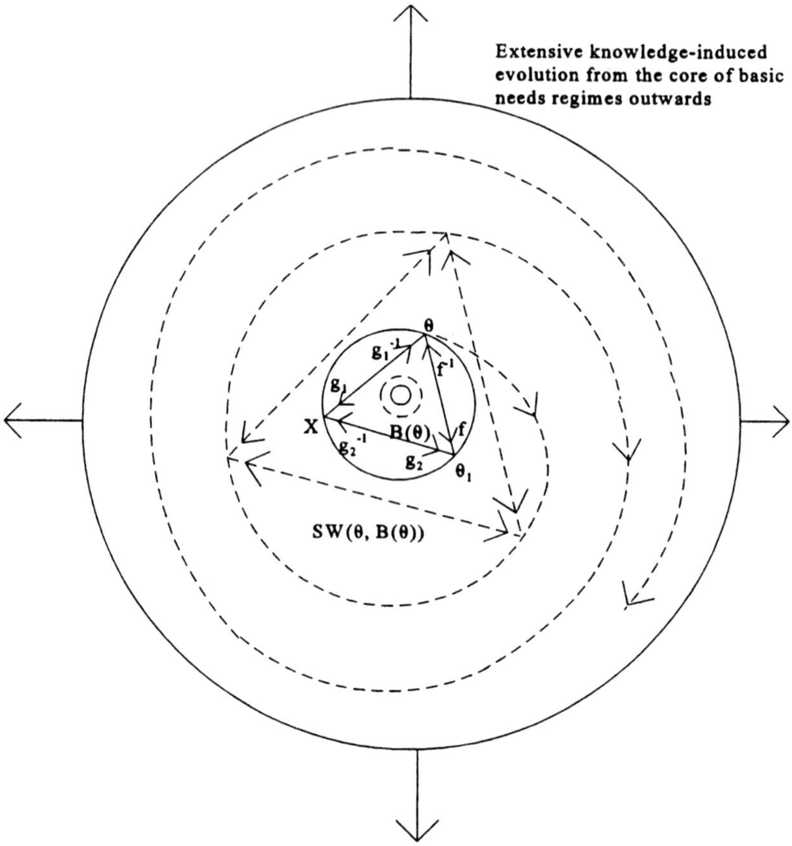

B(θ) denotes basic needs induced by θ.
SW(•) is the social well-being function induced by B(θ).

Figure 7.3: From limiting complementarity to increasing complementarity

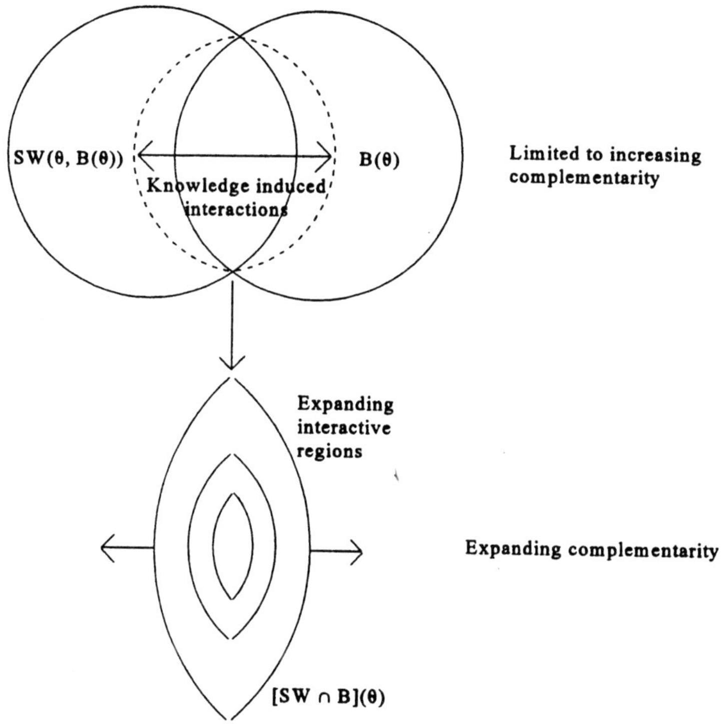

It is not difficult to note that figure 7.2 and the convergence of figure 7.3 to figure 7.2 are cross-sectional views of the Goodly Tree with multifarious interactions, integrations and evolutions. At the same time, each part of these figures is governed by the kind of interrelationships shown in figure 7.1.

RAZI-MASLOW SELF-ACTUALIZATION IN THE KNOWLEDGE-INDUCED FRAMEWORK

Maslow's self-actualization is based on the hierarchy of human fulfilment needs (Maslow 1968). These comprise, physiological needs at the base, followed consecutively by safety, belongingness, self-esteem, and higher moral needs in which are included social justice and truth. We find in such a hierarchy that the moral need at the highest level of self-actualization is made possible by the pre-condition of material need followed by social need. The implication is that physical aspects of basic needs precede the knowledge-induced substance of basic needs. Thus, the material premise of needs and not the primacy of knowledge, determines the epistemology of human consciousness and fulfilment. Now if a basic needs regime of development was to be built upon such a premise of materiality, there will permanently exist the problem as to how social justice and the efficiency component of economic growth are defined. We have noted that it is precisely the absence of a most reduced premise of unity of knowledge that leads into rationalistic ways of determining individual and group-specific preferences and rules of distribution and ownership according to competing individualism and pluralism.

The neoclassical economic school in this regard would equate income distribution with allocation of resources according to the marginal substitution theory of wages. The Marxist would equate wages to the labour theory of value that cannot be functionally determined endogenously in markets; hence, institutional determination of wages and prices becomes necessary. The bargaining between labour unions and management on wage determination is an example of bilateral monopsony, where no particular method of pricing is found to exist except by bilateral conflict resolution involving power and perks (Mansfield 1985).

At the very end, we find that the material premise of basic needs rendering the distribution questions to be decided by conflict between the agents and resources involved, causes trade-off to exist between competing ends. Now the marginal substitution principle of resource allocation enters the scene of decision-making. Interactions get wiped out due to the optimal methods of resource allocation and factor pricing. Even the possibility of incorporating ethical values and of causing evolution to higher levels of moral fulfilment needs, becomes methodologically impossible, unless they are enforced by institutions at the expense of ethical endogeneity. Maslow's hierarchical model of social decisions relating to a basic need regime of development, is now seen to lead into an independence of the knowledge function in the total social action.

Boulding looked at such a total social system in terms of independently constituted preferences of benevolent, malevolent and economic agents (Boulding 1971). The result is a methodological impossibility in explaining conflict resolution by taking recourse to ethical preferences of participation and cooperation as opposed to amoebic competition, which he treats in his knowledge formation concept (Boulding 1967).

Next turning to Razi, we find that there exists no Maslowian kind of hierarchy in Razi's human fulfilment pyramid. The levels of obedience to God (Ubudiyyah) now form a coherent interrelated body of knowledge evolution characterized simply by the intensifying belief system. The latter is simply the matter of evolutionary preferences caused by the induction of knowledge. The following are the levels of Ubudiyyah according to Razi's human fulfilment model. Noor refers to these as the five human attributes that simultaneously represent the universal human needs (Noor 1998): (1) devotional or servitude needs; (2) assistive or supportive needs; (3) uprightness; (4) need for guidance; (5) grace or benefaction needs. Now wherever is the starting point for a basic needs regime of development premised on human fulfilment in Razi's model, we find that an aspect of knowledge is considered to be primal.

We can now appropriately categorize an interrelationship among the θ-value and its derived and cognitive effects. The attribute (1) devotional or servitude needs, can be thought of as a level of Taqwa (God-consciousness) and hence equated to a θ-value. The principal manifestation of Taqwa is indeed to premise all of reality on Tawhid (Ω). (2) Assistive or supportive needs can be identified with the material effects of Shari'ah instruments to attain Justice ('Adl) and goodness (Ehsan). These are the knowledge-augmented goods and services, X(θ). (3) Uprightness is fairness and social justice in worldly dealings. These are the instruments of Shari'ah (Maqasid al-Shari'ah). They carry the precept of 'Adl and Ehsan into the formation of X(θ). (4) Guidance can denote the realization of Shari'ah and a community that gives rise to collective action according to discourse and participation (Shuratic Process). This process denotes the method of deriving rules of Shari'ah (Ahkam as-Shari'ah). Item (5) marks the enjoyment of felicity or social good. This is our social well-being function in terms of the θ-values and X(θ)-values via the route of Shuratic Process and recursive actions of the circular causation model of unified reality (Ω,θ).

In the circular causation and continuity model of unified reality, Razi's knowledge model is converted to the following form: {1: θ((3): 'Adl, Ehsan, Shari'ah instruments)} $\in \Omega \rightarrow_{(4)fs}$ {2:X(θ)}. At the end of this causal relation we obtain the social well-being function, {5:SW}={SW(θ,X(θ))}. Thus, once we have kept Tawhidi epistemology as the primal epistemology and knowledge flows as the starting point of the causal relation, then all other attributes can be combined in different ways to yield the second consequence in the sequence. This is to generate knowledge-induced cognitive forms, {X(θ)}, by basing the rules of social derivation and construction on Shari'ah (f_s). The end result is still the same, that is, the generation of the social product is determined by the same {θ,X(θ)}-tuples.

Such a re-combination of attributes in various ways to come up with the same causation chain as shown, presents a reflection of unity within diversity and the resulting order of complementarities among possibilities. However, Razi's model does not appear to incorporate the continuity feature in it, unless we extend the meaning of (5) to include such an evolutionary perspective with divine benefaction and grace. Then we could say that at the end of stage (5), Ω is reinvoked to give rise to fresh rounds of similar causation. If this extended inference can be made, then Razi's model also clearly manifests the circular causation and continuity of unification of knowledge across hierarchies of agents, variables, relations and systems. We can then re-establish the Qur'anic agricultural model and the Goodly Tree model on the framework of causation, interconnectedness and continuity of knowledge, as formalized before.

Maslow and Razi's self-actualization frameworks of basic need development perspectives can now be compared. In figure 7.4 we show that the premise of self-actualization in Razi's model is the knowledge base which is primordially derived from Tawhid. From such an epistemology, the subsequent knowledge-induced cognitive forms are derived. Hence a progressive self-actualization commences in Razi's model from the very inception of Divine Unity and its evolution across phases of unification of knowledge. The basic needs approach to socioeconomic development is then a progressive evolution of the knowledge-induced complementary processes across endogeneity of markets in conjunction with institutional guidance, interactive preference changes, policies and instruments of their mobilization over phases of change.

In figure 7.4, Maslow's and Razi's self-actualization model appear as inverted pyramids. Razi's model is once again of the tree-type, given either by the Goodly Tree or figure 7.1 in terms of the Qur'anic agricultural model. Maslow's model applied to the tree-type is of the nature of the Evil Tree discussed in the Qur'an (Chapter Ibrahim, verses). We will formalize it in Chapter 10. Its branches do not reach out to the heavens and soon die. This is inferred by the optimality of the self-actualization process at the apex of the triangle. The problem with Maslow's hierarchy is that, being premised on materially reduced concept of the basic need, the process to self-actualization becomes a perceptual experience in pluralism of competing approaches. There is no primal knowledge here to establish unity and complementarity in diversity. The endogenous nature of Maslow's model is based on the repetition of the perceptual experience of material rationality defining phases of moral conduct. Endogeneity in Razi's model is based on the repetition of the circular causation and continuity model of unified reality.

Figure 7.4: Maslow's and Razi's models of human fulfilment

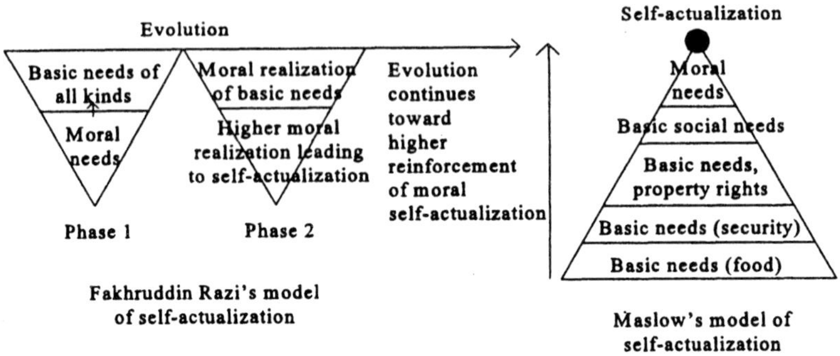

THE CONCEPT OF BASIC NEEDS REGIMES IN RAZI'S AGAINST MASLOW'S HUMAN FULFILMENT MODEL

The inversion of Razi's social pyramid against Maslow's at once reverses many of the implications of the basic needs fulfilment regimes of development and other categories that are linked with the self-actualization goal of human fulfilment. Razi's attributes of God-centred human consciousness make knowledge as the foundation for determining cognitive values. In the field of economics, such cognitive values become knowledge-induced socioeconomic variables. In the field of social security, this is also induced by knowledge. Since Razi pari passu relies on divine knowledge alone as the primordial category, therefore, the knowledge induction is by means of divine knowledge alone. In this system, the concept of basic needs is one of consumption and production of knowledge-induced cognitive forms for human fulfilment. We may say that such a human fulfilment is qualified by its social well-being function, Tazkiyyah and Falah. Dynamic basic needs regimes of development generating such social well-being, when derived from the knowledge-induced divine order, are sustained by the continuous reproduction of knowledge flows. Hence we find that Razi's knowledge model is cohesive in nature and not hierarchical, as in the case of Maslow's.

It is interesting to see that social contractarian models similar to Razi's were also thought out profoundly by Imam Shatibi (Shatibi undated), and in a psychological sense by Ghazzali (Karim undated). In either of these cases, the domain of Shari'ah remains primal in defining the nature of the goods and services with respect to the goal of attaining social well-being or individual well-being. It may however be pointed out that some kind of utilitarianism had entered Ghazzali's concept of ideal state of self-actualization (Fana) and the concept of a social utility state of happiness in Shatibi's Maslaha wal-Istihsan (public purpose) (Choudhury 1993, 1997b). Apart from these observations, Razi's, Ghazzali's and Shatibi's self-actualization models being premised on divine knowledge, were a priori premises for the a posteriori realization of cognitive forms. What we thus find missing in these thinkers is a formalization of the circular causation and continuity model of unified reality that always reproduces the a priori-a posteriori conditions of mind and matter continuity.

It is not that the lived experience of these great thinkers was delinked from Tawhid at each step and in this way combined with the Certainty of Akhira. The problem rather, was a lack of clear delineation of the method to be adopted to integrate the world with Tawhid and Akhira – the a priori with the a posteriori. This was also the deep problem of heteronomy in Kant; the loss of essence in Hume; the separation of matter and mind in Russell; and the continued quest for unification in the sciences (Barrow 1991).

According to Razi, dynamic basic needs regime are simply a production and sustenance of knowledge in all systems. From these emanate the cognitive order of physical reproduction. In Maslow, basic needs are primordial to an organized premise of Unity. Hence, a basic need although a necessity, is competed for. In such a competition, abundance is replaced by scarcity. Even basic needs become scarce commodities. The Qur'anic view on basic needs is that they have been made in abundance for all animate things. This can only be if knowledge is the conscious primal essence of such basic needs. Competition is now replaced by felicity – social well-being.

The agricultural model is one of abundance created by pervasive diversity and linkages. Hence by cause and effect in such a design, waste (Israf) must be reduced. The avoidance of waste for human ecological sustainability is a direct function of knowledge flows that generate consumption preferences in accordance with moderation, modesty and responsibility. In the dynamic basic needs model of human fulfilment, we can only have complementarities among participating entities that are opposed to the idea of competing dichotomy and pluralism. Thus, Maslow's model of human fulfilment is essentially yet another configuration of the occidental model of scarcity that breeds on competition and in turn causes more scarcity. The goal of self-actualization through the abundant reproduction of basic needs in this model, is limited by the occurrence and intensification of competition.

INTERLINKAGES AND DYNAMIC BASIC NEEDS IN MORAL SELF-ACTUALIZATION MODELS

The tree model and the agricultural model both exhibit universal complementarity. We have now also seen that they are models of dynamic basic needs of human fulfilment, as they are analytically premised on the unification of knowledge derived from Tawhidi epistemology. We can then say that the basic needs regime of development is causally premised on extensive sectoral and other interlinkages.

But to sustain interlinkages it is also necessary to generate price stability, efficient factor and capital mobilization and distributive equity. It is no surprise that the Qur'anic agricultural model realizes all these to logically establish sustainability overall.

Since prices, $p(\theta)$, are endogenous variables, they must be affected by θ-values. Hence, the characteristics of abundance, elastic demand and supply of basic needs and the feature of a non-competitive good when supplied in the absence of waste, mean that $p(\theta)$ must also be determined not by sheer unbridled market mechanism, but through the process of interactions as social contracts, between say, farmers and buyers. Such contracts far from being determined by the invisible-hand principle, are visible ones determined in the midst of the Shuratic

Process. For example, abundance of basic needs here does not mean that supply would be so low as not to sustainable prices in order to maintain the supply of basic needs. Hence, a sense of price maintenance is exercised to engender productive basic needs activities in the agricultural sector.

Price maintenance of basic needs means that such goods are to be diversified into resource-based and other sectoral production. Product diversification arising from agricultural inputs and sectoral interlinkages causes prices of such goods to be sustained through multimarkets, input-output characterization and product demand. At the same time, sectoral interlinkages mean that wages and rents, profit-sharing and cost-sharing in agricultural production, will all be causally interlinked with similar ones in other sectors. Choices of technology will be of the 'equally capital-labour-using' type, both of these factors being induced by a cooperative environment of decision-making (i.e induced by θ-values). Consequently, the diffusion of such technologies across interlinked sectors and factors markets, will cause wages and hence prices to be sustained at levels consistent with adequate supply of basic needs.

It is important to note that sustainability of basic needs depends upon fair price levels in the goods and factors markets. Without this, basic needs will not be evolving and hence would not be dynamic. On the other hand, basic needs supported by unsustainable prices and factors, must fall excessively upon the shoulder of governments for provision. This builds social costs. The result at the end would be a production and consumption of basic needs in a wasteful way.

In the Islamic literature, we therefore do not find a characterization of demand function with undue interference by institutions (Islahi 1995). It was also not the practice of Prophet Muhammad to allow undue interference of markets to happen. The non-functioning of due market processes is realized by knowledge-induction of preference changes, production and distributional menus. These in turn create ethicizing market orders. A good example of such ethicizing market conditions is sustainability of the ecological order (Choudhury 1994, Hawley 1986).

Finally, it is now time to bring together the above discussions here to define a dynamic basic need regime. A basic need as a knowledge-induced cognitive form for human fulfilment as a continuous sustainability of all levels of development, means that its diversity will change continuously with the diffusion of knowledge. Knowledge-induced basic needs as opposed to competing kinds of basic needs found in Maslow, and the diversities that knowledge-induced basic needs undergo through ethicizing markets, technology and sectoral linkages, characterize the dynamic nature of basic needs.

THE QUR'ANIC AGRICULTURAL MODEL OF HUMAN ECOLOGY

We will understand by human ecology the conditions of social well-being that are sustained by interrelationships within the political economy and between this and resource endowments. Characterization of the concept of human ecology by attributes of social justice and dynamic conditions, tie ecology to intertemporal frameworks of reference. But this intertemporality is much more in terms of interacting generations, rather than simply across all generations (Temkin 1995). The latter concept of saving has been found to be grossly inequitable and inefficient in present times. Examples are the inequitable collection of pension premiums from the young for old-age claimants; the tax burden on the young to take care of needs of the future generations that remain indeterminate (Phelps 1989, Gauthier 1986). Instead now, the knowledge-induced concept of ecological awareness means allocation of due resources across generations that can interact in direct interface. At best then, we can think of the present and the next generation of one's children and no further. This limited over-lapping generations outlook is necessary in order to make sense of the precision of intertemporal saving and equitable allocation.

In such a scale of knowledge-induced interactively determined distributions, sheer saving is replaced by responsibility of conduct at the present. Such responsibility translates into preference formation in favour of basic needs regimes of development and social change. The knowledge factor now transforms all consequential factors, such as, technology, pricing, polity-market-ecological interrelations. The concept of sustainability is to preserve the emergence of dynamic basic needs regimes of development under a human ecological order that is premised on knowledge generating possibilities. This does not mean cumbersome institutional levies on assets, incomes and wealth to unduly finance unknown targets of future generational needs.

Population relationships in the Qur'anic agricultural model of ecology and human needs fulfilment: economic demography of aging

One of the important issues to note in human ecology is population change. In a dynamic basic needs regime of development with its corresponding interrelationships among preferences, technology, resource allocation, consumption, production and distributional menus, population structure and size, are also accordingly affected while contributing to total sustainability in a complementary way. In this framework, dynamic basic need regimes of development is matched by a balance between population structure and size. This balance being determined by knowledge, is left to the choices of families under guidance and interactions on the basis of Shari'ah rules. Such rules now attend not merely to population planning as such, but rather to this in the perspective of the general systems of interrelationships that a human ecological orientation of dynamic basic needs contributes to a Shari'ah-based concept of sustainability. The Shuratic Process of the IIE-model once again becomes instrumental in determining the place of population structure and size in relation to the changing facets of the dynamic basic need regime with its extensive systemic interlinkages and sustainability criteria.

There is a close interrelationship between the nature of demographic transition and socioeconomic development. Such interrelationships have deepening impact on the institution of family, labour market and social interactions (Choudhury 1996, Coale 1989). The dynamic basic needs regimes of socioeconomic development in the Qur'anic agricultural model and the consequential balance between population size and structure, imply that population growth must be of the 'stable' type and not the 'stationary' type (zero rate of growth). Thus a young population structure, capable of generating a healthy social product for the well-being of the present generation and the immediately interacting future generation, sustains economic growth and distribution simultaneously. The stationary rate of growth is experienced by a population either at the earliest or during the aging phases of demographic transition. In either of these cases less social product is generated to finance the social security needs and entitlements of the dependent population.

With respect to labour force activities, the earliest phase of demographic change pushes children into the agricultural work force, whereby, human resource development remains low. In the fourth phase of aging demography, substitution of leisure for work lowers the saving ratio and causes higher claims on accumulated savings in social security fund. Now when labour productivity falls in this phase, there is a substitution of capital for labour in production. But overall productivity must yet remain low on its own, as the need for savings must be financed by higher interest rates. This will be to the detriment of spending in general. The resulting socioeconomic debilities are higher unemployment rate, lower total productivity, higher interest rate and lower investment and spending in general than in the case of the middle-aged structure of a stable population in demographic transition.

When the socioeconomic debilities arise in the demographic transition as characterized by stationary and stable population growth rates, complementarity and diversities cannot be sustained in production and distribution of resources. With this comes about inequitable distribution. But worse still, there is a decline in both economic efficiency (e.g. economic growth) and distributive equity (e.g. wealth and income distribution) across phases of stationary population growth in demographic transition.

It is worse still when mortality rate exceeds the fertility rate. This is particularly associated with the fourth phase of demographic transition. Now the problems noted with the aging population is accentuated to the extent that either government deficits associated with financing social security, increase phenomenally, or a privatization of the economy to take up the slack drives markets into unsustainability. The conditions of social equity and economic efficiency together worsen acutely. The environment and ecology fall at the mercy of the marginalizing market forces towards generating production, competition and economic growth.

Most Western nations today are in such an unsustainable social and economic predicament. Worse still, global capitalism is evidently driving developing countries into the same state by having them organize production around models and neo-liberal institutionalism, that in the first instance caused the impoverishing conditions of populations and adverse economic change to occur.

Economic demography in the Qur'anic systems model

The Qur'anic agricultural model of social well-being does not target the criterion of production and consumption but rather social well-being with social goods. In this way, the benefits of abundance in the dynamic basic needs regimes of socioeconomic development sustains complementarity between a stable population change and a robust economic growth with distributive equity. The youngness of population structure, the possibility to generate the social product and direct resources towards social security and entitlement, can sustain total productivity in the midst of extensive complementarities and diversities of linkages between the agricultural and other sectors. All these establish sustainability. Both the human ecological and physical ecology are now maintained by the very internal process of interactions, integration and evolution in the Qur'anic agricultural model. The interactive causation among the institutions of family, community, markets and polity would now respond with pervasive complementarities happening among themselves in the midst of sustainability.

If we are to interpret the stable population demographic transition and its epoch of abundance with the sign of divine bliss on earth, then the contrary kinds of demographic transition cannot enjoy the same bliss. The social implications of the latter on the institutions of family, community, markets, human relations and other, must be morally abhorring. The demographic transition model alternates between its phases, whereas the prescription of the Qur'anic agricultural model remains permanent in bliss. In this respect we can associate the following verse that carries this profound meaning respecting alternation in well-being as humanity abandons the path of dynamic basic need regimes of abundance, sustainability and divine bliss, and brings upon it deprivation (Qur'an 6, verse 6): 'See they not how many of those before them We did destroy? – Generations We had established on the earth, in strength such as We have not given to you – for whom We poured out rain from the skies in abundance, and gave (fertile) streams flowing beneath their (feet): yet for their sins We destroyed them, and raised in their wake fresh generations (to succeed them).'

In the end therefore, the picture provided in figure 7.5 can explain the system of interrelationships between population and the socioeconomic order in the light of the systemic interlinkages of a dynamic basic needs regime of development.

CONCLUSION

The Qur'anic tree model and agricultural model are rich systems of universal complementarities and diversities that explain the widest range of human realities. These span from the plane of thought being premised on Tawhidi epistemology to their positivistic application in the knowledge-induced cognitive order. Nothing seems to be left out from the rich embodiment of these models.

The discussions on dynamic basic needs and pervasive interlinkages that are generated by the Qur'anic tree model and agricultural model are found to have support in the works of the greatest of Islamic thinkers. Of these we have examined briefly Fakhruddin Razi's theory of knowledge and compared it to Maslow's self-actualization theory of social psychology. We concluded that only knowledge premised on a perfectly unified perspective of reality is made the epistemology and no other premise can generate a coherent view of human fulfilling reality. It is for this reason that the knowledge-centred worldview of the Tawhidi order remains by far a most significant epistemological breakthrough of any socio-scientific thought.

Figure 7.5: Population in the context of human ecological interrelationships

The concept of ethicized markets makes grassroots democracy and markets interact. Embedded in such ethicizing transformation are decision-making involving SD, HRD and POP, as shown by the directions of arrows.

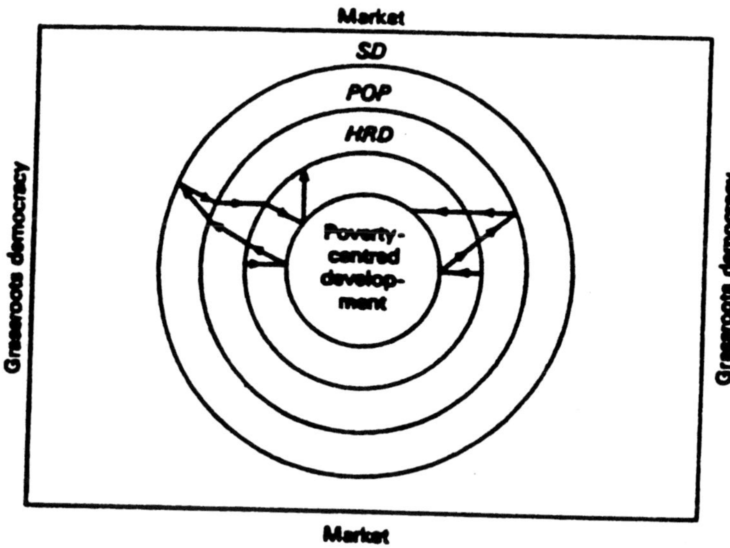

HRD : human-resource development
POP : population
SD : sustainable development

Source: Choudhury, M.A.. (1993). **Comparative Development Studies: In Search of the Worldview** (London, Eng.: Macmillan, New York, NY: St. Martin's Press) p. 2.

CHAPTER 8

DECISION-MAKING MODEL IN ISLAMIC POLITICAL ECONOMY

In this chapter a theory of decision-making in Islamic political economy is conceptualized in comparative perspectives to bring out the extensively complementary nature of the socioeconomic activities and relations underlying such decision-making. The central contrast between Islamic political economy and other ones in respect to the nature of decision-making is shown to be premised on the distinctive epistemology of the Oneness of God (Tawhid) that guides conduct and social action in the former.

PRINCIPAL OBJECTIVE OF THIS CHAPTER

The principal objective of this chapter is to place the field of decision-making within the broad framework of comparative political economy. We will then show by a natural process of analytical deduction that the only complete redress to such a treatment of socioeconomic decision-making can be accomplished in the Islamic political economy. This concept is explained as well in a comparative framework for our purposes. The natural and logical transmission of the methods of a knowledge-centred universe of Islamic political economy and decision-making in its midst, confirms that the precepts of Islamic political economy emanate from a logical and consistent analytical message arising from Qur'anic epistemology including the Prophet guidance (Sunnah) (Choudhury & Malik 1992, Choudhury et al 1997). No particular inhibitions and encumbrances need therefore be attached to the aura of the Islamic in such a knowledge-centred universe of political economy and decision-making in it.

A COMPARATIVE OUTLOOK ON POLITICAL ECONOMY

To start up our discourse on the nature of Islamic decision-making which is indispensably social in nature, one needs to understand the concept of the social and the embedding of the individual and groups within the nexus of the social whole in Islamic perspective. It is to explain such a nexus that we must correctly turn to the premise of political economy rather than simply to the economy, organization, institution or the polity taken separately.

The study of political economy has been differently invoked in the literature, ranging from it being treated as a study of the interrelationships between the laws of production and the ownership of wealth, the conflict between labour and capitalists on the issue of economic distributions, and the valuation of goods in terms of labour input that goes into the production of such a good (George 1925). Some writers have also characterized the study of political economy as the interface between economics and politics (Staniland 1985). Yet others have seen it as organizational behaviour influencing the social functions of distribution and control (Mommsen 1989). In the highly macroeconomic scale, political economy can also be construed as the study of power dynamics of world-systems that are formed by the fragmentation of the global region into capitalistic domination of smaller regions (Wallerstein 1979). Only recently do we find a treatment of political economy in terms of interdependence. But here too there are two approaches. First, there is the group of writers who treat political economy in the framework of dependency theory between the periphery and the centre and the role of polity in this relationship as a facilitator of transfer payments that sustains the periphery-centre dependency relationship (Matthews 1983). On the other hand, there is the group that examines the study of global interdependence as a nexus of interactions among polity, society, economy and the global order (Koizumi 1993, Choudhury & Hamat 1997).

On the issue of the political economy of decision-making one must consider organizational behaviour emanating from agent-specific preferences. Such individual preferences are then seen to be aggregated in some sense into the preferences of the organization. In this complex of agent-specific roles, organizational and institutional preferences reflect the aggregative behavioural attributes of the micro-agents. For example, in such a milieu, Sen points out that the concept of the moral standing of the market is a consequentialism of the basic preferences of transactors. If the consumer preferences are of the moral type, then Sen argues that their aggregation into market exchange will result in ethical markets, and vice versa (Sen 1985). The argument here is of an utilitarian or neoclassical economic sense. On the side of institutional utilitarianism, the deontological consequences of ethical decision-makers are seen here to be summed up by means of the utilitarian social utility function to yield a lateral aggregation of individual ethical utility functions (Harsanyi 1953, Hammond 1987). On the side of economic neoclassicism, the formation of underlying agent-specific preference maps assume transitivity of results to explain allocation of public goods and constitutional contracts as rational choices under condition of full information, even though this may be in a bounded sense (Buchanan 1975, Simon 1987).

In the field of comparative political economy the issue of resource allocation and control is an important one. It is around this area that some serious analytical discourse was carried out in the history of economic thought as problems of determining what are to be ownership controls, property rights, due and just pricing and wages. The theory of value has thus demanded the most significant attention in economic thought (Stigler 1960). In this area, prices and wages and through these, the determination of property and ownership, hence control and decision-making finally, are inextricably linked to the utility and utilitarian basis of exchange. Without the utility base in neoclassical economics and without the notion of market-clearance in classical economics, no prices and hence value of goods and services, can be conceived of. In either of these economic epistemology, rational, predictable behaviour of sorts, information-completeness and marginal substitution, are indispensable assumptions. Hence, complementarity cannot exist in the 'global' sense, although this may apply locally in special circumstances. On the other hand, marginal substitution applies universally.

The consequence of such approaches to valuation and decision-making is myopia to specific agent-centred, knowledge-centred and explicit reference to interactions in the decision-making process. Shackle points out the utter unrealism of such prescriptive models of human behaviour premised on optimality-equilibrium preconditions (Shackle 1971).

For our purposes, political economy will mean a study of 'global' interactions among generalized systems. In this framework are addressed the meanings of value, pricing, resource control and resource allocation within complexity. Therefore, a marginal substitution and optimality-equilibrium models of behaviour do not help. Much more, they destroy human realism of the cooperative worldview. Valuation of prices, socioeconomic decisions, property rights, organizational control and their embedding in the generic social contract, are not reflected in the reality of the process-centred dynamics and inherent ethical issues underlying conflict and conflict resolution. Such major issues can only be addressed by taking recourse to an interacting and cooperating model of man and the human ecology (Hawley 1986).

The ethically neutral element of socioeconomic decision-making is reflected even in alternative methods of comparative political economy. For instance, in the macroeconomic and institutional designs of Keynesianism, decision-makers remain absent. Governments do not appear as agents but as sources of stabilization policies. Monetarism too has nothing to do with decision-making as a behavioural concept. On the other hand, constitutional perspectives of public economics either become entrenched in benign market driven concepts of power-sharing, and this is the Hayekian market catallytic order (Hayek 1967); or else they remain competing models of public choice (Nordhaus 1975). None of the above works afford an explicitly interactive view of decision-making processes (Choudhury 1996a).

Thus at the end of the above discourse, we find that there is a keen interrelationship among the following premises: First is the nature of preference formation. Second is the nature of ensuing aggregation to define a social contract. Third is the determining causality generated by the domain of political economy. This is seen as a nexus of social, political and economic interactions in terms of preceding forms of preference formation and their social aggregations.

In the midst of these intrinsic relationships, it is clear that the study of decision-making is to be carried out in terms of the interrelationships caused by the embedding of group-specific preferences within social preferences. Just as social preferences are aggregatively formed by individual preferences, so also social decision-making must be studied in terms of an embedding of such group-specific decision-making within the social milieu. The process of such a decision-making must then be studied through hierarchies of organizations and institutions through which social decisions proceed while affecting the aggregation process (Fischer 1986). In this way, while the tripartite issues mentioned above, are taken up at each level of analysis and social hierarchy, the epistemological questions of neoclassicism and utilitarianism continue on to define the landscape of received economic doctrines (Quinton 1989).

THE POLITICAL ECONOMY OF DECISION-MAKING

Here is how socioeconomic decision-making is explained in an utilitarian framework with rational choice and information completeness either in symmetrical or asymmetrical situations (Hirschleifer 1987): Let there be n-number of agents (may be taken in the form of independent groups) each endowed by a utility function, $u_i(\mathbf{x}_i)$, where, $\mathbf{x}_i=\{x_{i1},x_{i2},..,x_{im}\}$ denotes a vector of m-number of goods or services, j=1,2,..,m, for the ith individual (group). From our previous arguments, it is possible that some of the goods and services in the $\mathbf{x}_{ij}$-bundle can be complements, but such complements will once again group themselves in substitutable bundles overall. Contrarily, if 'global' complementarity existed among the bundle of goods, then the income of the ith individual (group), Y_i, spent on the goods will be given by the equation,

$$Y_i=\Sigma_{j=1}^m p_{ij}.x_{ij}.$$

Now when, Y_i=constant for a given bundle, then $dY_i=0$. This implies that, $\Sigma_{j=1}^m p_{ij}.dx_{ij}=0$. If all goods were complements of each other, this equation would imply that, $p_{ij}.dx_{ij}=0$, for each j=1,2,..m. That is, either of the following conditions must hold: Every p_{ij}, i=1,2,..,n, j=1,2,..,m, is zero, implying free goods, and hence, no markets and exchange for such goods. Otherwise, $dx_{ij}=0$, for each i=1,2,..,n, j=1,2,..,m, implying a constant amount of each good bought. This is the case of equilibrium and optimality with full information .Furthermore, since this case is true for all levels of incomes, therefore, such continuous optimality-equilibrium states across all levels of incomes, suggest that no market transactions can exist. Only a hegemonic authority can cause such states to occur. Examples are the Communist Politbureau and the complete welfare state. Both of these are unreal and absurd cases of decision-making, which otherwise involve much interactions.

Consequently, some dx_{ij} must be negative, and this generates marginal substitution among the reconstituted bundle of goods. In such a case, optimality-equilibrium is once again established via the route of marginal substitution among bundles of goods. The muteness of interactions remains and some form of full-information condition must be assumed.

We cannot get out of such preconditions of optimality, equilibrium and independence, even by assuming information asymmetry, for consider $x_{ij}=x_{ij}(s_{ij})$, where, s_{ij} denotes information to the ith individual relating to the jth good, i=1,2,..,m, j=1,2,..,n. In such a state, $dY_i=0$, must once again imply that $dx_{ij}(s_{ij}) = (\partial x_{ij}/\partial s_{ij}).ds_{ij} = 0$. Thus the implication of constant asymmetric power once again results for each level of income. How can there be now a functional concept of power (information) asymmetry other than hegemony or pre-assignment of optimal-equilibrium states as mentioned above?

On the other hand, let us see what results in the general case, by making Y_i dynamic with respect to s_{ij}. Now, such an information-augmented variation in income is given by,

$$dY_i/ds_{ij} = \Sigma_{j=1}^{m} [p_{ij}(\partial x_{ij}/\partial s_{ij}) + x_{ij}(s_{ij})(\partial p_{ij}/\partial s_{ij})].$$

Applying rational choice theory to asymmetric information implies that, $\partial x_{ij}/\partial s_{ij} > 0$, $\partial p_{ij}/\partial s_{ij} < 0$, due to the effect of the information flow s_{ij}. Consequently, $[p_{ij}(\partial x_{ij}/\partial s_{ij}) + x_{ij}(s_{ij})(\partial p_{ij}/\partial s_{ij})]$ can attain all possible signs including the zero value. This result also implies that goods with all kinds of price elasticities of demand exist in the bundle. But since each such term cannot be individually positive or negative due to the existence of asymmetric information and its effect on the p_{ij} and x_{ij}, as shown above, therefore, a segmentation of the market between types of goods according to the effect of information asymmetry on them, must hold true. This is once again the meaning of marginal substitution between such goods.

The existence of moral hazards now also implies that risk-averters will control risk. Hence, Y_i will attain an optimal value with respect to s_{ij}. In such a situation of optimality and equilibrium, the conditions of risk-return trade-off exists. All the conditions of neoclassical economic rationality are now back in the analysis of the general case mentioned above. One cannot therefore, discern a case of complementarity at large under conditions of moral hazard and information asymmetry.

A UTILITY-BASED DECISION-MAKING CRITERION

Now let us narrow down the basket of goods $\mathbf{x}_i$ to risk and return for the ith investor, i=1,2,..,n. Since s_{ij} now denotes risk to the ith investor from the jth choice, therefore, $\mathbf{x}_i=(x_{ij},s_{ij})$. Because of the existence of marginal substitution between these ends, we describe the ith investor's utility function by, $u_i=u_i(x_{ij},s_{ij})$, i=1,2,..,n.

From these utility functions is constructed the organizational social utility function with regards to the jth good. That is,

$$w_j=\sum_{i=1}^{n} u_i(x_{ij},s_{ij}).$$

From this, the total welfare criterion of the organization with respect to all shareholders and risk-return tuples is given by (Mansfield 1990),

$$w=\sum_{j=1}^{m} w_j = \sum_{i=1}^{n}\sum_{j=1}^{m} u_i(x_{ij},s_{ij}).$$

The last expression can be interpreted in various ways under conditions of marginal substitution, optimality and equilibrium. All of these are consequences of the neoclassical form of rational economic behaviour. Let us look at these:

Let the decision-makers be divided into two categories – those with more information (R) and those with less information on alternatives (P). Because of the independence of the utility functions shown additively, we can write w in terms of separable functions with their own j-baskets of goods and services. Hence, $w=w_R(x_R,s_R) + w_P(x_P,s_P)$.

Furthermore, the marginal substitution between all the inner variables shown in the above expression means, that they are described along a well-determined welfare surface for the organization. Collective decision-making among the R and P types of shareholders is shown here to be subject to power conflicts based on the extent to which marginal substitution can be realized between the agents, their goods and risk-return preferences. The existence of well-determined surfaces is caused by the assumption of marginal substitution. This in turn leads to the existence of optimality and equilibrium for R, P and the collective.

While the above is a static form of resource and utility allocation among competing agents, a dynamic form can be similarly constructed in terms of technological change. The essential point to note is that despite any technological induction, the conditions of marginal substitution all through, cause well-determined surfaces to exist. This nicety consequently aids in pricing the risk-return to various agents and yields optimality-equilibrium state. Thus, decision-making must necessarily be governed by rational economic behaviour and must become benign of interactions at the points of optimality and equilibrium. Thus, decision-making must necessarily be governed by rational behavoiur and must become benign of interactions at the points of optimality and equilibrium. The well-determined surfaces are unreal creations of such interaction-benign decision-making generating market values of relative risk-return pricing. Besides, such prices must yield to market consequentialism and thus must marginalize at will the less productive and the less appealing to economically rational decisions. Nothing more moral can be expected from unbridled market competition and exchange (Sen 1990).

DIAGRAMMATIC EXPLANATION OF RESOURCE ALLOCATION IN NON-INTERACTIVE CASES

Figure 8.1 shows the two cases implied by welfare allocation among R and P by means of the risk-return choices across such shareholders. Due to market consequentialism, we have the following cases:

Case 1: Allocation in favour of R, is shown by x_R in diagram 8.1a. This in turn gives the welfare allocation in favour of R, as shown in diagram

8.1b. Such agents are also risk-averters because of their access to higher information. Similarly, we show the allocations for the P- shareholders.

Along the technological-induced trajectory, the allocations of welfare and goods with asymmetric information is shown by the trajectories OT_RT_R' for R, and by OT_PT_P' for P. Here the optimal welfare surfaces for R and P are l_Rl_R', L_Pl_P', respectively. Together the envelope of the two surfaces is l_Rl_P'

We note for each of these case there are corresponding optimal decision-making points on the surfaces of the production possibility curve L_1L_1', the corresponding L_2L_2' etc. The resource allocation (risk-return) trajectories are marked by OSS′ for R and by OQQ′ for P. Market consequentialism prevails to determine the selection of the mutually exclusive trajectories, OT_RT_R', OT_PT_P' etc.

Next in figure 8.1, we examine yet another kind of resource allocation under conditions of information asymmetry. When say, P gets disadvantaged by the information flows to R, although consequentialism would now rule out a moral standing of the market, yet governments may like to intervene in order to alter the allocation in ways that cause the welfare of the disadvantaged to be increased, even though this may be to the disadvantage of the more fortunate in society (those with more information). In such social allocations, Rawls' (1971) Original Position is a point like 'a' on or near to the 45-degrees line-trajectory from the origin. Rawls' Difference Principle states, that even if such a point was near to the 45-degrees line, OG, but in the interior of the surfaces L_RL_P', the allocation would be socially acceptable. Now the corresponding allocation of risk-return would also be near the 45-degrees line OH despite being inside the optimal production frontier L_1L_1' or L_2L_2'. There is obviously a loss of efficiency now in favour of social equity due to the above kinds of allocations. Indeed this is yet another example of marginal substitution or trade-off between economic efficiency and distributive equity.

Figure 8.1: Nature of optimal-equilibrium decision-making

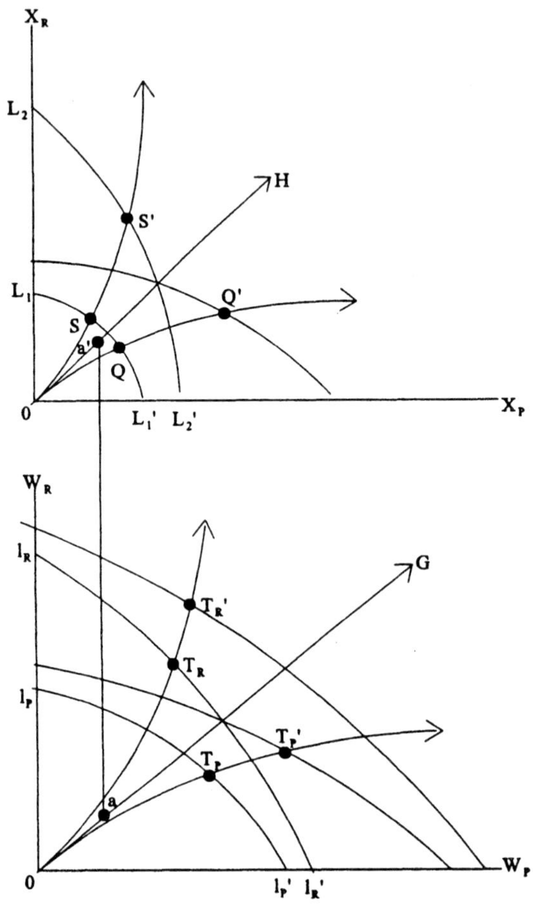

We now summarize by noting that neither for unbridled market transformation nor with policy interventions is it possible to resolve the problem of trade-off between economic efficiency and distributive equity that thoroughly pervades all of neoclassical economic reasoning and institutionalism, preference formation and the concept of optimality-equilibrium, as these are established by the interactions benign picture of decision-making in resource allocation. The case of information asymmetry does not help, as this is yet another manifestation of unbridled market exchange in which competition remains embedded in markets subjected to price discrimination monopoly behaviour.

In all of these, there is no redress to a meaningful concept of political economy of decision-making. Organizational behaviour is seen to be simply an aggregative transformation of individual or group-specific preferences. Fundamentally, such preferences and thereby, technologies and policies affecting institutional change, all remain exogenous factors in the transformation process. The micro-level picture remains epistemologically different from the macro-level picture and its treatment of the ethico-economic issues are disparate. Consequently, a permanent kind of dualism and methodological pluralism pervades economic theory. This is represented as much by methods that are differentiated between systems as those that embody system.

Despite the works of Collander (1984), Rawls (1971) North (1981), Olson (1965), Harsanyi (1955), Buchanan (1971), Arrow (1974), Hammond (1987) and Srinivasan (1985), to name a few [illegible] endogenous treatment of institutions and the political state in politi[illegible]conomy, the methodology of optimality-equilibrium in preferences formation and resource allocation remained unchanged. Consequently, it has not been possible for neoclassical economics and its prototypes to develop and explain a process-oriented theory of endogenous behaviour that would be relationally embodied in political economy.

SEARCH FOR THE EPISTEMOLOGY OF AN ENDOGENOUS POLITICAL ECONOMY OF DECISION-MAKING

We must therefore search for such a methodology of an inter- and intra-systemic process-oriented preference endogeneity that enables us to study decision-making within political economy as an endogenous epiphenomenon. It will be shown that the emergence of such a methodology epistemologically emanates from the principle of universal complementarity across hierarchies of agents (preferences), variables, relations and systems affecting resource allocation and social well-being functions. Such a methodology will logically annul traces of marginal substitution of resource allocation, and instead, premise the process-oriented study of resource allocation on interactions that lead to social integration and creative evolution across phases of decision-making. The social and private decision-making are now interactively unified together. Society, economy and polity are interactively made to establish rules of conduct and ethical guidance. Such an extensive methodology of unification through the process of interactions, integration and creative evolution would apply both to the market order and institutions at the micro- and macro-levels.

Epistemological inquiry involves theory construction from the premise of a worldview that subsequently governs every stage of a consistent treatment of and inferences drawn from such a worldview. The understanding of a process-oriented worldview of unification that is causally germane in an interactive, integrative and dynamically creative worldview, must thus be premised on a distinctive epistemology.

We will now define a few key concepts (Choudhury 1993). Other ones will be taken up as they arise:

Unity of systems in a 'globally' interrelated creative scenario will mean the Stock of Knowledge that can provide the epistemology and then guide it in understanding the intrinsic complementarity among agents, variables, relations and systems in hierarchies of change. The precept of Unity must thus be irreducibly unique, not rendered to the mental roaming of rationalism. This is because the Unitary irreducible premise is the essential premise of meanings and forms of the created order.

Unification of systems is the process premised on the derivation of knowledge flows from the Stock. It is thereby, the actual process that explains complementarity inter- and intra-systems. Since the flows of knowledge are derived from the Stock, they carry the essence of the Stock. This marks the principle of universal complementarity as the process that establishes endogenous inter-connectedness among hierarchies of agents, variables, relations and systems. But the interrelationships so formed, described and evolved, remain embedded in a domain of profound diversities within unity.

Interactions are discursive phenomena of the creative domain. They stand for the causation of endogeneity of knowledge flows, the resulting preference formation and continuity across hierarchies of agents, variables, relations and systems. When interactions occur simply in the human system, the generic system is taken as the nexus among polity, economy, society and science. When extensive forms of creative interactions are invoked, then too the anthropic presence is required to enable the observation, understanding and organization of rules of the creative order and the issues at hand. In this way, discursions form relational mappings between the natural world and the human domain. Now the concept of decision-making expands to the study of such extensive interrelations. Thereby, we come to have decisions on the nature of science, the ecological order and the role of morality in these.

Interactions being discursions in this broad sense of the term, are essentially knowledge flows. Hence, every interaction is a realization of a unit of knowledge flow. Since discursions in the relational order of creation must be pervasive, therefore, such a universe of functional forms is pervasive in knowledge flows. All of these uniquely emanate from the epistemology of Unity as the Stock of Knowledge.

Integration is a convergent stage of interactions leading to a consensus or agreement on issues at hand. Again in the human system, integration would apply to the convergence in decisions processed through the medium of interactions. In the creative domain, integration is the state of a knowledge-induced equilibrium attained by the functional forms of interrelationships between the human order and the creative order, as explained above. An integrative decision-making emanating from the process-oriented interactive order of knowledge flows, reflects the event of unification. The discursively process-oriented interrelationships establish the principle of universal complementarity. Now since knowledge flows remain pervasive across hierarchies of agents, variables, relations and systems, therefore, the epiphenomenon of complementarity, diversity and unification become pervasive as well.

Evolution is creative change to higher levels of knowledge flows. Evolution is the logical consequence of interactions leading to integration. Such a process now enables the pervasiveness of knowledge flows to carry the same process to higher levels of interactions followed by integrations, and so on. An evolution is thus a knowledge-induced creative change carried through in a process by means of the sequencing of interactions and integrations, as knowledge flows are pervasively derived from the epistemology of Unity and rendered functional in the real world.

In causing evolution, the pervasiveness of interactions transmit integration and evolutionary change via the medium of complementary interrelationships among knowledge-induced forms. Hence, evolution becomes the cause and effect of circular interrelations between knowledge flows and their induced cognitive forms across hierarchies of agents, variables, relations and systems.

Process is the completion of one circular relationship, such as, interactions → integration → evolution. The knowledge-centred universe is pervasive of such processes across hierarchies of agents, variables, relations and systems. Everywhere the principle of universal complementarity and diversity within unity prevails. This principle totally negates dualism and pluralism that are found in rationalist philosophy. Instead, the process-orientation establishes a circular causation and continuity model of unified reality of creation (Choudhury 1994a).

FORMALIZATION OF THE KNOWLEDGE-INDUCED PROCESS-ORIENTATION WORLDVIEW

We can now provide a more detailed formalization of the process-oriented worldview of the knowledge-centred universe. At the outset one notes that the concept of process and evolution here is not of the Darwinian category that results in systemic pluralism and not complementarities (Hull 1988). It is not of the type given by Whitehead (1979) and Riley on Kant (1993), in which ontological categories are premised on a rationalistic, and hence, pluralistic conception of God as the source of knowledge. It is also not of the type conceptualized by Bohr (Kafatos & Nadeau 1990), in which the concept of complementarity means a problem to see whether complete physical realities, such as quantum mechanics and relativity theory, can be unified together by means of space-time and position-momentum criteria. The duality of all such systems have persisted by the assumption of completeness of all such systems. On the other hand, in a knowledge-induced reality, no system can assume a completeness. Completeness exists only in the realm of the Stock.

In dynamical knowledge-induced systems, social and private decision-making are taken up in the unified framework of knowledge flows that interlink the epistemology of Divine Unity with the anthropic realization of all components of the socio-scientific order. The ontological question is now of prime importance, after it has been either left out or conjured to non-functionality in occidental and many Eastern epistemologies (Rucker 1983).

The following stages are considered for a formalization of the interactive-integrative-evolutionary (IIE) worldview of Divine Unity and unification of knowledge:

Stage 1 (S_1):

Knowledge flows are generated, starting by an elementary interaction (i, now i=1) across hierarchies of the following factors: agents (preferences) (a); variables considered in relation to an issue at hand, e.g. economic efficiency and distributive equity (j); functional relations as diversities, such as models of complementarity against neoclassicism of marginal substitution (k); given system (l). Now a unit of knowledge flow corresponding to the elementary interaction, i=1, is denoted by θ_{ajkl}^{1}. These are derived from the Stock (S) by means of appropriate rules (mappings), denoted by f_{s1} for the interaction 1:

$$S_1: \Omega \rightarrow_{fs1} \theta_{ajkl}^{1}. \text{ Hence, } f_{s1}(\Omega)=\theta_{ajkl}^{1} \in \Omega.$$

Stage 2 (S_2):

The knowledge flow, θ_{ajkl}^{1}, is now simultaneously mapped 'onto' creative order to generate a creative form as observation, X_{ajkl}^{1}, via a mapping denoted by f_1 for the interaction 1.

$$S_2: \theta_{ajkl}^{1} \rightarrow_{f1} X_{ajkl}^{1}. \text{ Hence, } f_1(\theta_{ajkl}^{1})=X_{ajkl}^{1}.$$

Stage 3 (S_3):

The interactions between S_1 and S_2 continue in circular fashion invoking greater comprehensions of f_{s1} and f_1, as such interactions continue by discursions across (a,j,k,l). We now generalize the interactions to i. i may assume values in the natural number system, when $i=1,2,..,N_1,..,N_2,...$ i may also assume values in the real number system or in higher space-systems (Dewitt 1992). Since an interaction is a unit of knowledge flow and a result of discourse taken in this broadest sense of the socio-scientific systems, therefore, both polity-economy-society interactions as well as scientific interactions with the human presence in it, are invoked as interactive decision-making.

The circular flows between S_1 and S_2 generate newer stages, S_1^i, S_2^i, according to increasing comprehensions of f_{s1} and f_1 with the diffusion of interactions (knowledge flows). We write the resultant socio-scientific order, $S(N_1)$, after N_1-number of interactions as follows:

$$S(N_1) = \lim(i \to N_1)[S_1^i \cap S_2^i] = \lim(i \to N_1)[(f_{si} \cap f_i)\{\theta_{ajkl}{}^i, X_{ajkl}{}^i(\theta_{ajkl}{}^{Ni})\}]$$

$$= (f_s(N_1) \cap f(N_1))\{\theta_{ajkl}{}^{N1}, X_{ajkl}{}^{N1}(\theta_{ajkl}{}^{N1})\}$$

$$= F(\theta_{ajkl}{}^{N1}, X_{ajkl}{}^{N1}(\theta_{ajkl}{}^{N1})\}.$$

Here, $F = (f_s(N_1) \cap f(N_1))$ forms composite mappings that are established by the necessary and sufficient conditions caused by the epistemological primacy of Ω over the entire domain of knowledge-induced created values, $\{\theta_{ajkl}{}^{N1}, X_{ajkl}{}^{N1}(\theta_{ajkl}{}^{N1})\}$. $S(N_1)$ denotes an integration over the limiting interactions taken from $i=1 \to N_1$. Such values taken over limiting interactions, such as N_1, N_2, etc. denote Integrations, $S(N_i)$, arising from the embedded interactions at the limiting points. One notes the importance of the functional forms like, f_{sNi} and f_{Ni}(implied), in deriving the rules of the interactions and integration to give ethical meaning to all knowledge-induced socio-scientific systems.

Stage 4 (S_4):

We note from Stage 3 that every integration, $S(N_i)$, is followed by newer integrations, as i=1,2,.., and each of these is a function of the

$\{\theta',X'(\theta')\}$-tuples coming from previous stages by the circular continuity of interrelationships through the medium of functional mappings. This is the knowledge-induced evolutionary phenomenon. Its intensity increases by the speed of generation of θ-values through the interrelationships of the circular causation and continuity model. Decisions are thus pervasively formed and evolved through such functional interrelationships. They are cause and effect of universal complementarities in the midst of diversities. Complementarity signifying the unification effect of knowledge, is denoted here by the composite mappings giving F(.), as mentioned above. Diversities are shown by the hierarchies (a,j,k,l) and their effects on evolving functional interrelationships. Thus complementarities and diversities are correlated realities of decision-making in these knowledge-induced systems.

Evolution is now defined by mappings, E(.), of interactively (N_i) attained integrations, $S(N_i)$:

$$E(S(N_i)) = E(\{F_{ajkl}(\theta_{ajkl}{}^{Ni}, X_{ajkl}(\theta_{ajkl}{}^{Ni}))\}).$$

Hence, an evolution is once again a composite mapping of (a,j,k,l)-specific integrations carried forward by the functional relations of complementarity, diversity and circular causation, F_{ajkl}. One can note how complex the system becomes at such a stage. An analytical theory of 'nexus' derived from Qur'anic epistemology is given by Choudhury (1995a).

A special case of F(.), and hence of E(F), is the social well-being function. Note that we use this social well-being function instead of the social welfare function, because of the intrinsic nature of universal complementarity in F(.) and E(F), whereas the universal nature of marginal substitution with local complementarities only, prevails in the social welfare function, w(.), as explained earlier.

With a simplification of symbols without loss in generality we write a summary of the above-mentioned knowledge methodology as follows:

Let, $SW=SW(\boldsymbol{\theta},\mathbf{X}(\boldsymbol{\theta}))$ denote the social well-being function, where, $\boldsymbol{\theta}$ and $\mathbf{X}(\boldsymbol{\theta})$ appear in their vector forms to imply IIE-phenomenon across (a,j,k,l) and i. Now by a combination of the stages 1-4 given above, we obtain the decision-making criterion for the knowledge-induced worldview (Choudhury 1996b):

$$\text{Simulate } \{\boldsymbol{\theta}\}\ SW(\boldsymbol{\theta},\mathbf{X}(\boldsymbol{\theta}))$$

$$\text{subject to, } \mathbf{X}'(\boldsymbol{\theta}') = f_1(\boldsymbol{\theta}, \boldsymbol{\theta}',\mathbf{X}(\boldsymbol{\theta}))$$
$$\boldsymbol{\theta}' = f_2(\boldsymbol{\theta}, \mathbf{X}(\boldsymbol{\theta}),\mathbf{X}(\boldsymbol{\theta}')),$$

where, $\boldsymbol{\theta}',\mathbf{X}(\boldsymbol{\theta}')$ are recursed values, starting from a given initial stage. The endogeneity of these variables is shown by the fact that policy or decision variables included in $\mathbf{X}(\boldsymbol{\theta})$, are knowledge-induced, and there exist recursive interrelationships among the decision variables and state variables through the medium of knowledge recursions.

Figure 5.1 (Chapter 5) denotes the simulative convergence and evolutionary processes signified by the above system. The subscripted variables and the SW-functional show the simulative stages of interactions leading to convergence and evolution. At this point, a particular simulated equilibrium solution is obtained temporarily.

Figure 8.2 further denotes the nature of evolution in knowledge-induced recursive interrelationships involving say, $X(\theta)$ as the only state variable, and θ as the decision variable. $SW(\theta,X_1(\theta))$ is the resulting social well-being function, also shown in the IIE context by points like e_1, e_2 etc. Equilibrium points attained by simulation are shown to be evolutionary in nature, moving from a_1 to a_2, b_1 to b_2, c_1 to c_2 etc. These allocation points are embedded in fuzzy spaces as a result of the IIE-disursions. The box, $\theta_1a_1X_1(\theta_1)b_1SW_1c_1$ comprises all possible dynamically complementary inter-relationships among the recursive variables and their resulting social well-being indexes. Thus, evolutions occur to higher levels of knowledge-induction shown by the dotted box, $\theta'a_2X_1'(\theta')b_2SW'c_2$ etc.

Figure 8.2: Evolutionary resource allocation and social well-being

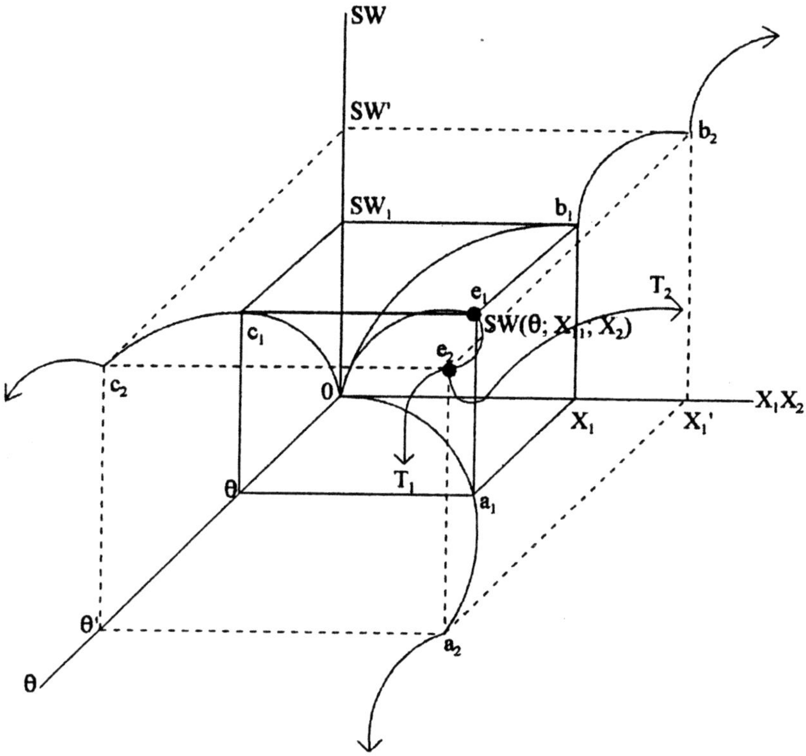

There are no steady-state equilibrium points anywhere. Thus, points like e_1 and e_2 that are embedded in fuzzy fields of decisions give rise to evolutionary knowledge-induced trajectories such as $0e_1e_2T_1$, $0e_1e_2T_2$, etc.

Clearly now, any of the mentioned allocation points and the resulting social well-being function being along IIE-spaces, cannot accept marginal substitution and optimality-equilibrium of the type shown earlier to be the case with neoclassicism and the Rawlsian form of social welfare analysis of social justice. This result is stronger and most general in negating marginal substitution and affirming the principle of universal complementarity in IIE-methodology. For instance, now the 'strategized' resource variation equation subjected to information asymmetry that we considered earlier, can be reconsidered by treating the s_{ij} as knowledge variables instead of the information variable in a competition system between those with more and less information accessibility (information asymmetry). We thus write that equation as,

$$dY_i/d\theta_{ij} = \Sigma_{j=1}^{m} [p_{ij}(\partial x_{ij}/\partial\theta_{ij}) + x_{ij}(\theta_{ij})(\partial p_{ij}/\partial\theta_{ij})].$$

All variables are induced by θ_{ij}-values. This expression is now decisively positive for reasons of monotonic induction of the variables by knowledge flows. Furthermore, because of complementarity among agents (i) and variables (j) as shown, each of these terms hold,

$$p_{ij}(\partial x_{ij}/\partial\theta_{ij}) + x_{ij}(\theta_{ij})(\partial p_{ij}/\partial\theta_{ij}) > 0,$$
$$\text{for, } \partial x_{ij}/\partial\theta_{ij} > 0,\ \partial p_{ij}/\partial\theta_{ij} > 0,\ x_{ij} > 0,\ p_{ij} > 0,\ Y_i > 0,$$

for all values of θ_{ij}. Consequently, we note that the price elasticity of demand for jth good is given by, ϵ_{ij},

$$0 \leq \epsilon_{ij} = -(p_{ij}/x_{ij})(\partial x_{ij}/\partial p_{ij}) < 1.$$

This implies that a mix of goods and services which are necessaries and comforts get dynamically evolved along basic needs regimes of development. Thus even in the general case of resource allocation, we find that certainty, predictability and consistency between the decision variables, basic needs transformation and the state variables, i.e. consumption of basic needs, establish complementarity along the evolutionary path of basic need regimes of development and social well-being.

PREFERENCE FORMATION IN THE IIE-METHODOLOGY

We have earlier claimed that in the endogenous knowledge-induced models, preference formation becomes endogenous as well. Such endogenous preferences would then establish endogenous institutions, regarding which Gottlieb (1984) and North (1981) say, would be a significant breakthrough in the study of political economy. We will consider here one such theory of social action for the political economy as an IIE-system (Parson 1937, Choudhury 1995b).

The primal functional f_s deriving rules from the epistemology of Divine Unity, set up and discourse out the rules of social action. In this way a precision is presented to the rules that emanate from and bring into effect the knowledge-induced unification process. Hence such unitary rules are polar to those derived by random, competing and conflicting rules of roaming rationalism and rational choice. The institutions, whose actions are signified by the policy variables p(θ), are established. They enact such rules by the process of participatory discourse; they present their preferences, initially $\{\succeq_p\}$, and which are subjected to final affirmation by the process of participatory and interactive discourse in social action.

From the primal rules arise instruments, policies and guidance to apply the rules to the political economy, seen here as a polity-market-society ecological system (θ). The rules thus influence consumer preferences taken initially to be $\{\succeq_c(\theta)\}$. Consumer preferences then establish production menus accordingly $\{X_1(\theta)\}$. The resultant economic distribution to factors of production through complementarity among them, $\{X_2(\theta)\}$, now reinforces complementarity between consumer choices and production menus. In this way, the functional 'f' of unification of knowledge emerges. That is, $\mathbf{X}(\theta) = (X_1(\theta),X_2(\theta)) = f$. We have observed above that in a knowledge-induced political economy, dynamic basic needs regimes of development will prevail. The IIE-model applied to the consumption, production and distributional sets, now comprise the corresponding concept of political economy.

The political economy now produces social goods, (SG=(SW(θ,X(θ))). Such a good provides social well-being rather than simply the physical value, because a social good is induced by rules that influence the composite processes according to knowledge that are pervasively induced by knowledge derived from the epistemology of Divine Unity. A social good is not necessarily a public good. Rather, the essence of complementarity between social and private economic menus makes the social good of a distinct type.

The responses from the political economy in respect to the preferences $\{\succeq_c \cap \succeq_p\}[\theta] = \succeq_1$, say, along with SW(θ,X(θ);≥), are post-evaluated in the institutions to re-start the earlier rules and instruments. Changes in f_s now undergo diversity rather than rejection, for the rules of Unity cannot be replaced, once they are formed by extensive discursions according to authentic texts.

At this stage a new round of interactions starts both intra-systems (institutionally, among consumers, producers and other agents) and inter-systems (polity-market ecological interrelationships). Thereafter, new interactive preferences of the nature of $\succeq_\theta$, of institutions and consumers, are interactively generated. We now define Social Action by the totality of the circular causation and continuity model of unified reality starting from actions at the institutional level, then proceeding on with the derived rules into the political economy at large. These actions are then combined with the responses from the political economy to the institutional order. The result is a continuous regeneration of more comprehensive rules and politico-economic transformations premised on the epistemology of Divine Unity and on the process of unification of knowledge. The social action is thus continuously applied and reinforced by the following process:

$$\Omega \succeq_{fs} \{\theta;\succeq_1\} \rightarrow_f \{X(\theta;\succeq_1)\} \rightarrow \text{in continuity}$$

$$\downarrow \quad \text{Process} \qquad\qquad \downarrow$$

$$SW(\theta,X(\theta);\succeq_1) \rightarrow \text{in continuity}$$

Such a process-oriented evolution of SW(.)-values through the social action is exactly the same as the one shown in figure A5.2 (Chapter 5).

DECISION-MAKING IN THE ISLAMIC POLITICAL ECONOMY

Since it was our objective in this chapter to derive the model of Islamic decision-making from a thoroughly analytical groundwork of Divine Unity, we have so far not invoked the Islamic nomenclature. But the precision and uniqueness of the IIE-worldview as premised on a functional precept of ontological Unity must suggest precise forms to f_s, f and all the connective variables and relations in the circular causation and continuity model of unified reality. We now use figures 8.2 and A5.2 to put down the Islamic nomenclature in gaining this analytical precision.

Ω denotes Divine Unity, Qur'anically referred to as Tawhid. The epistemology of Tawhid is principally the Qur'an and its explications by the Prophetic guidance called Sunnah and Ahadith.

f_s is Islamic Law termed as Shar'iah and its dynamic evolution through Ijtihad.

Interactions are termed as Ijtihad, meaning deriving rules from the epistemology of Tawhid.

Integration is termed as Ijma, social consensus.

Evolution is the Qur'anic meaning of re-origination (Khalq in-Jadid), which is pervasive in creation.

Knowledge-induced creative evolution comes about in continuously circular causation and continuity by means of the divine attributes (Asma ul-Husna). But while it would be too complex to include everyone of the ninety-nine praiseworthy names of Allah among these attributes that cause the circular causation and continuity model of unified reality to occur, therefore, we include the so-called 'basis vector' to which other attributes can be related. The selected attributes are, Just Balance (Mizan), Just Purpose (Maqasid), Certainty (Haqq al-Yaqin), and Felicity (Falah and Tazkiyyah). These are derived from the basis of Asma al-Husna.

Rules are termed as Ahkam and are discursively generated in the Islamic medium of discourse (Shura). The Process, Interactions → Integration → Evolution, forms the process of Shura, the consultative institution of Islam. This process is now taken up in the broadest sense of anthropic involvement in the socio-scientific order (invoking the Ayath al-Allah = Signs of Allah). In the Islamic political economy we note the primacy given to instruments of economic cooperation (Choudhury 1992) such as profit-sharing (Mudarabah), equity-participation (Musharakah), abolition of financial interest (Riba) in all shapes and forms, the participatory entrepreneurial spirit as a practical sign of Islamic solidarity, the institution of Zakah and the avoidance of waste (Israf) of all kinds. By using these Islamic politico-economic instruments an ethicizing market transformation toward achieving dynamic basic needs regimes of development comes about (Choudhury 1994b), as mentioned in the concept of public purpose (al-Maslaha) given by Imam Shatibi. The principle of universal complementarity with unity in diversity is pronounced in the integrated Tawhid-centred agricultural model presented in the Qur'an (Chapter 6, verse 99). See Chapter 7 of this book.

The social well-being is termed as Falah and its dynamic basic needs orientation is conveyed by the Qur'anic emphasis on necessaries and comforts of life through diversities of richness as found in the agricultural model. Imam Shatibi (Holland 1982) refers to these attributes as Dhururiyath (necessaries), Hajiyyath (comforts) and Tahsiniyyath (refinements).

The principle of universal complementarity is explained by the centrality of Tawhid in all things and by the precept of creation in complementing 'pairs' in the Qur'an. The meaning of 'pairs' is that of creative multiples, for pairs when compounded, rise exponentially to multiples of linkages.

Finally now, Islamic decision-making can be understood as the functional undertaking of the elements of the Shuratic Process in individual, organizational and socio-scientific preference formation. The Shuratic Process encompasses the totality of the knowledge-induced worldview as presented in this chapter.

CONCLUSION

We have shown in this chapter that knowledge-induced evolutionary processes are circular causation and continuity models of unification of knowledge across hierarchies of life and thought, where the transmission of the ontological completeness causes cognitive realities to appear and re-originate. They create a worldview of interactions, integration and creative evolution. These together define the concept of Islamic political economy as an extensively complementary system. Within this system, decision-making is carried out through precisely derived but discursively evolved rules. Neither rationalism nor ineffectual ontological reference to Unity can generate such general systems, for then marginal substitution, individuation, methodological pluralism and competition based on feigned notions of optimality-equilibrium, would logically prevail. On the other hand, the segregation of ontological Unity from the system of reality, partitions the whole into duality and pluralism.

The study of Tawhidi knowledge-induced worldview is a vast area of research. It is an area for deriving rules of life from the Qur'an and Sunnah. We have simply touched on this vast area by invoking a comprehensive theory of decision-making in Islamic political economy. Then too, a voluminous treatment remains incomplete.

Yet we have treated the model of rationalism and marginal substitution from the vantage point of the Tawhidi worldview as explained by the dialectics that exist between the planes of Truth (Unity) and Falsehood (pluralism and duality). The study of the latter is taken up in Chapter 10. We have also provided the pricing theory of the firm and an explanation of the organizational theory of the firm in the knowledge model of Chapter 5. The reader may wish to refer to my other works in these areas (Choudhury 1995-1998).

CHAPTER 9

ISLAMIC CONSUMPTION, PRODUCTION AND DISTRIBUTIONAL MENUS

In this chapter the methodology of interactions, integration and creative evolution as derived from Tawhidi epistemology and formulated in the IIE-model (the Shuratic Process) and as exemplified by the features of the tree and agriculture in Qur'anic terms, is applied to develop the consumption, production and distributional menus of the Islamic political economy. Our study once again invokes a general systems approach to bring out the pervasive complementarity and unity within diversity that defines the field of Tawhidi applications. Issues of social justice, fairness, social contracts and analytical methods are thus studied in a comparative framework to bring out the fecundity of the Tawhidi epistemic methodology in the study of strongly and pervasively interactive and dynamic general systems.

PREFERENCE FORMATION AND SOCIAL CONTRACT

Consumer Preference Formation According to Mainstream Economic and Political Theories

Consumer preferences in the utilitarian framework of decision-making are generated on the basis of methodological individualism. This is the consequence of the methodology of optimality, equilibrium and competing behaviour due to scarcity of resources and self-interest. Because of the independence of such attributes and tastes outside the market venue, consumer preferences in the utilitarian framework remain exogenously provided as datum. But the fact of the matter is that utilitarianism that is seen to give rise to methodological individualism, hedonic consumption and an idea of happiness that is centred on materiality, is also a kind of social contract (Quinton 1989). Then how can a social contract be premised on an ethically neutral epistemology?

We are led here to discourse the issue at an analytical level. Social contract is established by collective behaviour. Hence a collective preference is invoked. Rousseau said that by so forming collective preferences, individuals must give up part of their self-interest to gain security from the sacrifice (Rousseau 1968). In a framework of methodological individualism, the collective preference, say $\succeq$, becomes laterally aggregative over individual preferences, say $\succeq_i$. But the individuals, i=1,2,..,N, are assumed to be independent of each other, and their preferences are exogenously formed. Thus, $\succeq = \Sigma_{i=1}^{N} \succeq_i$. In a social contractarian sense, $\succeq$ gives rise to an optimal social welfare menu, while $\succeq_i$ individually give rise to optimal and competing utility functions in the goods that are socially allocated by means of competition over goods and resources. We can then consider the vector mappings,

$$\{\mathbf{x}_i; \succeq_i, i=1,2,..,N\} \rightarrow \{\mathbf{x}_1,\mathbf{x}_2,..,\mathbf{x}_N, \succeq\},$$

such that, $U_i(\mathbf{x}_i) \rightarrow_f W(\mathbf{x}_1,\mathbf{x}_2,..,\mathbf{x}_N)$.

That is, $f(U_i(\mathbf{x}_i)) = W(x_1,x_2,..,x_N)$, $i = 1,2,..,N$.

Hence, $\mathbf{W}(\mathbf{x}_1,\mathbf{x}_2,..,\mathbf{x}_N) = (1/N)\, \Sigma_{i=1}^{N} f(U_i(\mathbf{x}_i))$.

Harsanyi's (1955) special case of social aggregation of individual preferences leads to $f(U_i(\mathbf{x}_i)) = U_i(\mathbf{x}_i)$, i=1,2,..,N.

Now since the objective criterion of welfare economics is to optimize W(.), this implies that the corresponding aggregate social preference must also be optimized simultaneously. Otherwise, a change in preference would yield yet another level of W(.). Optimal preference must now result in competing individual preferences and utilities, as shown.

But the message of methodological individualism now extends from the level of preferences governing utilities to the level of competition for goods. We prove this fact as follows: In the state of maximum social welfare, dW = 0. Then,

$$\Sigma_{i=1}^{N} \Sigma_{j=1}^{m} (\partial U_i/\partial x_{ij}) dx_{ij} = 0, \text{ where, } \mathbf{x}_i = \{x_{i1}, x_{i2}, .., x_{im}\}, i=1,2,..,N.$$

Since, $\partial U_i/\partial x_{ij} \geq 0$, and $dx_{ij} \geq 0$, therefore, the only possibility is for $\partial U_i/\partial x_{ij} = 0$, for each i=1,2,..,n, and j=1,2,..,m. Hence, x_{ij} must also be at the optimal levels of consumption in order to make the individual utility functions optimal. x_{ij} must therefore be independent among the N-number of individuals and m-number of goods. The social contract of utilitarianism thereby, negates all traces of interactions in goods and individuals. The argument can be further extended 'globally' to systems and relations premised on utilitarian social contract.

Nature of utilitarian social contract

Much of economic and political theories have been premised on certain versions of utilitarian social contract. Neoclassical economics treats x_{ij} to be either all substitutes or substitutes in groups of complementarities. Not all goods can be complementary to each other in neoclassical resource allocation. Hence, there must exist trade-off among such marginal substitutes. Social choice theory determines an optimal social welfare function under conditions of dictatorial imposition of preferences (Arrow 1976). In such a situation, individual utility functions marginalize each other. This causes independence of preferences and hence of goods in the utility functions. Public choice theory is a version of neoclassical social utility analysis extended to formulate competing and self-interested behaviour of institutions (Nordhaus 1975). In institutional economic theory, constitutional matters are treated in the framework of a neo-liberal theory of market mechanism. Hayek's market 'catallaxy' theory, for example, applied to constitutional behaviour of institutions, reduces them to non-interacting states. Thereby, methodological individualism results (Hayek 1960).

Social contract in moral philosophy

In moral philosophy, social contract is intended to be of a different nature than utilitarianism. But we will now show that despite the moral basis in these social contractarian theories, the consequences of methodological individualism abides.

Consider importantly Kant's social contract. The problem of Kant's analytical synthesis lies in the impossibility to merge Kant's a priori philosophy (deductive) with the a posteriori philosophy (say of Hume's induction) through circularly interconnected relations (Seidler 1986). This discontinuity between the two kinds of reasoning – deductive and inductive – defines the problem of Kant's heteronomy.

Consequently, because of the disjointness between the two patterns of reasoning, a unification of knowledge cannot exist. The unitary precept of Divine Authority over all knowledge is abandoned by Kant as by Hume and by the chain of occidental philosophers toward premising knowledge derivation on any such unified origin. The epistemology of unified reality remains outside the sphere of action of pure reason in Kant. On the other hand, since practical reason cannot attain the a priori core of pure reason, therefore, Kant left God outside the realm of human inquiry. Subsequently, rationalism once again took hold of human reasoning. Now despite the categorical imperative that Kant bestowed on the moral order, it became impossible to derive the moral order from the roots of Divine Unity.

Kant's moral social contract on which so much has been written and that motivated Rawls to formulate his theory of justice (Rawls 1971), becomes subjected to the same problems of individual preference aggregation, conflict and hegemony by power, methodological individualism and pluralism. Since these problems have been discussed with respect to utilitarianism, we will now return to them.

It has been argued that rationalism, which swayed the debate between deductive and inductive reasoning and produced dichotomy in the matter-mind perception of reality, also found headway in the neoclassical dualism of marginal substitution through competition and self-interest. Neoclassicism itself shows strong aspects of Kantian dualism in its marginal substitution idea (Choudhury 1989).

Social contract in classical economic theory

Smith's moral contract found in his **Theory of Moral Sentiments** (1976a) was a good starting point of an ethical market order. But it lost steam when the market organization of the **Wealth of Nations** (1976b) completely marginalized all interactions among agents of exchange at the point of market equilibrium. Consequently, although Smith wrote on the need for human sentiments and cooperation, yet the atomism of exchange mechanism did not generate real interactions. Market equilibrium and optimality were methods to endow self-interested agents with complete knowledge. This made the agents finally benign of interactions. To Smith in the **Wealth of Nations**, market mechanism meant this end result of equilibrium. In **Moral Sentiments**, the theme of social interactions was central to Smith. But between the two works, moral sentiments become benign in **Wealth of Nations**. On the other hand, continuation of sentiments as interactions upon goodwill, cannot settle for the self-interested interactions-benign market equilibrium of the **Wealth of Nations** (Lutz & Lux 1988).

RATIONALISM AND SOCIAL CONTRACT

From all of the above discussion on social contractarianism, we note that any such idea that is premised on rationalism and causes methodological pluralism, is tantamount to dualizing our understanding of reality between morality and materiality, between mind and matter (Russell 1954). As long as the direct bearing of Divine Unity is not entered in the scientific complex of reasoning, there can exist no unification of knowledge either at the beginning or at the end of a series of causal relations (Davies 1990). This is the pervasive and inextricable problem in all kinds of occidental thought, despite the fact that the precept of moral autonomy has been raised by Kant and others.

Preference formation in Tawhidi perspective

To unify knowledge and present a unified picture of reality, we must return all reasoning to the epistemology of Divine Unity, Tawhid. Here we consider the approach of Imam Shatibi on the topic of the public purpose, Al-Maslaha wal-Istihsan. The juristic element of opinion, choice and decision was central to Imam Malik's concept of Istihsan, which was subsequently used by Imam Shatibi to construct his view of the Islamic social order based on the social structure of consumption and well-being. Imam Shatibi's three categories of consumer preferences, namely Dhururiyyath (necessary), Hajiyyath (comforts) and Tahsiniyyath (refinements) apply not simply to consumption menu, but also to the broad perspective of life, where the ordering of preferences in this order is required to build both the individual, familial and community identity and the national order. If we are to further add the great importance that Shatibi placed on the development of Shari'ah, we find that the same characterization can be applied to the politico-economic model of the Ummah, the world nation of Islam.

The above-mentioned three categories of praiseworthy items for consumption are like Fakhruddin Razi's delineation of the attributes of obedience to God in forming the Islamic theory of knowledge – the Tawhidi epistemology. Yet there exist interrelationships among these that can arise from any possible combination and ordering of the attributes while keeping primal the source of all knowledge as Tawhid. These thereby, characterize the unification of knowledge between the real world and its essence by means of knowledge flows across nexus of systemic interactions.

This observation on the diversity of possible combinations of the attributes of Razi's theory of knowledge leads us to infer that human preferences being perpetually influenced by knowledge flows and being embedded in a diversity of actions and reactions, they must be endogenously driven within a field of occurrences. Preference formation at no level – from the individual to the institution – can now be laterally aggregative, except when the condition of simultaneous evolution of the social preferences exists. This latter condition can then enable the evolution of all agent-specific preferences along with the evolution of social preferences at large.

The causation in such a relationship is two-directional – from the micro-level to the macro-level and vice versa. Thereby, when micro-preferences form social preferences, even though lateral aggregation is invoked, the evolution of social preference is at once enhanced by a locally limiting (consensual) knowledge flow. This simultaneously causes all preferences to evolve. Optimality and long-run steady-state equilibrium of all preferences are then annulled. Only instantaneous and evolutionary equilibria can exist. The field of preferences is thus spread over endogenous occurrences arising from knowledge-induced changes of the real world.

Preference aggregation in islamic political economy: the Islamic consumption menu

Now by invoking the same kind of aggregation methods as mentioned above, we note the profound changes that appear with regards to the consumption menu in the theory of Islamic political economy. Let, $\{\succeq(\theta)\}$ denote a class of aggregative social preference induced by a limiting value of consensual knowledge flow,

$$\theta.\succeq(\theta) = \Sigma_{a=1}^{N} \{\succeq_a(\theta), \text{where}, \theta = \lim(i \rightarrow N_1)[\{\cup_i \cap_{jkl} \theta_{(ijkl)}\}].$$

N_1 is the end of a consensual order (Ijma), and is followed by further Ijmatic evolutions of this kind. Thus, $\theta = \theta(N_1,N_2,..,)$. This value does not have a limiting point in a strictly evolutionary perspective of knowledge flows. It can acquire temporary equilibrium in the local sense of neighbourhood of the chain of consensual points.

Two cases can be considered. The first case is when the evolution of $\{\succeq_a(\theta)\}$, a = 1,2,..,N, determines the evolution of $\{\succeq(\theta)\}$. That is, the dynamism of Shuratic Process at the micro-levels determines the politico-economic health of the aggregative macrocosm. This can be a microenterprise, a business firm, a community, the Islamic state, or the integrated Islamic global order called the Ummah.

The second case is of the evolution of $\{\succeq(\theta)\}$ that determines the evolution of all $\{\succeq_a(\theta)\}$. This case happens when the Islamic state or an Islamic institution, enterprise, community, group etc. provides guidance to its members. The most important example in this case is the provision of rules (Ahkam) of Shari'ah to all component of the Islamic world-system. The dynamic linear aggregation of the type mentioned here applies most appropriately to decision-making in the short run, for now certain indecisive rules called Mubah can exist. Hence, $\cup_a\{\succeq_{,a}(\theta)\}$, can exist. Perfect consensus (unanimity) is then replaced by majority rule.

Between the above two cases there exists a perpetuity of interactive processes signified by the medium of interactions $i=1,2,..,N_1,..,N_2,..$ Only when a temporary equilibrium is established at a consensual point, can equality exist between the preferences on the two sides. Now the micro-level and the macro-level preferences have interactively established integration between themselves, before the next round of knowledge-induced evolution occurs. This is the completion of a round of knowledge formation in the IIE-model.

In the general case, the preference aggregation in the Shuratic Process is not linear albeit the dynamic type. The general form is given by, $\{\succeq(\theta)\} = \cap_a\{\succeq_a(\theta)\}$. This is the case of the long run. Now strict consensus exists. We note that if any of the intersecting preferences turn to be zero or winds down, the whole consensus formation is adversely affected. Besides, if the principle of complementarity is abandoned in consensus formation, then there will always exist the possibility of a null-value of $\{\succeq(\theta)\}$. Furthermore, if diversity of preference formation is not upheld, then the flexibility of the process must be abandoned. Now complementarity cannot be preserved. With the long-run preservation of complementarity and diversity the only possible evolution in the unanimity set can be by expanding the consensual sets with knowledge induction in themselves. Figure 9.1 explains such a consensual evolutionary case.

In figure 9.1, knowledge sets are shown to evolve from any given stage into higher stages either through a betterment of the previous knowledge stage or even by rejecting an earlier state of ignorance (Jahiliyyah). The evolutions continue toward cumulative expansion until the Tawhidi Stock is realized in fully realized only in Akhira.

Figure 9.1: Evolutionary epistemology of the knowledge-induced sets

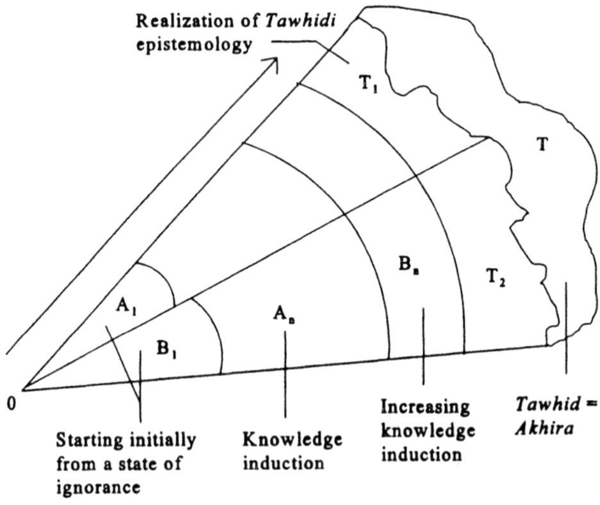

Preference formation is of primal importance in all subsequent politico-economic determinations. The Qur'an has laid far greater emphasis on the traits of consumption than on menus of production. Besides, every time a production menu has been invoked in the Tawhidi sense, consumption, distribution and social well-being have always been linked to consumption. The Qur'an refers to the act of production in terms of a creation that is abundant in rich diversities, ranging from primary, produced and intermediate goods and services to production of felicities. Hence our concept of the social good is derived from the Qur'an. For the sequencing among production, consumption and resources for production of felicity, one may refer to the Qur'an (Chapters 6, verses 95-99). For a just, fair and due distribution of the returns from production in the eyes of God against the inhumanity raised by pagan worships, refer to Chapter 6, verses 136-137.

We thereby now invoke the topic of production in logical relationship with consumption and preference formation in the Islamic political economy. The message of the IIE-worldview continues.

THE PRODUCTION MENU IN ISLAMIC POLITICAL ECONOMY

We will first examine a further breakdown of the preference formation internal to the ethico-economic general equilibrium of the Islamic political economy formed by the IIE-model being applied to the production menu. In this regard therefore, we are to examine the composition of the preference map of the market venue (M) pertaining to consumption behaviour, once the market preferences are induced by θ-values. Thus we determine $\{\succeq_M(\theta)\} \rightarrow_{Fc} \{\succeq_C(\theta)\}\cap\{\succeq_P(\theta)\}$, where, C denotes consumption-inducing consumer preferences. P denotes production-inducing production menus (here also subsumed with the generalized meaning of preferences). Fc determines the set expressing the consumption-production IIE-interrelationships.

Furthermore, when $\{\succeq_M(\theta)\}$ is interrelated with the polity-market (e.g. ecological) (p,M)-preferences, we obtain the generalized IIE-preferences in the domain of Islamic political economy as follows:

$$\{\succeq(\theta)\} \rightarrow_{F1} \{\succeq_M(\theta)\}\cap\{\succeq_p(\theta)\}.$$

That is, $F_1(\{\succeq(\theta)\}) \in \{\succeq_M(\theta)\}\cap\{\succeq_p(\theta)\}$;

but also, $F_c(\{\succeq_M(\theta)\}) \in \{\succeq_C(\theta)\}\cap\{\succeq_P(\theta)\}$.

Therefore, $F_1=F_c \text{ o } F_p$, where, $\{\theta\} \rightarrow_{Fp} \{\succeq_p(\theta)\}$.

Hence, $F_1(\theta)=(F_c \text{ o } F_p)[\{\theta\}] \in \{\succeq_C(\theta)\}\cap\{\succeq_P(\theta)\}\cap\{\succeq_p(\theta)\}$.

This final mapping suggests that preference formation in the Islamic political economy is not an automatic matter of optimal engineering systems and of prescriptive models of behaviour. Rather, it is established by a sequence of interrelated steps towards forming the interactive, integrative and evolutionary decision-making across hierarchies of agents, variables, relations and systems. This process gives rise to the θ-values. The underlying complex methodology was explained in details earlier.

There is yet another important meaning to $(F_c \text{ o } F_p)[\{\theta\}]$: In the iterative process of the IIE-model, {θ}-values simulatively form their cognitive values denoted by {X(θ)}. These in turn form recursive {θ}-values and so on, in circular causation and continuity model of unified reality. The {θ,X(θ)}-tuples give rise to the social well-being functions, {SW(θ,x(θ))}. All these were shown by means of the Goodly Tree of Knowledge and the Qur'anic agricultural model. $(F_c \text{ o } F_p)[\{\theta\}]$ can now be equated to a non-linear monotonic (denoted by A(θ)) transformation of the social well-being functional. We denote this by the polity-market (ecological) social well-being functional signifying the absolute need for the functionality and pervasiveness of the Shuratic Process in all ecological and socio-scientific issues. We thus obtain,

$$(F_c \text{ o } F_p)[\{\theta\}] = A(\{\theta\}).SW(\{\theta\},\{X(\{\theta\})\}).$$

This also means most importantly that knowledge flows as centred in Tawhidi episteme, form both the input and the output of all complexes of relations in Islamic world-systems. In respect to such a meaning of the divine worldview in creation, the Qur'an says (Chapter xli, verse 53): 'Soon will We show them Our Signs in the (furthest) regions (of the earth), and in their own souls, until it becomes manifest to them that this is the Truth. Is it not enough that thy Lord doth witness all things?'

To take account of specific cases, such as the production function alone now, $(F_c \text{ o } F_p)[\{\theta\}]$ can be further disaggregated into its finer components that can be explained in terms of the IIE-model, and so on. In Chapter 4 we undertook such a study in terms of the Islamic theory of value and factor utilization. Thus for instance, we can formalize,

$$(F_c \text{ o } F_p)[\{\theta\}] = F(\theta,L(\theta),K(\theta)).$$

In this production function we imply that labour (L(.)) and capital (K(.)) are complementary factors of each other, and this complementarity is made possible by the knowledge-induction process. This is as much a process ingrained in the diversity of creation that reflects in the market order, in a profound sub-system of the grand ecology and in institutional forms. The most important of the institutions is the pervasive and embryonic Shura. In this, the permanence of the Shuratic Process and of the endogenous policy and state variables is signified by the θ-values.

According to the complementary Qur'anic model of agriculture, F(.) would mean invoking particular branches of the Goodly Tree model that denote such systems interacting and integrating with other systems. In this way, we see that the consumption and production systems must be interactively integrated together to lead to a higher level of general ethico-economic system of the Islamic political economy.

FORMALIZING THE ISLAMIC PRODUCTION MENU

The model of such a general political economic system with consumption and production in it and as qualified by the properties provided above, is of the following form. Note here that all the variables are θ-induced, but we have suppressed this parameter with the variables.

$$\text{Simulate } \{\theta\} \; SW((\theta,C,P,L,K,p); \succeq(\theta)) \quad \ldots\ldots\ldots\ldots\ldots\ldots \quad (1)$$

$$\text{subject to, } C = f_{1(}(\theta,P,L,K,p,SW); \succeq(\theta)) \quad \ldots\ldots\ldots\ldots\ldots \quad (2)$$

$$P = f_2((\theta,C,L,K,p,SW); \succeq(\theta)) \quad \ldots\ldots\ldots\ldots\ldots\ldots \quad (3)$$

$$L = f_3((\theta,C,P,K,p,SW); \succeq(\theta)) \quad \ldots\ldots\ldots\ldots\ldots\ldots \quad (4)$$

$$K = f_4((\theta,C,P,L,p,SW); \succeq(\theta)) \quad \ldots\ldots\ldots\ldots\ldots\ldots \quad (5)$$

$$p = f_5((\theta, C, P, L, K, SW); \succeq(\theta)) \ldots\ldots\ldots\ldots\ldots\ldots (6)$$

$$\theta_+ = f_6(\theta) \ldots\ldots\ldots\ldots\ldots\ldots\ldots\ldots\ldots\ldots (7)$$

$$\succeq(\theta)\} \in \succeq_C(\theta)\} \cap \{\succeq_P(\theta)\} \cap \{\succeq_p(\theta)), \ldots\ldots\ldots\ldots\ldots (8)$$

Expression (1) suggests that the social well-being function of the Islamic general system in production and consumption is circularly interrelated with the distributional variables that exist in complementarity as well as among themselves and the rest. Joint ventures in an ecological environment of responsible consumption and production can characterize such a production-consumption menu of social well-being. There is also the important and indispensable presence of the policy variables that emanate endogenously from the interactive preferences. Such policy variables, instruments, institutional variables and programmes, are all of the type promoting cooperation and joint ventures in the Islamic political economy (Siddiqi 1985, Chapra 1985, Choudhury 1992a). Policy variables are carriers of the rules, Ahkam, that are formed by the discourse in the Shuratic Process across institutions, firms and relevant groups of agents. They impact upon markets, causing transformation of consumption and production preferences.

Expression (2) explains that consumption is related positively with the following:

(a) production through the Qur'anic implication of the dynamic basic needs regimes of development;
(b) an increased labour force that brings about spending through earnings and productivity while an increasing size of the population brings about higher labour force participation;
(c) an increased capital expenditure that augments with labour in the joint production menus, decision-making and control;
(d) endogenous policy variables that bring about other complementarities through the Shuratic discursive process;
(e) an evolutionary epistemology of the IIE-framework that is permanently premised on Tawhidi epistemology.

Expressions (3)-(8) now invert the relationships with the other variables according to the same principle of universal complementarity as shown in expression (2).

The dynamic evolutionary nature of the above-mentioned general system is explained by iterations among the θ-variables. At all phases of such discourse there exist converging tendencies brought about by the ecological Ijma or interactions as signified by expression (8).

The presence of the simulated value of SW(.) in each of the expression means that new and evolutionary θ-values emerge from the combination of the attributes of knowledge formation when derived from the Tawhidi premise. These attributes are, Just Balance (Mizan 'Adl), Purpose (Maqasid), Certainty (Haqq al-Yaqin), Felicity (Falah) and Evolution (Khalq in-Jadid). Finally, when recursive knowledge, state variables and policy variables enter the expressions (2)-(8), an iterative process is established as signified by the Shuratic Process and governed by the principle of universal complementarity. This also signifies the circular causation and continuity model of unified reality (Choudhury 1993, Smith 1992).

Figure A5.1 (Chapter 5) shows the iterative procedure of the system (1)-(8). Most important to note here is that two kinds of methods are explained. First, and most importantly, is the human participatory process either in a political economy or in observing, analyzing and unravelling the interactive process of creation through a medium of discourse in science and society. Hence we develop the concept of the socio-scientific order. In such an application of the system (1)-(8) and similar systems on other and more extended socio-scientific problems, it is not so much the exact measurement of the various variables by engineering methods that is so important. Rather, it is the structure and configuration of such variables through the human discourse medium that remains central, as in organizational behaviour.

The second implication of the above-mentioned system is of course also the underlying engineering application to estimate θ-values through methods of artificial intelligence and then to simulate the whole system. The engineering approach is both difficult and socially unrealistic, as robust methods of simulating such large systems do not exist. Besides, endogenizing all variables, except of course the Ω-premise and the lagged recursive variables, is a difficult mathematical exercise. As an example, a similar kind of embarrassment with engineering methods occurs for the theory of superstrings with respect to its infinities in the solutions of large systems of cosmological equations (Hawking 1988).

The method of endogenizing all variables in terms of recursive θ-values, and conversely, endogenizing the θ-values in terms of the other variables, is the essence of circular causation and continuity in the IIE-model of unified reality. This feature of endogeneity is a direct result of the principle of universal complementarity. We call such a principle of pervasive endogeneity of the complementary system as the principle of ethical endogeneity (Choudhury 1995, James 1996).

Ethical endogeneity is conveyed in the above-mentioned diagram by θ-induction and reproduction between X(θ)-values and evaluation by means of SW-functions. In this way, interactively convergent values are generated. This process conveys the idea of simulation.

THE DISTRIBUTION MENU IN ISLAMIC POLITICAL ECONOMY

Distribution and allocation of resources are the natural consequences of the combined menus of consumption and production. We have noted this above in terms of the presence of the L(.) and K(.) variables in the SW(..) function. But the concept of distribution must also lead to a well-determination of payments to factors of production. It is narrated by a saying of the Prophet Muhammad that the dues of labour must be paid even before his sweat from the work runs dry. This is a simile to the generalized fact that wages and other due factor payments are to be paid without delay. The Qur'an says (Chapter 55, verse 9): 'So establish weight with justice and fall not short in the balance.'

How must wages as payments to labour be defined now? We have expounded a Fitra theory of value for wages for the Islamic political economy in Chapter 4. Briefly stating that theory, we note in it that according to the extension of the system (1)-(8) distribution enters this system in terms of wages and profit-shares. However, wages must now be payments to labour in an ethicizing market for goods and labour that endlessly interact with each other to extract the Fitra value of such a market order.

We can determine factor payments from the following simultaneous system (θ-values associated with the variables have been suppressed):

$$Q = F_P(\theta, L, K) \quad \ldots\ldots (9)$$

$$D_L(K, w, r) = S_L(K, w, r) \quad \ldots\ldots (10)$$

$$D_K(L,w,r)=S_K(L,w,r) \quad \text{......} \quad (11)$$

$$w.L + r.K = Q \quad \text{......} \quad (12)$$

where, $D_L(.)$ denotes demand function for labour; S_L denotes the supply function of labour. Likewise, there are D_K, S_K for capital. w denotes wages; r denotes yield on capital. Q is given. We then have four unknowns in four equations. The solution of the simultaneous equations system is thus determinate, for universal complementarity among all variables exists once a knowledge-value is endogenously assigned through the medium of discourse.

In the above kind of market determination of wages and yields, the Qur'anic and Sunnatic rules promoting market mechanism as a rich embodiment of the Signs of God (Ayath al-Allah), is applied. Despite these, the same sources also advocate justice and goodness to prevail in markets, thus transforming them into ethicizing markets. In this respect, the θ-values become carriers of the Shari'ah rulings on attaining the attributes of justice ('Adl) and compassion (Ehsan) in the market of social goods.

There are specific instruments in the Islamic political economy that bring about these attributes of ethicizing market order. Among them are, profit-sharing in cooperative ventures between labour and capital (Mudarabah), joint-ventures among capital and labour in and between themselves (Musharakah), promoting permissible goods and services (Halal), avoidance of forbidden goods and services (Haram) and waste (Israf), adopting the gold standards of monetary numeraire, and so on.

For the very unskilled in specific kinds of production and technological environments where market-determined wages will not suffice to deliver economic and social security, there the Islamic wealth tax called Zakah, levied on the firm's production and on the well-to-do income earners, can be directed into productive activities to absorb and train the needy and unskilled. Now just as with any employment subsidy, Zakah enters the labour demand and supply functions and capital demand and supply functions. But it is also independently determined both by existing wages as well as recursive wages on the basis of productivity gained from the medium of training in which Zakah is spent. Hence the additional factor market equation relating to Zakah (z) is,

$$z = Z(w,r,K,L)[\theta] \quad (13)$$

In Islamic history, the institution of social guidance of market functions, called al-Hisbah fil Islam, was well-known to guide markets according to Shari'ah rules. It is also well-known that when the Mamluke Government in Eqypt went astray from the gold standard of monetary numeraire, then inflation became rampant in the Mamluke kingdom (Alouche 1994, Choudhury 1997a).

Through the presence of θ-values, determination of factor payments by the firm in the Islamic political economy is to be centred on decision-making that combines promotion of market transactions with ethical values. This leads to the realization of ethicizing markets and social contracts in all dealings between labour and capital. The firm's production menu is thus induced by the underlying complementarities. It takes up an organizational meaning in the labour-capital interactive and consensual bargaining process. Its dynamic form is shown by the existence of θ-values as they get recursive in the Shura of the firm within the broader framework of the Islamic political economy (Choudhury 1997).

In other cases of unskilled labour that is not of the needy category, training costs may be covered by general revenues and personal expenditure on general training. There is no limit to the extent that such principles can be extended at the highest levels of modern organizations (Weitzman 1984, Wisman 1991, Choudhury 1996). Examples in the U.S.A. are industrial democracy now becoming popular in Employee Savings and Ownership Plans (ESOP) (Ellerman 1991).

PROFIT-SHARING AND ECONOMIC DISTRIBUTION

By using the nature of universal complementarity and diversity of the tree model and the agricultural model, we can further explain the role of the important institution of profit-sharing in Islamic enterprise. Profit-sharing and cost-sharing are part of the broader institution of cooperative ventures or joint ventures in Islam that logically emanate from and then strengthen the Shari'ah tenet of abolition of interest-based transactions. It is not our objective here to re-write here what comprises volumes that have been already accomplished on the topic of interest (Riba) and profit-sharing mechanism of Islamic financing (Chapra 1985, Siddiqi

1985). We will dwell instead on the analytics of the profit-sharing and cost-sharing (risk-diversification) variables in the system (1)-(8).

Because of complementarity between labour and capital, we can write, L=L(K), K=K(L), both of which are primarily induced by θ-values. These expressions mean that labour comes to own directly the tools and equipments. In capitalism, such tools and equipments are taken away from workers by dint of the skewness in the capital ownership problem and the sustaining of the unequal ownership between workers and capitalists (owners of capital) that must be sustained for the continuation of capitalism (Heilbroner 1986). On the other hand, we also note in the above expressions that the Marxist concept of organic capital is reproduced by means of the cooperation of labour in the production menu. This condition breaks down the Marxist argument, according to which the organic composition of capital generates the surplus for capitalist and denies labour its due share in the production of profits (Blaug 1968). The organic composition of capital is defined by Marx to be the ratio of machine cost (r.K) to labour cost (w.L). Hence as labour cost declines due to the capitalist accumulation of capital and lower wages paid to labour (exploitation of labour theory), (rK/wL) increases.

In our case, we cannot totally rely on wages and rents but on profit-shares. In a cooperative production menu, total profit (π) is given by,

$$\pi = \pi_K(K(L)) + \pi_L(L(K)) \quad \ldots\ldots (14)$$

$$\text{Now, } d\pi/\pi = d\pi_K/\pi + d\pi_L/\pi \quad \ldots\ldots (15)$$

We will define the profit-shares for capital and labour, respectively by,

$$s_K = \pi_K/\pi;\ s_L = \pi_L/\pi \quad \ldots\ldots (16)$$

Thereby, $d\pi_K/\pi = s_K.d\pi/\pi_K = s_K.\pi_K\hat{};\ d\pi_L/\pi = s_L.\pi_L\hat{}$.

The hatted variables denote percentage changes of the respective variables.

$$\text{Thus, } \pi\hat{} = s_K.\pi_K\hat{} + s_L.\pi_L\hat{} \quad \ldots\ldots (17)$$

$$s_K + s_L = 1 \quad \ldots\ldots (18)$$

One can note that all the π^-variables are functions of θ-values. Then s_i, i=K,L, being determined by the θ-value through the π^-values, become endogenous in terms of θ-values. This means that profit-shares must be determined through cooperation between labour and capital in order to lead to fair and stable rates. This is also the result of frequent re-contracting made possible in Islamic profit-sharing and cost-sharing enterprises called Mudarabah/Musharakah (Choudhury 1986). The ideal case would be for s_L and s_K to settle down to a 50-50 per cent value.

We also note that the π and π^ values being monotonically affected by θ-values, expression (17) would be dynamic with respect to such evolutionary 2-values that emanate from the underlying Shuratic Process. It is through such a dynamic nature of the Shuratic Process that a continuous nature of re-contracting in Mudarabah/Musharakah is possible. Now shares tend towards near equality as the complementarity between capital and labour in the above kind of production menus is enhanced. Profit-sharing rates and the profit-rates, thus become important endogenous policy variables in the Islamic political economy.

PROFIT-SHARING AND COST-SHARING

Cost-sharing is a natural corollary to profit-sharing model. This can be noted by alternatively writing the profit-sharing ratios in terms of cost-sharing. Owners of capital and workers now share profits in proportion to how much they put into the production. The valuation here is not limited to capital investments alone. Wages foregone by workers and input of human capital can be included in the asset-shares. In the general case therefore,

$$s_L = \pi_L/\pi = C_L/C;\ s_K = \pi_K/\pi = C_K/C, \quad \ldots\ldots\ldots\ldots \quad (19)$$

where, C_i, i = K,L, denote cost contributions by capital and labour, respectively. C denotes the total cost of the venture. By working out in the same way as before, we obtain,

$$C = C_K(K(L)) + C_L(L(K)) \quad \ldots\ldots\ldots\ldots \quad (20)$$

$$C\hat{}= s_K.C_K\hat{} + s_L.C_L\hat{} \quad \ldots\ldots\ldots\ldots \quad (21)$$

$$s_K + s_L = 1 \quad \ldots\ldots\ldots\ldots \quad (22)$$

All variables in the above equations are defined as before with the change in terminology to costs rather than profits. The hatted variables denote the percentage change of costs in total and to partners in Mudarabah/Musharakah partnerships. In terms of knowledge formation through the Shuratic Process, an increasing entitlement by labour would enable them to participate on fairly equal terms with capital. This will stabilize the cost-sharing ratios.

Thus, like the profit-sharing ratios and profit-rates, the cost-sharing ratios and percentage changes in costs, become important endogenous policy variables in the Islamic political economy. Stabilization of the cost structure in equations (19)-(22) depends upon the principle of universal complementarity, which is causally interrelated with product diversification and risk-diversification. All of these are both the result of cause and effect in the circular causation and continuity model of the Shuratic Process.

THE ORGANIC COMPOSITION OF CAPITAL IN ISLAMIC DISTRIBUTIONAL MENU

By contrasting with the Marxist concept of organic composition of capital as the ratio of machine cost to labour cost, which increases only by the force of capitalistic substitution of capital for labour, we now formalize a different concept of organic capital in Islamic political economy. Here we refer to Chapter 4 of this book with regards to the Fitra theory of value in Islamic political economy that we referred to above. We proceed as follows:

The production and distribution in an Islamic political economy are intrinsically interlinked with the sharing of costs and profits as shown above. But we will also assume the existence of a partly wage-economy with a cooperative economy. Indeed, in Islamic history, as elsewhere, the wage-paying economy was never completely replaced by Mudarabah/Musharakah enterprises. With this combination of the two kinds of factor payments the relative factor costs in the Islamic political economy is denoted by the ratio,

$$R=[r(w).K(L) + C_K(C_L)]/[w(r).L(K) + C_L(C_K)] \quad \ldots\ldots\ldots (23)$$

where, $C_i(C_j)$, i,j = K,L, i...j, denote interdependent factor costs. K(L) and L(K) denote capital stock and quantities that are interdependent on each other. Each of the variables is thus made complementary to the other variable through the cooperative and interdependent nature of ownership in the Islamic cooperative enterprise.

Equation (23) can be re-written as,

$$R = (s_K'.C' + s_K.C)/(s_L'.C' + s_L.C) \quad \ldots\ldots\ldots\ldots\ldots\ldots \quad (24)$$

where, dashed symbols denote the counterparts of the profit-share and cost-share variables, for the wage-rent part of output distribution. C′ is the total cost in the wage-rental production; C is the total cost in the profit-sharing and cost-sharing production. The principal connection between these two parts of production shows how the sharing-ratios are determined by the underlying Shuratic Process, and how in this way, more of labour is transformed into participatory Mudarabah/Musharakah contracts.

A special feature of the profit-sharing and cost-sharing enterprises is the establishment of a retained income fund. This reduces the need for external capital for future investments (Choudhury 1992b, Siddiqi 1983). But the same is not true of a wage-rent economy, for marginal substitution is a function of relative wage/rental ratio and profits. Hence under the Shuratic Process with the advance of θ-values, the wage-rent part of production is opposed to the profit-sharing and cost-sharing part. Besides, within the wage-rent part, there exists marginal substitution (trade-off). Whereas, within the profit-sharing and cost-sharing part, there is pervasive complementarity.

R, the organic composition of capital in the Marxist sense of increasing variable cost of capitalist production, now declines in the Islamic political economy, as the profit-sharing and cost-sharing enterprise perpetuate. This replaces much of the wage-rent economy; stabilizes the need for external cost while using internal retained earnings or the internal Islamic financing sources of the dual Islamic transformation. The latter is the case with Islamic banks that today function in the midst of a dual financial set-up. Yet Islamic banks by themselves finance Islamic enterprise.

The above result on R is also reinforced by the fact that the Marxist organic composition of capital is inversely related to profits. Hence, it is logical that in the Islamic political economy, where enterprises are driven by the profit-sharing and cost-sharing motives, the concept of organic composition of capital in the Islamic political economy must remain opposite to the Marxist concept. These observations suggest us to abandon the term organic composition of capital and call R as the 'transformation ratio' of the Islamic enterprises as they move from wage-paying ones to predominantly but not solely, profit-sharing ones. It may be said generally, that the only kind of enterprise in the Islamic political economy at all levels is of the Mudarabah/Musharakah type with extensive participation and cooperation.

The transformation to Mudarabah/Musharakah is endogenously realized by the primacy of θ-values in the Shuratic Process. Without these knowledge values no possible learning process, complementarity, diversities or Shari'ah-based policies, guidance and ethical values, can be fused into the decision-making processes.

CONTROLLING THE TRANSFORMATION RATIO IN THE ISLAMIC POLITICAL ECONOMY

Distribution in the Islamic political economy hinges upon several factors: First, there must be complementarity among factors of production. This itself is causally linked with diversities in the production menus and as risk-diversification arises from cost-sharing. Second, the Shuratic Process must continuously transform an enterprise into a Mudarabah/Musharakah one. It must thereby marginalize the wage-paying and rent-seeking economy. Third, there must be the possibility for continuous re-negotiation of Mudarabah/Musharakah contracts so that workers can increasingly gain ownership of capital in the joint venture. This would dynamically set the profit-sharing and cost-sharing ratios until they together tend towards a 50-50 per cent sharing.

Keeping these points in mind, we now consider equation (24). We re-write it as,

$$R=(s_K'C'/s_LC)[(1 + s_KC/s_K'C')/(1 + s_LC/s_L'C')] \quad\ldots\ldots\ldots (25)$$

By a logarithmic differentiation over θ-values, we obtain,

$$\lim(\theta \to \infty)[(1/R)(dR/d\theta)]$$

$$= \lim(\theta \to \infty)[(s_L C/s_K'C')((d/d\theta)(s_K'C'/s_L C))$$
$$+ \lim(\theta \to \infty)(1/(1 + s_K C/s_K'C')).[(d/d\theta)(s_K C/s_K'C')]$$
$$- \lim(\theta \to \infty)(1/(1 + s_L C/s_L'C')).[(d/d\theta)(s_L C/s_L'C')] \quad \ldots\ldots (26)$$

In the limit, as R increases substantially, implying a transformation to the profit-sharing enterprise at large, then the first term on the right-hand-side must decline substantially. Thus the dominating factor in determining the positive value of the transformation rate given by the left-hand-side term of equation (26), would be for,

$$\lim(\theta \to \infty)(1/(1 + s_L C/s_L'C')).[(d/d\theta)(s_L C/s_L'C')]$$
$$- \lim(\theta \to \infty)(1/(1 + s_K C/s_K'C')).[(d/d\theta)(s_K C/s_K'C')] > 0 \quad .. (27)$$

That is, in the limit, as

$$\theta \to \infty,$$

$$(d/d\theta)(s_L C/s_L'C')/(d/d\theta)(s_K C/s_K'C') > (1+s_L C/s_L'C')/(1+s_K C/s_K'C') > 0 \quad (28)$$

Expression 28 means that with the progress of the Shuratic Process, the gains in retained earnings making up the internal sources of financing, the empowerment and human resource development obtained through participatory enterprise and mobilization of Zakah funds from the enterprise, must simultaneously reduce the costs of labour and capital in the profit-sharing and cost-sharing enterprise relative to the wage costs and capital costs, respectively. A major source of such cost reduction is the progressive eradication of interest-based financing in the Islamic cooperative enterprise. A complete transformation to an efficient interest-free economy cannot occur unless simultaneously a substantial gain has been obtained in transforming the enterprises into profit-sharing and cost-sharing ones.

We have thus noticed that the transformation ratio is an important measure of the effectiveness of fair distribution, which to the Islamic political economy means a progressive dismantling of the capitalist relationship of wages to rents. It also means a rejection of the concept of value and organic composition of capital as held by the Marxist theory of capital. Distribution in the Islamic political economy is therefore, not to be construed as being mid-way between the capitalist and Marxist orders as some have implied (Behdad 1989). Rather, it emanates from an epistemological root of unity and unification of knowledge that can only be activated in an actual process-oriented system called the Shuratic Process. Distribution is also not unduly conducted by governmental and institutional intervention. Rather, governments and institutions play the major role in knowledge formation in the IIE-system. Whereas, the flow of resources entering fair distribution and establishing a simultaneity between economic efficiency and distributive equity, mainly takes place in the ethicizing market order.

The last point can be readily noticed by introducing state-run distributional flows as additional social costs in the system of equations (25)-(28). But this component of the cost eventually disappears in the limit, as $\theta \to \infty$. That is, now integration, social contract and dynamic evolution to higher levels of realization of the same become pervasive in the economy. The very presence of risk-diversification, cost-sharing and ethical transformation of markets by means of the pervasiveness of θ-values, make state presence unnecessary, except by way of guidance, defence, foreign affairs and protection of Shari'ah by the Islamic State.

THE GENERAL SYSTEM: CONSUMPTION, PRODUCTION AND DISTRIBUTIONAL INTERRELATIONSHIPS IN THE ISLAMIC POLITICAL ECONOMY

In the model of social action in Islamic political economy, the IIE-model applies in integrating the consumption, production and distributional menus. As we mentioned earlier that like the overall interactive preference map, $\{\succeq\} = \{\succeq_M\}\cap\{\check{s}_P\}$, there must exist finer disaggregation of this and of the same type at all levels of decision-making. Thus with the distributional menus in place now the consumption-production preference map is now,

$$\{\succeq\} = \{\succeq_M\}\cap\{\succeq_P\}\cap\{\succeq_D\}\cap\{\succeq_p\},$$

where, $\{\succeq_D\}$ denotes distributional preferences.

We can furthermore write,

$$\{\succeq\} = \cup_i[\cap_j\{\succeq\}\cap_k\{\succeq_k\}\cap_l\{\succeq_l\}\cap_s\{\succeq_p\}] = \cup_i\cap_{jkls}\{\succeq_{jkls}\},$$

with $i = 1,2,..,N_1,..,N_2,..$ denoting increasing numbers of interactions;

$$j \in M,\ k \in P,\ l \in D,\ s \in p.$$

The total polity-market interactions with further disaggregations in the socioeconomic side, have thus been complemented by interactions within and across the Islamic political economy. The interactive preferences of consumption, production and distribution have thus been accounted for.

The idea of preferences have been explained earlier. Distributional preference means choice of menus of production and consumption that enable a fair distribution to factors of production to take place. It is of course a consequence, that if consumption and production menus are ethical in nature, then the distributional menu that so emanates will also be of an ethical nature (Sen 1985). Yet in the IIE-model, it is important to recognize the circular causation and continuity model of unified reality. In the general systems network, this methodology suggests that an action can start from any part of the general systems and then circularly interrelate with the whole. That is because the unique knowledge formation that complements all systems according to the perspective of unification of knowledge in the episteme of Tawhid, activates a response from any sub-systems to the rest. In the IIE-model this is obviated by the fact that circular causation can start any where in the closed chain (i.e. from Ω to Ω=Akhira), as shown below (also Chapter 3):

$$\Omega \rightarrow \{\theta\} \rightarrow \{X(\{\theta\})\} \rightarrow \{\theta_+\} \rightarrow \{X_+(\{\theta_+\})\} \rightarrow \text{etc.....} \rightarrow \Omega$$

Within this chain, all possible disaggregations can be further considered and the interconnections either of the Qur'anic tree model or the agricultural model, can be invoked. Although diversity is an essential aspect of this circular causation as exemplified by {.}, yet as was mentioned earlier, there is a reverse map of each of the mappings ($\rightarrow$) shown, to its preceding set. This establishes a necessary and sufficient condition of knowledge input-output in the entire system. In Shari'ah terms this means that a rule (Ahkam) has unique backward and forward linkages to generate a consensus (Ijma) or analogy (Qiyas). This is also the meaning of the well-defined continuity that the Tawhidi worldview generates, as opposed to the delinked and random roots of pure and instrumental rationalism (Etzioni 1988) conjectured in occidental epistemology (Radnitzky & Bartley III 1988).

We now use the nodes of the Qur'anic tree model and the interconnections of the Qur'anic agricultural model, where there appear moral-material, i.e. knowledge-induced ethicizing tuples, such as, $\{\theta, X(\theta); \succeq\}$, with their fruits in abundance, $\{SW(\theta, X(\theta); \succeq\}$. These variables and their functionals mean that there must exist unique forward and backward mappings that are governed by underlying preferences, all causally connected with knowledge flows.

In Shari'ah terms this means that a unifying experience is generated across hierarchies of agents, variables, relations and systems, as the Tawhidi epistemology is carried by Sunnah into practical aspects of life. Through such a medium, the Shuratic Process is established and discourse of and for the development of Shar'iah, are continuously evolved. It is equally possible now that agents can determine the need for ethicizing market interactions commencing from discourses around fair distribution of income and wealth, as in the case of Zakah and its organization. This subsequently finds its effect on a production of social good that complements with economic efficiency at the production level. Subsequently, interactive consumption and production menus carry the Zakah-related preferences in this case, into a general system of interrelationships in the Islamic political economy.

It is well-known that Zakah payment remains dependent on the order of consumption and production menus by way of avoidance of waste (Israf) or appropriateness of the goods. In both of these, God-consciousness (Taqwa formation) is essential to establish knowledge. The requirement of Taqwa formation in any of the consumption, production and distributional domains of human activity thus integrates Zakah with the other menus through the medium of avoidance of Israf and the appropriateness of goods.

A COMPARATIVE VIEW OF GENERAL ECONOMIC EQUILIBRIUM SYSTEMS AND THE GENERAL SYSTEMS STUDY IN ISLAMIC POLITICAL ECONOMY

The above-mentioned feature of circular causation and unified interlinkages among consumption, production and distributional menus, is not to be found in other general systems approaches and in the general economic equilibrium models (Eatwell et al 1989). The problem of non-integration is centred on the fact that social discourse remain exogenous to the economic system: Family is an exogenous institution to preference formation; technology is exogenous in the production and distributional menus. Learning-by-doing is an engineering mechanism, not a social process in economic models of iterations. Transactions costs are always subjected to minimization or to bounded uncertainty (Simon 1957, Williamson 1987).

In Walrasian general economic model, which is among the most important for conceptualization of the social economy (Rugina 1983, Benasy 1986), there is the need for a numeraire, often taken to be currency money. The system of n equations in (n+1) unknowns (demand and supply of goods, demand and supply of factors and the monetary aggregate, given their prices) is solved by assigning a standard reference value (say a value of unity) to currency base (Allingham 1989, Choudhury 1992c). In this way, the currency base is made the starting point of the general economic equilibrium system of linkages.

A reverse inference can be drawn: If each of the n markets of goods and services (factors) remains in equilibrium, then the monetary sector must also have been in equilibrium (Henderson & Quandt 1971) – a necessary condition but not a sufficient one for general economic equilibrium.

When Walrasian general equilibrium model is macroeconomically extended to Leontief type input-output models, there too, the technological coefficients remain exogenously fixed. For dynamic input-output coefficients there is simply the time-dependency, not policy-perturbations (Choudhury 1994). Thus all such variations of Walrasian general economic equilibrium models become engineering applications of assumed socioeconomic preferences. They are not actually generated under a process of social interactions.

In Keynesian general equilibrium analysis, the price-level is introduced exogenously. This causes underemployment equilibrium to result. If the market process was fully relied upon, the price flexibility of classical and neoclassical economics would be allowed for, but this would result in wages that would not be institutionally sustainable (e.g. by unions). Consequently, we find that the Keynesian general economic equilibrium model always commences from the side of household (marginal propensities to consume and save) and labour-market relationships (full employment) (Fusfeld 1986).

In all of received systems and cybernetic studies, it is central to introduce exogenous equations that control the entire system. We might question that even in the IIE-model we have Tawhidi exogeneity but knowledge flows (θ) are endogenous. But the neighbourhood of θ-values and hence of the knowledge-induced cognitive $X(\theta)$-values, remains an open one. Thereby, the concept of general equilibrium assumes an evolutionary nature, unlike the optimal steady-state conditions of economic equilibrium based on other numeraire concepts. Besides, unlike the evolutionary equilibrium models of some economic equilibrium models in the literature (Grandmont 1989), the Tawhidi evolutionary model is closed with respect to Akhira. Hence random conjectures and random rationalism are absent in this model.

THE PERMANENCE OF TAWHID IN THE EVOLUTIONARY KNOWLEDGE MODELS

We can explain the above-noted essential feature of Tawhidi evolutionary models in the following way by noting the processes in figure 9.2.

Figure 9.2: Certainty and evolution in the Tawhidi worldview

Process, P_1 $P_2 \rightarrow$

$\Omega \rightarrow_{fs} \{\theta\,(S)\}$ $\rightarrow_{f1} \{\theta\}$ $\rightarrow_{f2} \{X(\{\theta\})\} \rightarrow$ etc.

$\downarrow$ $\downarrow$ $\downarrow$ $\downarrow$

$fs(\Omega) \in Nbd.\Omega = \{\theta(S)\};$

$f1(\{\theta(S)\}) = \{2\} \in Nbd.\Omega;$

$f2(\{\theta\}) = \{X(\{\theta\})\} \in Nbd.\Omega.$

continuity
until Akhira=Ω.

Thus, Ω-episteme reappears at every stage of the IIE-model but in terms of the neighbourhood concept of knowledge evolution. Every step of the transformation shown here across the Shuratic Process, implies the permanent appearance of Tawhid in such world-systems by virtue of the Divine Laws. No cognitive implication of the Oneness of God is possible in such knowledge-induced order, for reality is realized by derivation of knowledge from the Ω-topology. Hence the mapping of $Nbd.\Omega \rightarrow Nbd.\Omega$ at each step of the process (say P_i, $i=1,2,..$) shown above, causes evolutionary equilibrium to appear and be sustained by the necessary and sufficient conditions of forward and backwards interrelationships in the mappings shown. Now, $\{P_1,P_2,...\} \in \Omega$-topology. Since the Ω-topology is neither infinite nor cognitive in the sense of materiality, therefore, it must be a topology of supercardinal measure to allow for all possible neighbourhoods of knowledge-induced realities within it. Ω completes itself only in Akhira, which according to Qur'an is Certainty. Hence a historical process of sustainability is established by the Tawhidi worldview instead of a perception of reality as generated by rationalism. Here randomness causes perception to descend to the lowest state of the mind (Bergson quoted by Russell 1990).

THE GENERAL SYSTEM OF INTERRELATIONSHIPS AMONG CONSUMPTION, PRODUCTION AND DISTRIBUTION IN THE IIE-MODEL

Evolutionary equilibria are momentary in nature. In the language of Shari'ah, this means that the Shuratic Process yields discourses (Ijtihad), which in turn leads to consensus (Ijma). Subsequently, a sequence of Ijmas is evolved by similar Shuratic Processes as the unification of knowledge proceeds on, generating dense knowledge-sets (Choudhury 1997). There exists linear or higher order monotonicity in such processes ($\{P_i\}$) 'almost everywhere' in the measure-theoretic sense (Halmos 1974). This case can be interpreted by noting that sparingly wrong Ijmas in Islamic history have not altered the overall methodology; subsequent corrections were made. The example here is the erroneous Ijmas of the dialecticians (Kalam scholars, the rationalists), which were later on corrected by the Ijmas of the truly Islamic scholars (Mutakallimun) (Muslehuddin undated).

CONSUMPTION - PRODUCTION - DISTRIBUTION GENERAL SYSTEM IN ISLAMIC POLITICAL ECONOMY

Arguing in the same way as we established the consumption-production general system we can now include economic distribution in it and write the general system of interrelationships among consumption, production and distribution as follows, having suppressed the θ-values in the variables.

This system is to,

Simulate$\{\theta\}$

$$SW = SW(\theta,C,P,D,L,K,\pi(L),\pi(K),p; \succeq(\theta))$$

subject to,

$$C = f_1(\theta,P,D,L,K,\pi(L),\pi(K),p,SW; \succeq(\theta))$$

$$P = f_2(\theta,C,D,L,K,\pi(L),\pi(K),p,SW; \succeq(\theta))$$

$$D = f_3(\theta,C,P,L,K,\pi(L),\pi(K),p,SW; \succeq(\theta))$$

$$L = f_4(\theta,C,P,D,K,\pi(L),\pi(K),p,SW; \succeq(\theta))$$

$$K = f_5(\theta,C,P,D,L,\pi(L),\pi(K),p,SW; \succeq(\theta))$$

$$p = f_6(\theta,C,P,D,L,K,\pi(L),\pi,(K),SW; \succeq(\theta))$$

$$\theta_+ = f_7(\theta,C,P,D,L,K,\pi(L),\pi(K),p,SW; \succeq(\theta))$$

$$\{\succeq(\theta)\} \in \{\succeq_C(\theta)\}\cap\{\succeq_P(\theta)\}\cap\{\succeq_D\}\cap\{\succeq_p(\theta)\} = \cup_i[\cap_j\{\succeq_j\}\cap_k\{\succeq_k\}\cap_l\{\succeq_l\}\cap_s\{\succeq_p\}] = \cup_i\cap_{jkls}\{\succeq_{jkls}\},$$

with $i=1,2,..,N_1,..,N_2,..$ denoting number of interactions; $j\in M$ (market=consumption),

$k\in P$ (production), $l\in D$ (distribution), $s\in P$ (polity)

The simulation of this system can be initiated by assigning the initial <u>Sharee</u> values to $\{\theta\}$, i.e. ordinal values assigned to a socio-scientific event by the learned in Shari'ah pertaining to a Shuratic discourse on the issues and problems at hand. For these discourses there will also exist an assigned value of the policy variable, p(θ). Examples of such cases are assignment of principal policy goals such as, Zakah, avoidance of interest (Riba), avoidance of waste (Israf), profit-sharing (Mudarabah/Musharakah) in accordance with an assigned ordinal θ–value, say on a numeral scale. The system thereafter iterates itself. All this is to present an engineering mechanism for the recursive system above. But engineering mechanisms would often be imprecise for large scale systems.

If such system were simulated, the results will be indicative of guidance on the actions to be undertaken and on post-evaluation of past actions in the social action of complementarity among the polity-market variables. The essential meaning conveyed by the above simulation system is one of anthropic presence in the process of decision-making and choices. Now the political economy of such a decision-making process in the above system simply conveys an organized way of viewing how the Shuratic Process is to be guided.

Many different kinds of simplifications can be derived from the above general system. For instance, the L(.), K(.) variables can be replaced by the technological choice capital/labour ratio, (K(L)/L(K))[θ], which may also be taken in the cost-sharing form, (C(L)/C(K))[θ]. The relative profit-sharing ratio, (π(L)/π(K))[θ], could replace the individual profit-shares. D(θ) could be subsumed in the π(.)-values. θ-values can be assigned ordinal values at the post-evaluation stage according to the level of knowledge perceived to have been reached. Now a much neater system of iterative relationships can be generated. The levels of knowledge in the unification process attained will be reflected and be assigned according to the stable nature of the ratios mentioned above, nearing unity in the ideal case. Since θ-values are ordinal in nature, precision is not required in determining such values. It is the monotonicity of the values corresponding to the positive changes in the socioeconomic variables and policy variables that is important.

Yet again, a greater degree of specification can be built into the system by introducing the combination of wage-rent and profit-sharing/cost-sharing system. Now the transformation ratio, R, can be introduced and the θ-values will be monotonically related with the values of R as the wage-rental kind of production menu is progressively replaced by the profit-sharing and cost-sharing types. This property would also be reflected in the ratios mentioned above nearing unity. In this way, a number of controls can guide the simulation of the system as an indicative one for real process-oriented presence by agents, issues and systems in the enacting scene.

CONCLUSION

It now remains to be seen how the general system of Islamic political economy fits into the Qur'anic tree model or agricultural model. The tree model was rich in describing the universal complementarities among hierarchies of agents, variables, relations and systems. This was in polar contrast to the marginal substitution principle of neoclassicism and rationalistic principles of evolutionary social and economic Darwinism (Georgescu-Roegen 1971, Nelson & Winter 1982). The Qur'anic tree and agricultural model is rich in diversities and interlinkages. It presents a model of dynamic basic needs regimes of development. As opposed to such a model is the alienating model of industrialization that replaces agriculture for the sake of manufacturing and heavy industries. The consequences of such an alienating development extend to the side of capital-labour strife that is pronounced by the capitalist hegemony on the one hand, and Marxist unrealism on the other.

The simulation properties of the consumption-production-distribution model in the IIE-framework points to the combination of complementarities and diversities in the context of unification of knowledge understood as interrelations and interactions. The moral aspects of the Qur'anic tree and agricultural models are now seen in terms of fairness of distribution in the profit-sharing, cost-sharing systemic nexus that is generated by interlinkages in the Islamic political economy.

These kinds of interrelationships themselves do not arise from void. Rather, they are causally related to the Shari'ah instruments, such as, the institution of charity (Zakah), avoidance of interest (Riba), avoidance of waste (Israf), and the profit-sharing/cost-sharing institution (Mudarabah/Musharakah). The system we have delineated along with their further possible extensions and simplifications, have positivistic implications premised on the normative framework of Divine Unity. They thus apply practically to the human discursive processes, rather than being limited to engineering mechanisms of optimal and steady-state physical systems.

CHAPTER 10

CONTRASTING MODELS OF KNOWLEDGE AND 'DE-KNOWLEDGE'

For every knowledge flow, $\{\theta\}$, there is its mathematical complementation denoted by $\{\theta'\}$. The totality of these two constitute total reality that is distinctly partitioned between Truth and Falsehood. The Qur'an says in this regard (Chapter 10, verse 32): 'Apart from Truth, what (remains) but error? How then are ye turned away?' We will call the Falsehood space as 'de-knowledge' and explain its structure, dynamics and implications with respect to a distinct kind of its own world-system. The totality between $\{\theta\}$ and its complementation $\{\theta'\}$ forms the topology of knowledge space. Likewise, it also establishes the topology of the 'de-knowledge' space. The Goodly Tree along with its structure and model underlying the IIE-configuration of the universe and its world-system has now its mathematical complementation. We will call such a tree of 'de-knowledge' as the Evil Tree. The Qur'an characterizes the Evil Tree in Chapter 14 (verse 26-27).

In Chapter 3 we showed that the Evil (Falsehood) has no creative power of its own. It is a subordinate of the Supreme Tawhidi creation and is created by God for the purpose of distinguishing the only substance of ultimate reality, that is Truth, when knowledge is completed in Akhira. Thus, for the Evil Tree of Knowledge, all that was true of the Goodly Tree are negated and reversed. Consequently, a complete mathematical complementation exists between Truth and Falsehood and all their manifestations. In this chapter, we will go through the process of constructing the Evil Tree i.e. the model of 'de-knowledge,' and explain the analytical raison detre of its fundamental weakness.

THE EVIL TREE OR THE MODEL OF 'DE-KNOWLEDGE'

Our starting point is to recognize that Ω remains the epistemological origin of Goodness as characterized by the bundle, $\{\theta^*, X^*(\theta^*),$

$SW(\theta^*,X^*(\theta^*))\}$, the disaggregate level of knowledge-induced variables, flowers and fruits of branches, and the transmission mappings emanating from the inherent complementarities. Ω also explains Falsehood, $\{\theta'\}$. Falsehood, on the other side, is characterized by the following 'de-knowledge' bundles and their induced forms:

$$\{\theta^{*\prime},X^{*\prime}(\theta^{*\prime}),SW'(\theta^{*\prime},X^{*\prime}(\theta^{*\prime}))\}.$$

For this bundle,

$$\{\theta^*\}\cap\{\theta^{*\prime}\} = \varphi,\ \{X^*(\theta^*)\cap X^{*\prime}(\theta^{*\prime})\} = \varphi,$$
$$\{SW(\theta^*,X^*(\theta^*))\}\cap\{SW'(\theta^{*\prime},X^{*\prime}(\theta^{*\prime})) = \varphi,$$

where, φ denotes nullity.

The question then is: How can θ^* and $\theta^{*\prime}$ both emanate from Ω, a uniquely creative origin? The answer sought in economic terms is that substitution and replacement of a thing depend upon its relative value. For the case of a well-determined falsehood (or 'untruth'), the measurable value of its space of truth to that of untruth as a variable, is infinite. Hence, untruth cannot be 'substituted' for truth, in the sense of partial replacement, as along a neoclassical production possibility curve (Rhoads 1985, Hobbes 1958). Rather, untruth must be completely 'replaced' by truth. Thus truth and untruth must emanate from the same production function in respect to their relative values. In the case of Mubah, which though is only a temporary phenomenon of learning in knowledge-induced world-systems, a non-zero or non-infinite relative value of the two measures can be determined.

Mathematically speaking, a topology is complete by virtue of the existence of complementation of sub-sets. In the Truth-Falsehood dichotomy, this complementation is signified by the existence of $\theta^{*\prime} \in \Omega$. Hence, the null-point, N, must belong to the topology of $\{\theta^*\}$ and $\{\theta^{*\prime}\}$. That is, $\{\theta^*\}\cap\{\theta^{*\prime}\} = \varphi \in \Omega$. For this reason, $\{\theta^*\}$ and $\{\theta^{*\prime}\}$ must both belong to Ω. Subsequently, all monotonic and continuous transformations, say, $X(\{\theta^*\cap \theta^{*\prime}\}) = X^*(\{\theta^*\})\cap X^{*\prime}(\theta^{*\prime})$. Thereby, $X^*(\theta^*)$ and $X^{*\prime}(\theta^{*\prime})$, define their own topologies defined on the derived spaces from $\{\theta^*\}$ and $\{\theta^{*\prime}\}$. This is likewise true of $SW(\theta^*,X^*(\theta^*))$ and $SW'(\theta^{*\prime},X^{*\prime}(\theta^{*\prime})$. We can extend this argument to hierarchies of agents, variables, relations and systems for the two cases of knowledge and 'de-knowledge.'

The Qur'anic explanation given is that God is the Supreme Absolute and Complete in Knowledge. The devil has no power of its own, but contracts it from the divine will for the testing of truth against falsehood. This test results in the unravelling of the only two ultimate realities, namely, Truth (Haqq) and Falsehood (Batil). Hence in the Qur'an, just as the Sidra is the Goodly Tree and domain of complete knowledge, so also is Zakkum the Evil Tree and domain of 'de-knowledge.' Just as the Illihin is the totality of all truth-based entities, so is Sijjin the totality of all falsehood-based entities. According to the Qur'an, such realities were revealed to the Prophet Muhammad during his flight to the Sidrathul Muntaha, the realm of complete knowledge. This Qur'anic fact establishes the conditions of disjointness that is otherwise now proven by economic and mathematical reasoning.

Apart from truth and falsehood, there is the kind of human preference that remains indeterminate in the short-run (Mubah). A Mubah preference remains in this state until it is well-determined either as truth or falsehood with the progress of knowledge. Here too we note that the presence of knowledge is required to discern truth from falsehood and to well-determine a Mubah either as truth or falsehood eventually.

The intersecting nature of the falsehood-sets appears similar to that of the truth-sets. This is due to the same unifying and interacting nature of these domains in their own disjoint selves. But one now needs to examine the inner structure of the falsehood-set.

Since falsehood is created by its claim to self-generated knowledge that it treats independently of Ω, therefore, the nature of this individuating epistemology starts from $\{\theta^{*\prime}\}$, and pervades through and through its structure. Consequently, every branch, node, and transmission mechanism, all that we have earlier explained for the case of the knowledge-centred worldview, now transmit increasing rationalism in 'de-knowledge.' Rationalism by the force of its perceptual and competing egoism generates individualism and differentiation within the structure of the falsehood-set. The individuating characteristic increases and intensifies with the growth of 'de-knowledge.' The result is that 'atomism' caused by continuous refutation, falsification and individualistic power and perception, now pervades the 'de-knowledge' structure.

The limiting nature of 'de-knowledge' in its inner structure is shown by means of figure 10.1. The falsehood-set, F, is shown to give rise to sub-sets that though intersecting ones, are so in intensifying the regimes of falsehood. But within these sub-sets and the parent F, the ever-presence of individuation and individualism makes the inner structure pervasively atomistic. This feature is shown by the dotted sub-sets. In all, the world-system of the falsehood-set is an endogenous embedding of individualism and individuation, hence of non-interaction, within the evolution of 'de-knowledge.' Such an evolution is caused by non-interactions, and in turn sustains the same.

What does it mean for interactions to prevail in the 'de-knowledge' space and yet individualism to pervade in the inner structure of 'de-knowledge'? The answer is as follows: Each individuated (atomistic) pattern creates its replications over the evolutionary path of 'de-knowledge.' We show this in figure 10.1. The idea then is that the space of 'de-knowledge' experiences its interactive evolution in the sense of perpetuating the methodological individualism or pluralism of the inner structure (Choudhury 1995).

SOME MATHEMATICAL IMPLICATIONS OF INDIVIDUATING CONDITIONS OF 'DE-KNOWLEDGE' VERSUS THE INTERACTIVE PROCESSES OF THE KNOWLEDGE-INDUCED WORLDVIEW: PERMANENT SUPERIORITY OF THE GOODLY TREE.

The Evil Tree

The implication continues on to point out that the transmission mappings between branches lead to separable functions. Hence, a composite mapping fails to exist. The social aggregation in 'de-knowledge' space will be linearly additive across branches of the Evil Tree. Note the following type:

$$f(\theta_1',\theta_2',\ldots,\theta_n') = \Sigma_{i=1}^{n} f_i(\theta_i').$$

Consequently, since $f_i(\theta_i) = X_i$, therefore, $f(\theta_1',\theta_2',\ldots,\theta_n') = \Sigma_{i=1}^{n} X_i$.

Finally, $SW((\theta_1',X_1'(\theta_1)), (\theta_2',X_2'(\theta_2')),..,(\theta_2',X_n'(\theta_n')))$
$= \Sigma_{i=1}^{n} SW_i(\theta_i',X_i'(\theta_i'))$.

On the other hand, the aggregation principle of the knowledge space is quite the contrary. Now well-defined composite mappings act as the transmission mechanisms of pervasively complementing branches of the Goodly Tree. For instance, between i=1,2, we would obtain,

$$f = (f_2 \circ f_1)[\theta],\ \theta=\theta_1 \cap \theta_2 \neq \varphi.$$

Hence, aggregation is given by,

$$f_{agg} = \int_{\theta 1 \cap \theta 2} f(\theta)d\theta.$$

In figure 10.2, we explain the evolutionary transformation of interacting knowledge sets by means of composite mappings. The intersecting sub-set is shown here to evolve with increasing knowledge production. Consequently, there exist necessary and sufficient (cause-effect) conditions between knowledge tuples, such as $\{\theta_1 \cap \theta_2\}$ and $\{f_2 \circ f_1\}$ etc.

In figure 10.2, the continuity of the composite mappings shows the evolving $\{X(\theta)\}$-sets in relation to evolving $\{\theta\}$-sets. The dotted arrows show the necessary and sufficient conditions of circularity of interrelations. None of these can exist in the case of linear additivity. The implication on the side of the knowledge plane is that aggregation proceeds by cumulation of sets over interactions, i.e. of knowledge-formation. This is just the opposite of what happens in the inner structure of the 'de-knowledge space.'

Figure 10.1: The atomistic structure of 'de-knowledge'

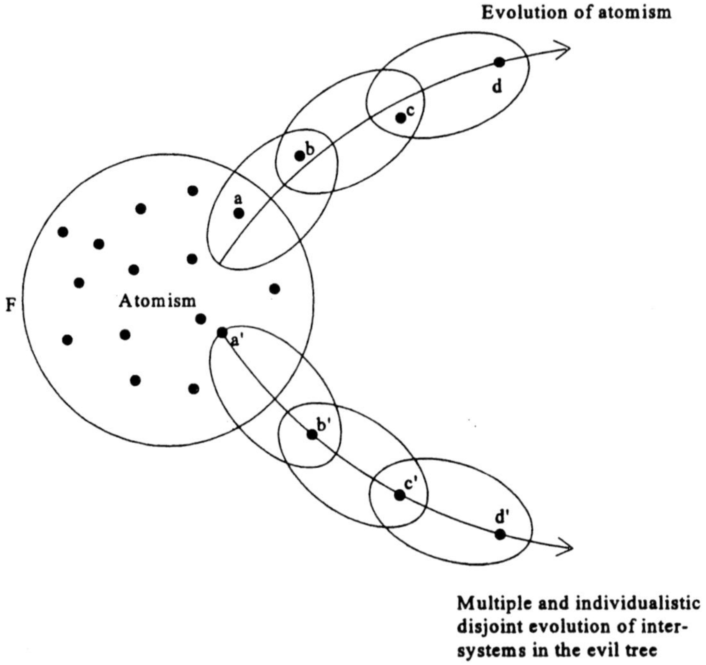

Figure 10.2: Extensively evolutionary nature of knowledge-induced sub-sets with transmission mechanisms

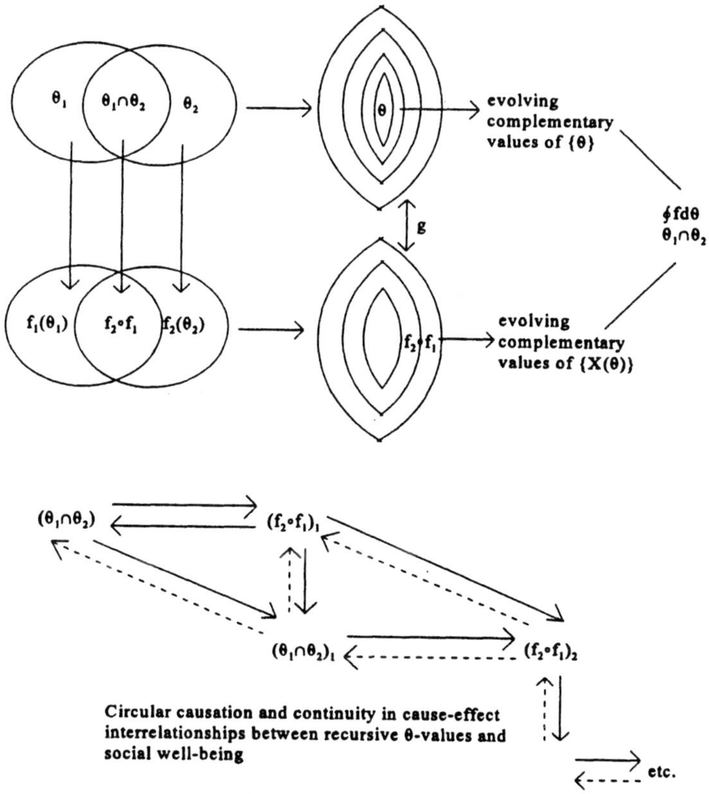

The examples of methodological individualism and falsified perceptions arising from these are well-known in the literature on the methodology of science in the West (Popper 1987, Campbell 1987, Nagel 1961). The continuity of such a premise is to be found pervasively in the dualistic, pluralistic and differentiated systems created by Western scientific reductionism (Dampier 1961). Darwin to Popper, Kuhn to neoclassicism, institutionalism and public choice theory, are a few examples in this group of processes signifying rationalism, pervasive methodological individualism, pluralism and individuation. In the modern scientific literature we find systemic and analytical dichotomy between micro- and macro- systems, microeconomics and macro-economics, Quantum theory and Relativity theory (Thurow 1983, Weinberg 1992). Even in epistemological and ontological arguments we find a dichotomy between a priorism such as of Kant's and a posteriorism such as of Hume's (Seidler 1986). We find the dichotomy also in the mind-matter separation by Russell (1991) and in the biblical metaphysical partitioning of Trinity.

With the above characteristics of the Evil Tree, we can now formalize on its stems and branches. Here we will allow for short-run and limited interactions in the inner structure at the early stages, followed by increasing individuation. This is the case of Darwinism that today pervades scientific and social literature in the West. The branches are linear and not spanning outward and upwards as earlier shown for the Goodly Tree. This feature indicates the kind of linear aggregation and systemic independence that exist in the relationships arising from induction by 'de-knowledge.' Since the roots of 'de-knowledge' are premised on competition, self-interest, egoism, optimality and axioms of independence, therefore, they remain weak as a structure with respect to growth, stability, and richness.

The Measurability of Truth Versus Falsehood

To show that the measurability (μ) of $\{\theta_1 \cap \theta_2\}$ is greater than that of simply $\{\theta_1'\}$, we proceed as follows:

$$\lim(i \rightarrow N)\{\theta_{1i} \cap \theta_{2i}\} = \mu(\theta_N), \text{ and } d\mu(\theta_N)/dN > 0,$$
since N is evolutionary.

Whereas,

$$\lim(i \to N)\mu(\{\theta_{1i}'\}) = \mu(\epsilon_N), \text{ and } d\mu(\epsilon_N)/dN = 0,$$
since ϵ_N is a singleton.

Now over all interactions with expanding θ-set due to monotonicity of θ-values, we obtain,

$$\Sigma_{N=1}^{N1} (d/dN)(\mu(\theta)-\mu(\varepsilon)) > 0, \text{ since each } (d/dN)(\mu(\theta)-\mu(\epsilon)) > 0.$$

Hence by the monotonicity of the continuous functions we obtain, $\mu(\theta) > \mu(\epsilon)$ for $\forall\ \theta$ and $\forall\ \epsilon$ belonging to Ω in the disjoint sense of mathematical complementation applied to $\{\theta\}$ and $\{\theta'\}$.

Clearly then, $\mu(\epsilon)/\mu(\theta) < 1$, for $\forall\ \theta$ and $\forall\ \epsilon$, implying the permanence of the superiority of Truth over Falsehood – the Goodly Tree over the Evil Tree or of Knowledge over 'De-Knowledge.' Thus for different evolutionary values of θ and ϵ, we will have $\{\mu(\epsilon)/\mu(\theta)\}$ continuously decreasing as θ increases. That is,

$$(d/d\theta)(\mu(\epsilon)/\mu(\theta))$$
$$= ((1/\mu(\theta)).(d\mu(\epsilon)/d\theta) - (\mu(\epsilon)/\mu(\theta)^2).(d\mu(\theta)/d\theta))) < 0,$$

since each term is negative for $d\mu(\epsilon)/d\theta < 0$. Hence in the limit of all composite evolutionary functionals of knowledge tending to Akhira, $\mu(\theta) \to$ supercardinal measure. Thereby, the right hand side runs down to zero. That is,

$$\mu(\epsilon) \to 0, \text{ as } \mu(\theta) \to \text{supercardinality at the event of Akhira.}$$

Two important implications can be drawn from the above result. First, the end of time, called Kiyamah in the Qur'an, is characterized by the Great Equilibrium of complete destruction of Evil (meaning $\mu(\epsilon) = 0$, as $\mu(\theta) \to$ supercardinal measure) by the complete victory of Truth ($\mu(\theta)$ = supercardinal measure). Second, since $\mu(\Omega) = \mu(A)$, where A denotes Akhira as manifestation of the Complete Stock of Knowledge, therefore, the final weakness of Falsehood is established from the Beginning to the End. The power of falsehood thus remains permanently weak. The Qur'an says in this regard (Chapter 21, verse 18): 'Nay, We hurl the Truth against falsehood, and it knocks out its brains, and behold, falsehood doth perish! Ah! Woe be to you for the (false) things ye ascribe (to Us).'

PERVASIVE WEAKNESS OF 'DE-KNOWLEDGE'

To prove the pervasive nature of such a weakness of 'de-knowledge,' we will formalize at the disaggregate levels of the branches of the Evil Tree. This is brought out in figure 10.3. The arrows indicate the branches of the Evil Tree. They appear as linear and separable. The interrelationships between them by virtue of their essences, reinforce the individuating character, and hence the linearity and isolation of the branches. In this way, methodological individualism endogenously deepens the same.

To formalize we proceed as follows:

$$\theta_1^{*\prime} \rightarrow_{f1'} \theta_2^{*\prime} \rightarrow_{f2'} \theta_3^{*\prime} \rightarrow \ldots$$

$$\theta_1^{*\prime} \rightarrow_{f1''} \theta_2^{*''} \rightarrow_{f2''} \theta_3^{*''} \rightarrow \ldots$$

We must first prove that the above two relations are not possible simultaneously with the common base of $\theta_1^{*\prime}$. Consider in the contrary, that this is possible. Then examine the relations,

$$\theta_2^{*\prime} = f_1'(\theta_1^{*\prime}),\ \theta_2^{*''} = f_1''(\theta_1^{*\prime}).$$

Also, by non-zero inverse mappings we have,

$$\theta_1^{*\prime} = f_1^{\prime -1}(\theta_2^{*\prime}) = f_1^{''-1}(\theta_2^{*''}) \text{ i.e. } f_1''(\theta_2^{*''}) = f_1'(\theta_2^{*\prime}).$$

But since, $f_1''(\theta_1^{*\prime}) = f_1'(\theta_1^{*\prime})$, therefore, $\theta_1^{*\prime} = \theta_2^{*''} = \theta_2^{*\prime} = \theta_1^{*\prime}$.

Now from the above formalization and figure 10.3 we note that the two rays will converge to a unique one. This is the result of methodological individualism or pluralism that cannot give rise to anything else but its own individuated prototype along the same trajectory. A distinct branch exists for each individuated node.

Now if we assume limited interactions at the earlier stages of evolution of 'de-knowledge,' as in the case with the initial Darwinian stages, then the following picture emerges, as shown in figure 10.4. This is similar to the interconnection between the branches of the Goodly Tree in the sense of their complementary (Qur'anic 'parts') essences. But the difference in the case of the Evil Tree is that the dynamics of the transmission mechanisms are provided by 'de-knowledge.' This differentiates and individuates, as 'de-knowledge' proceeds in the system. Mubah now succumbs to 'de-knowledge' and is then well-determined as a falsehood.

Figure 10.3: The character of linearity through independence of the branches of the evil tree

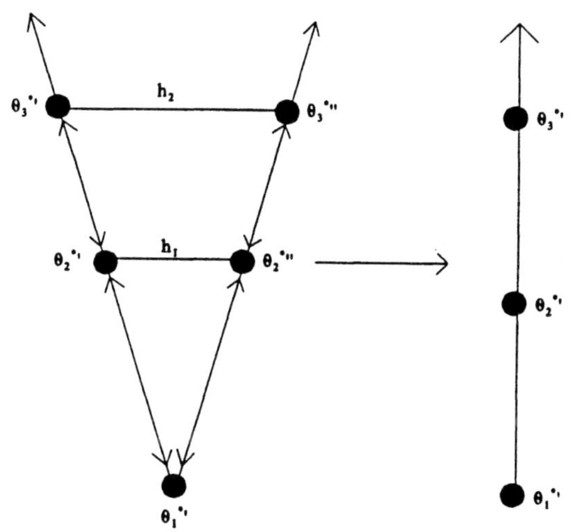

Interactions within systems (branches) to reinforce isolation between branches of the evil tree

Singularly lean branches of the evil tree

Figure 10.4: Limited initial interactions in the evil tree

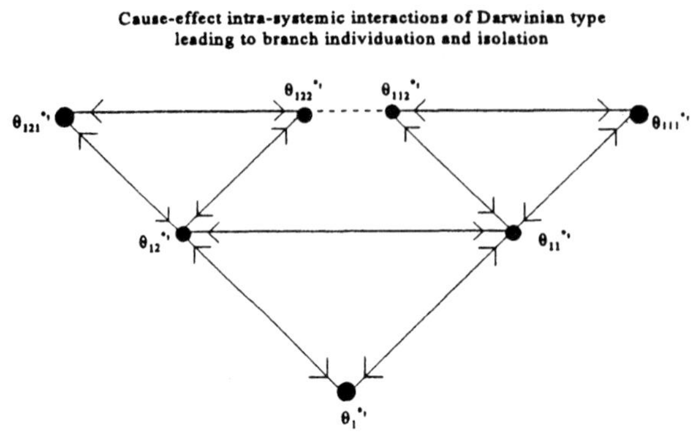

So far the formalization is exactly similar to that for the knowledge branches. As mentioned above, the difference is that the transmission mappings interrelating branches, become increasingly weak with the evolution of 'de-knowledge.' Consequently, the evolutionary branches merge into singular ones. The passage from limited interactions to individuation is very localized. For instance,

$\lim(n \to N)\ f_n' \circ f'_{n-1} \circ \ldots \circ f_2' \circ f_1' = \varphi$,
even if only one of the $f_i' \circ f'_{i-1} = \varphi$, $i = 1,2\ldots$

Now, by transitivity, the null mapping can be generalized for all i =1,2,...

Another argument for the localized and limited interactions in the inner structure of 'de-knowledge' can be made. First consider the case where knowledge-values increase continuously. Then, $(d\mu(\in)/d\theta) < 0$ continuously. Since a transmission mapping is a positive transformation of $\mu(\in)$, therefore, such an f'-transmission also reduces to zero. Second, consider the case where θ′ increases over θ-values for sometime. Now, $(d\mu(\in)/d\theta) < 0$, once again, but f_i', for i=1,2,.., become separable functionals. Then the localized initially interactive branches of the Evil Tree are finally reduced to the same linear individuation kind as shown in figure 10.3. The final picture of localized interactions yielding separable functionals based on individuation of decisions is shown in figure 10.5.

Figure 10.5: Reversal to linear individuation of the branches of the localized initially interactive branches of the evil tree

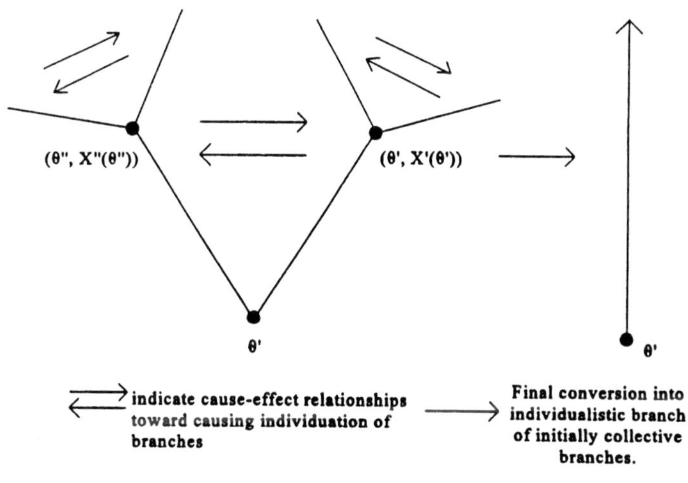

The localized and limited interactions during early stages of interactions, signified by neighbourhoods, Nbd($\in(\theta')$), can be removed from effectiveness. This will leave the total 'de-knowledge'-set measurably individuated 'almost everywhere' in the measure-theoretic sense (Halmos 1974).

EPISTEMOLOGICAL ROOTS OF 'DE-KNOWLEDGE'

Now we will examine the epistemological root of 'de-knowledge.' The definition for this is based on an extension of mappings backwards, as in the case of deriving $\mu(\Omega)$, shown in Chapter 3. But in the case of 'de-knowledge,' any θ', not a unique one, can be the root of an independent and competing epistemology in its own rationalistic, individuated and competing plane. Hence the definition of the root of such an individuated epistemology is $\mu'(\theta')$.

But like the separability of the f_i'-functionals of 'de-knowledge,' $\mu'(\theta')$ as a functional of 'de-knowledge' at the epistemological level, is a separable form. In figure 10.6, we show rising individuated branches of the Evil Tree based on their separable $\{\theta'\}$-bases. It is important to note here that a separable branch and interconnected branches cannot exist in the same tree. Otherwise, two nodes, one for knowledge and the other for 'de-knowledge' will contradict each other through irreconcilable transmission mappings. Furthermore, the complete independence, i.e. disjunction between truth and falsehood, cannot allow for the two types of branches to co-exist in the same structure.

Figure 10.6: Separable branches of the evil tree

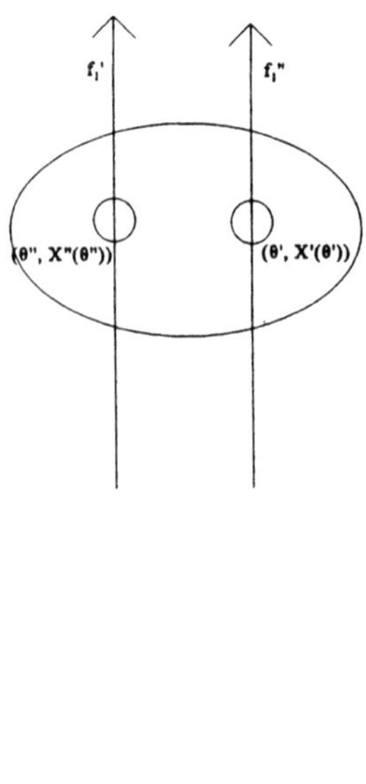

This furthermore means, that the Mubah case must be interpreted as one of temporary interactions in the $Nbd(\in(\theta\cap\theta'))$, which in the long run becomes $Nbd\in(\theta)\cap Nbd\in(\theta') = \varphi$. Hence, Mubah, M, belongs to either $Nbd(\in(\theta))$ or to $Nbd(\in(\theta'))$ but not to both. From here on, the evolution of M belongs to either of these. It becomes either a truth or a falsehood finally. Thus, once again in the measure-theoretic language, Mubah is a subset of the total knowledge space that can be enclosed in a set of relatively zero measure compared to the measure of the total knowledge space. Hence, even with the temporary existence of Mubah in the knowledge space, this remains measurable 'almost everywhere' For the 'de-knowledge' space, we explained in a similar way with respect to the temporary, local, and initial stages of interactions. In this way, the complete disjointness between the Good Tree and the Evil Tree is fully established. The important distinctness of the two processes must be noted. Localized interactions in the case of 'de-knowledge' evolve into non-interaction in the Evil Tree. On the other hand, a Mubah converted into a knowledge space evolves in the long run into perpetually interactive domains.

We can now move from the domain of $\theta^{*\prime}$-values to their cognitive values, $X^{*\prime}(\theta^{*\prime})$ and of the corresponding criterion function, $SW'(\theta^{*\prime},X^{*\prime}(\theta^{*\prime}))$. The properties of independence, competition, marginalism, and methodological individualism are transmitted from θ^{*}-values to the other variables and criterion function. The property of independence or preference exogeneity of relationships makes the aggregation of such functions to be additive and lateral. This signifies the absence of interactions or the limiting role of interaction as the optimal condition of independence and individuation is attained. But the consequences of such properties are extensive.

We begin first with the criterion function,

$$SW'(\theta^{*\prime},X^{*\prime}(\theta^{*\prime})) = \Sigma_{i=1}^{n} SW_i'(\theta_i^{*\prime},X_i^{*\prime}(\theta_i^{*\prime})),$$

along with every monotonic transformation of these functions being similarly related in the aggregative sense. We must understand how θ_i' affect X_i' in the reverse relations of 'de-knowledge.' Increasing values of $\theta_i^{*\prime}$ generate increasing non-interactive domains till the interactions are methodologically eliminated in the state of optimality. This conclusion is obvious for the steady-state equilibrium. But even for evolutionary optimal-equilibrium states, the delineation of the Evil Tree suggests, that new states will break away from the older ones and become independent branches describing evolutionary states that remain repetitive in themselves but are different and disjoint from other bases of evolution. Darwinian natural selection governs such evolutionary states. The best state of such evolutions of 'de-knowledge' is ethical neutrality. The worst state is methodological individualism or ethically degeneration characterized say, by the Hobbesian nature of selfish human preferences (Parson 1964). In either case, with optimal conditions of $\theta_i^{*\prime}$, the above expression becomes,

$$SW'(X^{*\prime}(\theta^{*\prime}) = \Sigma_{i=1}^{n} SW_i'(X_i^{*\prime}(\theta^{*\prime})),$$

with the independence from θ_i^* for reasons either of constancy of $\{\theta_i^{*\prime}\}$-values or of ethical neutrality. The point to note then is that the branches of the Evil Tree now remain structurally unchanging. The only way that the $X_i^{*\prime}$-values can evolve now is by the force of time as an independent variable. But the effect of time is to structurally embed the system of evolutions in the state of ethical neutrality or 'ignorance' ('de-knowledge' non-interactions in gaining unification of knowledge or complementarity).

In the Evil Tree this looks as shown in figure 10.7. Every level of evolutionary optimum of these variables. Thereby, only time as an independent variable, affects the evolution of $X'(t)$- values along their time paths. These paths are shown in the (X',T)-axis. But the arrow shows that such an independent concept of time is a consequence of $\{\theta^{*\prime}\}$ evolving by stages. Therefore, just like $\theta^{*\prime}$, time, t, as so derived, is also a non-systemic variable.

ROOTS OF THE EVIL TREE

The roots of the Evil Tree extend its structure backwards to determine the total worth of this tree and its capacity to advance across events. The measurability concept of roots is now extended to study the dimensionality of 'de-knowledge.' This along with the branch structure of the Evil Tree can now configure the Evil Tree in its totality against the structure of the Goodly Tree. Figure 10.8 shows how the Goodly Tree and the Evil Tree will look like when placed side by side.

Figure 10.7: Treatment of time against 'de-knowledge' and its induced forms

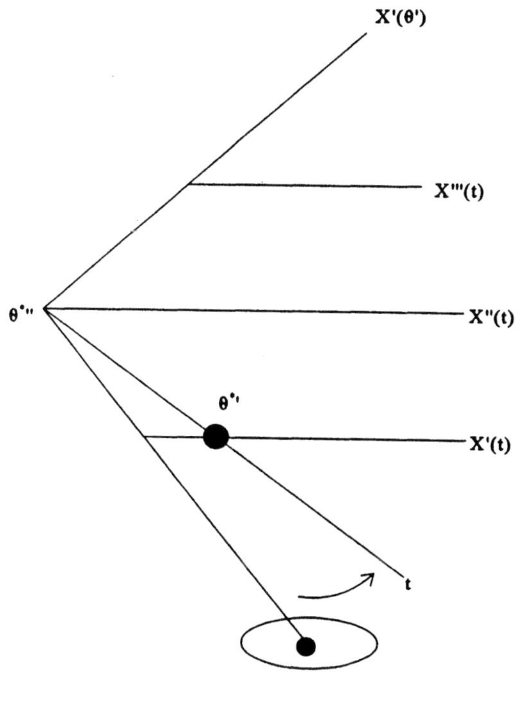

Figure 10.8: Contrasting the evil tree from the goodly tree

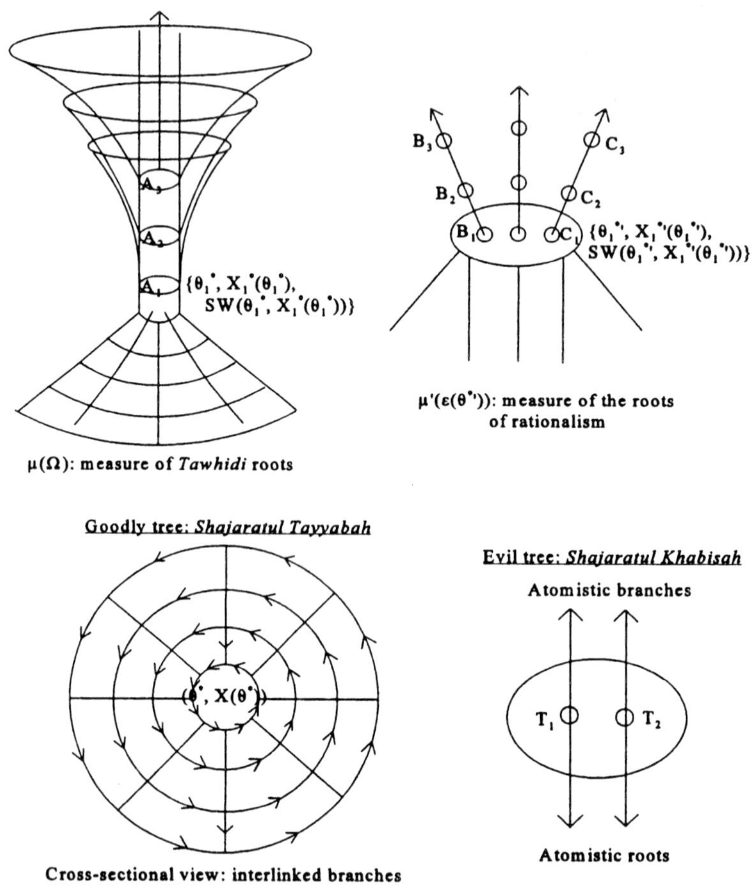

We note in figure 10.8 that a point like, $A_i = (\theta_i^*, X_i^*(\theta_i^*), SW_i(\theta_i^*, X_i^*(\theta_i^*)))$ $i=1,2,..,n$, for which formalization of branch nodes, transmission mechanisms were done in Chapter 3. Formalization for the Evil Tree will be contrary to this. The branches for the Evil Tree are defined by, $B_i = (\theta_i^{*\prime}, X_i^{*\prime}(\theta_i^{*\prime}), SW_i'(\theta_i^{*\prime}, X_i^{*\prime}(\theta_i^{*\prime})))$. But because of competition between B_i and C_i belonging to the Evil Tree, the consequential marginalization between these will cause $dSW_i'/dSW_i'' < 0$, where SW_i'' denotes the value for the criterion function associated with $\{\theta^{*\prime\prime}, X''(\theta^{*\prime\prime})\}$. This means that there can exist choices between 'bads' in the Evil Tree. Furthermore, since each branch is constantly integrated within itself while maintaining independence, methodological individualism and rationalistic perceptions, this causes $d\theta_i/d\theta_i'' < 0$ and $dX_i'(\theta_i')/dX_i''(\theta_i'') < 0$, i=1,2,..,n. Now with lim(i→N), the marginalist consequences are extended to the base values $(\theta_i^{*\prime}, \theta_i^{*\prime\prime})$ and their functional relations in the neighbourhoods shown by $Nbd(\in(\theta_i^{*\prime}, \theta_i^{*\prime\prime}))$. Consequently, the roots, $\mu(\in(\theta_i^{*\prime}, \theta_i^{*\prime\prime}))$, also remain dissociated.

We now obtain the limiting sense of independent branches as shown by T_1, T_2, T_3, etc. along with their independent bases and roots. Since the total root of the Evil Tree becomes a countably finite set of separable roots, we can treat this countable measure as a given datum when maximized in finitude. Hence with competition between trees and roots we obtain,

$$\mu(\in(\theta^{*\prime})) = \Sigma_{i=1}^{n} \mu_i(\in_i(\theta_i^{*\prime})), \text{ and } d\mu(\in(\theta^{*\prime})) = 0.$$

That is, $\Sigma_{i=1}^{n} (\partial\mu_i(\in_i^*(\theta_i^{*\prime})))/\partial\in_i^*(\theta_i^{*\prime})).(d\in_i^*(\theta_i^{*\prime})/d\theta_i^{*\prime}) = 0.$

But each of the terms in this summation for independent branches is non-negative. This can only be true if each of the terms is independently zero. This implies a condition of no growth for the separable roots. Such a tree must necessarily be impoverished. The Qur'an says that the Evil Tree is 'torn up by the root from the surface of the earth: It has no stability' (Chapter 14, verse 26).

COMPLETE DEFINITIONS OF THE GOODLY TREE AND THE EVIL TREE

The Goodly Tree

Definitions of the Goodly Tree (GT) and the Evil Tree (ET) can now be given in their limiting sense as follows:

$GT(\{R \cup T \cup B\} \leftrightarrows F\};$
such that, $R = \mu(\Omega)$, $T = \{\theta^*, X^*(\theta^*), F = SW(T))\}$.

The branches of GT are defined by,

$$B = [\{\cup_i \cap_{jkl}\{\theta_{ijkl}\}\}, \{\cup_i \cap_{jkl}\{\theta_{ijkl}\}\}].$$

Flowers and fruits as social well-being criterion are defined by,

$$F = \cup_i \cap_{jkl}[\{SW^{(s)}_{ijkl}(\theta^{*(s)}_{ijkl}, X^{*(s)}_{ijkl}(\theta^{*(s)}_{ijkl}))\}].$$

The following conditions hold:

$$\lim(i,j,k,l)\ [\cup\cap\{\theta^{(s)}_{ijkl}\}] = \theta^*,$$

$$\lim(i,j,k,l)\ [\cup\cap\{X^{(s)}_{ijkl}(\theta_{ijkl})\}] = X^{*(s)}(\theta^{*s})$$

$R \in H(i,j,k,l)$, hierarchies; $\{\theta^*\} \in \Omega$.

The total value of the Goodly Tree is thus evaluated in terms of the real-valued mappings, which are the transmission mechanisms mapped 'onto' the social well-being functions.

The Evil Tree

$ET: \{R' \cup T' \cup B') \leftrightarrows F'\},$
such that $R' = \mu'(\theta^{*\prime})$, $T = \{\theta^{*\prime}, X^{*\prime}(\theta^{*\prime})\}$, $B_i = T_i$,

$$F = \cup_i SW_i'(\theta_i^{*\prime}, X_i'(\theta_i^{*\prime}))\}.$$

$\theta_i^{*\prime}$ are exogenously assigned to $X_i^*(\theta_i^{*\prime})$, where,

$X_i^*(\theta_i^{*\prime})$ = exogenously derived from $\theta_i^{*\prime}$, or is independent of $\theta_i^{*\prime}$, in which case it is an ethically neutral value generated endogenously.

$$\theta_i^{*\prime}, \{\theta_1^{*\prime}, \theta_2^{*\prime}, \ldots\}, i = 1,2,\ldots$$

The total value of the Evil Tree is evaluated in terms of the real-valued mappings, which are now separable transmission functions, into the mathematical 'complementation of the social well-being' function of 'de-knowledge.' These too are separable functions.

One must note here as to how the measurability of the mathematical union of T_i-evil trees must always be a decreasing and finally a vanishing functional, relative to the increasing measure of the Goodly Tree. To prove this we proceed as follows:

For a sample case, we write $\mu(SW(\theta^*)) = \cup^N_{i=1}\cap^2_{j=1}SW_{ij}(\theta_{ij}^*)$, depicted by the representation of figure 3.13 in Chapter 3. Here the intersection of the two systems, S_1 and S_2 evolves by being induced commonly by the θ^*-values. Thus, $(S_1 \cap S_2)[\theta^*]$ increases monotonically with increasing interactions that accompany the $\{\theta^*\}$-values. Thereby, $d\mu(SW(\theta^*))/d\theta^* > 0$. Hence, $\mu(SW(\theta^*))$ is an increasing function of knowledge, θ^*.

Conversely, for the Evil Tree we have, $\mu'(SW'(\theta^{*\prime}))$ as a linear monotonic function of $\Sigma_{j=1}{}^2\, SW'(\theta_j^{*\prime})$, due to competition, marginalism, and methodological individualism (across systems, S_j and within S_j, $j=1,2$). Thus, $\mu'(SW'(\theta^{*\prime}))$ = constant. For the more general case before a limiting value of θ^* or $\theta^{*\prime}$ is arrived at, we write,

$$[d\mu'(SW'(\theta'))/d\theta']/[d\mu(SW(\theta))/d\theta] =$$
$$[(d\mu'(SW'(\theta'))/(d\mu(SW(\theta)).(d\theta/d\theta'))].$$

But since $d\theta/d\theta' < 0$, therefore, $d\mu'(SW'(\theta'))/d\mu(SW(\theta)) < 0$ as well. Now in the limit of $i \to N$ (interactions leading to consensus), we would have, $\theta \to \theta^*$. Whereas, either $\theta^{*\prime}$ = constant, or SW' is ethically neutral. Hence, $d\mu'(SW'(\theta^{*\prime}))/d\mu(SW(\theta^*)) \to 0$. This proves our assertion.

CONTRASTING THE SYSTEMIC VIEW OF BRANCHES OF THE GOODLY TREE AND EVIL TREE

The systemic views of the branches of the Goodly Tree and the Evil Tree appear as follows in figure 10.9. We have already studied the evolutionary equilibrium processes in the IIE-model of the Goodly Tree in Chapter 3. Thus we need simply to look at the disjointly recursively adaptive equilibrium within closed and non-interacting systems of the Evil Tree. These are shown by the cobweb type adaptations shown in figure 10.9 along branches of the Evil Tree. This phenomenon contrasts with the interconnected recursive equilibria signifying systemic ethical endogeneity but Tawhidi exogeneity in the Goodly Tree. The convergences of such equilibrium processes occur at nodes like $\{\theta^*, X^*(\theta^*)\}$ for the Goodly Tree; and at nodes like $\{\theta^{*\prime}, X^{*\prime}(\theta^{*\prime})\}$ in the Evil Tree.

Figure 10.9: Contrasting equilibriums between the goodly tree and evil tree

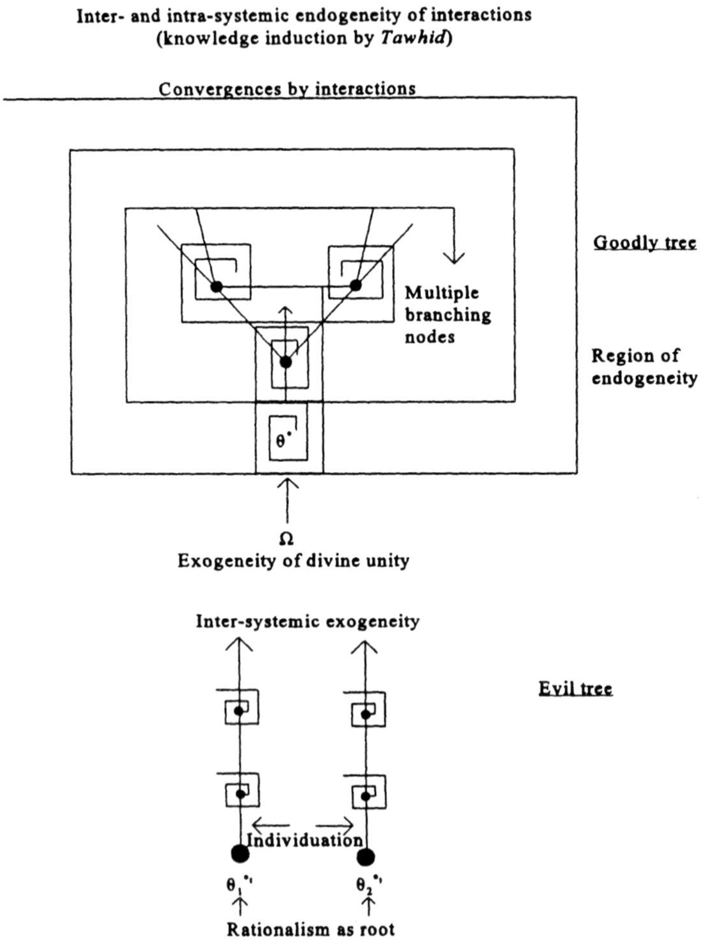

In the knowledge-centered Goodly Tree, interrelations are permanently and pervasively endogenous. Exogeneity of relations in such a worldview occurs due to two factors only. First, there is the exogeneity of God as the episteme of Divine Unity. But here too, in the supercardinal sense, the strict equivalence between Akhira and the Beginning establishes functional identity between the two. But between the world and Tawhidi (Akhira) epistemology, the latter is uncreated; but it bestows reality. Within the world that carries the unification essence of Divine Unity, endogeneity of knowledge-induced processes is a universal and abiding attribute of the Islamic worldview. The other kind of exogeneity occurring in Tawhidi systems is associated with temporary conditions of Mubah (indeterminacy).

EXAMPLES OF MATHEMATICAL ALGORITHMS IN THE GOODLY TREE AND THE EVIL TREE

Examples of mathematical forms that can appear in the two cases given above are as follows: For the Goodly Tree, the IIE-model of the Shuratic Process would suggest the simulation problem:

Simulate $\{\theta_{ij}\}$ $SW(\theta_{ij},X(\theta_{ij}))$ as a complex function of $(\theta_{ij},X_{ij}(\theta_{ij}))$ as endogenous knowledge-induced tuples.

The simulation is carried out subject to the following types of constraints:

$$\theta_{+ij} = f_1(\theta_{ij})$$

$$\theta_i = f_2(\theta_{-ij})$$

$$X_{+ij}(\theta_{+ij}) = f_3(f_1(\theta_{ij}))$$

$$X_{ij}(\theta_{ij}) = f_4(f_2(X(\theta_{-ij})))$$

$$\theta_{ij} = f_5(X(\theta_{ij})).$$

For the Evil Tree, the optimal-equilibrium models of non-interactions and ethical exogeneity would suggest its following objective criterion:

Optimize $\{\theta\}$ $W(\theta',X'(\theta'))$
as a linear function of $(\theta_{i.}',\theta_{.j}',X_{i.}'(\theta_{i.}'), X_{.j}'(\theta_{.j}'))$,
as a mix of endogenous and exogenous variables.

The constraints of the optimization problem are,

$$\theta_{+i}' = f_1'(\theta_{i.})$$

$$\theta_{.j}' = f_2'(\theta_{.j})$$

$$X_{i.} = f_3'(\theta_{i.}')$$

$$X_{.j} = f_4'(\theta_{.j}').$$

When the above two different systems are depicted in the Goodly Tree and the Evil Tree, respectively, they look as shown in figure 10.10. The arrows denote the cobweb type recursive equilibria in the two cases of the Goodly Tree and the Evil Tree. Evolutions of these equilibria cause an outwardly and richly branching Goodly Tree, whereas a linear paucity for the Evil Tree.

The complexity of the Goodly Tree needs complex and sophisticated methods for tractability. The receptacle treatment of time is not acceptable, except for a local treatment of operations over Euclidean spaces. Hence, human involvement in such processes are at the centre of the meaning of interactions, integration and evolution. On the other hand, the non-existence of causality shown by a one-way arrow in the simplicity of the Evil Tree, shows the inherent exogeneity (non-relational order) of such a system. Engineering tractability as a method now becomes important but human realism is lost.

In the Goodly Tree we also note the middle two-directional arrows. This implies two results. First, within temporality there is endogeneity across hierarchies. Between supercardinalities of Ω and Akhira there is a unique endogeneity. But since the measurability of the temporal domain of 'unknowns,' $\mu(\theta,X(\theta))$, must always be less than the supercardinal measure, $\mu(\Omega)$. Therefore, $\{\theta,X(\theta)\} \in \Omega$ always. Hence, there will always exist $\{\theta,X(\theta)\}$-tuples that cannot fully span the topology of Ω. Now the transmission mapping of complete nature cannot exist from the domain of such 'unknowns' to the manifestation of the Complete Stock in Akhira (Ω).

The nature of systemic relationships in the Goodly Tree (simulation and evolutionary equilibria) and the Evil Tree (optimization and recursive relationships in adaptive planes of linearity) can be seen in figure 10.10.

Figure 10.10: Representing the recursive relations of the goodly tree and the evil tree

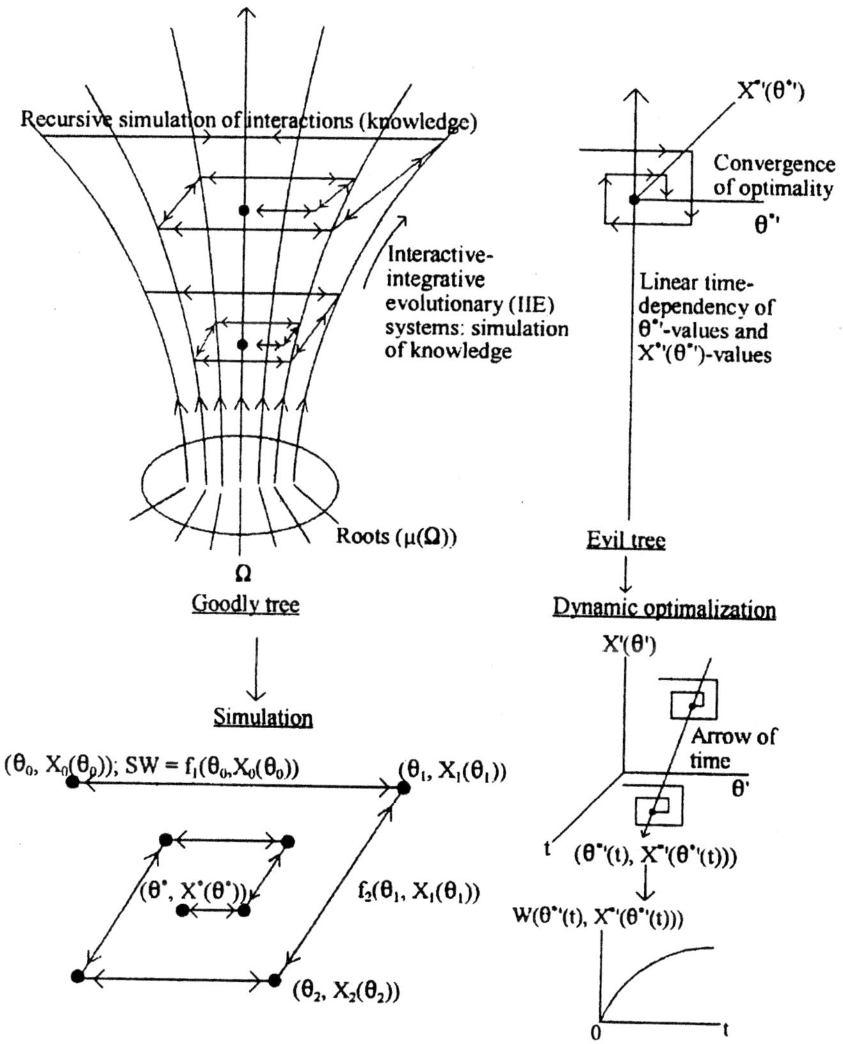

CONCLUSION: CONTRASTING THE PRINCIPAL ELEMENTS OF THE GOODLY TREE AND THE EVIL TREE- THE MODELS OF KNOWLEDGE AND 'DE-KNOWLEDGE'

The results we have discussed in this chapter are suggestive of the fact that two conditions characterize the decision-making processes in the knowledge-induced plane in contrast to the 'de-knowledge' plane. First, there is a continuous dissociation between Truth and Falsehood as knowledge increases. In this, Mubah is a temporary state associated with incomplete knowledge on a given issue at hand. Second, whatever is the nature of change, i.e. from truth to truth, from falsehood to falsehood, or between these states – either through the medium of Mubah or through a determinate move, there are always interactive and evolutionary fields around the decision-making points. The consequence of these two conditions is that interactive processes remain at the root of discernment between the states of truth and falsehood. But once these states have been established, the evolutions continue to be increasingly interactive across hierarchies of agents, variables, relations and systems in the case of the knowledge-induced change.

For 'de-knowledge,' endogeneity of interactive evolution applies only in the sense of repeating the nature of methodological individualism of systems. Within such systems there are no interactions. The resulting sheer linearity of the 'de-knowledge' process, i.e. individualism, optimality, and steady-state equilibrium process, is due to their operations across receptacle time (al-Azm 1967).

Finally, the question of unity in diversity on the one hand, and the idea of methodological individualism and pluralism on the other hand, need to be noted. We have shown before that the transmission mappings of interrelated branches of the Goodly Tree increase diversity. This is also the reason why linearity in systems is replaced by complexity of increasing returns in the interactive, integrative and evolutionary order premised on Divine Unity and unification of knowledge. The question still to be answered is this: Can such a rich diversity can be obtained even without the primal epistemology of Divine Unity? As we have shown in Chapter 6, the principle of universal complementarity can emanate necessarily and sufficiently from the episteme of Tawhid and no other premises. It is also this very principle that establishes by a necessary and sufficient condition, the pervasive nature of interactive, integrative and evolutionary sequences by means of transmission mappings.

On the other hand, when the episteme of Divine Unity is abandoned and the premise of rationalism is assumed as the episteme of a system of methodological individualism and pluralism, then the consequential isolation of the Evil Tree as shown above, cannot enrich its roots and hence its flowers and fruits. The result then is a logical demise of diversity. This is at once signified by the linearity of the process according to time, when 'de-knowledge' causes repetition of its own prototype across hierarchies of systems, variables, and agents.

Reductionism, dualism and now pluralism have characterized the rationalistic models of man and the universe for a long time. Their roots lie in an essentially delinked and dissociative perception of reality. Such a perception is endogenously reinforced by the philosophy of methodological individualism, pluralism and systemic independence that underlies rationalism. This kind of perception and philosophy has been instilled into individual behaviour as preferences. Through the lateral aggregation method of independently existent Evil Trees, reductionism has been transformed into their own corresponding social preferences and social contracts. So much so that reductionism, which has been the foundation of Western science, carried with it the Darwinian natural selection throughout the concept of systems (Hull 1988). Systems in such cultures remain linearly aggregative or simply non-linearly adaptive in the linear sense to additive preferences. The so-called interrelationships among systems are now interpreted as dichotomy between endogenous and exogenous variables. Within the independently dissociative systems, socio-scientific variables and instruments remain endogenous. That is, such systems are shown to evolve intertemporally in the framework of reductionism across domains of interconnected 'de-knowledge.' Whereas, across such inherent systems within the domains, ethical exogeneity or neutrality in their variables and relations prevails.

In the knowledge-centred Goodly Tree, interrelationships remain permanently and pervasively endogenous. Exogeneity in such a worldview occurs due to two factors only. First, there is the exogeneity of God as Divine Unity that is never created but always creates. However, here too in the supercardinal sense, the strict equivalence between Akhira and the Primordial Beginning, establishes functional identity between these two Events. But between the world and these endpoints, Divine Unity remains uncreated while bestowing all of

Reality. Within the world that carries the unification essence of Divine Unity, endogeneity of unifying processes remains a universal and intrinsic attribute. The other kind of exogeneity that can occur in the Tawhidi worldview is associated with the temporary conditions of Mubah (indeterminacy).

CHAPTER 11

CONCLUSION

This book has been a study on the conceptualization of the socio-scientific epistemology of Divine Unity, also termed as the Tawhid and as derived from Qur'an and Sunnah. In this, we paid particular attention to the knowledge-based world-systems that get depicted in terms of the framework of unity and unification of knowledge within the tenets of Shari'ah. Such a generalization was shown to apply to both the natural order and the human order, in each case requiring linkages with and discourse within the human world with regards to the epiphenomenon of unification of knowledge. Such a unification agenda was shown to exist pervasively in systemic complementarity while admitting rich diversities among possibilities. We termed that guiding principle of unification of knowledge within diversity of possibilities as the principle of universal complementarity. This was shown to give rise to a socio-scientific universe that differed in most respects from the rationalistic premises of dualism and pluralism. Examples of marginal substitution in the neoclassical methodology with respect to the latter kind of methodology was found to be confronted and replaced by the principle of universal complementarity among Shari'ah-based possibilities.

Using the Qur'anic Chapter entitled, **Ibrahim**, we developed a systems model of the complementary process-oriented worldview. In this we found that while Divine Unity remains as the Absolute and Complete domain of Knowledge as Stock, yet from this epistemological and ontological roots emanate flows of knowledge that follow a process. Such a process was substantively described by interactive, integrative and evolutionary interrelationships between knowledge flows premised on Divine Unity and their induced forms in world-systems. We called such a world-system as the socio-scientific order by virtue of its universally systemic uniqueness of unification of knowledge as described by the process-oriented worldview. Knowledge flows were thus endogenous to systems in terms of unification, while the premise of

Divine Unity remained exogenous but it permanently determined the course of the knowledge-induced world-systems.

Contrary to the worldview of unity and unification of knowledge with its own dynamics and structure, explanation and analytic, we also treated the individuating processes of 'de-knowledge' world-systems. We contrasted the two in the light of ethical perspectives of social well-being. The latter concept was substantively defined and used to construct the simulative dynamics of the underlying processes of the knowledge-based world-system. On the other hand, the methodology and methods of optimality and steady-state equilibrium were found to delineate the analytical structure of the rationalistic order. Neoclassical economics was shown to be a prime example of such a world-system. The 'de-knowledge' world-system was also derived from the Qur'anic Chapter, **Ibrahim**. Thus, the same epistemological basis was used to evaluate both the systems, even though we undertook fairly detailed discussions of the rationalistic order.

The basis of the knowledge-centered interactive, integrative and evolutionary worldview of unity and unification of knowledge was used to study several topics of the Islamic political economy. These were organizational theory of decision-making, which we referred to as the Shuratic Process, a theory of systems, simulative social well-being function, knowledge-induced consumption, production and distribution menus, pricing and resource allocation, and problems of scientific methodology. These studies were intended to show the widely extended applications of the knowledge-based interactive, integrative and evolutionary model of unity and systemic unification in varied fields, all having a deeply moral implication.

In the study of these topics, a widely comparative perspective was maintained both with mainstream economics and Islamic economics. The inference derived from these investigations was that Islamic political economy as an example of the interactive, integrative and evolutionary world-system of the socio-scientific order, emerges with a methodology and explanatory power that is singularly its own, being derived epistemologically from the fundamental Islamic sources, namely, Qur'an and Sunnah.

At the end, we come up with the subtle conclusion that a new paradigmatic shift has occurred with the emergence of thinking in the area of knowledge-centered interactive, integrative and evolutionary methodology derived from the epistemology of Divine Unity. Such an epistemology is functionally applied to the world-systems via unification of knowledge. In the economic, social and institutional fields, where such a methodology becomes the groundwork of a theory of Islamic political economy. In the natural sciences, it provides a theory of systems. Thus there exists a unique methodology that applies to various world-systems. This uniqueness is precisely because of the emerging worldview that relates epistemologically to the premise of Divine Unity, which in turn defines laws for human thought and guidance. Thereby, the conduct of human action in all systems is determined by the precepts of unification of knowledge. We found thereby, that the central role of knowledge lay in inducing participatory enterprises, the consensual decision-making arising out of discourse, polity-market interactive transformation of knowledge-induced preferences and their relationships to moral conduct in ethicizing markets and social order. These were all studied in this book as part of a project on a theory of everything that is not epistemologically premised on materiality but on divine essence, i.e. knowledge flows with their substantive analytical and applied capability in the material order.

Being lectures given at learned conferences and a collection of additional chapters that were presented at various occasions, this book is not meant to be exhaustive in the fields of Islamic political economy and interactive systems. But it marks an additional step towards the building of a Qur'anic systems-based worldview. Many other aspects of such systems have been covered in other scholarly contributions by the author. Some of these have been referred to in this book.

Finally, one notes the strongly normative nature of the theory developed here. Yet this is not to underscore the strongly positivistic implications of the same. The normative aspect gains grounds on the basis of a need for transforming a deeply entrenched rationalistic thinking in the global order today by something that is different and humanly more objective. The theory is normative by being strictly epistemological at each step. Hence it requires compliance with its epistemic roots while developing and formalizing the various systems under study. The positivistic aspects of the theory and system arise by virtue of their simulative description of human actions instead of an optimal and steady-state one. The simulative approach signifies a better configuration of the socio-scientific world, where discourse and interactions become permanently endemic. The strength of the positivistic aspect being of an empirical nature, it will of course require development of institutions and preference changes that are treated here as being of a normative nature. Such institutions would yield data and information as a result of their progressive change.

The positivistic aspect as an empirical one, will also rely on sophisticated computer programs that are not simply based on non-linear optimal processes. Rather, even the parameters of the process-oriented relations of simulative systems become knowledge-induced. Yet at the end, as it has been pointed out in this book, it is the power of information flow through discourse, consensus and evolution, and its impact on an ethicizing world-system, that is far more interesting an outlook than an engineering approach. However, the two approaches remain complementary ones in the study of our knowledge-centered integrative, integrative and evolutionary world-systems by means of the epistemology of Divine Unity and its formalism in a universe that continuously unifies through complementarity and diversity of opportunities as delineated by Shari'ah and its endless dynamic possibilities.

REFERENCES

INTRODUCTION

Carnap, R. (1966). "Causality and determinism," in his **Philosophical Foundations of Physics** (New York, NY: Basic Books, Inc).

Choudhury, M.A. (1993). **Islamic Socio-Scientific Order and World Systems** (Lanham, Maryland: University Press of America).

Hawking, S.W. (1983). " Our picture of the universe," in his **A Brief History of Time** (New York, NY: Bantam Books).

Kant, I. (Ed. Friedrich, C.J. 1977) [1780]. "Critique of pure reason," in **The Philosophy of Kant** (New York, NY: The Modern Library).

Penrose, R. (1989). **The Emperor's New Mind** (Oxford, Eng: Oxford University Press).

Rucker, R. (1983). "The one and the many," in his **Infinity and the Mind** (New York, NY: Bantam Books).

Smith, H. (1986). **The Religions of Man** (New York, NY: Harper Perennial).

CHAPTER 1: GENERAL PERSPECTIVES: THE WORLDVIEWS OF ISLAM AND THE OCCIDENT

Ali, A. (1989). **The Spirit of Islam** (Lahore, Pakistan: Islamic Book Service) Chapters X & XI.

Asad, M. (1987). **This Law of Ours** (Gibraltar: Dar al-Andalus).

Bayrakli, B. (1992). "The concept of justice in the philosophy of Al-Farabi," **Hamdard Islamicus**, Vol. XV, No. 3, Autumn, pp. 21-31.

Bhaduri, A. & Steindl,J. (1985). "The rise of monetarism as a social doctrine" in Arestis, P. & Skouras, T. eds. **Post-Keynesian Economic Theory** (Armonk, NY: M.E. Sharpe, Inc.) pp. 56-78.

Chittick, W.C. (1989). **Sufi Path of Knowledge** (Albany, NY: State University of New York)..

Choudhury, M.A. (1998). **Reforming the Muslim World** (London, Eng.: Kegan Paul International).

----- (1995). "Ethics and economics: a view from ecological economics," **International Journal of Social Economics**, Vol. 22, No. 2, pp. 40-60.

----- (1991). "The Tawhidi precept in the sciences," **MAAS Journal of Islamic Science**, Vol. 7, No. 1, Jan-June, pp. 20-44.

Dawkins, R. (1976). **The Selfish Gene** (New York, NY: Oxford University Press).

Drucker, P.F. (1993). **Post-Capitalist Society** (New York, NY: HarperCollins Publishers).

Ferry, L. trans. Philip, F (1992). **The System of Philosophies of History** (Chicago, ILL: The University of Chicago Press).

Ferry, L. & Renault, A. (1992). **From the Rights of Man to the Republican Idea** (Chicago, ILL: The University of Chicago Press).

Fukuyama, F. (1992). **The End of History and the Last Man** (New York, NY: The Free Press).

Giddens, A. (1983). **A Contemporary Critique of Historical Materialism** (Berkeley, California: University of California Press).

Hegel, G.W.F. trans. Sibree, J. (1956). **The Philosophy of History** (New York, NY: Dover Publications, Inc.).

Heilbroner, R. & Milberg, W. (1995). **The Crisis of Vision in Modern Economic Thought** (Cambridge, Eng.: Cambridge University Press).

Holland, M. trans. (1982). **Public Duties in Islam: The Institution of Al-Hisbah** (by Ibn Taimiyyah) (Leicester, Eng.: The Islamic Foundation).

International Monetary Fund (1995). **International Capital Markets, Developments, Prospects, and Policy Issues** (Washington D.C.).

Independent Commission on Population and Quality of Life (1996). **Caring for the Future** (Oxford, Eng.: Oxford University Press).

Jalbani, G.N. trans. (1985). **Al-Fauz Al-Kabir Fi-Usul Al-Tafsir** (by Shah Walilullah) (Islamabad, Pakistan: National Hijra Council).

Kant, I. trans. Friedrich, C.J. (1987). "Critique of pure reason," in **The Philosophy of Kant** (New York, NY: The Modern Library) pp. 24-39.

Karim, F. trans. (undated). **Imam Ghazzali's Ihya Ulum-Id-Din, Vol. I: The Book of Worship** (Lahore, Pakistan: Sh. Muhammad Ashraf Press).

Korten, D.C. (1995). **When Corporations Rule the World** (London, Eng.: Earthscan Publications Ltd.).

Mahdi, M. (1964). **Ibn Khaldun's Philosophy of History** (Chicago, ILL: The University of Chicago Press).

Marcuse, H. (1964). **One Dimensional Man** (London, Eng.: Routledge & Kegan Paul).

Nabi, M.B. trans. Kirkary, A.B. (1983). **The Quranic Phenomenon** (Indianapolis, IN: American Trust Publications).

Naisbitt, J. & Aburdeen, P. (1990). **Ten New Directions for the 1990's Megatrends 2000** (New York, NY: William Morrow & Company, Inc.).

Nasr, S.H. (1978). **An Introduction to Islamic Cosmological Doctrines** (Boulder, CO: Shambhala).

Nordhaus, W. & Tobin, J. (1972). "Is growth obsolete?" in **Economic Growth**, Vol. 5 (New York, NY: Oxford University Press).

Ongun, T. (1994). "Uruguay Round Agreements: an evaluation," **Journal of Economic Cooperation Among Islamic Countries**, Vol. 15, Nos. 1-2, pp. 113-35.

Parikh, J.K. (1992). "Restructuring consumption patterns for sustainability," **Network**, No. 20, Oct.

Penrose, R. (1989). **The Emperor's New Mind** (Oxford, Eng.: Oxford University Press).

Quinton, A. (1989). **Utilitarian Ethics** (La Salle, ILL: Open Court).

Rahman, F. (1958). **Prophecy in Islam, Philosophy and Orthodoxy** (London, Eng.: George Allen & Unwin Ltd).

Russell, B. (1990). "Bergson," in **A History of Western Philosophy** (London, Eng.: Unwin Hyman Ltd.) pp. 756-65.

Schumpeter, J.A. (1950). **Capitalism, Socialism, and Democracy** (New York, NY: Harper & Row).

Shackle, G.L.S. (1972). **Epistemics and Economics** (Cambridge, Eng.: Cambridge University Press).

Siddiqi, A.H. (1979). **A Philosophical Interpretation of History** (Lahore, Pakistan: Kazi Publications).

Staniland, M. (1985). **What is Political Economy? A Study of Social Theory and Underdevelopment** (New Haven, CON: Yale University Press).

Stockholm Initiative on Global Security and Governance (1991). **Common Responsibility in the 1990s** (The Prime Minister's Office, Govt. of Sweden, April 22).

Sullivan, W.M. (1982). "The contemporary crisis of liberal society," in McCullough, H.B. ed. **Political Ideologies and Political Philosophies** (Toronto, Ont: Wall & Thompson) pp. 57-9.

Urquhart, B. & Childers, E. (1996). **A World in Need of Leadership: Tomorrow's United Nations** (Uppsala, Sweden: Dag Hammarskjold Foundation).

Wallerstein, I. (1979). **The Capitalist World-Economy** (Cambridge, Eng.: Cambridge University Press).

Walzer, R. trans. (1985). **Al-Farabi on the Perfect State** (Oxford, Eng.: Clarendon Press) pp. 1-18.

Weldon, J.E.C. trans. (1987). **The Nicomachean Ethics** (by Aristotle) (Buffalo, New York: Prometheus Books).

White, H. (1989). "New historicism," in Veeser, H.A. ed. **The New Historicism** (New York, NY: Routledge).

CHAPTER 2: THE QUR'ANIC WORLDVIEW IN THE SCIENCES

Barrow, J.D. (1991). **Theories of Everything, the Quest for Ultimate Explanation** (Oxford, Eng.: Oxford University Press).

Breuer, R. (1990). tr. Newman, H. & Lowery, M. **The Anthropic Principle, Man as the Focal Point of Nature** (Boston, MA: Birkhauser).

Busuttil, S. Agius, E. Inglott, P.S. & Macelli, T. (eds.) (1990). **Our Responsibilities Towards Future Generations** (Malta: Foundation for International Studies).

Cantor, G. (1955). **Contributions to the Founding of the Theory of Transfinite Numbers**, (ed.) P. Jourdain (New York, NY: Dover Publications).

Charon, J. (1975). tr. by Moore, P. **Cosmology, Theories of the Universe** (New York, NY: McGraw Hill).

Choudhury, M.A. (1996a). "A Theory of social systems: family and ecology as examples," **Kybernetes: International Journal of Systems and Cybernetics,** Vol. 25, 1996.

----- (1996b). "Markets as a system of social contracts," **International Journal of Social Economics**, Vol. 23, No. 1, pp. 17-36.

----- (1995a). **The Epistemological Foundations of Islamic Economic, Social and Scientific Order, 6 Vols plus Booklet** (Ankara, Turkey: Statistical, Economic & Social Research and Training Centre for Islamic Countries).

----- (1995b). **The Islamic Socio-Scientific Order and World-System** (Penang, Malaysia: Secretariat for Islamic Philosophy and Science, Universiti Sains Malaysia).

----- (1994). **The Unicity Precept and the Socio-Scientific Order** (Lanham, MD: The American Press of America).

----- (1991). "The Tawhidi precept in the sciences," **MAAS Journal of Islamic Science**, Vol. 7, No.1, Jan-June.

Cohen, J.S. & Hogan, M.E. (1994). "The new genetic medicines," **Scientific American**, December.

Coveney, P. & Highland, R. (1990). **The Arrow of Time** (New York, NY: Fawcett Columbine).

Dampier, W.C. (1961). **A History of Science and Its Relations with Philosophy and Religion** (Cambridge, Eng.: Cambridge University Press).

Davies, P. (1983). **God and the New Physics** (London, Eng.: Penguin Books).

Dawkins, R. (1976). **The Selfish Gene** (New York, NY: Oxford University Press).

Dewitt, B. (1992). **Supermanifolds** (Cambridge, Eng.: Cambridge University Press).

Einstein, A. (1960). **Relativity** (London, Eng.: Methuen).

Garber, D. (1992). **Descartes' Metaphysical Physics** (Chicago, ILL: University of Chicago Press) Also see for Copernicanism in this book, "The Mature Section," pg. 20-29.

Hawking, S.W. (1988). **A Brief History of Time, From Big Bang to Black Holes** (New York, NY: Bantam Books).

----- (1980). "Is the end in sight for theoretical physics?" (Cambridge, Eng.: Cambridge University Press).

Heiserman, D.L. (1992). **Exploring Chemical Elements and Their Compounds** (Blue Ridge Summit, PA: Tab Books).

Hirsch, M.W., Marsden, J.E. & Shub, M. (eds. 1993). **From Topology to Computation: Proceedings of the Smalefest** (New York, NY: Springer-Verlag).

Hubner, K. (1983). tr. Dixon, P.R. Jr. & Dixon, H.M. **Critique of Scientific Reason** (Chicago, ILL: University of Chicago Press).

Hull, D.L. (1988). "Conceptual interaction," in his **Science as a Process** (Chicago, ILL: University of Chicago Press).

Kakutani, S. (1941). "A generalization of Brouwer's fixed point theorem," **Duke Mathematical Journal**, Vo. 8. No.3, pg. 457-9.

Koizumi, T. (1993). "Economic development as a cybernetic process," in his **Interdependence and Change in the Global System** (Lanham, MD: University Press of America).

Kosko, B. (1993). **Fuzzy Thinking, the New Science of Fuzzy Logic** (New York, NY: Hyperion).

Mahmood, S.B. (1991). **Doomsday and Life After Death, the Ultimate Fate of the Universe as Seen Through the Holy Qur'an** (Islamabad, Pakistan: Holy Qur'an Research Foundation).

Nasr, S.H. (1968). **Science and Civilization in Islam** (New York, NY: Barnes & Noble).

Neurath, O. Carnap, R. & Morris, C. (1970). **Foundations of the Unity of Science, Vol. II** (Chicago, ILL: University of Chicago Press).

Russell, B. (1990). **A History of Western Philosophy** (London, Eng.: Unwin Paperbacks).

Skinner, R. (1969). **Relativity** (Waltham, MA: Blaisdell Publishing).

Wallerstein, I. (1989). **The Modern World-System III** (New York, NY: Academic Press, Inc.).

Walzer, R. (trans. 1985). **Al-Farabi on The Perfect State** (Oxford, Eng.: Clarendon Press).

A. Yusuf Ali (1946). **The Holy Qur'an, Text. Translation and Commentary** (New York, NY: McGregor & Werner, 1946) was used for deriving meaning of referred to Qur'anic verses.

CHAPTER 3: THE QUR'ANIC MODEL OF KNOWLEDGE: THE INTERACTIVE, INTEGRATIVE, AND EVOLUTIONARY PROCESS

Breuer, R. (1991). **The Anthropic Principle, Man as the Focal Point of Nature** (Boston, MA: Birhauser).

Cantor, G. trans. Jourdain, P.E.B.(1955). **Contributions to the Foundations of the Theory of Transfinite Numbers** (New York, NY: Dover Publications).

Choudhury, M.A. (1995). **The Epistemological Foundations of Islamic Economic, Social and Scientific Order**, Six Vols (Ankara, Turkey: Statistical, Economic & Social Research and Training Centre for Islamic Countries).

----- (1994). "The epistemic-ontic circular causation and continuity model of socio-scientific reality: the knowledge premise," **International Journal of Social Economics**, Vol. 21, No. 1, pp. 2-18.

Choudhury, M.A. & Malik, U.A. (1992). **The Foundations of Islamic Political Economy** (London, Eng.: Macmillan & New York, NY: St. Martin's Press).

Descartes, R. (1954). "Discourse on methods," in Commins, S. & Linscott, R.N. eds. **Man and the Universe: The Philosophers of Science** (New York, NY: The Pocket Library).

Halmos, P.R. (1974). **Measure Theory** (New York, NY: Springer-Verlag).

Hume, D. trans. Bigge, S. (1988). **Treatise on Human Nature** (Oxford, Eng.: Oxford University Press).

Husserl, E. trans. Alston, W.P. & Nakhnikian, G. (1964). **The Idea of Phenomenology** (The Hague, Netherlands: Martin Nijhoff).

McCloskey, D.N. (1985). **The Rhetoric of Economics** (Wisconsin, Minnesota: The University of Wisconsin Press) pp. 36-61.

Moore, A.W. (1991). **The Infinite** (London, Eng.: Routledge).

Qadri, C.A. (1990). **Philosophy and Science in the Muslim World** (London, Eng.: Routledge).

Rucker, R. (1983). **Infinity and the Mind, the Science and Philosophy of the Infinite** (New York, NY: Bantam Books).

Russell, B. (1970). **A History of Western Philosophy** (London, Eng.: Unwin Hyman).

Sherover, C.M. (1972). **Heidegger, Kant and Time** (Bloomington, IN: Indiana University Press).

Wilkinson, D. (1991).**Our Universes** (New York, NY: Columbia University Press).

CHAPTER 4: COMPARATIVE POLITICAL ECONOMY: ISLAM AND THE OCCIDENT

Bentham, J. (1789). **An Introduction to the Principles of Morals and Legislation** (London, Eng.: T. Payne & Sons).

Blaug, M. (1968). **Economic Theory in Retrospect** (Homewood, Ill: Richard D. Irwin) Chapter 7.

Choudhury, M. A. (1996a). "Markets as a system of social contracts," **International Journal of Social Economics**, Vol. 23, No. 1. pp. 17-36.

----- (1996b). "Why cannot neoclassicism explain resource allocation and development in the Islamic political economy?" in Ahmed, E. ed. **Role of Private and Public Sectors in Economic Development in an Islamic Perspective** (Herndon, VA: International Institute of Islamic Thought) pp. 17-44.

----- (1995). "Epistemology and science," **Arademika**, No. 46, pp. 89-116.

----- (1994a). "An Islamic theory of moral entitlement in comparative perspective," in Nitsch, T. O. Phillips, L. M. Jr. & Fitzsimmons, E. L. eds. **On the Conditions of Labor and the Social Question One Hundred Years After** (New York, NY: The Edwin Mellen Press) pp. 351-366.

----- (1994b). "The Muslim republics of the CIS: their political economy under communism, capitalism and Islam,," **The Evils of Soviet Communism and Other Critical Essays: Part II, The International Jornal of Social Economics**, Vol. 21, Nos. 5 & 6. pp. 2-32.

----- (1994c). **Economic Theory and Social Institutions** (Lanham, MA: The University Press of America).

----- (1993). **The Unicity Precept and the Socio-Scientific Order** (Lanham, MD: University Press of America).

----- (1991). "The endogenous theory of money and Islamic capital markets," **The Journal of Economic Cooperation Among Islamic Countries**, Vol. 12, Nos. 3-4, pp. 75-97.

Coase, R. H. (1994). "Adam Smith's view of man," in **Essays on Economics and Economists** (Chicago, ILL: The University of Chicago Press) pp. 95-116.

Cole, G. D. H. (1966). "The theory of value," in **The Meaning of Marxism** (Ann Arbor, Michigan: Michigan University Press).

Ekelund Jr., R.E. & Hebert, R.E. (1990). **A History of Economic Theory and Method** (New York, NY: McGraw-Hill Publishing Co.) p.274.

George, H. (1897). **The Science of Political Economy** (New York, NY: Robert Shaclkenbach Foundation) pg. 76.

Haddad, L. (1995). "Ethics as generalise economics: a conceptual framework for dealing with choices between economic and non-economic activities," **Humanomics**, Vol. 11, No. 4, pp. 7-28.

Johnston, J. 1984, **Econometric Methods** (New York, NY: McGraw-Hill) Ch. 11.

Kant, I. trans. Freidrich, C. (1987). "Critique of pure reason," in **The Philosophy of Kant** (New York, NY: The Modern Library) pp. 24-39.

Lutz, M. (1997). "The Mondragon cooperative complex: an application of Kantean ethics to social economics," in Choudhury, M.A. ed. **Fertschrift in Honour of Immanuel Kant: Socio-Economics of Community Development in Global Perspectives II**, (W. Yorkshire, Eng.: MCB University Press).

Mansfield, E. (1985). **Microeconomics** (New York, NY: W. W. Norton) Ch. 13.

Martin, S. (1988). **Industrial Economics, Economic Analysis and Public Policy** (New York, NY: MacMillan Publishing Co.) Chapter 5.

Martinez-Alier, J, (1990). "Marxism and ecology" in **Ecological Economics, Energy, Environment, and Society** (Oxford, Eng.: Basil Blackwell) pp. 218-225.

Mill, J. S. (1994). **Principles of Political Economy** (Oxford, Eng.: Oxford University Press).

Minford, P. & Peel, D. (1983). "The political economy of democracy" in **Rational Expectations and the New Macroeconomics** (Oxford, NY: Martin Robertson & Co.) Chapter 8.

The Holy Qur'an, Text, Translation and Commentary by A. Yusuf Ali, (1989). (Brentwood, Maryland: Amana Corporation).

Quinton, A. (1989). **Utilitarian Ethics** (LaSalle, ILL: Open Court).

Sen, A. (1990). "Freedom and consequences," in **On Ethics & Economics** (Oxford, Eng.: Basil Blackwell) pp. 58-89.

Shackle, G. L. S. (1971) **Epistemics and Economics** (Cambridge, Eng.: Cambridge University Press).

Smith, A. (1790). **The Theory of Moral Sentiments**, Raphael, D. D. & Macfie, A. L. eds. (Oxford, Eng.: Clarendon Press, 1976).

---- (1976)[1776]. **An Inquiry Into the Nature and Causes of the Wealth of Nations.** Campbell, R. H. and Skinner, A. S. eds. (Oxford, Eng.: Clarendon Press).

Solow, R. M. (1970). **Growth Theory, An Exposition** (Oxford, Eng.: Clarendon Press).

Srinivasan, T. N. (1985). "Neoclassical political economy, the state and economic development," **Asian Development Review**, Vol. 3, No. 2, pp. 38-58.

Staniland, M. (1985). **What is Political Economy? A Study of Social Theory and Underdevelopment** (New Haven, CO: Yale University Press) Ch. 6.

Stigler, G. J. (1960). "The influence of events and policies on economic theory," **The American Economic Review**.

Thurow, L. (1983). **Dangerous Currents, The State of Economics** (New York, NY: Random House).

Tribe, K. (1999). "Adam Smith: critical theorist?" **Journal of Economic Literature**, Vol. XXXVII, June pp. 609-32.

Vanek, J. (1975). "The basic theory of financing of participatory firms," in Vanek, J. ed. **Self-Management (Economic Liberation of Man)** (London, Eng.: Penguin).

Zimbalist, A. Sherman, H & Brown, S. (1989). **Comparing Economic Systems, A Politico-Economic Approach** (New York, NY: Harcourt Brace Jovanovich, Publishers) Chapter 8.

CHAPTER 5: ISLAMIC POLITICAL ECONOMY, A CRITIQUE OF ISLAMIC ECONOMICS

Ahmad, M. (1986). "Islamic political theory: current scholarship and future prospects," in Ahmad, M. ed. **State Politics and Islam** (Indianapoils, IN: American Trust Publication) pp. 1-22.

Allouche, A. (1994). **Mamluk Economics, a Study and Translation of Al-Maqrizi's Ighathah** (Salt Lake City, Utah: University of Utah Press) Chapter, "Currency [Islamic Currency]".

Ansari, J.A. (1986). **The Political Economy of International Economic Organization** (Boulder, CO: Rienner) pp. 1-32.

Anwar, M. (1987) **Modelling an Interest-Free Economy: A Study in Macroeconomics and Development** (Herndon, VA: International Institute of Islamic Thought) 119 pp.

Ariff, M. (1982). "Monetary policy in an interest-free Islamic economy: nature and scope," Ariff, M. ed. **Monetary and Fiscal Economics of Islam** (Jeddah, Saudi Arabia: International Center for Research in Islamic Economics) pp. 287-309.

Ariff, M. & Mannan, M.A. (1990). **Developing a System of Financial Instruments** (Jeddah, Saudi Arabia: Islamic Research and Training Institute, Islamic Development Bank & Kuala Lumpur, Malaysia: Ministry of Finance).

Asad, M. (1980). **The Principles of State and Government in Islam** (Gibraltar: Dar al-Andalus).

Bashir, A-H,M. & Darrat, A.F. (1992). "Equity participation contracts and investment: some theoretical and empirical results," **The American Journal of Islamic Social Sciences**, Vol. 9, No. 2, Summer, pp. 219-32.

Becker, G. (1989). "Family," in J. Eatwell, M. Milgate & P. Newman eds. **The New Palgrave: Social Economics** (New York, NY: W.W. Norton) pp. 64-76.

Blaug, M. (1968). **Economic Theory in Retrospect** (Homewood, ILL: Richard D. Irwin, Inc) pp. 1-9.

Boulding, K.E. (1967). "Evolution and revolution in the developmental process," in **Social Change and Economic Growth** (Paris, France: Development Center of the Organization of Economic Cooperation and Development) pp. 219-29.

Bowles, S. (1991). "What markets can – and cannot – do," **Challenge**, Vol. 34, No. 4, pp. 11-16.

Buchanan, J.M. (1975). **The Limits of Liberty, Between Anarchy and Leviathan** (Chicago, ILL: The University of Chicago Press).

Buchanan, J.M. & Tullock, G. (1962). **The Calculus of Consent** (Ann Arbor, Michigan: The University of Michigan Press).

Cantor, G. trans. Jourdain, P.E.B. 1955, **Contributions to the Founding of the Theory of Transfinite Numbers** (New York, NY: Dover Publications).

Chapra, M.U. (1985). **Towards a Just Monetary Society** (Leicester, Eng.: The Islamic Foundation).

----- (1992). **Islam and the Economic Challenge** (Leicester, Eng.: The Islamic Foundation & Herndon, VA: International Institute of Islamic Thought) Ch. 5.

Chittick, W.C. (1989). **Sufi Path of Knowledge** (Albany, NY: State University of New York).

Choudhury, M.A. (1986). "Macroeconomic relations in the Islamic economic order," in **Contributions to Islamic Economic Theory: A Study in Social Economics** (London, Eng.: Macmillan Press Ltd. & New York, NY: St. Martin's Press Ltd) pp. 166-87.

----- (1989a). "An Islamic econometric model for Malaysia with policy conclusions," **Journal of Economic Cooperation Among Islamic Countries**, Vol. 10, No. 2, pp. 23-53.

----- (1989b). **Islamic Economic Co-operation** (London, Eng.: Macmillan & New York, NY: St. Martin's Press).

----- (1990a). "Syllogistic deductionism in Islamic social choice theory," **International Journal of Social Economics**, Vol. 17, No. 11, pp. 2-20.

----- (1990b). "Islamic economics as a social science," **International Journal of Social Economics**, Vol. 17, No. 6, pp. 35-59.

----- (1990c). "Price, value and social equilibrium in ethico-economics," **Journal of the Social Sciences**, Vol. 18, No. 1, pp. 268-79.

----- (1991a). "The Tawhidi precept in the sciences," **MAAS Journal of Islamic Science**, Vol. 7, No. 1, Jan-Jun, pp. 19-44.

----- (1991b). "Micro-macro interface in Islamic economic theory," **The Middle East Business and Economic Review**, Vol. 3, No. 1, Jan. pp. 29-38.

----- (1991c). "The endogenous theory of money and Islamic capital markets," **Journal of Economic Cooperation Among Islamic Countries**, Vol. 12, Nos. 3-4, pp. 75-97.

----- (1992a). **The Principles of Islamic Political Economy: A Methodological Enquiry** (London, Eng.: Macmillan Press Ltd. & New York, NY: St. Martin's).

----- (1992b). "A theory of moral entitlement in resource allocation," in Sattar, Z. ed. **Resource Mobilization and Investment in an Islamic Economic Framework** (Herndon, VA: International Institute of Islamic Thought) pp. 45-70.

----- (1993a). "Towards a general theory of Islamic social contract," in Choudhury, M.A. **The Unicity Precept and the Socio-Scientific Order** (Lanham, MA: The University Press of America) pp. 105-48.

----- (1993b). "Conflict resolution and social consensus formation in Islamic social choice and welfare menu," **International Journal of Social Economics**, Vol. 20, No. 1, pp. 64-77.

----- (1993c). **Comparative Development Studies: In Search of the World View** (London, Eng.: Macmillan & New York, NY: St. Martin's Press).

----- (1994a). **Economic Theory and Social Institutions: A Critique With Special Reference to Canada** (Lanham, MA: The University Press of America) Chapter 11: "Social Contractarianism for Humanistic Institutionalism."

----- (1994b). "Islamization of knowledge, the epistemological question," **Journal of the Faculty of Islamic Studies and Arabic**, Vol. 1, No. 2, pp. 168-215.

----- (1994c). "The epistemic-ontic circular causation and continuity model of socio-scientific reality: the knowledge premise," **International Journal of Social Economics**, Vol. 21, No. 1, pp. 3-18.

----- (1994d). "Labour market," in **Economic Theory and Social Institutions** (Lanham, MA: The University Press of America) pp. 281-320.

----- (1995a). **The Epistemological Foundations of Islamic Economic, Social and Scientific Order, 6 Vols** (Ankara, Turkey: Statistical, Economic and Social Research and Training Centre for Islamic Countries, Organization of Islamic Conferences).

----- (1995b). **The Epistemological Foundations**, Vol. 5, Chapters 9 & 10.

----- (1995c). "A systems model of the Malaysian macro-economy," **Kybernetes: The International Journal of Systems & Cybernetics**, Vol. 24, No. 7, pp. 75-90.

----- (1996a). "Islam, Economics and Society by Professor S.N.H. Naqvi: a critical review," **Hamdard Islamicus**, Vol. XVIV, Nol 1, Spring, pp. 99-122.

----- (1996b). "Markets as a system of social contracts," **International Journal of Social Economics**, Vol. 23, No. 1, pp. 17-36.

----- (1996c). "Why cannot neoclassicism explain resource allocation and development in the Islamic political economy?" in Ahmed, E. ed. **Role of Private and Public Sectors in Economic Development in an Islamic Perspective** (Herndon, VA: International Institute of Islamic Thought) pp. 17-44.

----- (1997). **Money in Islam** (London, Eng.: Routledge).

----- (1997b). "Theory and practice of Islamic political economy," in Choudhury, M.A. Abdad, M.Z. & Salleh, M.S. eds. **Islamic Political Economy in Capitalist-Globalization, An Agenda for Change** (Kuala Lumpur, Malaysia: Utusan Publications) pp. 3-39.

---- (1997c ed.). **Comparative Political Economy**, being a special issue of **Humanomics**, Vol. 13, No. 3 & 4 (Hull, Eng.: Barmarick Publications).

----- (1997d ed.). **Festschrift in Honour of Imam Ghazzali: Socioeconomics of Community Development in Global Perspective I** (West Yorkshire, Eng.: MCB University Press).

----- (1998a). **Studies in Islamic Social Sciences** (London, Eng.: Macmillan & New York, NY: St. Martin's).

----- (1998b). **Reforming the Muslim World** (London, Eng.: Kegan Paul International).

Choudhury, M.A. & Malik, U.A. (1992). **The Foundations of Islamic Political Economy** (London, Eng.: Macmillan & New York, NY: St. Martin's Press).

Cole, G.D.H. (1966). "The theory of value," in **The Meaning of Marxism** (Ann Arbor, Michigan: The University of Michigan Press).

Condorcet, M.J.A.N. de Caritat, M. (1785). **Essai sur l'application de l'analyse a la probabilite des decisions rendues a la pluralite des voix** (Paris, France: Imprimerie Royale).

Desai, M. (1989). "Endogenous and exogenous money," in J. Eatwell, M. Milgate & P. Newman eds. **The New Palgrave: Money** (New York, NY: W.W. Norton) pp. 146-50.

Dewitt, B. (1992). **Supermanifold**, Cambridge, Eng.: Cambridge University Press.

Ekelund Jr R.B. & Hebert, R.E. (1990). "Karl Marx and scientific socialism," in **A History of Economic Theory and Method** (New York, NY: McGraw-Hill Book Co.) pp. 261-85.

Ellerman, D. (1991). "The democratic firm: a cooperative-ESOP model," in Wisman, J.D. ed. **Worker Empowerment** (New York, NY: The Bookstrap Press) pp. 83-96.

Etzioni, A. (1988). "Instrumental rationality: supportive condition," in **The Moral Dimension, Toward a New Economics** (New York, NY: The Free Press) pp. 151-65.

Faruqi, B.A. (1977). **The Mujadid's Conception of Tawhid** (Delhi, India: Idarah i-Adabiyat i-Delhi).

Friedman, M. (1989). "Quantity theory of money," **The New Palgrave: Money**, op cit. pp. 1-40.

Grandmont, J.-M (1989). "Temporary equilibrium," in J. Eatwell, M. Milgate & P. Newman eds. **The New Palgrave: General Equilibrium** (New York, NY: W.W. Norton) pp. 297-304.

Gray, A. (1967). **The Development of Economic Doctrine** (London, Eng.: Longmans) pp. 2-3.

Haddad, L. (1995). "Ethics as generalised economics: a conceptual framework for dealing with choices between economic and non-economic activities," **Humanomics**, Vol. 11, No. 4, pp. 7-28.

Hasan, Z. (1986). "Distributional equity in Islam," in Iqbal, M. ed. **Distributive Justice and Need Fulfilment in an Islamic Economy** (Islamabad, Pakistan: International Institute of Islamic Economics & Leicester, Eng.: The Islamic Foundation) pp. 35-62.

Hayek, F.A. ed. S. Kresge (1999). "Theory and the trade cycle," **Good Money**, (Chicage, Ill.: University of Chicago Press).

----- (1937). "Economics and knowledge," **Economica**, Vol. 4, 33-54.

Henderson, J.M. and Quandt, R.E. (1971). **Microeconomic Theory: a Mathematical Approach** (New York, NY: McGraw-Hill, Inc.).

Holland, M. trans. (1982). **Public Duties in Islam: The Institution of Al-Hisbah** (Leicester, Eng.: The Islamic Foundation).

Ibn Taimiyyah (1967). **Al-Hisbah Fil Islam** (Beirut, Lebanon: Dar al-Kutb al-Arabiyyah).

Iqbal, J. (1986). "The concept of state in Islam," in Ahmad, M. ed. **State Politics and Islam** (Indianapolis, IN: American trust Publication) pp. 37-50.

Intrilligator, M.D. (1971). **Mathematical Optimization and Economic Theory** (Englewood Cliffs, NJ: Prentice-Hall, Inc.) Ch. 12.

Islahi, A.A. (1995). "Market mechanism in Islam: a historical perspective," **Journal of Islamic Economics**, Vol. 1, No. 1, Jan. pp. 1-13.

Islamic Development Bank Oct. (1995). **Annual Report 1994-95** (Jeddah, Saudi Arabia: Islamic Development Bank).

Ismail, S.M. (1989). "Musharekat and muzarebat," in **Capitalism, Socialism and Islamic Economic Order** (Lahore, Pakistan: Oriental Publications) pp. 440-74.

Jahri, M.A.M.M. (1980). "The relative efficiency of interest-free monetary economics: the fiat money case," in Ahmad, K. ed. **Studies in Islamic Economics** (Jeddah, Saudi Arabia: International Center for Research in Islamic Economics & Leicester, Eng.: The Islamic Foundation) pp. 85-118.

Jalbani, G.N. trans. (1985). **Al-Fauz al-Kabir Fi Usul al-Tafsir** (Islamabad, Pakistan: National Hijra Council).

Kahf, M. (1978). **The Islamic Economy: Analytical Study of the Functioning of the Islamic System** (Plainfield, IN: The Muslim Students' Association of the United States and Canada).

----- (1982a). "Saving and investment function in a two-sector Islamic economy," in Ariff, M. ed. **Monetary and Fiscal Economics of Islam** (Jeddah, Saudi Arabia: International Center for Research in Islamic Economics) pp. 107-23.

----- (1982b). "Fiscal and monetary policies in an Islamic economy," in Ariff, M. op cit. pp. 125-37.

Karim, M.F. trans. undated, **Imam Ghazzali's Ihya Ulum-id-Din, Vol. 1: The Book of Worship** (Lahore, Pakistan: Sh. Muhammad Ashraf Press).

Khan, A. (1983). **Islamic Economics: Annotated Sources in English and Urdu**, Vol. 1 (Leicester, Eng.: The Islamic Foundation).

----- (1991). **Islamic Economics: Annotated Sources in English and Urdu**, Vol. 2 (Leicester, Eng.: The Islamic Foundations).

Khan, F. (1986). "Macroeconomic consumption function in an Islamic economy," in Choudhury, M.A. **Contributions to Islamic Economic Theory: A Study in Social Economics** (London, Eng.: Macmillan) pp. 140-65.

----- (1991). "Time value of money and discounting in Islamic perspective," **Review of Islamic Economics**, Vol. 1, No. 2, pp. 35-45.

Khan, W.M. (1985). **Towards an Interest-Free Islamic Economic System** (Leicester, Eng.: The Islamic Foundation & Islamabad, Pakistan: The International Association of Islamic Economics) Ch. 4.

Khan, M.S. & Mirakhor, A. (1987). **Theoretical Studies in Islamic Banking and Finance** (Houston, Texas: Book Distribution Center).

Kirzner, I.M. (1997). "Entrepreneurial discovery and the competitive market process: an Austrian approach," **Journal of Economic Literature**, Vol. XXXV, No. 1, March, pp. 60-85.

Koizumi, T. (1993). **Interdependence and Change in the Global System** (Lanham, MA: The University Press of America).

Lucas, R.E. & Sargent, T.J. 1978, "After Keynesian macroeconomics," in **After the Phillips Curve: Persistence of High Inflation and High Unemployment** (Boston, Massachusetts: Federal Reserve Bank of Boston).

Lutz, M. (1994). "Instrumental rationality and the human dimension," **Humanomics**, Vol. 10, No.4, pp. 49-75.

Mansfield, E. (1985). **Microeconomicc, Theory and Applications** (New York, NY: W.W. Norton) Ch. 13.

Masud, M.K. (1984). **Islamic Legal Philosophy** (Islamabad, Pakistan: Islamic Research Institute).

Mehmet, O. (1990). **Islamic Identity & Development** (London, Eng.: Routledge) Ch. 8: "Islam, the modern state and imperfect competition: to ban or to regulate?"

Metwally, M.M. (1980). "A behavioural model of the Islamic firm" (memeo) (Jeddah, Saudi Arabia: International Center for Research in Islamic Economics, King Abdulaziz University).

----- (1989). "The role of the rate of interest in contemporary Islamic societies," **The Middle East Business and Economic Review**, Vol. 1, No. 1, pp. 32-53.

----- (1991). "The humanomics of a Muslim consumer," **Humanomics**, Vol. 7, No. 3, pp. 63-72.

Minford, P. & Peel, D. (1983). **Rational Expectations and the New Macroeconomics** (Oxford, Eng.: Martin Robertson) Chapter 2: "Solving rational expectations models".

Muslehuddin, M. (undated). **Philosophy of Islamic Law and the Orientalists** (Lahore, Pakistan: Islamic Publications Ltd.).

Nagel, E. (1981). "Reduction of theories," in **The Structure of Science** (New York, NY: Harcourt, Brace & World) pp. 336-97.

Naqvi, S.N.H. (1994). **Islam, Economics, and Society** (London, Eng.: Kegan Paul International) Ch. 3-5.

Nasr, S.H. (1987). "Science education," **Muslim Education Quarterly**, Vol.5, No.1, pp. 4-14.

----- (1996). "The Islamic worldview and modern science," **Islamic Thought and Scientific Creativity**, Vol. 7, No. 1, March, pp. 7-22.

Neurath, O. Carnap, R. & Morris, C. eds. (1970). **Foundations of the Unity of Science Vol. 2** (Chicago, ILL: The University of Chicago Press).

Nikaido, H. (1989). "Fixed point theorems," in Eatwell, J. Milgate, M. & Newman, P. eds. **The New Palgrave: General Equilibrium**, New York, NY: W.W. Norton, pp. 139-44.

Noor, H.M. (1998). "Fakhruddin Razi's theory of knowledge and its implications in ethico-economics," **Humanomics**, Vol. 14, No. 1, pp. 59-96.

Osborne, M.J. & Rubinstein, A. (1994). "Knowledge and equilibrium," in **A Course in Game Theory** (Cambridge, Massachusetts: The MIT Press) pp. 67-85.

Parsons, T. (1964). **The Structure of Social Actions** (New York, NY: The Free Press of Glencoe).

Phelps, E.S. (1970). "The new microeconomics in employment and inflation theory," in Phelps, E.S. **Microeconomic Foundations of Employment and Inflation Theory** (New York, NY: W.W. Norton) pp. 1-27.

Popper, K. (1982). "Scientific reduction and the essential incompleteness of all sciences," in Bartley, W.W. ed. **The Open Universe: An Argument for Determinism**, Totowa, NJ: Rowman & Littlefield.

Post, J.F. (1988). "Paradox in critical rationalism and related theories," in Radnitzky, G. & Bartley III, N.W. eds. **Evolutionary Epistemology, Rationality and the Sociology of Knowledge**, La Salle, ILL: Open Court, pp. 223-51.

Qadri, C.A. (1988). "Muslim philosophers and their problems," in **Philosophy and Science in the Islamic World** (London, Eng.: Routledge) pp. 70-88.

Quinton, A. (1989). **Utilitarian Ethics** (La Salle, ILL: Open Court).

Romer, P.M. (1986). "Increasing returns and long-run growth," **Journal of Islamic Political Economy**, Vol. 94, pp. 1002-1037.

Samuelson, P.A. (1970). **Foundations of Economic Analysis**, New York, NY: Atheneum, p. 6.

Sen, A. (1970). "The impossibility of a Paretian liberal," **Journal of Political Economy**, Vol. 72.

----- (1977). "Rational fools: a critique of the behavioural foundations of economic theory," **Philosophy and Public Affairs**, Vol. 6.

----- (1985). "The moral standing of the market," in Paul, E.F. Miller, F.D. & Paul J. eds. **Ethics and Economics** (Oxford, Eng.: Blackwell).

----- (1985). "Well-being, agency and freedom," **Journal of Philosophy**, Vol. 82.

----- (1987). "Freedom and consequences," in **On Ethics & Economics** (Oxford, Eng.: Basil Blackwell) pp. 58-88.

Shackle, G.L.S. (1972). **Epistemics and Economics** (Cambridge, Eng.: Cambridge University Press).

Shakun, M. (1988). **Evolutionary Systems Design** (Oakland, CA: Holden-Day) Ch. 1.

Siddiqi, M.N. (1983). **Banking Without Interest** (Leicester, Eng.: The Islamic Foundation).

----- (1991). "Some economic aspects of Mudarabah," **Review of Islamic Economics**, Vol. 1, No. 2, pp. 21-33.

Simon, H. (1957). "A behavioural model of rational choice," in **Models of Man** (New York, NY: John Wiley & Sons, Inc.) pp. 241-60.

Smith, T.S. (1992). **Strong Interaction** (Chicago, ILL: The University of Chicago Press).

Stigler, G.J. (1960). "The influence of events and policies on economic theory," **American Economic Review**, May.

Sullivan, W.M. (1989). "The contemporary crisis of liberal society," in McCullough, H.B. ed. **Political Ideologies and Political Philosophies** (Toronto, Ont: Wall & Thompson) pp. 57-9.

Taj El-Din, S.I. (1991). "Risk-aversion, moral hazard and financial Islamization policy," **Review of Islamic Economics**, Vol. 1, No. 1, pp. 49-66.

Taylor, O.H. (1967). "The future of economic liberalism," in **Economics and Liberalism** (Cambridge, Massachusetts: Harvard University Press) pp. 294-311.

Tinbergen, J. (1987). "The optimum order revisited," in Feiwel, G.R. ed. **Arrow and the Foundations of the Theory of Economic Policy** (London, Eng.: Macmillan) pp. 281-327.

Tobin, J. (1969). "A general equilibrium approach to monetary theory," **Journal of Money, Credit and Banking**, Vol. 1, Feb. pp. 15-29.

Tobin, J. & Brainard, W.C. (1968). "Pitfalls in financial model building," **American Economic Review**, Vol. 58, May, pp. 99-122.

Tschiderer, W. (1996). "The development of Professor Hayek's research programme," **International Journal of Social Economics**, Vol. 22, No. 6, pp. 65-80.

Turnovsky, S.J. (1995). "An introduction to endogenous growth models," in **Methods of Macroeconomic Dynamics** (Cambridge, Massachusetts: The MIT Press) pp. 391-425.

von Mises, L. (1976). **The Ultimate Foundation of Economic Science** (Kansas City, Missouri: Sheed Andrews and McMeel, Inc.) p. 16.

Yadegari, M. (1984). "Shariati and the reconstruction of the social sciences," **American Journal of Islamic Studies**, Vol. 1, No. 1, Spring, pp. 53-9.

Zaidi, I. & Mirakhor, A. (1991). "Stabilization and growth in an open Islamic economy," **Review of Islamic Economics**, Vol. 1, No. 2, pp. 1-20.

Zarqa, M.A. (1983). "An Islamic perspective on the economics of discounting in project evaluation," in Ahmed, Z. Iqbal, M. & Khan, M.F. eds. **Fiscal Policy and Resource Allocation in Islam** (Jeddah, Saudi Arabia: International Centre for Research in Islamic Economics, King Abdulaziz University) pp. 203-34.

CHAPTER 6: KNOWLEDGE AND INTERACTIONS IN POLITICAL ECONOMY AND ECONOMIC THEORY

Amin, S. (1989). **Eurocentrism** (New York, NY: Monthly Press).

Arrow, K.J. (1963). **Social Choice and Individual Values** (New York, NY: John Wiley).

----- (1972). "The economic implications of learning by doing," **Review of Economic Studies**, Vol. 29, pp. 155-73.

Barrow, J.D. (1991). **Theories of Everything, the Quest for Ultimate Explanation** (Oxford, Eng: Oxford University Press).

Becker, G.S. (1989). "Family," in Eatwell, J. Milgate, M. & Newman, P. eds. **The New Palgrave: Social Economics** (New York, NY: W.W. Norton) pp. 64-76.

Boland, L.A. (1989). **The Methodology of Economic Model Building, Methodology After Samuelson** (London, Eng: Routledge).

Bordo, M. (1989). "The contribution of 'A Monetary History of the United States, 1867-1960' to monetary history," in Bordo, M. ed. **Money, History, and International Finance: Essays in Honour of Anna J. Schwartz** (Chicago, ILL. University of Chicago Press) pp. 15-75.

Boulding, K.E. (1967). "Evolution and revolution in the development process," in **Social Change and Economic Growth** (Paris, France: Organization for Economic Cooperation and Development).

Campbell, D.T, (1988). "Evolutionary epistemology," in Radnitzky, G. & Bartley, W.W. III eds. **Evolutionary Epistemology, rationality, and the Sociology of Knowledge** (La Salle, ILL: Open Court) pp. 47-89.

Casti, J.L. (1990). "Proof or consequences," in **Searching for Certainty** (New York, NY: William Morrow & Co. pp. 323-403.

Choudhury, M.A. (1992). **The Principles of Islamic Political Economy** (London, Eng: Macmillan & New York, NY: St. Martin's).

----- (1993). **The Unicity Precept and the Socio-Scientific Order** (Lanham, MA: The University Press of America).

----- (1994). "The epistemic-ontic circular causation and continuity model of socio-scientific reality: the knowledge premise," **International Journal of Social Economics**, Vol. 21, No. 1, pp. 3-18.

----- (1995). "Reality and Tawhidi timal topology embedded in supermanifold of knowledge," in **The Epistemological Foundations of Islamic Economic, Social and Scientific Order, Vol. 5 of Six Vols.** (Ankara, Turkey: Statistical, Economic and Social Research and Training Centre for Islamic Countries, Organization of Islamic Conferences).

----- (1995b). **The Epistemological Foundations of Islamic Economic, Social and Scientific Order, Six Vols.** (Ankara, Turkey: Statistical, Economic and Social Research and Training Centre for Islamic Countries, Organization for Islamic Conferences).

----- (1996). "Why cannot neoclassicism explain resource allocation and development in the Islamic political economy?" in Ahmed, E. ed. **Role of Private and Public Sectors in Economic Development in an Islamic Perspective** (Herndon, VA: International Institute of Islamic Thought) pp 17-44.

----- 1997a, **Money in Islam** (London, Eng: Routledge).

----- (1997b). "Theory and Practice of Islamic Political Economy" in Choudhury, M.A. Abdad, M.Z. & Salleh, M.S. eds. **Islamic Political Economy in Capitalist-Globalization, an Agenda for Change** (Kuala Lumpur, Malaysia: Utusan Publications) pp. 2-39.

----- (1998). **Studies in Islamic Science and Polity** (London, Eng.: Macmillan & New York, NY: St. Martin's Press).

Daly, H.E. (1992). "From empty-world to full-world economics: recognizing an historical turning point in economic development," in Goodland, R. Daly, H.E. el-Serafy, S. & von Droste, B. eds. **Environmentally Sustainable Economic Development: Building on Brundtland** (Paris, France: UNESCO) pp. 29-38.

Dasgupta, A.K. (1985). **Epochs of Economic Theory** (Oxford, Eng: Basil Blackwell).

Dawkins, R. (1976). **The Selfish Gene** (Oxford, Eng: Oxford University Press).

Debreu, G. (1959). **Theory of Value, an Axiomatic Analysis of Economic Equilibrium** (New York, NY: John Wiley).

Denison, E.F. 1962, **The Sources of Economic Growth in the U.S. and the Alternatives Before Us** (New York, NY: Committee for Economic Development, Supplementary Paper No. 13).

Desai, M. (1989). "Endogenous and exogenous money," in Eatwell, J. Milgate, M. & Newman, P. **The New Palgrave: Money** (New York, NY: W.W. Norton) pp. 146-150.

George, H. (1897). **The Science of Political Economy** (New York, NY: Robert Schalkenbach Foundation).

Dewitt, B. (1992). **Supermanifolds** (Cambridge, Eng: Cambridge University Press).

Drucker, P.F. (1990). **The New Realities** (New York, NY: Harper & Row).

Etzioni, A. (1988). "Instrumental rationality: supportive conditions," in **The Moral Dimension, Toward a New Economics** (New York, NY: The Free Press) pp. 151-65.

Ferry, L., Philip, F. (1992, trans). **The System of Philosophies of History** (Chicago, ILL: The University of Chicago Press).

Frenkel, J.A. & Razin, A. (1989). **Fiscal Policies and the World Economy** (Cambridge, MA: The MIT Press).

Friedman, M. (1989). "Quantity theory of money," in **The New Palgrave: Money**, op cit.

Georgescu-Roegen, N. (1971). **The Entropy Law and the Economic Process** (Cambridge, MA: Harvard University Press).

Griclichez, Z. (1970). "Notes on the role of education in production function and growth accounting," in Hansen, L.W. ed. **Education, Income and Human Capital** (Washington D.C.: National Bureau of Economic Research.

Haines, W.W. (1987). "A society without money: reflections on Jacques Maritain," **Festschrift in Honour of Anghel N. Rugina, Part I, International Journal of Social Economics**, Vol. 14, Nos. 3-5, pp. 97-104.

Halmos, P.R. (1959). **Measure Theory** (Princeton, N.J: D. van Nostrand Co).

Hammond, P.J.(1987). "On reconciling Arrow's theory of social choice with Harsanyi's fundamental utilitarianism," in Feiwel, G.R. ed. **Arrow and the Foundations of the Theory of Economic Policy** (London, Eng: Macmillan) pp. 179-221.

Harsanyi, J.C. (1954). "Cardinal welfare, individualistic ethics, and interpersonal comparisons of utility," **Journal of Political Economy**, Vol. 61, pp. 309-21.

Hawley, A.H. (1986). **Human Ecology** (Chicago, ILL: The University of Chicago Press).

Hayek, F.A. (1945). "The use of knowledge in society," **American Economic Review**, Vol. 35, No. 4, pp. 519-30.

Hull, D.L. (1988). **Science as a Process, An Evolutionary Account of the Social and Conceptual Development of Science** (Chicago, ILL: The University of Chicago Press).

Khan, T. (1984). **Islamic Economics: A Bibliography** (Jeddah, Saudi Arabia: Islamic Research and Training Institute).

Koizumi, T. (1993). **Interdependence and Change in the Global Order** (Lanham, Madison: The University Press of America).

Korten, D.C. (1995). **When Corporations Rule the World** (London, Eng: Earthscan).

Kosko, B. (1993). **Fuzzy Thinking, the New Science of Fuzzy Logic** (New York, NY: Hyperion).

Krugman, P. (1996). **The Self-Organizing Economy** (Oxford, Eng: Blackwell).

Laidler, D. (1990). "The quantity theory is always and everywhere controversial – why?" **Atlantic Canada Economic Association Papers**, Vol. 18, pp. 98-122.

Maddox, I.J. (1970). **Elements of Functional Analysis** (Cambridge, Eng: Cambridge University Press).

Mill, J.S. (1994 reprinted). **Principles of Political Economy** (Oxford, Eng: Oxford University Press).

Miller, G.J. (1997). "The impact of economics on contemporary political science," **Journal of Economic Literature**, Vol. XXXV, No. 3, Sept. pp. 1173-1204.

Morishima, M. (1964). **Equilibrium, Stability and Growth** (Oxford, Eng: Oxford University Press).

Nelson, R.R. & Winter, S.G. (1982). **An Evolutionary Theory of Economic Change** (Cambridge, MA: The Belknap Press of Harvard University Press).

Nordhaus, W.D. (1975)." The political business cycle," **Review of Economic Studies**, Vol. 42, pp. 169-90.

North, D.C. (1981). **Structure and Change in Economic Theory** (New York, NY: W.W. Norton).

Osborne, M.J. & Rubinstein A. (1994). **A Course in Game Theory** (Camridge, MA: The MIT Press).

Penrose, R. (1989). **The Emperor's New Mind** (Oxford, Eng: Oxford University Press).

Pheby, J. (1988). **Methodology and Economics, a Critical Introduction** (London, Eng: Macmillan).

Popper, K. A. "Scientific reduction and the essential incompleteness of all sciences," in Bartley, W.W. III ed. **The Open Universe: An Argument for Indeterminateness** (Totowa, N.J: Rowman & Littlefield).

Prigogine, I. (1980). **From Being to Becoming: Time and Complexity in the Physical Sciences** (San Francisco, CA: Freeman).

Rawls, J. (1971). **A Theory of Justice** (Cambridge, MA: Harvard University Press).

Rhoads, S.E. (1985). "Kind hearts and opportunity costs," in **The Economist's View of the World: Government, Markets, and Public Policy** (Cambridge, Eng: Cambridge University Press).

Romer, P.M. (1986). "Increasing returns and long-run growth," **Journal of Political Economy**, Vol. 94, pp. 1002-37.

Schumpeter, J.A. (1962). "The theory of economic development" in **Capitalism, Socialism and Democracy** (New York, NY: Harper & Row Torchbooks).

Sen, A. (1986). **Poverty and Famines, an Essay on Entitlement and Deprivation** (Oxford, Eng: Oxford University Press).

Shackle, G.L.S. (1972). **Epistemics and Economics** (Cambridge, Eng: Cambridge University Press).

Shakun, M. F. (1988). **Evolutionary Systems Design** (Oakland, CA: Holden-Day, Inc).

Smith, T.S. (1992). "Dynamics of strong interactions," in **Strong Interactions** (Chicago, ILL: The University of Chicago Press) pp 67-104.

Srinivasan, T.N. (1985). "Neoclassical political economy, the state and economic development," **Asian Economic Review**, Vol. 3, No. 2, pp. 38-58.

Stigler, G.J. (1966). **The Theory of Price** (London, Eng: Collier-Macmillan Ltd).

Thurow, L. (1996). **The Future of Capitalism** (London, Eng: Nicholas Brealey).

von Mises, L. (1976). **The Ultimate Foundation of Economic Science** (Kansas City, Missouri: Sheed Andrews & McMeel, Inc).

Wolf, R.P. (1977). **Understanding Rawls** (Princeton, N.J: Princeton University Press.

CHAPTER 7: COMPLEMENTARITY IN THE QUR'ANIC ECOLOGICAL MODEL

Ahmad, Z. (1991). **Islam, Poverty and Income Distribution** (London, Eng.: The Islamic Foundation).

al-Jawziyya, Ibn Qayyim trans. al-Akili (1993). **Natural Healing with the Medicine of the Prophet** (Philadelphia, PA: Pearl Publishing House).

Barrow, J.D. (1991). **Theories of Everything** (Oxford, Eng.: Clarendon Press).

Boulding, K.E. (1972). "Economics as a social science," in Globe, F.R. ed. **Boulding: Collected Papers, Vol. 2** (Boulder, CO: Association of University Press).

Boulding, K.E. (1967). "Evolution and revolution in the development process," in **Social Change and Economic Growth** (Paris, France: Development Centre of the Organization for Economic Cooperation and Development).

Choudhury, M.A. (1999). "Regulation and deregulation in the Islamic political economy: comparative perspectives," forthcoming, **Journal of King Abdulaziz University: Islamic Economics.**

----- (1997). "Islamic scientific epistemology: two alternative views with applications to curriculum development and the economy," paper presented in the Second International Conference on Values and Attitudes in Science and Technology, International Islamic University Malaysia, 1996; now in a revised form in **Reforming the Muslim World** (London, Eng.: Kegan Paul International, 1998).

----- (1996). "A theory of social systems: family and ecology as examples," **Kybernetes: The International Journal of Systems & Cybernetics**, Vol. 25, No.5, pp. 21-37.

----- (1995). **The Epistemological Foundations of Islamic Economic, Social and Scientific Order**, Six Vols. (Ankara, Turkey: Statistical, Economic and Social Research and Training Centre for Islamic Countries, Organization of Islamic Conferences).

----- (1994). "The concept of sustainable development: from Rio to ethics," **Jurnal Ekonomi Malaysia**, No. 28, pp. 69-92.

----- (1993). "Toward a general theory of Islamic social contract," in **The Unicity Precept and the Socio-Scientific Order** (Lanham, MD: The University Press of America) pp. 105-48.

----- (1992). "A theory of moral entitlement in resource allocation, in Sattar, Z. ed. **Resource Mobilization and Investment in an Islamic Economic Framework** (Herndon, VA: International Institute of Islamic Thought) pp. 45-70.

Coale, A.J. (1989). "Demographic transition," in J. Eatwell, M. Milgate & P. Newman eds. **The New Palgrave: Social Economics** (New York, NY: W.W. Norton) pp. 16-23.

Gauthier, D. (1986). **Morals by Agreement** (Oxford, Eng.: Oxford University Press).

Hawley, A.H. (1986). **Human Ecology** (Chicago, ILL: The University of Chicago Press).

Ibn Taimiyyah (1967). **Al-Hisbah fil Islam** (Beirut, Lebanon: Dar ul Kutb al-Arabiyyah).

Islahi, A.A. (1995). "Market mechanism in Islam: a historical perspective," **Journal of Islamic Economics**, Vol. 1, No.1, pp. 1-13.

Karim, F. (undated). **Imam Ghazzali's Ihya Ulum-Id-Din Vol. I: Book of Worship** (Lahore, Pakistan: Sh. Muhammad Ashraf Press).

Lancaster, K.J. (1966). "A new approach to consumer theory," **Journal of Political Economy**, Vol. 74, April, pp. 132-57.

Mansfield, E. (1985). **Microeconomics** (New York, NY: W.W. Norton) Ch. 13.

Maslow, A.H. (1968). **Toward a Psychology of Being** (New York, NY: Van Nostrand Reinhold).

Masud, M.K. (1984). **Islamic Legal Philosophy** (Islamabad, Pakistan: Islamic Research Institute).

Nasr, S.H. (1978). **An Introduction to Islamic Cosmological Doctrines** (Boulder, CO: Shambhala).

Noor, H.M. (1998). "Razi's human needs theory and its relevance to ethics and economics," **Humanomics**, Vol. 14, No. 1, pp. 59-96.

Phelps, E.S. (1989). "Distributive justice," in J. Eatwell, M. Milgate & M. Milgate eds. **The New Palgrave: Social Economics** (New York, NY: W.W. Norton) pp. 31-34.

Rucker, R. (1983). **Infinity and the Mind, the Sciences and Philosophy of the Infinite** (New York, NY: Bantam Books).

Russell, B. (1954). **The Analysis of Matter** (New York, NY: Dover Publications, Inc).
Schuon, F. (1989). "The way," in **Understanding Islam** (London, Eng.: Unwin Hyman Ltd.) pp. 106-59.

Shatibi [Imam] (undated). **Al-Muwafaqat fi Usul al-Shariah,** Abdallah Draz ed. (Cairo, Egypt: Al-Maktabah al-Tijariyyah al-Kubra).

Temkin, L.S. (1995). "Justice and equality: some questions about scope," in Paul, E.F. Miller Jr. F.D. & Paul, J. eds. **The Just Society** (Cambridge, Eng.: Cambridge University Press) pp. 72-104.

CHAPTER 8: DECISION-MAKING IN ISLAMIC POLITICAL ECONOMY

Arrow, K.J. (1974). **The Limits of Organization** (New York, NY: W.W. Norton).

Buchanan, J.M. (1975). **The limits of Liberty, Between Anarchy and Leviathan** (Chicago, IL: The University of Chicago Press).

Buchanan (1971). **The Basis for Collective Action** (New York, NY: General Learning Press).

Choudhury (1998). **Reforming the Muslim World** (London, Eng.: Kegan Paul International).

----- (1996a). "Markets as a system of social contracts," **International Journal of Social Economics**, Vol. 23, No. 1, pp.17-36..

----- (1996b) ."A theory of social systems: family and ecology as examples," **Kybernetes: The International Journal of Systems & Cybernetics**, Vol. 25, No. 5, pp. 21-37.

----- (1995b) .**The Epistemological Foundations of Islamic Economic, Social and Scientific Order, Six Volumes** (Ankara, Turkey: Statistical, Economic and Social Research and Training Centre for Islamic Countries, Organization of Islamic Conferences).

----- (1995a). **Islamic Socio-Scientific Order and World System** (Penang, Malaysia: Secretariat for Islamic Philosophy and Science, Universiti Sains Malaysia) Chapter 4: "The Nature of Relations Between Science, Technology and Organization in Islamic World View."

----- (1994a). "The epistemic-ontic circular causation and continuity model of socio-scientific reality: the knowledge premise," **International Journal of Social Economics**, Vol. 21, No. 1, pp. 3-18.

----- (1994b). "An Islamic Theory of Moral Entitlement in Comparative Perspectives," in Nitsch, T.O. Phillips, J.M. Jr. & Fitzsimmons, E.L. eds. **On the Condition of Labor and the Social Question One Hundred Years Later** (Commemorating the 100th Anniversary of Rerum Novarum, and the Fiftieth Anniversary of the Association of Social Economics) (New York, Lewiston: The Edwin Mellen Press).

----- (1992). **The Principles of Islamic Political Economy: A Methodological Enquiry** (London, Eng.: Macmillan Press & New York, NY: St. Martin's Press).

----- (1993). **The Unicity Precept and the Socio-Scientific Order** (Lanham, MA: The University Press of America).

Choudhury, M.A. Abdad, M.Z. Salleh, M.S. eds. (1997). **Islamic Political Economy in Capitalist Globalization: An Agenda for Change** (Kuala Lumpur, Malaysia: Utusan Publications & Penang, Malaysia: The International Project in Islamic Political Economy, Universiti Sains Malaysia).

Choudhury, M.A. & Hamat, A.F.C. (1997). "Markets, globalization and structural change," in Gupta, D. & Chaudhry, N.K. eds. **Political Economy Perspectives of Globalization** (New York, NY: Kluwer).

Choudhury, M.A. & Malik, U.A. (1992). **The Foundations of Islamic Political Economy** (London, Eng.: Macmillan & New York, NY: St. Martin's Press).

Collander, D. ed. (1984). **Neo-Classical Political Economy** (Cambridge, Eng.: Ballinger Publishing Co).

Dewitt, B. (1992). **Supermanifolds** (Cambridge, Eng.: Cambridge University Press).

Fischer, C.C. (1986). "The nature and implications of a process conception of rationality based on social learning," **Forum for Social Economics**, Spring 1986, pp. 63-73.

George, H. (1925). **The Science of Political Economy** (New York, NY: Robert Schalkenbach Foundation).

Gottlieb, M. (1984). **A Theory of Economic Systems** (New York, NY: Academic Press, Inc.

Hammond, P.J. (1987). "On reconciling Arrow's theory of social choice with Harsanyi's fundamental utilitarianism," in Feiwel, G.R. ed. **Arrow and the Foundations of the Theory of Economic Policy** (London, Eng.: Macmillan Press Ltd.) pp. 179-221.

Harsanyi, J.C. (1955). "Cardinal welfare, individualistic ethics, and interpersonal comparisons of utility," **Journal of Political Economy**, Vol. 63, pp. 309-21.

Harsanyi (1953). "Cardinal utility in welfare economics and the theory of risk-taking," **Journal of Political Economy**, Vol. 61, pp. 434-35.

Hawley, A.H. (1986). **Human Ecology, A Theoretical Essay** (Chicago, IL: The University of Chicago Press).

Hayek, F.A. (1967). **Studies in Philosophy, Politics and Economics** (Chicago, IL: The University of Chicago Press).

Hirschleifer, J. (1987). "Evolutionary models in economics and law: cooperation versus conflict strategies," in his **Economic Behaviour in Adversity** (Chicago, IL: The University of Chicago Press) pp. 211-72.

Holland, M. (trans.) (1982). **Public Duties in Islam: The Institution of Al-Hisbah** (Leicester, Eng.: The Islamic Foundation).

Hull, D.L. (1988). "A general analysis of selection process," in his **Science as a Process, An Evolutionary Account of the Social and Conceptual Development of Science** (Chicago, IL: The University of Chicago Press) pp. 397-431.

Kafatos, M. & Nadeau, R. (1990). "Changing the rules: the new epistemology of science," in their **The Conscious Universe** (New York, NY: Springer-Verlag) pp. 75-89.

Koizumi, T. (1993). **Interdependence and Change in the Global System** (Lanham, MA: University Press of America).

Mansfield, E, (1990). **Managerial Economics** (New York, NY: W.W. Norton).

Matthews, R. (1983). **The Creation of Regional Dependency** (Toronto, Ont: University of Toronto Press).

Mommsen, W.J. (1989). **The Political and Social Theory of Max Weber** (Chicago, IL: The University of Chicago Press).

Nordhaus, W. (1975). "The political business cycle," **Review of Economic Studies**, Vol. 42, pp. 169-90.

North, D.C. (1981). **Structure and Change in Economic History** (New York, NY: W.W. Norton).

Olson, M. (1965). **The Logic of Collective Action** (Cambridge, Mass: Harvard University Press).

Parson, T. (1937). **The Structure of Social Action** (New York, NY: McGraw-Hill Book Co).

Quinton, A. (1989). **Utilitarian Ethics** (LaSalle, IN: Open Court).

Rawls, J. (1971). **A Theory of Justice** (Cambridge, Mass: Belknap Press at Harvard University Press).

Ripley, P. (1993). "The elements of Kant's practical philosophy," in Beiner, R. & Booth, W.J. eds. **Kant & Political Philosophy, the Contemporary Legacy** (New Haven, CONN: Yale University Press) pp. 7-37.

Rucker, R. (1983). "The one and the many," in his **Infinity and the Mind, the Science and Philosophy of the Infinite** (New York, NY: Bantam Books) pp. 203-37.

Sen, A. (1985). "The moral standing of the market," in Paul, E.F. Miller, F.D. Jr. & Paul, J. eds. **Ethics and Economics** (Oxford, Eng.: Basil Blackwell).

Sen, A. (1990). "Economic behaviour and moral sentiments, freedom and consequences," in his **On Ethics and Economics** (Oxford, Eng.: Basil Blackwell).

Shackle, G.J.S. (1971). **Epistemics and Economics** (Cambridge, Eng.: Cambridge at the University Press).

Simon, H. (1987). "Decision making and organizational design," in Pugh, D.S. ed. **Organization Theory** (Hammondsworth, Middlesex, Eng.: Penguin Books, pp. 202-23).

Srinivasan, T.N. (1985). "Neo-classical political economy, the state and economic development," **Asian Development Review**, Vol. 3, No.2, pp. 38-58.

Staniland, M. (1985). **What is Political Economy? A Study of Social Theory and Underdevelopment** (New Haven, CONN: Yale University Press).

Stigler, G.J. (1960). "The influence of events and policies on economic theory," **American Economic Review**, May, 36-45.

Wallerstein, I. (1979). **The Capitalist World-Economy** (Cambridge, Eng.: Cambridge University Press).

Whitehead, A.N. edited by D.R. Griffin & D.W. Sherburne (1979). **Process and Reality** (New York, NY: The Free Press of Glencoe).

The Qur'anic verses and terms are in reference to A. Yusuf Ali, **The Holy Qur'an, Text, Translation and Commentary** (Brentwood MA: Amana Corporation, 1989).

CHAPTER 9: ISLAMIC CONSUMPTION, PRODUCTION AND DISTRIBUTIONAL MENUS

Allingham, M. (1989). "Numeraire," in J. Eatwell, M. Milgate & P. Newman eds. **The New Palgrave: General Equilibrium** (New York, NY: W.W. Norton) pp. 202-4.

Allouche, A. (1994). "Currency" in **Mamluk Economics, a Study and Translation of Al-Maqrizi's Ighathah** (Salt Lake City, Utah: University of Utah Press).

Arrow, K.J. (1976). **Social Choice and Individual Values** (New York, NY: John Wiley & Sons).

Behdad, S. (1989). "Property rights in contemporary Islamic thought: a critical perspective," **Review of Social Economy**, Vol. XLVII, No. 2, Summer).

Benasy, J.P. (1986). "The basic concepts," in **Macroeconomics: an Introduction to the Non-Walrasian Approach** (New York, NY: Academic Press, Inc).

Blaug, M. (1968). "Marxian conomics," in **Economic Theory in Retrospect** (Richard D. Irwin: Homewood, ILL) pp. 227-97.

Chapra, M.U. (1985). **Towards a Just Monetary System** (London, Eng.: The Islamic Foundation).

Choudhury, M.A. (1997a). **Money in Islam** (London, Eng.: Routledge).

----- (1998a). **Reforming the Muslim World** (London, Eng.: Kegan Paul International).

----- (1998b). **Studies in Islamic Social Sciences** (London, Eng.: Macmillan & New York, NY: St. Martin's Press).

----- (1996). "The nature of globalization and the Muslim world," in Choudhury, M.A. ed. **Topics in Globalization and Structural Change** (Hull, Eng.: MCB University Press).

----- (1995). **The Epistemological Foundations of Islamic Economic, Social and Scientific Order**, Six Vols. (Ankara, Turkey: Statistical, Economic and Social Research and Training Centre for Islamic Countries, Organization for Islamic Conferences).

----- (1994). **Economic Theory and Social Institutions** (Lanham, MA: The University Press of America).

----- (1993). **The Unicity Precept and the Socio-Scientific Order** (Lanham, MA: The University Press of America) Chapters 4 & 6.

----- (1992a). **The Principles of Islamic Political Economy** (London, Eng.: Macmillan & New York, NY: St. Martin's Press) Chapter 4.

----- (1992b). "The Islamic profit sharing system in comparative perspective," **The Middle East Business and Economic Review**, Vol. 4, No. 2, July, pp. 14-18.
----- (1992c). "The ethical numeraire," **International Journal of Social Economics**, Vol. 19, No. 1, pp. 60-72.

----- (1989). "Kantian perspectives and ethical alternatives in social contract theory," **Atlantic Canada Economic Association Papers**, Vol. 18, pp. 164-86.

----- (1986). "An analytical model of profit-sharing in an Islamic economy," in **Contributions to Islamic Economic Theory, A Study in Social Economics** (London, Eng.: Macmillan & New York, NY: St. Martin's Press) Chapter 6.

Davies, P. (1990). **God and the New Physics** (London, Eng.: Penguin Books).

Ellerman, D. (1991). "The cooperative firm: a cooperative-ESOP model," in Wisman, J.D. ed. **Worker Empowerment, the Struggle for Workplace Democracy** (New York, NY: The Bookstrap Press) pp. 83-100.

Etzioni, A. (1988). "Beyond rationalism: the role of values and emotions," in **The Moral Dimension** (New York, NY: The Free Press) pp. 88-165.

Fusfeld, D. (1986). "The Keynesian revolution," in **The Age of the Economist** (Glenview, ILL: Scott, Foresman and Co.) Chapter 9.

Georgescu-Roegen, N. (1971). "Science: a brief evolutionary analysis," in **The Entropy Law and the Economic Process** (Cambridge, Mass: Harvard University Press) Chapter 1.

Grandmont, J.-M. (1989). "Temporary equilibrium," in J. Eatwell, M. Milgate & P. Newman eds. **The New Palgrave: Social Economics** (New York, NY: W.W. Norton) pp. 297-304.

Halmos, P.R. (1974). **Measure Theory** (New York, NY: Springer-Verlag).

Harsanyi, J.C., (1955). "Cardinal welfare, individualistic ethics, and interpersonal comparison of utility," **Journal of Political Economy**, Vol. 6, pp. 309-21.

Hawking, S.W. (1988). "The unification of physics," in **A Brief History of Time** (New York, NY: Bantam Books).

Hayek, F.A. (1960). **The Constitution of Liberty** (Chicago, ILL: The University of Chicago Press).

Heilbroner, R. (1986). **The Nature and Logic of Capitalism** (New York, NY: W.W. Norton).

Henderson, J.M. & Quandt, R.E. (1971). **Microeconomic Theory, a Mathematical Approach** (New York, NY: McGraw-Hill).

James, B. (1996). "Knowledge and memory," **Kybernetes: The International Journal of Systems and Cybernetics**, Vol. 25, No. 5, pp. 63-66.

Lutz, M. & Lux, K. (1988). **Humanistic Economics, the New Challenge** (New York, NY: The Bookstrap Press).

Muslehuddin, M. (undated). **Philosophy of Islamic Law and the Orientalists** (Lahore, Pakistan: Islamic Publications Ltd).

Nelson, R.R. & Winter, S.G. (1982). **An Evolutionary Theory of Economic Change** (Cambridge Mass: Harvard University Press).

Nordhaus, W.D. (1975). "The political business cycle," **Review of Economic Studies**, Vol. 42, pp. 169-90.

Quinton, A. (1989). **Utilitarian Ethics** (LaSalle, ILL: Open Court).

Radnitzky, G. & Bartley III, N.W. eds. (1988). **Evolutionary Epistemology, Rationality and the Sociology of Knowledge** (LaSalle, ILL: Open Court).

Rawls, J. (1971). **A Theory of Justice** (Cambridge, Mass: Harvard University Press).

Rousseau, J-J. trans. Cranston, M. (1968). **The Social Contract** (London, Eng.: Penguin Books).

Rugina, A. (1983). "Toward a third revolution in economic thinking," **International Journal of Social Economics**, Vol. 10, No. 1, pp. 3-46.

Russell, B. (1990). "Bergson," in **A History of Western Philosophy** (London, Eng.: Unwin Hyman) pp. 756-65.

----- (1954). **The Analysis of Matter** (New York, NY: Dover Publications).

Seidler, V.J. (1986). **Kant, Respect and Injustice, the Limits of Liberal Moral Theory** (London, Eng.: Routledge & Kegan Paul).

Sen, A. (1985). "The moral standing of the market," in Paul, E.F. Paul, J. & Miller Jr. F.D. eds. **Ethics and Economics** (Oxford, Eng.: Basil Blackwell).

Siddiqi, M.N. (1985). **Partnership and Profit-Sharing in Islamic Law** (London, Eng.: The Islamic Foundation).

----- (1983). "Economics of profit-sharing," in Ahmed, Z. Iqbal, M. Khan, M.F. eds. **Fiscal Policy and Resource Allocation in Islam** (Jeddah, Saudi Arabia: International Centre for Research in Islamic Economics & Islamabad, Pakistan: Institute of Policy Studies) pp. 163-96.

Simon, H.A. (1957). **Models of Man** (New York, NY: John Wiley & Sons).

Smith, A. (1976a) [1790]. **The Theory of Moral Sentiments** Raphael, D.D. & Macfie, A.L, eds. (Oxford, Eng.: Clarendon Press).

Smith, A. (1976b) [1776]. **An Inquiry into the Nature and Causes of the Wealth of Nations,** Campbell, R.H. & Skinner, A.S. eds. (Oxford, Eng.: Clarendon Press).

Smith, T.S. (1992). **Strong Interaction** (Chicago, ILL: The University of Chicago Press).

Weitzman, M.L. (1984). **The Share Economy** (Cambridge, Mass: Harvard University Press).

Williamson, O.E. (1987). "Kenneth Arrow and the new institutional economics," in Feiwel, G.R. ed. **Arrow and the Foundations of the Theory of Economic Policy** (London, Eng.: Macmillan Press Ltd).

Wisman, J.D. ed. (1991). **Worker Empowerment, the Struggle for Workplace Democracy** (New York, NY: The Bookstrap Press).

CHAPTER 10: CONTRASTING MODELS OF KNOWLEDGE AND 'DE-KNOWLEDGE'

al-Azm, S.J. (1967). **Kant's Theory of Time** (New York, NY: The Philosophical Library, Inc).

Campbell, D.T. (1987). "Evolutionary epistemology," in Radnitzky, G. Bartley III, W.W. eds. **Evolutionary Epistemology, Rationality, and the Sociology of Knowledge** (LaSalle, ILL: Open Court).

Choudhury, M.A. (1995). "The process-centered worldview," **Proceedings of the Pakistan Academy of Sciences**, Vol. 32, No. 1-4, pp. 123-26.

Dampier, W.C. (1961). **A History of Science and Its Relations with Philosophy and Religion** (Cambridge, Eng.: Cambridge University Press).

Halmos, P.R. (1974). **Measure Theory** (New York, NY: Springer-Verlag).

Hobbes, T. (1958). **Leviathan** (Indianapolis, IN: Bobbs-Merrill, reprint).

Hull, D.L (1988). **Science as a Process** (Chicago, ILL: The University of Chicago Press).

Nagel, E. (1961). "Methodological problems of the social sciences," in **The Structure of Science, Problems in the Logic of Scientific Explanations** (New York, NY: Harcourt, Brace & World, Inc).

Parsons, T. (1964). "Some phases of the historical development of individualistic positivism in the theory of action," in **The Structure of Social Action** (New York, NY: The Free Press of Glencoe).

Popper, K.R. (1972). **Conjectures and Refutations: The Growth of Scientific Knowledge** (London, Eng.: Routledge & Kegan Paul).

Rhoads, S.E. (1985). "Kind hearts and opportunity costs," **Across the Board**, Dec. 1985, pp. 40-7.

Russell, B. (1991). **A History of Western Philosophy** (London, Eng.: Unwin Hyman).

Seidler, V.J (1986). **Kant, Respect and Injustice, the Limits of Liberal Theory** (London, Eng.: Routledge & Kegan Paul).

Thurow, L. (1983). **Dangerous Currents, the State of Economics** (New York, NY: Random House).

GLOSSARY OF ARABIC TERMS

'Adl - social justice.

Afw - floor of giving charity.

Ahkam - rules derived by discourse and consensus according to Qur'an and Sunnah (see below).

Akhira - Hereafter.

al-Adl wal Ehsan - justice with compassion.

al-A'lamin - Islamic world-system governed by the Qur'an the Sunnah (see below).

al-Hisbah fil Islam - public duties in Islam, also the social control of markets in Islam.

Allah - God, having no gender attached to this terminology and centrally implicating Oneness of God.

Aql - intellect.

Asma al-Husna - Blessed names conveying the attributes of Allah. Although reduced to ninety-nine in number, these attributes are indefinitely many more.

Ayath (Ayath Allah) - Signs of Allah (God) as reflections of Divine Unity in the order of things,

Barzakh - the universe of existence of the soul between death and resurrection.

Batil - untenable as falsehood and bound for destruction.

Bayyanah - unveiling of knowledge and reality according to Qur'an.

Burhan Aqli - the rationalist way of deriving reason.

Dhururiyyath - necessaries of life, basic needs.

Falah - felicity.

Fana - complete surrender to Allah causing the state of self-annihilation in the face of humility and Divine submission.

Fard - mandatory practices under Islamic Law.

Fitra - primordial nature of things.

Hajiyyath - comforts of life.

Halal - recommended and permissible acts and consumption according to Islamic Law.

Haqq al-Yaqin - the inexorable nature of Divine Truth.

Haram - forbidden acts and consumption under Islamic Law.

Ibrahim - Abraham, a chapter of Qur'an.

Ijma - consensus of the Islamic community, taken in this work in reference to Qur'anic interpretation to mean complementary processes being formed and reformed in the natural and cosmic universes as in the Islamic social structure of Shura (consultation, see below).

Ijtihad - authoritative research based on Qur'an and Sunnah (see below).

Ikhtiyar - free will.

Illihin - Divine record of all good deeds of individuals.

Israf - waste and prodigality.

Istidlal - reflection and reasoning.

Jahannum - Hell.

Jahiliyyah - condition of ignorance and falsehood.

Jannah - Heaven.

Kalam - rationalism.

Khalq in-Jadid - re-origination both in the sense of recreation in the Hereafter and in the sense of continuous re-origination of Divine manifestations in the order of things encompassing knowledge and observations.

Kiyamah - Doomsday or the end of the temporal order followed by resurrection.

Lauh Mahfuz - the Divine Tablet in which the Essence of the Qur'an is embalmed, also called the Mother of the Book.

Maqasid al-Shari'ah - the purpose of Shari'ah (Islamic Law).

Maslaha wal-Istihsan - the public purpose based on social preferences.

Miraj (see Sidarthul Muntaha): The most important event of Miraj is the revelation of the Islamic mode of prayer to the Prophet Muhammad and the change of Qibla from the Dome of the Rock to Makkah for all times.

Mizan - balance (also used with the sense of justice and equilibrium in human and cosmic orders).

Muamalat - worldly matters.

Mubah - indeterminate events between permissible and forbidden ones according to Islamic Law.

Musharakah - equity financing in Islam.

Mutakallimun - Islamic epistemologists who denied the rationalist basis of knowledge as being unacceptable in deriving Islamic thought.

Mudarabah - profit-sharing financing instrument in Islam.

Naba al-Azim - the great event of Kiyamah and Akhira.

Qibla - direction of prayer of Muslims towards Makkah. It is also taken here to mean the Islamic versus the non-Islamic premises of belief.

Qiyas - analogy.

Qur'an - the Divine revelation in the form of a book to the Prophet Muhammad.

Riba - in excess of the due value of an exchange, financial interest being an example of this excess.

Shari'ah - Islamic Law.

Shura (also Shuratic) - extensive consultation and discourse leading to consensus in the Islamic community over all matters of Islamic thought and actions. According to the understanding of the Qur'an, we take this in the extensive sense of interactions within and between human and non-human domains.

Sidrathul Muntaha - the domain of absolute and fullness of Divine Knowledge to which the Prophet Muhammad was carried in his celestial journey of Divine communication with reality.

Sijjin - Divine record of all bad deeds of individuals.

Sirathul Mustaqim - the straight path of righteousness in the sense of its uniqueness and unity of purpose for truth.

Sunnat al-Allah - the Divine Law.

Sunnat al-Rasul (also Sunnah) - recommendations and practices of the Prophet Muhammad.

Tahsinyyath - refinements of life.

Taqwa: God-consciousness.

Tazkiyyah - purification and solace of the soul.

Tawhid - Oneness of God as the Absolute in Knowledge, Creator and Cherisher of the universe.

Ubudiyyah - obedience to God.

Ummah - the conscious world nation of Islamic.

Zakkum - the evil tree of Hell.

SUBJECT INDEX